# Labor Market Dynamics in Turkey during the Last 100 Years

# Labor Market Dynamics in Turkey during the Last 100 Years

Edited by Meltem İnce Yenilmez and M. Çağlar Özdemir

LEXINGTON BOOKS
*Lanham • Boulder • New York • London*

Published by Lexington Books
An imprint of The Rowman & Littlefield Publishing Group, Inc.
4501 Forbes Boulevard, Suite 200, Lanham, Maryland 20706
www.rowman.com

86-90 Paul Street, London EC2A 4NE



British Library Cataloguing in Publication Information Available

**Library of Congress Cataloging-in-Publication Data Available**

ISBN 978-1-66695-617-7 (cloth)
ISBN 978-1-66695-618-4 (electronic)

*This book is dedicated to all women in the world who are the foundation stone and architects of society.*

# Contents

# Preface

The evolution of the labor market is a complex thread woven into the fabric of a nation always undergoing change, forming a dynamic tapestry of Turkey's social and economic history. This important thread is thoroughly explored in this book, *Labor Market Dynamics in Turkey during the Last 100 Years*, which charts its course through a century's worth of ups and downs. Using thorough investigation and examination, we endeavor to shed light on the evolving forms of Turkey's labour market. We navigate the maze of labor dynamics from the early twentieth century, when the Republic was founded, to the modern period of globalization, technological breakthroughs, and economic complexity. It is a trip through societal changes, legislation, culture, and time that has radically altered the nature of employment.

Comprehending the workings of the labor market is crucial for comprehending the socioeconomic advancement and progress of any country. Due to its strategic location at the intersection of two continents and several cultures, Turkey has seen an unprecedented influx of labor trends. Turkey's labor market has changed together with the country, reflecting its historical, political, and economic shifts from an agricultural economy to the dynamic, varied workforce of today.

This book aims to provide an in-depth study of the dynamics of the labor market in Turkey, looking at the important changes, laws, and social factors that have influenced the nature of work. Through an in-depth analysis of labor mobility, employment sectors, educational influences, and policy impacts, our goal is to present a comprehensive perspective that will benefit scholars, policymakers, economists, and anyone else interested in Turkey's socioeconomic development.

This book is the result of the hard work and enthusiasm of a group of academics and researchers who are passionate about learning about the complexities of Turkey's labor market dynamics. Their dedication, experience, and painstaking investigation have all contributed to the story's enrichment, making this book an invaluable resource for information. Turning the pages of this book will allow you to think back on the past, comprehend the present, and imagine a future in which Turkey's labor market will keep developing and guaranteeing prosperity and well-being for all of its residents.

M. Çağlar Özdemir
Meltem İnce Yenilmez

# Acknowledgments

I want to thank my family for their unlimited tolerance for my long working hours during my academic studies. I hope I have not alienated my children, Çınar Alp and Elif Duru, from academic studies. I especially want to thank my wife, Tuna, whose support I feel endless every moment. Without her compassion, at least half of my enthusiasm for work would have been exhausted. I want to thank my loyal mother and father and my sister Pınar, who made me proud by receiving her professorship last month. Finally, of course, I want to thank all my colleagues who contributed to the writing of this book. They spent months devoted to this book.

I hope this book will become an essential resource for researchers conducting studies on the Turkish labor market in the coming decades.

*M. Çağlar Özdemir*

Words cannot express how grateful I am to my mother, father, mother-in-law, and father-in-law for all of the sacrifices that they have made on my behalf and whose love and guidance are with me in whatever I pursue. They are the ultimate role models. I wish to thank my sisters,. I have no words to describe the meaning of your love and support. Most importantly, I owe my deepest gratitude to my loving and supportive husband, Özgür, and my wonderful beloved son, Bryan Poyraz, who provides unending inspiration and is such a good boy who always cheers me up. You are the best thing that is still happening to me. Last but not least, I am so grateful to my dear teacher, colleague, and more than a relative, Prof. Dr. M. Hulusi Demir, whose supportive approach and encouragement have guided me throughout the process.

*Meltem İnce Yenilmez*

## *Chapter 1*

# Youth Labor Force in Turkey

Beril Baykal[1]

The aim of this study is to reveal the status of the youth labor force in Turkey since the establishment of the republic in 1923), specifically focusing on the period 2010–2020and to evaluate the policies for the youth labor force implemented during this period. In this study, a general evaluation was carried out regarding the status of the youth labor force from the republic's founding until 2010, including labor force participation rates, employment rates, unemployment rates, labor force participation by education level, employment and unemployment status, job search duration, and underemployment of youth in the 2010–2020 period. Furthermore, a general assessment was made from relevant literature and development plans. The data for 2010–2020 were obtained from the research reports of TURKSTAT, ILO, and DİSK-AR . The measures taken and policies implemented, especially after 2000, for the youth labor force in Turkey were also mentioned.

## INTRODUCTION

Young people, who represent the dynamic structure of society, are important to both society and the economy today and in the future. They make valuable contributions to both society and the economy by fostering vitality, innovation, and creativity. The youth labor force is of great importance for a stronger country. Even in the aftermath of the 2008 global economic crisis, the labor market's prospects for young people continue to be inadequate. According to the Global Employment Trends for Youth 2022 published by the International Labour Organization (ILO), youth unemployment has become a chronic problem, and the inadequacy of quality employment opportunities continues to prevent young people from settling in decent jobs. Considering the current employment opportunities for young people, the weight of informal, low-paid, and irregular/temporary jobs draws attention. This situation also directly affects the quality of jobs that can be created for young people in the future. Conversely, the distinction between youth and adults in terms of employment and unemployment trends has not changed much in the last decade. Also, the Covid-19 crisis exacerbated labor market challenges generally faced by young people (ILO, 2022). In this context, young people are in a disadvantaged position in many countries. In an open economy, where tough competition conditions and standards are high and the competencies and skills demanded are constantly changing, it becomes more difficult for young people to take part in employment. Therefore, the disadvantaged situation of young people in the labor market has become a wide-ranging and permanent problem.

As is the case worldwide, the Turkish labor market is in disequilibrium. Turkey possesses an advantage in terms of its youth labor force that very few countries in the world have. However, from the perspective of the youth labor force, youth participation, employment, and unemployment constitute significant problem areas, indicating youth cannot use their potential to the maximum. Furthermore, rates of youth participation in the labor force and their employment are lower when compared to the overall working-age population, but their unemployment rates are higher than the general unemployment rates. The main factors leading to this disequilibrium are Turkey's demographic structure, education policies, and labor policies.

## CONCEPT OF YOUTH

The developmental stages of human life include childhood, youth, maturity, and old age. Although all these stages have some unique and important features, it can be said that "youth" is the most significant and productive stage of human life, necessitating a special focus and in-depth research as compared to the other stages (Murat & Şahin, 2011).

The definition of youth differs from country to country, depending on cultural, institutional, and political factors. One of the most important criteria considered when defining the concept of youth is age range. The age range is 12–30 in some countries (Uganda), whereas in other countries it is 18–35 (Nigeria and Bangladesh) (ILO, 2005, 3). While developed countries have different upper and lower limits for the age range, the age at which compulsory education finishes is often the lowest limit. For example, in England, the Youth Employment Policy is generally aimed at the 16–18 age group; in Northern Italy, the youth policies refer to the 14–29 age group; and in Southern Italy, policies target the 14–32 age group (O'Higgins, 1997, 1). On the other hand, Australia defines the 12–25 age group as young (O'Higgins, 2001). At the international level, those defined as young by the United Nations (UN) and the ILO are people in the 15–24 age group. In the statistics of the Turkish Statistical Institute (TURKSTAT), the definition of youth includes the population between the ages of 15 and 24.

In terms of labor force, Article 71 of Labour Law No. 4857 states that the lower limit for the working age is 15: "It is forbidden to employ children under the age of fifteen." Similarly, in ILO Convention No. 138, employees between the ages of 15 and 24 are considered "young workers." Although the upper limit for the definition of a young worker in industrialized countries changes frequently, the lower limit is generally accepted as the age at which compulsory education ends (Erol, 2013, 17; Gündoğan, 1999, 65).

## YOUTH POPULATION AND YOUTH LABOR FORCE

### The Situation between 1923 and 2010

In the early yearsof the republic, especially after the 1929 economic crisis, the state-sponsored industrialization policies led to a significant increase in the labor force and the number of employees. Nevertheless, the labor force and employees in this period were far from the norms demanded by industrialization in terms of education and work experience. As the Ottomans were late to industrialize, had an agriculture-based economy, and so on, the labor force was predominantly unqualified and uneducated in this period. This labor force, which lacked continuity and was unsuitable for industrial establishments equipped with modern technology, also created serious limitations and problems. In addition, low wages in the industrial sector, lack of social security opportunities, lack of occupational health measures, and the problem of housing in the cities also affected the formation of the labor force. Therefore, obtaining data on the labor force for this period is highly challenging (Makal, 1999, 295–300). It is worth noting that, in addition to these problems, there have been positive developments with the the labor market, such as Turkey's accession to the ILO in 1932, the formulation of the First Five-Year Industrial Plan in 1934, and the enactment of the Labour Law in 1936. However, with the outbreak of World War II, progress of the labor force were interrupted.

The developments in the economic policies implemented worldwide after World War II also impacted Turkey. During this period, mechanization in production life increased, the industrial sector expanded, and, therefore, the number of paid employees increased. The increase in migration from rural to urban areas as a result of increased mechanization in agriculture reduced wage levels in cities and signaled possible unemployment.

By the 1960s, the economy entered a phase of planned development, and industrial investments increased under the leadership of the public sector. This situation did not only affect the sectoral distribution of employment but also led to a significant increase in the number of employees. While there was no mention of any measures for the employment of young people in the early stages of planned development, the measures for young people were mostly in the field of education. However, these measures have been planned in a way that will enable young people to overcome the obstacles of the social environment and rise to the levels they deserve so that the manpower resource is used in the best way and in line with other economic resources (First Five-Year Development Plan, 1963). The Second Five-Year Development Plan (1968) introduced a separate section to address the challenges faced by youth. The objective of the plan was to provide training to young people in order to meet the quantity and quality standards necessary for development initiatives, with the training to be given after completion of basic education. Therefore, during this period, it was observed that young people were perceived as lacking the qualifications required for development. Again, this plan aimed to organize programs that enable young girls and women to adapt to the requirements of developing economic and social life, as well as increase education and job orientation services. In other words, insufficient participation of young women in education and employment was seen as a problem. The Third Five-Year Development Plan (1973) indicated that the share of young people in the population was quite high and that Turkey held an advantageous position in terms of its youth labor force. The plan aimed to train young people to be highly qualified citizens and be the main driving force in development. Furthermore, the necessity of an education system that supports the development efforts, in which the preference for industrialization is emphasized and the vocational skills and abilities of the young people for economic activities were mentioned, indicating that the targets of the previous plans had not been achieved and the structural problems regarding the youth labor force still persist in this period.

Neo-liberal policies and technological developments that started with the globalization process after 1980 have significantly affected the labor force, and unemployment has become an important problem. The decisions of January 24, 1980, transformed Turkey into country that is committed to adapting to market economies and using neo-liberal policies and tools to achieve this goal. During this period, the sectoral distribution of the labor force was altered, unemployment increased, the qualification level of the labor force changed, and polarization commenced (Sapancalı, 1998). In addition, regulations protecting the labor force were restricted to allow the capital to move freely, flexible work began to become widespread, and real wages decreased. Young, old, and low-qualified employees were affected the most because of these technological developments and neo-liberal policies. In this period, the ratio of the young population that is economically active to the active population decreased, and youth unemployment increased considerably (Fourth Five-Year Development Plan, 1979; Fifth Five-Year Development Plan, 1985).In the 1990s, the impact of neo-liberal policies continued. During this period, the percentage of the young population in Turkey was around 20%, and the increasing unemployment among the youth continued to be a significant issue. As it can be understood from the labor force statistics published by TURKSTAT since 1988, although education level of the youth were increased in these years, unemployment rates did not decrease; in fact it increased (Sixth Five-Year Development Plan, 1990; Seventh Five-Year Development Plan, 1996). Continuing its young population advantage in the 2000s, Turkey could not prevent the problems related to the youth labor force. It is seen that the measures taken to increase youth employment are not effective, and the problem of youth unemployment, especially educated youth unemployment, continues. TURKSTAT data also confirm this situation.

## The Situation between 2010 and 2020

According to the address-based population system, as of 2020, the young population, which constitutes 15.4% of the total population in Turkey, is 12,983,750, and the youth labor force population is 4.573.000. Accordingly, from 2010 to 2020, the young population increased from 12,544,000 to 12,983,750, and the youth labor force increased from 4,426,000 to 4,573,000. Although the number of young male and female populations in Turkey is close to each other, it is striking that the female youth labor force is only about half of the male youth labor force (figure 1.1).

The data for the young population show that young people are not included in the labor force mostly because of their studentship. While more than 50% of young people were not included in the labor force in 2010 because of being students, this rate increased to 60% in 2020. Of course, it is gratifying that young people continue their education. However, there is a growing perception that education systematically hinders participation in the labor force as a voluntary field.

Another important reason for the barriers to the participation of young people in the labor force in Turkey is "domestic/housework responsibilities." It should be emphasized that this reason belongs only to women. Gender roles are also listed among the factors that prevent youth from being included in the labor force.

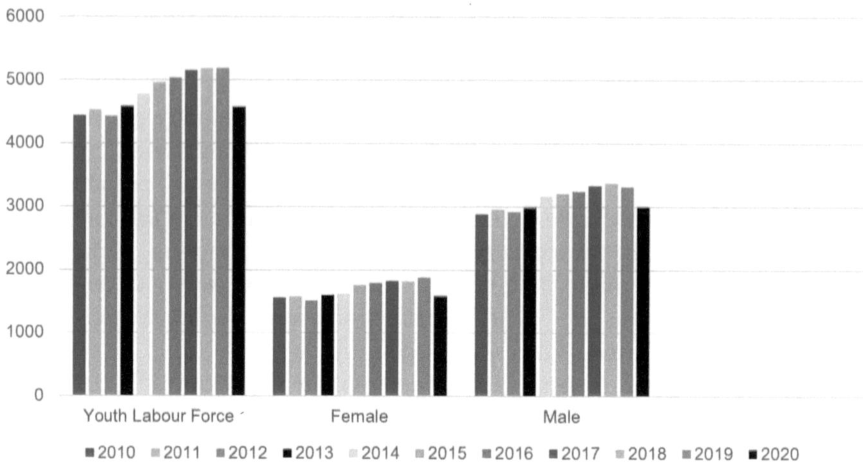


**Figure 1.1 Status of Youth Labor Force By Gender.** *Source*: Prepared from TURKSTAT Labour Force Statistics data.

Furthermore, there has been a significant increase in the number of young people who have become hopeless over the past decade. This segment, which is not generally included in the unemployment calculation, consists of young people who are not looking for a job and are ready to work but have no hope of finding a job.

The education level of the youth labor force has changed between 2010 and 2020. The majority of the youth labor force (46%) were primary school graduates in 2010. However, by 2020, there was a decrease in the number of young people who graduated from primary education. Instead, the number of young people who graduated from secondary or equivalent schools increased approximately 24 times, constituting 28.5% of the total youth labour force. This rate is followed by high school and equivalent school graduates, with approximately 21%, and higher education graduates, with approximately 20%. This shows that the education level of the youth labor force in Turkey has increased in the last ten years.

## Labor Force Participation of Youth

The labor force participation of youth increased by approximately 6 points from 2010 to 2019, reaching 44.4%. The labour force participation of women and men has been on the rise during the same period. However, in 2020, the labor force participation rate seems to have decreased by approximately 5% for both men and women in total (figure 1.2).

There has been an upward trend in the labor force participation rate according to the education level. The education group with the highest increase in

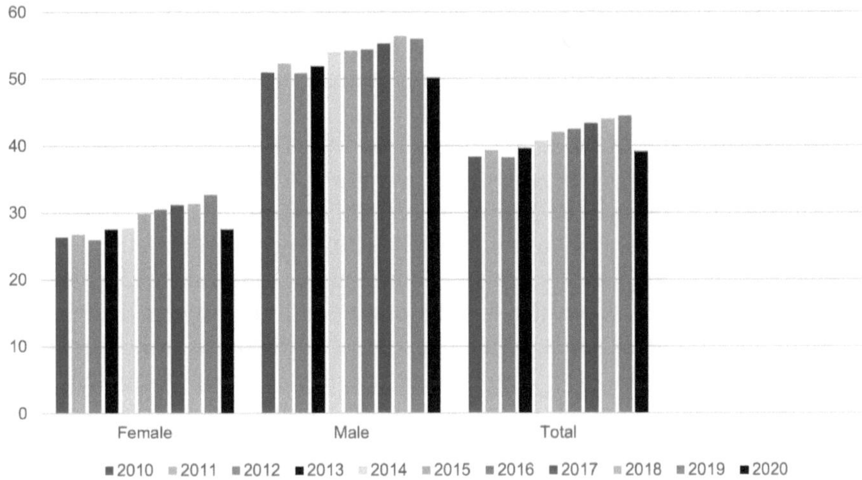


**Figure 1.2 Labor Force Participation.** *Source*: Prepared from TURKSTAT Labour Force Statistics data.

labor force participation in the last ten years is primary school graduates. In this group, the labor force increased from 34.1% to 63.3%, with an increase of approximately 30 points in the 2010–2020 period. On the other hand, the labor force participation of youth who graduated from secondary school or its equivalent decreased drastically, falling from 71% to 26.6%. The group with the highest labor force participation is higher education graduates.

## Employment Status of Youth

For young people, employment is the most important factor that shapes their social identity and determines their lives, independence, development, self-confidence, and economic and political identities. Therefore, ensuring the participation of young people in employment is very important for both the youth and the welfare of the country. Economic policies that do not create employment, mismatch of employment opportunities in the fields young people receive education, discriminatory policies applied in the recruitment process (lack of experience, sexist policies, education), directing young people to low-paid and informal jobs, the inability of young people to keep up with technological changes and developments, or the fact that there is a certain limit of employment in the public sector that is still widespread in Turkey can be listed as some of the obstacles to youth employment.

The youth employment rate in Turkey followed a fluctuating course in the 2010–2019 period and fell behind the general employment rate, with 29.2% in 2020. Likewise, the employment rate of men and women followed a fluctuating course in the same period and decreased in 2020. The employment rate of women in Turkey is almost half that of men. The employment rate, which is already low among young people, has remained even lower among young women.

The upward trend in the employment rate varies according to the education profile. The education group with the highest employment rate in the last ten years is primary school graduates. In this group, the employment rate increased from 27.8% to 49.6% in the 2010–2020 period. The second group with an increased employment rate is young people who can read and write but have not finished schooling. On the other hand, the highest decrease in the employment rate is among young people who graduated from secondary school or its equivalent. The employment rate in this group decreased from 63.2% to 21.4%. In general, the group with the highest employment rate is higher education graduates.

The majority of employed youth are employed on a wage/salary basis. It is observed that young people are mainly employed in manufacturing, agriculture, and wholesale and retail trade.

However, while employment in agriculture has decreased in the last ten years, it is observed that youth employment has increased in manufacturing, wholesale and retail trade. In addition, it is seen that youth employment is inadequate in areas where many young people receive education, such as administrative sciences, finance, and information and communication technologies. As in general employment, there is a general downward trend in youth employment in 2020.

Youth employment data by occupation has been encouraging since 2014. Between 2014 and 2020, young people were mainly employed as service and sales personnel. The number of young people employed as service and sales personnel increased every year, except for 2020. The second occupational group, in which young people are heavily employed, is jobs that do not require qualifications. However, it is seen that the number of young people employed in jobs that do not require qualifications has decreased in the last two years. In addition, when 2014 and 2020 are compared, although the number of young people working as professionals is relatively low, the same is expected to increase while employment in other occupational groups decreases.

Data from 2010 to 2020 show that while the number of informally employed youth has decreased, the number of informally employed youth has increased. It can be said that the measures taken and the policies implemented to encourage youth employment are effective here. However, it is noteworthy that the number of young people working informally and those working formally is close to each other. Therefore, it is an important problem that the number of young people working informally is still high.

## Unemployment of Youth

Young people are the group most affected by the overall increase in unemployment. Because young people have just entered the labor market, they are inexperienced, have no or short terms of service, or there is a mismatch between the skills demanded and the skills possessed. Since young people are the most junior members of the labor market, they may be more affected by unemployment during periods when the unemployment of adults who are more experienced than them increases (Dursun & Aytaç, 2009; Işık, 2016).

Youth unemployment is higher than adult unemployment in Turkey. It is seen that there has been no improvement in youth unemployment between 2010 and 2020. Considering the phenomenon of youth unemployment in terms of gender, more important dimensions of the issue emerge. Unemployment of young women is higher than that of young men in Turkey, as in many parts of the world. In Turkey, where youth unemployment reached 25.3% in 2020, youth unemployment rose to 30.3% (figure 1.3). These rates show that Turkey, which has a high young population, cannot use the advantage of the youth labor force effectively in working life.

TURKSTAT uses the concept of narrowly defined unemployment as per ILO standards in the calculation of the unemployment rate. In a narrow definition of unemployment calculation, job seekers who are ready to work and those who have applied for a job in the last four weeks are taken into account. However, those who have lost hope of finding a job, those who are not looking for a job but are ready to work, and those who

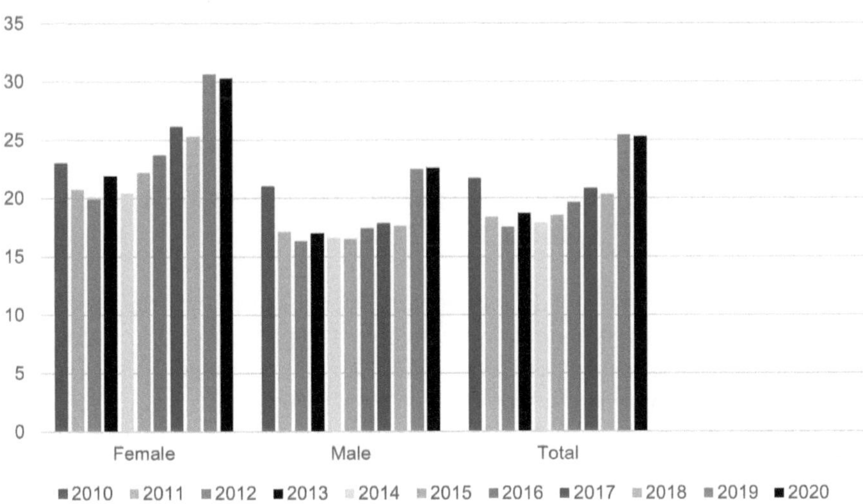


**Figure 1.3 Youth Unemployment Rate.** *Source*: Prepared from TURKSTAT Labor Force Statistics data.

are underemployed due to time are not included in the calculation. ILO defines a broad definition of unemployment as labor underutilization and calculates alternative/broad definition unemployment rates for countries as well as standard unemployment rates. Within the scope of a broad definition of unemployment, ILO includes those who are underemployed based on time (short-time workers, seasonal workers), standard unemployed, and potential workforce (those who are still not working and want to work if they find a job) (DİSK-AR, 2019). According to this calculation, broad youth unemployment was 30.3% in 2010, while it was 41.1% in 2020. This rate is 46.9% for young women and 37.8% for young men in 2020. Unemployment among young women tends to increase over the years, and it is understood that almost half of the young female workforce was unemployed in 2020.

Youth unemployment has taken a fluctuating course over the years in high school and below education levels. In Turkey, where almost one in four young people is unemployed, even in narrow-defined unemployment, it is seen that the highest youth unemployment rate is among higher education graduates. Although the unemployment rate, which was 32.5% in 2010, decreased to 28.5% in 2014, it increased to 35.8% in 2020 and created a very important picture. In this context, in terms of labor demand in Turkey, it is possible to say that especially the educated labor force has difficulty finding a job.

When the reasons for the unemployment of young people are examined, the number of people who were unemployed due to entering the labor market for the first time in 2010 is higher than other groups. This situation is followed by the termination of the employment contract becauseof being employed in a temporary job. As the years progressed, the reason for unemployment among young people was leaving their jobs against their own will and working in a temporary job.

## POLICIES IMPLEMENTED FOR THE YOUTH LABOR FORCE IN TURKEY

The fact that Turkey has important potential in terms of the young population can be expressed as a demographic window of opportunity. It is stated that this window of opportunity will close in 2040, and if the youth labor force is well trained and channeled into production until this year, Turkey can achieve considerable economic growth, and the youth unemployment problem can be solved. It is predicted that until 2023, Turkey's working-age population will increase and reach approximately 70%, and after this date, it will continue to increase at a decreasing rate until 2040. After 2040, it is expected that the population will tend to age, and the demographic window of opportunity will close (UNDP, 2008). When evaluated within this framework, the importance of youth for Turkey emerges once again. If Turkey does not adoptspecial policies foryoung people, it will not be able to turn the potential of the young population into an advantage and will face significant challenges in the near future. Therefore, special protection of young people is necessary and important. Starting from the Fifth Five-Year Development Plan (1985–1989), the aim has been to reduce youth unemployment, with incentives for youth employment and vocational training, and to increase youth employment by educating them under market requirements and changing technologies. In the 9th and 10th Development Plans and in the National Employment Strategy that came into effect in 2017, young people were included in the groups that should be specially protected.

The Turkish Employment Agency (IŞKUR), which is the most important institution in the implementation of employment policies for young people, directs young people to the most suitable jobs for them as soon as possible with its job placement services, provides young people with qualifications suitable for market requirements with vocational and on-the-job training activities, enables individuals to reveal their talents and capacities with consultancy services, and assists in career choices. Youth employment is also supported by entrepreneurship training and work programmes for the benefit of society. In addition, experiences and practices are shared with national and international partners under the coordination of IŞKUR, and more young people benefit from grants and consolidations for employment (Kılıç & Bülbül, 2012).

The Young Entrepreneur Training Programme, one of the projects, directed university graduates to start their businesses. The Grant Program for Supporting Youth Employment in Sectoral Investment Areas, another project carried out by IŞKUR and implemented with European Union financing, aimed to improve the employability of young people, increase their entrepreneurial skills, and improve the guidance and consultancy services provided for young people in this direction. Within the scope of the project, 56 grant projects in 33 provinces were supported. With the supported grant projects, the private sector representatives in the local priority and developing sectors were also included in the grant projects, providing young people with professional skills and experience, on-the-job training and internship opportunities to facilitate the transition from school to work, and entrepreneurship training were organized (https://www.iskur.gov.tr/kurumsal-bilgi/uluslararasi-iliskiler-ve-projeler/projeler/).

The National Youth Employment Action Plan prepared on November 16, 2011, within the framework of the United Nations Joint Program "Decent Work for All: National Youth Employment Programme," aimed to increase the employment of young people who are among the disadvantaged groups in the labor market and ensure their integration into economic and social life. With this action plan, it is aimed to employ more young women and men in decent jobs in Turkey. At this point, IŞKUR, which plays an active role, employs job and vocational consultants, organizes visits to workplaces in every sector operating in the labor market, determines vacant jobs (labor demands), and directs unemployed youth to these vacancies suitable for their qualifications (Kılıç & Bülbül, 2012).

Between 2010 and 2013, it was aimed at encouraging the participation of young people in the labor market and increasing their employability and entrepreneurial capacity with the "Youth Employment Support Project." Within the scope of the project, 127 grant projects were supported to facilitate youth employment; entrepreneurship training, guidance and consultancy services for young entrepreneurs who will set heir own businesses, internship opportunities to facilitate the transition from school to work, entrepreneurship, and career days were organized (https://www.iskur.gov.tr/kurumsal-bilgi/uluslararasi-iliskiler-ve-projeler/projeler/).

Another policy implemented for the employment of young people is insurance premium incentives. In Turkey, insurance premium incentives have been implemented for young people since 2011. The most comprehensive and important incentive work is the regulations introduced by Law No. 6111 published in the Gazette on February 25, 2011. With the aforementioned law, insurance premium incentives have been introduced to be valid for the recruitment of men aged 18–29 and women over the age of 18. In addition to the specified gender and age requirements, the duration of the insurance premium incentive is further increased for those who get a job as a certificate holder in the relevant profession after completing the vocational qualification certificate or workforce training courses. Therefore, in order to increase employment, encourage the employment of young people and women and vocational training, incentives have been introduced for the payment of employer premiums of the Social Security Institution from the Unemployment Insurance Fund for a period of up to 54 months.

Policies have also been developed to reduce the rate of informal employment among young people. Giving the right to benefit from general health insurance for two years for young people who will enter the labor market for the first time, and the regulations that the death pensions of the young people who receive survivors' pensions are not cut even if they start working in the education process are direct applications for areas where unregistered employment is common. In this way, it is aimed to decrease the unregistered employment rate among the young population. Although the data show that the number of young people working informally is decreasing, the high number of young people working informally indicates that more measures are needed (Specialization Commission Report, 2018).

Establishing the relationship between education and the labor market is also very important in terms of youth employment. Of course, the only function of education is not to equip people with skills demanded by the labor market. However, an economy needs to be designed in such a way that it determines the necessary human resources and education to a certain extent to meets this need. Only in this way can an education-employment relationship be established. In this context, there is a need for education policies that are based on the needs of the labor market to a certain extent and that are implemented consistently. In this context, practices such as the dissemination of internship practices, facilitating social security practices of interns and state support for intern wages have been developed and have produced partially positive results (Specialization Commission Report, 2018).

## CONCLUSION

The challenges faced by the youth labor force have been concerning since the establishment of the republic. The structural problems persisted until the globalization process, although the measures to address the youth labor force issue, which began to be discussed more frequently with the Fifth Five-Year Development Plan, were implemented. The changes that started with the globalization process in the labor market and still continue as a result of technological transformations especially affect the young labor force. It is possible to say that young people are at a disadvantage in the labor market in Turkey as in the world. The data between 2010 and 2020 examined within the scope of this study also reveals that this situation is still valid.

Between 2010 and 2020, it was observed that the labor force participation and employment rates of the youth labor force increased. Particularly in 2019, the labor force participation rate reached the highest level for both men and women. Although this is seen as a positive trend, the continuous increase in youth unemployment rates, which reached 25.4% in the past 2 years, casts a negative light on the situation. When evaluated in terms of broad-defined unemployment, this rate is alarming. In this context, it can be concluded that the active employment policies implemented between 2010 and 2020 were partially effective but mostly insufficient.

Another striking point in the data is that the labor force participation and employment rates of young women are lower than those of men, but their unemployment rates are higher than those of men. Whether it is due to the sexist division of labor or the prevalence of precarious forms of employment, this situation causes the young female labor force to become vulnerable. Although young people are among the groups that need special protection, it is seen that a separate heading and separate measures are required for young women.

Another important issue is that although the labor force participation rate and employment rate of higher education graduates are high, the unemployment rate is higher than other education groups. Educated unemployment is an important problem that has been mentioned frequently in recent years. The fact that the relationship between education and employment has not been established has an important place among the causes of youth unemployment in Turkey. Thus, it can be concluded that an education system that does not take into account the expectations and needs of the labor market is the primary cause of unemployment.

As a result, because youth labor force participation and employment rates are below the general rates in Turkey, unemployment rates are above the general unemployment rate, and the sector in which they are employed and employment conditions, the situation of the youth labor force reveals that it has a structural problem and the policies implemented are inadequate. In addition, the fact that the education required by the constantly developing and changing technological environment is still insufficient in Turkey, young people have limited opportunities to benefit from these educational opportunities, and the Turkish economy and labor market are slow to adapt to the constantly developing and changing technologies, threatening the situation of the youth labor force. The inability to follow the developments in technology and education causes young people to make preparations in terms of employment expectations according to traditional sectors, which, in turn, limits their development potential.

In this context, the effectiveness of the policies implemented should be analyzed, the development scenario (especially economic and technological developments) should be evaluated well, and based on data and results appropriate policies should be framed. Unless structural problems are addressed, young people will always encounter obstacles in the labor market. As a result, it will not be possible to build a stronger economy and so a better future, and social welfare will not be achievable.

## NOTE

1. Asst. Prof., Kocaeli University Faculty of Economics and Administrative Sciences, Department of Labour Economics and Industrial Relations, Turkey, berilbaykal81@gmail.com

## REFERENCES

DİSK-AR. (2019-Aralık). İşsizlik ve İstihdam Raporu (Unemployment and Employment Report). http://arastirma.disk.org.tr/?page_id=1295. https://ilostat.ilo.org/topics/youth/#

Dursun, S. & Aytaç, S. (2009). Üniversite Öğrencileri Arasında İşsizlik Kaygısı (Unemployment Anxiety Among University Students), Uludağ *Üniversitesi İktisadi ve İdari Bilimler Fakültesi Dergisi, 28*(1), 71–84. https://www.acarindex.com/dosyalar/makale/acarindex-1423935894.pdf

Erol, S. I. (2013). Gençlere Yönelik Aktif İstihdam Politikaları: Japonya, Kore, Çin Ve Türkiye Örnekleri (Active Employment Policies for Youth: Examples of Japan, Korea, China and Turkey). *TÜHİS İş Hukuku ve İktisat Dergisi, 24*(6) / *25*(1–2), 15–43. https://tuhis.org.tr/upload/dergi/1389608428.pdf

Gündoğan, N. (1999). Genç İşsizliği ve Avrupa Birliği'ne Üye Ülkelerde Uygulanan Genç İstihdam Politikaları (Youth Unemployment and Youth Employment Policies in the Member States of the European Union). *Ankara Üniversitesi SBF Dergisi, 54*(1), 63–79. https://doi.org/10.1501/SBFder_0000001932

ILO (2005). *Youth: PathwaystoDecentWork.* Genava: International Labour Office. https://learning.itcilo.org/ilo/youthemployment/PDF/rep-vi_en.pdf

ILO (2022). *Global Employment Trends for Youth 2022.* Geneva: International LabourOrganization. https://www.ilo.org/wcmsp5/groups/public/---dgreports/---dcomm/---publ/documents/publication/wcms_853321.pdf

Işık, V. (2016). Türkiye'de Genç İşsizliği ve Genç Nüfusta Atalet(Youth Unemployment And Youth Inertia In Turkey). *Hak-İş Uluslararası Emek ve Toplum Dergisi, 5*(11), 130–145. https://dergipark.org.tr/tr/pub/hakisderg/issue/24441/259081

Kılıç, C. & Bülbül, O. (2012). Genç İşsizliğine İlişkin Teorik Çerçeve Dünyada Genç İstihdamının Durumu (Theoretical Framework on Youth Unemployment Status of Youth Employment in the World), *İstihdamda, 3i*(7), 40–41. https://media.iskur.gov.tr/15353/istihdamda-3i-sayi-7.pdf

Makal, A. (1992). *Türkiye'de Tek Partili Dönemde Çalışma.* İstanbul: İmge Kitabevi.

Murat, S. & Levent Ş. (2011). Gençlerin İstihdamı/İşsizliği bakımından Türk Eğitim Sisteminin Değerlendirilmesi(The Failure Of The Turkish Educational System For Creating Youth Employment). *Çalışma ve Toplum,* 3, 96. https://www.calismatoplum.org/Content/pdf/calisma-toplum-1377-d80d44e9.pdf

O'Higgins, N. (1997). The Challenge of Youth Unemployment. *International Social Security Review, 50*(4), 63–93. http://dx.doi.org/10.1111/j.1468-246X.1997.tb01084.x

O'Higgins, N. (2001). *Youth Unemloyment and Employment Policy: A Global Perspective.* ILO. https://www.researchgate.net/publication/44829351_Youth_unemployment_and_employment_policy_A_global_perspective

Sapancalı, F. (1998). 1980 Sonrası Ekonomik Gelişmelerin İşgücü Ve İstihdama Etkisi (The Effects of Economic Developments After 1980 on Labour and Employment). *Kamu İş - İş Hukuku Ve İktisat Dergisi, 4*(3), 131–159.

T.C. Başbakanlık Devlet Planlama Teşkilatı. (1963). Birinci Beş Yıllık Kalkınma Planı (1963–1967). (First Five-Year Development Plan). https://www.sbb.gov.tr/kalkinma-planlari/

T.C. Başbakanlık Devlet Planlama Teşkilatı. (1968). İkinci Beş Yıllık Kalkınma Planı (1968–1972). (Second Five-Year Development Plan). https://www.sbb.gov.tr/kalkinma-planlari/

T.C. Başbakanlık Devlet Planlama Teşkilatı. (1973). Üçüncü Beş Yıllık Kalkınma Planı (1973–1977). (Third Five-Year Development Plan). https://www.sbb.gov.tr/kalkinma-planlari/

T.C. Başbakanlık Devlet Planlama Teşkilatı. (1979). Dördüncü Beş Yıllık Kalkınma Planı (1979–1983). (Fourth Five-Year Development Plan). https://www.sbb.gov.tr/kalkinma-planlari/

T.C. Başbakanlık Devlet Planlama Teşkilatı. (1985). Beşinci Beş Yıllık Kalkınma Planı (1985–1989). (Fifth Five-Year Development Plan). https://www.sbb.gov.tr/kalkinma-planlari/

T.C. Başbakanlık Devlet Planlama Teşkilatı. (1990). Altıncı Beş Yıllık Kalkınma Planı (1990–1994). (Sixth Five-Year Development Plan). https://www.sbb.gov.tr/kalkinma-planlari/

T.C. Başbakanlık Devlet Planlama Teşkilatı. (1996). Yedinci Beş Yıllık Kalkınma Planı (1996–2000). (Seventh Five-Year Development Plan). https://www.sbb.gov.tr/kalkinma-planlari/

TURKSTAT Labour Force Statistics for 2013 and Before. https://biruni.tuik.gov.tr/isgucuapp/isgucu.zul

TURKSTAT Labour Force Statistics for 2014 and After. https://biruni.tuik.gov.tr/medas/?kn=72&locale=tr

UNDP. (2008). Turkey Human Development Report Youth in Turkey. http://hdr.undp.org/sites/default/files/turkey_2008_nhdr_en.pdf

*Chapter 2*

# Unionization and Collective Bargaining in Turkey

Ekrem Erdoğan[1]

This chapter analyses the situation of unionization and collective bargaining in Turkey. Turkey's unionization and collective bargaining process have been evaluated historicallyand statistically. The research is limited to the emergence of public institutions regulating labor relations, unionization of workers and public servants, collective bargaining processes, disputes, and dispute resolution. A voice mechanism enables employees to participate in decisions that affect them. The existence of representation mechanisms that emerge with the initiative of the employees in a country also positively affects the democratization process. Unionization and collective bargaining are the most basic mechanisms for the right to speak of employees. However, the number of people who can exercise this right is even more essential. In the research, firstly, the institutionalization process of these representation mechanisms is discussed, and then, statistics by periods. The data were obtained from official institutions and trade unions. The data on unionization, collective bargaining, mediation, strikes, and lockouts have been interpreted within this framework. The emergence and use of union rights operate separately for workers and public servants in Turkey. Unionization rates of workers and the number of workers covered by collective bargaining are low in Turkey. Despite the high unionization rate of public officials, they do not have the legal right to strike.

## INTRODUCTION

The labor problem that emerged due to poor working conditions after the Industrial Revolution led to the emergence of industrial relations and social policy discipline. This process also formed the basis of European democracy. The employees' solidarity and their role as a pressure group have increased the managers' sensitivity to these problems. What is important here is whether this solidarity process takes place naturally. Workers made positive contributions to the democratization process when they formed a solidarity with which they could resist adverse conditions at the request of the working class. The organization of employees, who force the system as a power factor, has led to the emergence and development of collective bargaining and struggle processes. All this has led to the institutionalization of industrial relations. Today, many countries accept trade union rights within the framework of social rights. However, there are some differences in the use of these rights, as each country's level of development and practice is different.

The Türk industrial relations system has been institutionalized in parallel with industrialization. The right of workers to organize and bargain collectively has been established by the public authority rather than by the coercion of the working class. Therefore, its contribution to the democratization process is limited. The regulation of social rights in working life started with an individual dimension in 1936 and a collective dimension in 1946. The laws have been revised many times, and this process has continued with the changes made in 2012. Since the establishment of the Republic of Turkey, there have been significant political and socioeconomic developments that affectsworking life. These changes, which significantly affect the collective rights of employees, have accelerated, especially in recent years.

This study examines the main features of working life in Turkey within the framework of actors, institutions, developments, and data. Thus, the situation of the Türk labor market in the context of industrial relations at the threshold of the new digital world has been revealed. However, here, it has been tried to convey the process and the current situation as it is rather than making comparisons with good practice examples.

In this chapter, organization, collective bargaining, dispute, and resolution processes in the Türk industrial relations system are discussed within the institutionalization of industrial relations. The data obtained from the Türk Statistical Institute, the Ministry of Labor and Social Security of the Republic of Turkey, the Official Gazette, and the trade unions were analyzed.

## INSTITUTIONALIZATION OF THE INDUSTRIAL RELATIONS SYSTEM

The functionality of the components that make up industrial relations depends on these components gaining an institutional character. This becomes possible by accepting the elements that make up industrial relations in the social and legal framework. However, this process progresses in direct proportion to industrialization and, therefore, the increase in the number of employees in terms of quantity and quality.

One of the most critical stages in institutionalization is the organization of the parties. At this stage, the organization of the state, employees, and employers is expressed as the triple pillar of industrial relations. This tripartite structure consists of specialized public institutions representing the state, unions and confederations representing employees, and trade unions representing employers and employers' associations. The second stage is the collective bargaining process. Here, we mean a method in which the parties accept each other as negotiable elements. The next phase includes resolving disputes and is divided into two separate processes. These establish peaceful and combative resolution methods in case of conflict.

## ORGANIZATION OF THE PARTIES OF WORKING LIFE IN TURKEY

Workers' and employers' organizations and specialized public institutions play an essential role in managing industrial relations and regulating working conditions. They form parts of this management system at the national, sectoral, and workplace levels in Turkey. This section examines the main actors, institutions, and their roles in regulating the working life in Turkey.

### Public Institutions Authorized to Regulate Working Life

The Ministry of Labor and Social Security in Turkey is the most basic public institution that regulates and supervises working life. The ministry undertakes the tasks of solving the structural problems of the labor market, increasing employment and qualified human resources, and taking measures to improve social security and OHS (Occupational Health and Security).

In the historical process, it was first established in 1945 as the Ministry of Labor. In 1974, the Ministry of Social Security was established, and the Social Insurance Institution and the Social Security Organisation for Artisans and Self-Employed (Bağ-Kur) were affiliated with this ministry. In 2018, the Ministry of Family, Labor and Social Services was established by merging the Ministry of Family and Social Policies and the Ministry of Labor and Social Security during the transition to the Presidential Government System. Finally, in 2021, it was divided into the Ministry of Family and Social Services and the Ministry of Labor and Social Security (ÇSGB, 2022a).

The most critical units regulating working life within the ministry are the Directorate General of Labor, the Directorate General of Occupational Health and Safety, and the Directorate General of International Labor Force. Social

Security Institution, Turkey Employment Agency (İŞKUR), and Vocational Qualifications Institution are related institutions.

The Directorate General of Labor serves as the central service unit of the ministry and consists of various departments. These include collective bargaining, trade unions, official mediation, individual labor law, labour statistics, public collective agreements, and employment policies departments. Each department has expertise, regulatory, and supervisory authority on the relevant subject. In this context, the duties of the directorate can be summarized as follows (ÇGM, 2022):

- To form an opinion on law proposals.
- To carry out the procedures for determining and implementing the minimum wage.
- To carry out the works envisaged in Trade Unions and Collective Bargaining Agreement Law No. 6356 (determination of authority, collective bargaining agreement, extension, strike-lockout, determination of the sector, determination of unionized workers and public officials, mediation).
- Creating and implementing a policy on increasing employment and improving working conditions.
- To produce policies on child labor, women's employment, discrimination, and disabled people in working life.

Accordingly, the Directorate General of Labor fulfils the duties of minimum wage, union rights, employment policies, improvement of working conditions, regulation, and supervision in terms of disadvantaged groups.

With the establishment of the Ministry of Labor in 1945, the "Directorate General of Occupational Health" was established as the central service unit. It was restructured as the Directorate General of Occupational Health and Safety in 2003. Most recently, in 2018, its duties and authorities were redefined as follows (ISGM, 2022):

- To prepare and implement a programme in the field of occupational health and safety.
- Checking the suitability of protective equipment.
- Ensure that necessary measures are taken to protect all employees against work accidents and occupational diseases.
- To carry out the measurement, technical control, risk analysis, training, and consultancy services in this field.
- Authorizing and issuing documents.

The Directorate General of Occupational Health and Safety fulfils the duties of implementing occupational health and safety in workplaces and supervising these processes in terms of suitability.

The Directorate General of the International Labor Force carries out the task of regulating the work permits and occupations of the foreign workforce. It is also an authorized institution for social security of foreigners, terms of opening a business, and bilateral agreements (UIGM, 2022).

Social insurance in Turkey has been established in 1945. In 2006, with the Social Security Reform, the Social Insurance Institution (SSK), Bağ-Kur, and the Pension Fund, which provide services according to different norms and standards, were combined under one roof. The institution makes payments according to the risks faced by individuals within the scope of short- and long-term insurance branches, attaches income, and provides health services to the insured and their dependents within the scope of general health insurance (SGK, 2022).

The legal infrastructure of the Vocational Qualifications Authority, which was established as the Vocational Standards Commission in 1992, was completed in 2006. VQA has the following duties and authorities (R.G., 2018):

- To manage the national vocational qualification system.
- To determine occupational standards and national qualifications.
- To accredit the institutions that will test the determined standards.

VQA carries out national standardization and accreditation services for occupations within the framework of international criteria.

In 1946, the Employment and Employment Agency (İİBK) was established to provide public employment services. The institution, whose primary duties were defined in 1971, was reorganized as the Turkey Employment Agency (İŞKUR) in 2000. The institution, which initially served as a classical job and worker finder, has now gained a structure that can implement active and passive labor force policies (İŞKUR, 2022). With the change in 2003, Private employment agencies and İŞKUR were provided to mediate employment services.

When evaluated in general, as one of the triple pillars of industrial relations, the state maintains a specialized public institution within the system. In particular, the issues of the organization, collective bargaining, disputes, and establishment of solutions, that form the basis of this study, fall under the scope of the Directorate General of Labor within the Ministry of Labor and Social Security. Other specialist units undertake supporting tasks regarding collective rights in working life.

## Trade Unions

Constitutions have been influential in the construction of workers' collective rights in Turkey. In this context, enacting these rights was delayed because there was no direct regulation on trade union rights in the 1924 Constitution. Of course, it is incorrect to explain this situation only with the Constitution. The factors that delay the achievement of union rights in Turkey are primarily hidden in the quantitative and qualitative problems related to capital accumulation and the working class. Naturally, the delays in capital accumulation, industrialization, and the formation of the working class caused the regulations in this area to appear later.

Unionization in Turkey should be handled separately in terms of workers and public officials. Trade union rights for those with worker status have been enacted in Turkey before. The transition to a multiparty political life in 1946 initiated a change in the democratization process. During this period, the ban on class-based organizations was lifted. Thus, the establishment of political parties and trade unions accelerated. This situation pushed the public authority to make regulations in this area. The collective rights of those with worker status were first regulated in 1947 with law no. 5018. According to this law, workers were deprived of fighting means (strike, lockout) (R.G., 1947). These were the years when Turkey's international integration started to increase. In 1951, ILO Convention No. 98 was ratified, broadly defining freedom of association outside of the civil service and private-sector. This convention mainly aims to protect union rights against private sector employers (R.G., 1951).

The 1961 Constitution granted all wage earners the right to form trade unions and associations and to freely join and withdraw from membership. However, in Article 47, collective bargaining and the right to strike were granted only to those with worker status. Following the Constitution, Trade Unions Law No. 274 and the Collective Bargaining Agreement, Strike, and Lockout Law No. 275 came into effect in 1963. These regulations define the means of combat (strike, lockout) for the first time for those with worker status. Thus, the institutionalization of the Türk Industrial Relations System was fully ensured for the workers (R.G., 1963) and established organizing, collective bargaining, and peaceful and combative means.

After the 1980 military coup, the collective rights of workers were reorganized in 1983 with laws numbered 2821 and 2822. These regulations naturally have a structure that reflects the coup mentality and restricts employees from exercising their collective rights. Notary requirements for union membership, the establishment of a confederation as an umbrella organization, only interest strikes, and thresholds related to the collective bargaining power of unions (10 percent in the branches of activity and 50 percent+1 in the workplace) can be counted among these (R.G., 1983).

In 1983, ILO Convention No. 87 on Freedom of Association and Protection of the Right to Union was enacted. Unlike contract No. 98, this contract guarantees the union rights and freedom of all employees without discrimination (R.G., 1993). Finally, Trade Unions and Collective Bargaining

Agreement Law No. 6356 was adopted in 2012. This law reduced the number of branches of activity from twenty-eight to twenty, which can make membership transactions via e-government. The thresholds have been rearranged for the unions' authority to bargain collectively. This reduced the business line threshold to 1 percent and determined the workplace threshold as 50 percent+1 and the enterprise threshold as 40 percent. In addition, the unionization of flexible and subcontracted workers was regulated (R.G., 2012a).

The unionization of public servants came to the fore with the 1961 Constitution. In Article 46, employees and employers are given the right and freedom to form trade unions. The phrase "employees" here means public servants also have this right. In the same article, it is foreseen that the rights of public servants who are not workers will be regulated by law (R.G., 1961). This context put Law No. 624 on Public Servants Unions into effect in 1965. Accordingly, organizing public servant personnel other than workers has become possible. However, other collective rights, such as collective bargaining, strike, and lockout, are not defined (R.G., 1965).

After 1971, a controversial period began in the unionization of public servants. With the amendment made on this date, the phrase "all employees and employers" in Article forty-six of the 1961 Constitution was changed to "workers and employers," thus preventing the unionization of public servants (R.G., 1971). This situation continued until the constitutional amendment in 1995. In this period, public servants organized under the umbrella of associations. The constitutional amendment in 1995 paved the way for the unionization of public servants. However, six years later, in 2001, the Law on Public Servants Unions No. 4688 was adopted. Accordingly, public servants had the right to unionize and have collective discussion meetings. In the 2001 version of the law, public servants did not have collective bargaining and strike rights (R.G., 2001). However, with the change made in 2012, public servants also had the right to collective bargaining. Public servants who are legally deprived of the right to strike have to apply to the Public Servants Arbitration Board in case of disagreement in collective bargaining negotiations (R.G., 2012b).

In Turkey, labor unions are organized based on the branch of activity, and public servants are based on the branches of service. This framework determined twenty branches of activity and eleven branches of service. Only confederations can be established as umbrella organizations.

Unionization data of workers in Turkey have been problematic for specific periods. Data from 1947 to 1963 are relatively safe. However, between 1963 and 2012, the the number of trade union members is overestimated. Since 2012, the implementation of the membership process through the e-Government portal has allowed instant tracking of data.

It would be more accurate to evaluate the unionization rates according to the stages of the unionization process for those with worker status in Turkey. Firstly, 1947–1963 is when the unions gained experience without combative means. During this period, workers increased by approximately 2.5 times, while unionized workers increased by about five times. This situation has led to an increase in unionization rates. The unionization rates were 26.65 percent in 1950, 45.57 percent in 1960, and 36.53 percent at the end of the period. During the period, the number of unions increased from 73 in 1948 to 432 in 1960 (Mahiroğulları, 2010: 163; Talas et al., 1965: 96). During this period, Turkey's membership in international organizations accelerated, implemented a liberal development program, and thus industrialization accelerated. In addition, Türk-İş was established, and Press and the Code on Sea Labor were adopted. All these have led to an increase in the number of unionized workers. However, this increase is minimal. As a result, there were just over 710,000 workers and approximately 260,000 unionized workers in 1963.

In 1947–1960, the unions focused on social aid activities rather than their economic and political roles. Unionism could not develop due to laws, practices of power, and structural problems. Private sector organizations remained very low compared to the public sector. Employers also started to organize in 1948 and became more effective after 1954 (Güzel, 1996: 166–167).

The 1961 Constitution and the subsequent laws numbered 274 and 275 initiated a new era by providing workers with combative means. According to the Ministry of Labor data, there were 511 unions and 298,000 members in 1961. This figure rose to 835,000 in 1967 and over 2 million in 1970. It increased from 3.3 million in 1975 to 5.7 million in 1980. However, it is claimed that these figures need to be corrected. The main reasons for this difference include membership in more than one union and the unions' failure to report resignations, deaths, and dismissals. DİSK was founded in 1967, MİSK in 1970, and Hak-İş in 1976. In addition, the introduction of certain thresholds to be able to operate nationwide in 1970 increased trade union competition. This situation has led to the fact that the number of members is much higher than the truth (Koç, 2003: 50). There are different figures for the number of unionized workers during this period. The number of workers covered by SSK was just over 920,000 in 1965, 1.3 million in 1970, and 2.2 million in 1980. Therefore, considering that the number of unionized workers cannot exceed the total number of workers, it is impossible to obtain the correct data during the period (Mahiroğulları, 2010: 170).

The ideology of the 1980 military coup was influential in establishing the 1982 Constitution, the 2821 Trade Unions Law, and the 2822 Collective Bargaining Strike Lockout Laws. These laws have a restrictive approach to certain rights provided to workers.

According to the Ministry of Labor and Social Security data, there were 1,427,000 unionized workers in 1984. In 2001, this figure exceeded 2.5 million. In January 2003, the total number of workers was 4,686,618, the number of unionized workers was 2,717,326, and the unionization rate was 57.98 percent. The authenticity of these data is also doubtful. It is claimed that the number of union members paying dues in 2003 was around 1.2–1.3 million (Koç, 2003: 106). According to the statistics of July 2009, there were 5.3 million workers, 3.2 million unionized workers, and a unionization rate of 59.88 percent. This number is higher than the actual figure because the ministry could not detect the excess in the notifications of the unions promptly (Mahiroğulları, 2010: 174). On the other hand, the Ministry of Labor and Social Security did not publish data in 2010–2011 and 2012.

After 2012, it is accepted as a new phase in terms of unionization. The e-Government gateway was put into service in Turkey in 2008. This system, in which hundreds of public institutions are integrated, is essential in terms of working life. With Law 6356, entered into force in 2012, workers can become union members via e-Government. This system, where notifications can be seen instantly, allows the number of trade union members to be determined accurately.

According to the labor force statistics of the Türk Statistical Institute, there was an increase in employment of more than 8.7 million people in the period of 2011–2022. This increase in employment increased the number of workers with worker status. Between 2013 and 2022, the total number of workers increased from 11,628,000 to 15,987,000. At the same time, the number of unionized workers increased from 1,032,000 to 2,280,000. While the total number of workers increased by approximately 50 percent, the number of unionized workers increased by more than 100%. This situation also reflected positively on unionization rates.

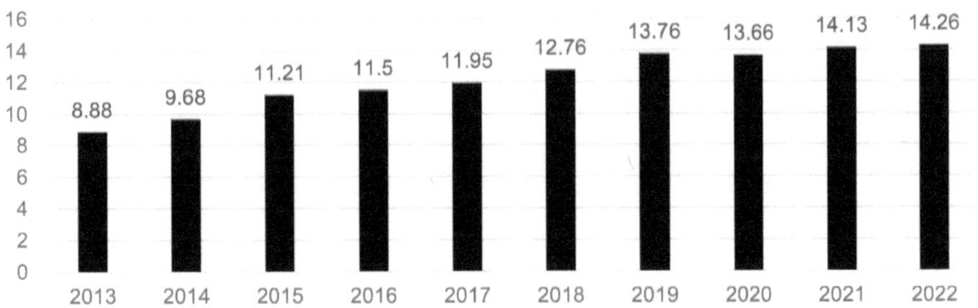


**Figure 2.1 Unionization Rate in 2013–2022 (%).** *Source*: ÇSGB (2022b). Note: It has been produced based on the Official Gazette communique on the number of workers and union members between 2013 and 2022.

According to figure 2.1, the unionization rate of workers increased from 8.88 percent to 14.26 percent during the period. Although this increase is significant, we can say that the unionization rate is still low.

Another factor that determines the power of the working class, apart from the organized workers, is the number of unions. The large number of unions plays a role in dividing the power of the working class. The number of labor unions between 1963 and 2022 can be evaluated in three periods. The first period was 1963–1983, when union inflation was experienced. During this period, the lowest number of unions reached 565 in 1963 and the highest 912 in 1978. The average for the period is 719. A significant problem arises when unions increase rapidly, and the working class rises quantitatively at a different rate. This situation dramatically divides the power of the working class, which faces the same problems. As it is known, accepting a union's demands at the collective bargaining table and before the society depends on the number of its members. The more members it has, the more it can play the role of a pressure group. The high number of unions reverses this situation. The second period is the period between 1984 and 2012. Compared to the 1963–1984 period, the average number of trade unions was around 100. Since 1984, the number of trade unions has decreased rapidly. This number dropped to eighty, the lowest, in 1988. One reason for this is the prohibitive understanding of the 1980 coup. Apart from this, adopting the principle of solid unionism can also be cited as a reason. The third period is between 2013 and 2022. In this period, when the new trade union law came into effect, the number of unions increased by more than 80 percent, from 121 to 218 (ÇSGB, 2022c).

As stated before, employees with worker status have the right to establish unions based on branches of activity. In this context, workers in Turkey are organized into twenty branches of activity.[2] The highest number of workers are in the 10, 12, 13, 5, and 18 branches of activity. On the other hand, the highest number of unionized workers are in the 20, 12, 10, and 17 branches of activity. The highest unionization rate is in the 20 branches of activity. More than half of the employees in this branch of activity are unionized. The branch of activity follows this numbered 17. These are followed by branches of activity 9 and 19, respectively. The lowest unionization rate is in the 13, 18, and 10 branches of activity (R.G., 2022b).

In Turkey, there are differences in unionization rates by gender. The high unionization rate among men is suitable for a male-dominated capitalist society. In Turkey, men's labor force participation and the employment rate are higher than women's. This situation is naturally reflected in the number of organized female workers. Unionization data by gender have been published regularly since 2014. Accordingly, the unionization rate of men increased from 9.9 percent in 2014 to 15.57 percent in 2021. For women, this rate increased from 4.05 percent in 2014 to 10.41 percent in 2021. However, in recent years, it has been seen that the gender gap has closed in favor of women. The unionization rate of men increased by 57.2 percent between 2014 and 2021. In women, this increase was 157 percent (ÇSGB, 2022c).

Public servants in Turkey continue their working lives within the framework of a separate regulation. Public sector unionization has not been welcomed in Turkey since the Ottoman Empire. After the Republic of Turkey was established, it continued this practice until 1961 (Tuncay, 2007: 160). In Turkey, public servants began to exercise their union rights, which were devoid of collective bargaining and strikes, in 1965. By 1971, 658 unions were established. After the prohibition of the unionization of public servants in 1971, an association period, including political division, began (Koç, 2003: 51–52). With the legal amendment in 1995, the unionization of public servants was made possible, and it entered into legal force in 2001 with the law numbered 4688. For this reason, unionization statistics of public servants have been given since 2002.

From 2002 to 2022, there was an increase of more than 1,389,000 in the employment of public servants. In the same period, unionized public servants increased by more than 1,344,000. This situation shows us that there is an increase in the number of union members almost as much as the increase in employment. Currently, 1,994,845 of 2,746,681 public officials are organized.[3] This figure is the highest unionized number of all time (ÇSGB, 2022d). This situation is also reflected in the unionization rates of public servants. Figure 2.2 shows the unionization rates of public servants.

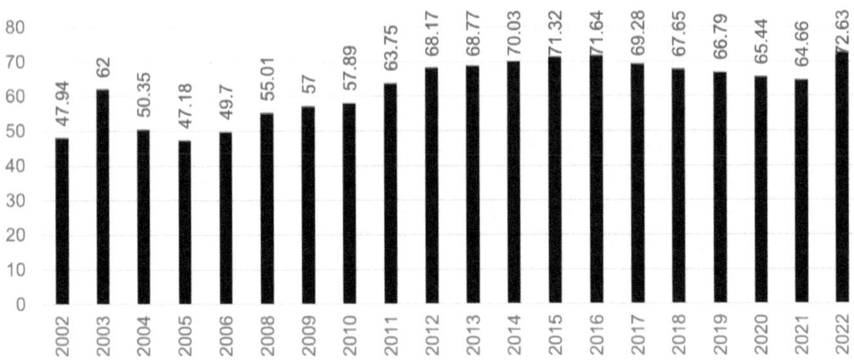


**Figure 2.2 Unionization Rate of Public Servants (%).** *Source*: ÇSGB (2022d). Note: It was produced based on the Official Gazette communique on the number of members of public servants' unions between 2002 and 2022. Since statistics were not produced in 2007, they are not shown here.

According to figure 2.2, unionization rates of public servants increased from 47 percent in 2002 to 71.6 percent in 2016. In 2020, it decreased slightly to 65 percent. In 2022, it reached the highest level, 72.63 percent. Compared to workers, unionization rates of public servants have always been higher. The most important reason for this is that employees in the public sector have job security.

*Main Union Confederations*

There are currently seven confederations and independent trade unions representing workers in Turkey. However, over 98 percent of unionized workers are organized by three confederations. These are Türk-İş, Hak-İş, and DİSK, respectively. Apart from these, there are currently TÜM-İŞ, ÜLKEM-İŞ, ANADOLU-İŞ, YENİDEN MİSK, and independent labor union confederations.

Türk-İş, the confederation with the highest number of members, was founded in 1952. There are thirty-four unions affiliated with the confederation, which is organized into twenty branches of activity, one of which is in the Türk Republic of Northern Cyprus (HÜR-İŞ). In 2022, thirty-two of these unions had collective bargaining power. Türk-İş is a member of ETUC, ITUC, and TUAC (TÜRK-İŞ, 2022).

Hak-İş, the confederation with the second-highest number of members, was established in 1976. The confederation, which is organized in all branches of business, has a total of twenty-one member unions, one of which is in the Türk Republic of Northern Cyprus (KKTC KAMU-SEN). In 2022, seventeen of these unions had collective bargaining power. Hak-İş is a member of ETUC, ITUC, and TUAC (HAK-İŞ, 2022).

DİSK (Confederation of Progressive Trade Unions of Turkey) was established in 1967. There are twenty-two member unions. In 2022, six of these unions had collective bargaining authority. It is a member of ETUC and ITUC (DİSK, 2022).

All Trade Unions Confederation (TÜM-İŞ) was established in 2019 and has eleven unions. The Anatolian Confederation of Trade Unions (ANADOLU-İŞ), which was established in 2020, has four, and the Re-Nationalist Confederation of Trade Unions (YENİDEN MİSK) has six unions. None of these confederations had unions with collective bargaining power in 2022. Ülkem Trade Unions Confederation (ÜLKEM-İŞ), which was established in 2020, has a total of ten unions, one of which has collective bargaining power. Independents, which has 113 unions, has four unions with collective bargaining power.

Türk-İş is the largest trade union confederation regarding the number of members. Between 2013 and 2022, the number of members increased from approximately 726,000 to over 1,256,000. Türk-İş has been organized primarily in public workplaces, preserving its nationalist-conservative line without experiencing significant conflicts with the governments. On the other hand, Hak-İş increased the number of its members more than three times during the period. Between 2013 and 2022, the number of members increased from approximately 178,000 to over 762,000. It is argued that the main reason for this rise seen in Hak-İş is related to the political support of the current government and its organization in the public sector. It is seen that there was a rapid increase in Hak-İş until 2019, but after 2019, the rate of growth in members slowed down. It can be said that the most important reason for this is the government's loss of metropolitan municipalities in local elections. On the other hand, DİSK, unlike other confederations, has been on the left politically and tends to organize in the private sector. Between 2013 and 2022, the members increased from approximately 103,000 to over 220,000. Although the number of members increased slightly more than two times during the period, it has the lowest number of members among the three powerful confederations (ÇSGB, 2022b).

While Türk-İş was in a position to represent 70.4 percent of unionized workers in 2013, its representation power decreased despite increasing the number of its members during the period. The representation rate fell to 52.5 percent of workers in 2020 and increased slightly to 55.1 percent in 2022. The main reason for the decrease in the rate of Türk-İş during the period is the increase in Hak-İş. Hak-İş's membership rates increased from 17.3 percent in 2013 to 36.4 percent in 2018. It decreased to 33.5 percent in 2022 in direct proportion to the loss of local elections by the government. DİSK maintains its current status in terms of member rates. The membership ratio of DİSK decreased from 10 percent in 2013 to 9.6 percent in 2022.[4]

There are currently twelve confederations and independents representing those with public servant status in Turkey. However, 91.2 percent of unionized public servants are organized by three confederations. These are Memur-Sen, Turkey Kamu-Sen, and KESK, respectively. Apart from these, there are BASK, BİRLEŞİK KAMU-İŞ, HAK-SEN, ÇALIŞAN-SEN, TUM MEMUR-SEN, ANADOLU-SEN, ŞEHİT GAZİ-SEN, MIL-SEN, and YURT-SEN (ÇSGB, 2022e).

The largest confederation of public servants, MEMUR-SEN (Confederation of Public Servants Trade Unions), was established in 1995. It has eleven member unions (MEMUR-SEN, 2022). The second largest confederation, Turkey Kamu-Sen, was established in 1992. It has thirteen member unions (TÜRKİYE KAMU-SEN, 2022). KESK, the third-largest confederation, was established in 1995. It has eleven member unions (KESK, 2022). The confederation, which ranks fourth, was founded in 2008 by unions that left KESK. There are nine member unions (BIRLEŞİK KAMU-İŞ, 2022).

It is seen that the three main confederations organize public officials to a large extent. These are Memur-Sen, Turkey Kamu-Sen, and KESK. According to figure 2.2, the number of public servants organized in Memur-Sen has increased significantly. Memur-Sen increased the number of unionized public servants more than 2.5 times, reaching over 1 million. While Turkey Kamu-Sen maintains its members, KESK has lost many members, especially since 2015 (ÇSGB, 2022d).

The change in the number of members of public servants before the confederations was reflected in the member rates. While Memur-Sen organized 36.9 percent of all unionized public servants in 2009, it organized 58.5 percent in 2021. This situation provides a significant representation ability in collective bargaining on behalf of public servants. During the same period, Turkey Kamu-Sen experienced a decrease of 12 percent, and KESK experienced a reduction of approximately 15 percent. Birleşik Kamu-İş, Independents, and Others increased their membership rates during this period. Currently, Memur-Sen represents 58.5 percent of unionized public servants. Turkey Kamu-Sen represents 25 percent, KESK 7.7 percent, and Birleşik Kamu-İş 4 percent of unionized public servants[5] (ÇSGB, 2022d).

## Employers' Organizations

Employers in Turkey have the right to organize by Law 5018 adopted in 1947. However, they were not organized in a significant way until 1961. It is seen that after the workers are organized in the world, employers also accelerate their organizing activities. This is also the case for employers in Turkey. While employers in Turkey were organized under the roof of unions and confederations, on the other hand, they took part in compulsory and voluntary employers' associations that were not unions.

The Union of Chambers and Commodity Exchanges of Turkey was established in 1950 as the leading professional organization and legal representative of the private sector in Turkey. TOBB is the parent organization of 365 chambers and commodity exchanges (Chambers of Commerce, Chambers of Industry, Chambers of Commerce and Industry, Chamber of Shipping and Commodity Exchange) in 81 provinces and 160 districts. In Turkey, tradespeople, artisans, merchants, and industrialists must register with the chamber. TOBB is rather a parent organization representing small- and medium-sized enterprises. Membership is mandatory (TOBB, 2022; Ticaret Bakanlığı, 2022). Here, we can say that the main reason for the state is to establish a solidaristic working life.

Founded in 1962, TİSK (Türk Confederation of Employer Associations) has been the only leading organization authorized to represent Türk employers in industrial relations at home and abroad until 2019. It aims to bring solutions to macro problems in labor relations. There are twenty-one member employers' unions operating in various sectors of the economy and industry, including public service. It covers approximately 10,000 workplaces where 2 million employees are employed. It represents the employer segments in all platforms where the principle of tripartite representation is valid, such as the Economic and Social Council, the Tripartite Advisory Board, and the Labor Council at the national level. At the international level, it represents Türk employers on global platforms such as ILO, IOE, BUSINESSEUROPE, and more (TİSK, 2022).

TÜSİAD was founded in 1971. This organization is an association established based on voluntary representation. It has international representations in Brussels, Washington, DC, Berlin, London, and Paris. It has networks in China, Silicon Valley, and the Gulf. It is a member of BUSINESSEUROPE. It has members representing nearly 4,500 companies. These companies provide 85 percent of foreign trade, excluding energy imports, and 50 percent of registered employment, excluding public and agriculture (TÜSİAD, 2022). Another employer organization accepted within this framework was MUSIAD, established in 1990. MUSIAD, which employs approximately 1.8 million people, represents about 60,000 enterprises. It performs this representation task nationally all over the country and internationally in eighty-one different countries (MÜSİAD, 2022). Finally, the Confederation of All Employers' Unions was established in 2019. It has nine unions (TİSKO, 2022).

While there were 78 employer unions in 1963, this number increased to 120 in 1970 and 102 in 1983. This was a period in which the number of trade unions increased significantly. The number of employer unions also increased depending on the increase in trade unions. After 1983, the prohibitive practices of the coup mentality led to a decrease in the number of trade unions. Accordingly, the number of employer unions decreased between 1983 and 2002. This number, which was sixty in 1984, dropped to forty-nine in 2002. Since 2008, the number of trade unions has shown an increasing trend. While there were 94 trade unions in 2007, this figure reached 218 in 2022. Accordingly, the number of employer unions reached eighty-four in 2022 (ÇSGB, 2022c).

## COLLECTIVE BARGAINING

According to Sidney and Beatrice Webb, collective bargaining is the process of determining working conditions between employers and their representatives and employee representatives, that is, unions. Collective bargaining is a negotiation process that produces two results. The first is the state of agreement. This is called a collective agreement. The second is the conflict situation. In this case, a collective labor dispute arises.

Authorized trade unions carry out collective bargaining for those with worker status in Turkey. For a union to conclude a collective bargaining agreement, it is necessary to organize at least 1 percent of the workers working in the sector in which it is established and more than half of the workers in the workplace that the collective agreement will cover. On the other hand, if that employer is to conclude a collective bargaining agreement covering more than one workplace, then the bargaining process must be carried out by the union that organizes more than 40 percent of the workers working in the enterprise (Law no: 6356, Article: 41-1) (R.G., 2012a).

The total number of unions doubled between 2013 and 2022 by branches of activity. While there were 92 trade unions in 2013, this number increased to 218 in 2022. This is directly proportional to the increase in the number of unionized workers. The most important weapon of the unions in voicing their demands is the number of members. In other words, unions with more members have the potential to obtain more rights. Here, the increase in the number of unions at the same rate as the increase in the number of unionized workers weakens the potential of the working class to increase its power (ÇSGB, 2022b).

On the other hand, the number of authorized unions is increasing partially. This number increased from forty-four in 2013 to sixty in 2022. Although the total number of unions increased by 80 percent during the period, the rate of increase in the number of authorized unions remained around 54 percent. The ratio of the total number of unions to the number of unions that passed the threshold decreased from 36.4 percent in 2013 to 27.5 percent in 2022. Since the number of new unions increased, the rate of authorized unions is decreasing. This means that the scope of collective bargaining is narrowing.

The Public Employers' Board, on behalf of the public administration, and the Public Servants Unions Board, on behalf of the public servants, participate in the collective bargaining negotiations for public servants. The Public Employers' Board consists of representatives of public institutions to be determined by the competent authority. The chairman of the Public Servants Unions Board is the confederation with the highest number of members. In addition, it consists of fifteen members, one representative from the union with the highest number of members in each branch of service, and one representative from the first, second, and third confederations with the highest number of members (Law No. 4688, Article 29) (R.G., 2012b).

From this point of view, it can be said that MEMUR-SEN, which has the highest number of members in the collective bargaining of public servants in Turkey, both chairs the Public Servants Unions Board and has a predominantly representative authority within this structure.

## Level and Scope of Collective Bargaining

Collective bargaining can be done at different levels, usually local, regional, national, or international. However, this situation becomes more difficult as you go from local to international levels. This means that global collective bargaining is theoretically possible but very difficult in practice. In Turkey, workers and public servants participate in the collective bargaining process and have the right to conclude a collective bargaining agreement. However, there are differences in practice for both groups.

Workers can make collective bargaining agreements at the workplace, enterprise, and industry levels. These are defined in Article 2 of Law No. 6356. Enterprise collective agreements can be arranged if there is more than one workplace belonging to an actual or legal person or a public institution or organization in the same branches of activity. A group collective bargaining agreement covering workplaces and established companies in the same line of business belonging to more than one employer can also be drawn up between the labour union and the employers' union. The trade union in all contract types must represent the workers. In contrast, the employer is freer. Especially in workplace and enterprise collective bargaining agreements, the employer can participate directly. The employer doesn't need to be represented by a union. However, if a group collective bargaining agreement is to be made, then the employer's union must become a party on behalf of the employer.

In addition, the parties can also draw up a framework contract. According to Article 2-b of Law No. 6356, a framework contract is defined as the contract made at the branches of activity level between the employee and employer unions that are members of the worker and employer confederations represented in the Economic and Social Council. However, we should evaluate this contract within the scope of social dialogue. Because framework contracts should include regulations regarding vocational education, occupational health and safety, social responsibility, and employment policies. In these contracts, there should be no provisions regulating the mutual rights and obligations of the parties in the collective bargaining agreement, the implementation and control of the deal, and the ways to resolve disputes (Law no: 6356, Article: 33-2/3) (R.G., 2012a).

The members of the labor union that make collective bargaining primarily benefit from the collective bargaining agreement. Others can benefit from the collective bargaining agreement only by paying solidarity dues to the union that is a party to the collective bargaining agreement (Law No. 6356, Article 39-1/4). There is also an extension practice in Türk working life. The extension is the implementation of a collective bargaining agreement signed by the union with the highest number of members in the workplace where there is no collective bargaining agreement in branches of activity. The implementation of the extension is at the discretion of the president. However, for it to be implemented, it is necessary to have the request of the worker or employer representatives in that sector or the Minister of Labor and Social Security and the favorable opinion of the Supreme Arbitration Board (Law no: 6356, Article: 40–1) (R.G., 2012a).

In general, collective bargaining agreements can be made in one- to three-year periods. They are usually signed for two years in Turkey. The number between 1963 and 1983 tended to increase when evaluated in terms of periods. In 1979, nearly 3,000 collective bargaining agreements were signed. It can be said that the most crucial reason for the decrease in 1981 was the prohibitive attitude of the military coup administration. In 1982, it quickly increased to 3,221. This situation may be due to delays from the previous year. The average of the period is 1,650. From 1984 to 2002, an annual average of 2,447 collective bargaining agreements were made. They were signed at most in 1991, 2001, and 1993, respectively. In the 2003–2021 period, the annual average number is 2,314. Although fewer collective bargaining agreements were signed compared to the previous period, it has been an increasing trend in recent years (ÇSGB, 2022c).

The number of collective bargaining agreements has been separated into public and private sectors since 1984. Except for 2001, the majority of collective bargaining agreements between 1984 and 2002 were signed in the private sector. During this period, 66 percent of the contracts were signed in the private sector. Apart from 2005, more collective bargaining agreements were signed in the public sector during 2003–2015. It has increased again in the private sector since 2015. The number of collective bargaining agreements signed in the private sector in 2003–2021 decreased to 50.5 percent on average (ÇSGB, 2022c).

In addition, the number of workers covered by the signed collective bargaining agreements should also be evaluated. The number of workers covered by the collective bargaining agreements signed in the 1963–2021 period tended to increase until 1991, decreased from 2012, and started to increase again from then to the present. The number of workers covered by the collective bargaining agreements signed in the 1963–1983 period has increased. This increase occurred in parallel with the rise in collective bargaining agreements. In this period, an annual average of 408,857 workers were covered by collective bargaining agreements. From 1984 to 2002, a yearly average of 635,771 workers were covered. In the 2003–2021 period, this number was 535,831. These data show that although there has been an upward trend in recent years, the scope of collective bargaining has narrowed[6] (ÇSGB, 2022c).

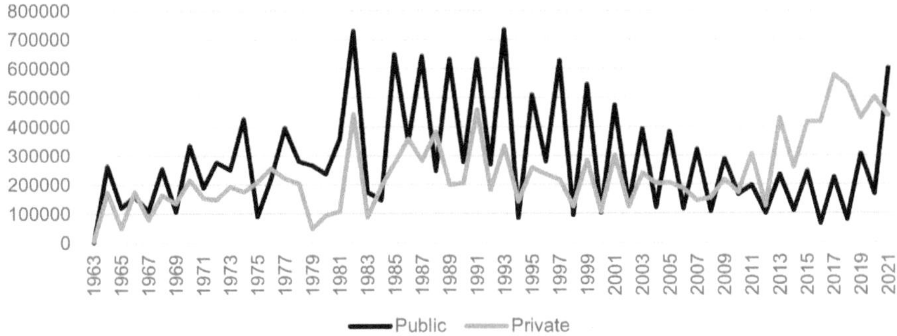


**Figure 2.3 Number of Workers Covered by Collective Bargaining Agreements by Public and Private Sector (1963–2021).** *Source*: ÇSGB (2022c). Note: Produced from work-life statistics books in 1989, 1998, 2009, 2010, and 2021.

Most workers covered by collective bargaining agreements from 1963 to 2010 were in the public sector. Since 2010, there has been a contraction in the public sector and an increase in the private sector. About 61.1 percent of the workers covered by the collective bargaining agreements signed in the 1963–1983 period were in the public sector. This rate was 61.5 percent in 1984–2002 and 41.5 percent in 2003–2021 as seen in figure 2.3. The scope of collective bargaining agreements changes in favor of the private sector.

To fully understand the scope of collective bargaining, looking at the ratio of total and unionized workers and workers covered by collective bargaining agreements would be more accurate. How many of the total and unionized workers are within the scope of collective bargaining gives us information about the functioning of the right-to-speak mechanism.

Although the collective bargaining data are more reliable, the problems in the unionization statistics, especially in the period until 2012, necessitate an evaluation since 2013 in calculating the ratio of the total number of workers within the scope of collective bargaining to the unionized workers. Since the data for 2022 have yet to be published, the evaluation was made from 2013 to 2021. Accordingly, an average of 4.97 percent of total workers and 42.1 percent of unionized workers are within the scope of collective bargaining during the period[7] (ÇSGB, 2022c).

Another issue is the extension when evaluated in terms of the scope of the collective bargaining agreement. The extension means expanding the size of the collective bargaining agreement. Although it is not a common practice in Turkey, it is regulated in Article 40 of Law No. 6356. Accordingly, the extension is made in the branches of activity where the workplace where this transaction is to be made is established. A collective bargaining agreement signed by the union with the highest number of members in that branch of activity is taken as a basis. This collective bargaining agreement may be extended to workplaces that do not have a collective bargaining agreement, upon request of the Minister of Labor and Social Security, by amending it entirely or partially after the opinion of the Supreme Arbitration Board. Here, the president has the authority to apply and remove the extension. It becomes official by entering into force in the official gazette together with the reason for its extension. The extension automatically ends if the extended collective bargaining agreement expires and a collective bargaining agreement is made in that workplace.

Making a collective bargaining agreement for those with the status of public servants is possible differently than for those with the status of a worker. Accordingly, at the end of the collective bargaining of public servants, a collective agreement is signed, consisting of a general section on economic and social rights and areas on financial and social rights specific to each branch of service. A contract can be signed to determine the amount of social balance compensation in local administrations within a maximum of three months after the signing of this contract. However, this agreement is not accepted as a collective agreement (4688, Article 31). Unlike the worker status, no distinction can be made between public servants in terms of union members and nonunion members in the implementation of the collective agreement provisions, except the collective agreement bonus (4688, Article 28). Collective bargaining agreements can be concluded for a minimum of one year and a maximum of three years for those with worker status. However, it is usually done for two years. The shorter-term collective bargaining agreements can be drawn up for businesses whose activities last less than one year (Law No. 6356, Article 35-2/3). After the collective agreement is signed, this period cannot be changed and expires at the end of this period. Collective bargaining negotiations in public servants are held in years with odd numbers, and the provisions of collective agreements are valid for two fiscal years (4688, Article 28/31).

## COLLECTIVE LABOR DISPUTE

During the collective bargaining process, a collective labor dispute arises if the parties do not come to the meeting, do not participate even if they come, or cannot agree within the collective bargaining period. In Turkey resolution of collective labor disputes primarily requires using peaceful means (Law No. 6356, Article 35-2/3). This issue should be handled separately for worker and civil servant status. Because civil servants lack combative means, this process ends for them at the first stage.

## Means of Peaceful Resolution

In the first stage of collective labor disputes, there are two options for those who have the worker's status. These are mediation and arbitration processes. There is a special arbitrator and a High Arbitration Board in the arbitration process also. Mediation is the search for a solution to the dispute by appointing one of the official mediation lists of the competent authority. Here, the official mediator tries to reach an agreement between the parties and makes suggestions to them. However, the mediator's decision is not binding. In other words, the parties do not have to comply with the decision (Law No. 6356, Article 50). Mediation figures in Turkey have been reached since 1989. Between 1989 and 2014, the total number of mediations was mostly at the same level. The average number of mediations in this period is 554. It increased significantly in 2016 and 2017 and reached 3,578. Later, in 2020, this figure decreased to 984. It grew to 1,432 in 2021.

On the other hand, another important indicator is the number of workers covered by the mediation process. During this period, the number of workers covered by mediation decreased until 2012. In this period, the number fell from 700,000 to 90,000. Due to the increase in total mediation after 2012, the number of workers covered by mediation has also increased. In 2021, the number of workers covered by mediation increased to over 805,000. How this process ends is also an important issue. Although the mediation rates that resulted in an agreement have increased partially until 2011, the primary trend is stagnant. As of 2012, despite the increase in mediation and the number of workers under its scope, the agreement rate has been decreasing. Although the number of mediation was the highest in 2016 and 2017, it was in these years that the rate of mediation concluded with an agreement was the lowest. The average rate of mediation that resulted in a deal in the 1989–2021 period is 25 percent[8] (ÇSGB, 2022c).

The second way to resolve disputes is through the arbitration process. In conflicts where strikes and lockouts are prohibited, and in cases where the decision is not to hold a strike as a result of the strike vote, one of the parties may apply to the Supreme Arbitration Board. If the application is not made, the authority of the labor union is lost. On the other hand, the parties may, by mutual agreement, apply to a special arbitrator at every stage of the disputes of collective rights or interests. They can also choose the Supreme Arbitration Board as a special arbitrator. Unlike mediation, the decisions taken at the end of the arbitration process bind the parties since they have the force of a collective bargaining agreement (Law No. 6356, Article 51/52).

Considering the collective bargaining agreement concluded by the Supreme Arbitration Board, the workplace it covers, and the number of workers it covers, immediately after the 1980 coup, the number of collective bargaining agreements concluded by the Supreme Arbitration Board increased significantly. In addition, there was a significant increase in 2016–2017 and 2018. It is observed that these increases are caused mainly by the private sector. Apart from that, the average number resolved by the Supreme Arbitration Board follows a standard course. In parallel with the increase in collective bargaining agreements concluded by the Supreme Arbitration Board, the number of workers it covers has also increased. While these increases were caused by the public sector in the 1981–1982 and 1983 periods, they were caused by the private sector in the 2016, 2017, and 2018 periods[9] (ÇSGB, 2022c).

The situation is different for public servants. If one cannot reach an agreement during the collective agreement negotiation process, the State Personnel Presidency keeps a report stating that the negotiations resulted in a disagreement. In the following procedure, the signatory parties must apply to the Public Officials Arbitration Board for the dispute settlement. Decisions made by the board have the force of a collective agreement and are binding on the parties (Law No. 4688, Article 33/34).

## Means of Combative Solution

What is meant as a means of the combative solution is the right to strike and lockout. However, in Turkey, these rights are granted to workers and employers. It is not legal for public servants to use combative methods.

Law 5018, which came into force in 1947, gave workers the right to organize but did not define the means of struggle they could use in case of conflict. The right to strike began to be used as a legal right in 1963, with its inclusion in the 1961 Constitution. The regulation of collective bargaining and the right to strike continued with the laws numbered 275 in 1963, 2822 in 1983, and 6356 in 2012.

A strike is a walkout of workers doing the job by not working collectively to stop the activity in the workplace or to significantly disrupt it, depending on the nature of the work, by agreeing among themselves or by following an organization's decision (Law No. 6356, Article 58). For the workers to go on strike in Turkey, a disagreement must arise in the collective bargaining process and then complete the mediation process. Otherwise, the strike is not considered legal. In other words, at the first stage, a labor union that has the authority to make a collective bargaining agreement must also complete the mediation process after it fails to reach an agreement during the collective agreement. If they cannot agree on this process, a strike decision can be taken by complying with the legal deadlines. In some places, even if a strike decision has been taken, a strike may not be held. For example, one can annul a strike decision at a workplace by making a strike vote. A decision is made for a strike vote within six working days from the announcement of the decision to strike and with a written application of one-fourth of the employees in that workplace. As a result of the voting, the decision made by the majority of the voting participants is followed. If the decision not to strike has been taken, a strike cannot be held (Law No. 6356, Article 61).

During the period, the number of strikes tended to increase until 1990. This increase has accelerated, especially since the late 1970s. It has been in a decreasing trend since 1990, except for 1995. The number of workers participating in the strike followed a course parallel to the number of strikes. The number of workers participating in the strike increased until 1996. Starting from 1996, except for the years 2000–2007 and 2013, there has been a decrease in the number of workers participating in the strike[10] (ÇSGB, 2022c).

The number of working days lost in a strike has also developed in line with the strike trend. However, although the number of strikes was low in 1995 and 2007, the number of workers participating in the strike and the number of lost workdays were higher. It is possible to evaluate strikes in three periods in Turkey. These periods are 1963–1980, 1984–2002, and 2003–2021. These periods are the ones in which there is a break in Türk history.

During the 1963–1980 period, a total of 1,440 strikes took place. Approximately 10.2 million working days were lost in these strikes, in which 290,554 workers participated. The average number of workers per strike was 201. The number of working days lost per striker was 35. The average number of working days lost per strike was 7,076. According to Güzel (1996: 210–248), the number of strikes was less in 1963–1970, but the strike duration per worker was longer because of law no. 3008. This situation increased the cost of the strike for all parties. In the 1973–1980 period, the strike, the workforce participating in the strike, and the number of workdays lost during the strike increased considerably. It can be said that the increase in violence in strikes since 1975 is related to the role played by DİSK. Although there were few strikes in the public sector, the average number of workers participating was higher. On the other hand, the number of lost working days in the private sector was more elevated. Among the reasons for this situation were the aggressive, anti-union, and anti-strike attitudes of the employers.

Due to the ban on September 12, 1980, there were no strikes or lockouts in 1981, 1982, and 1983. A total of 2,106 strikes took place in the 1984–2002 period. About 87.9 percent of these strikes were in the private sector. The total number of workers participating in the strike was over 775,000. Workers in the public sector constituted 56.6 percent of this number. The total number of working days lost in the strike was approximately 2.3 million. About 50.9 percent of this occurred in the public sector. The number of workers per strike increased compared to the previous period and reached an average of 368. This number was approximately 182 in the private sector and 1,733 in the public sector. From this, it can be concluded that there were strikes with more involvement in the public sector. The average number of working days lost per strike was 29.5. This number was 26.6 in the public and 33.4 in the private sector. The average number of working days lost per strike was 10.898. Of these, 46.165 occurred in the public and 6.083 in the private sector.

In 2003, the period of the Justice and Development Party began. There were a total of 343 strikes during the period. Most (91.3 percent) of these strikes were in the private sector. A total of 87,428 workers participated in the strike, of which 95 percent were private sector workers. In these strikes, 3,684,599 working days were lost, with 99 percent of this number occurred in the private sector. The number of workers per strike decreased compared to the previous period and became 254.8 on average. This number was 265.4 in the private sector and 145.1 in the public sector. The average number of working days lost per strike was 42.1. This number was 7.78 in the public sector and 43.9 in the private sector. The average number of working days lost per strike was 10.742. This number was 1.129 in the public and 11.663 in the private sector.

When evaluated in general, lockout practices are not seen very often in the Türk Industrial Relations system. Of the 463 lockouts in total, 453 were before 2000. There were lockout applications most intensely between 1987 and 1993. In these seven years, a total of 426 lockouts were implemented. The number of people locked out and the number of days lost in the lockout followed a course parallel to this trend. Although there were more lockouts in the private sector until 1992, the number of people locked out and the number of days lost in the public sector were higher[11] (ÇSGB, 2022c).

## CONCLUSION

In Turkey, the process of unionization, collective bargaining, and dispute resolution is applied separately as it is subject to different regulations for workers and public servants. While workers have all the rights in terms of institutionalization, public servants need combative means. The pressure of the working class has not fully formed the institutionalization of industrial relations in Turkey. In this process, the influence of the state was more significant. In addition, the interruptions (coups) in Türk political life effectively limited the demands of the employees. The triple pillar of industrial relations in Turkey consists of specialized public institutions representing the state, trade unions and confederations representing workers, trade unions representing employers, and employers' associations. Public institutions authorized to regulate working life are gathered under the Ministry of Labor and Social Security. These are the General Directorate of Labor, the General Directorate of Occupational Health, the General Directorate of International Labor

Force, the Social Security Institution, the Türk Employment Agency, and the Vocational Qualifications Institution. In the issue of unionization, collective bargaining, and dispute resolution, the main task is the General Directorate of Labor and its subordinate departments.

Unionization in Turkey started legally in 1947 with the law numbered 5018 and is carried out according to the rule that entered into force in 2012. Accordingly, trade unions are established based on the branches of activity. There are twenty branches of activity. Membership in the trade union is done via e-Government. Only authorized unions can conduct collective bargaining. For a trade union to be authorized to bargain collectively, it must organize a certain percentage of the workers in the branches of activity and workplace where the trade union is established. These rates are 1 percent for the branches of activity, 51 percent for the workplace, and 41 percent for the enterprise. The unionization of public officials came to the fore with the 1961 Constitution. It started legally in 1965 with Law No. 624 on State Personnel Unions. The unionization of public servants became controversial with the legal amendment in 1971, which continued until 1995. The constitutional amendment in 1995 removed the legal obstacle to the organization of public officials. The law regulates trade union rights of public officials numbered 4688 in 2001 and the amendments in 2012. Although public officials have the right to organize collective bargaining, they do not have the right to strike in a disagreement, so they have to apply to the Public Servants Arbitration Board. Public officials are organized based on service branches, with eleven service branches.

The tendency to unionize in Turkey has generally increased due to the increase in the total number of workers. While the number of workers increased 2.5 times in the 1948–1963 period, the number of unionized workers increased five times. However, the increase in the number of unionized workers is limited. In 1963, there were approximately 710,000 workers and 260,000 unionized workers. For this reason, unions have focused on social aid rather than their economic and political roles. Unionization data for the 1963–2012 period are problematic. Because in this period, notifications of resignation, death, and dismissal due to competition between unions are problematic. Data have become more secure since 2012, with the membership being made through the e-Government gateway. Between 2011 and 2022, employment in Turkey increased by more than 8.7 million. This was reflected in the number of workers and the increase in unionized workers. While the total number of workers increased by 50 percent, unionized workers increased by more than 100%. The unionization rate increased from 9.21 percent in 2013 to 14.32 percent in 2022. Although this increase is significant, it should be said that the rate of unionization among workers is still low. The highest number of unionized workers is in general works and metal branches of activity. The highest rate of unionized workers is in general works and health and social services branches of activity. The fewest unionized workers are in the media, broadcasting, journalism, and shipbuilding and shipping branches of activity. In terms of percentage, it is lowest in the construction branches of activity. When evaluated according to gender, the unionization rate for men is 15.58 percent, and for women, it is 9.45 percent. The increase in unionization in recent years has helped to close this gap in favor of women.

The unionization rate of public servants is higher than that of workers, mainly due to the job security factor. This rate increased from 47.94 percent in 2002 to 72.63 percent in 2022. In 2022, approximately 2 million of the 2.7 million public servants were union members.

In Turkey, workers are represented by seven confederations and independents. Currently, Türk-İş (55.1 percent), Hak-İş (33.5 percent), and DİSK (9.6 percent) organize 97.2 percent of organized workers. From 2013 to 2022, all confederations increased the number of members. The highest increase was experienced in Hak-İş. DİSK, on the other hand, kept its number of members. Twelve confederations and independents represent public servants in Turkey. Currently, Memur-Sen (58.5 percent), Turkey Kamu-Sen (25 percent), and KESK (7.7 percent) have organized 91.2 percent of the total organized public servants. While Memur-Sen increased the number of its members significantly during the period, the others experienced decreases at the same rate. Employers in Turkey also have the right to organize since 1947, and they have been organized in three ways. These can be listed as compulsory membership system (TOBB), associations (TÜSİAD and MÜSİAD), and union system (Union system, TİSK, and TİSKO).

The period 1963–1983 was when the number of trade unions increased significantly in Turkey. There were an average of 719 trade unions during this period. The extremely high number of trade unions in a place where the working class does not increase quantitatively at the same rate divides the power of the working class. Since 1984, there has been a severe decrease in unions. From 1984 to 2012, there were an average of 101 labor unions. The number of trade unions, 103 in 2012, increased to 218 in 2022. The number of authorized trade unions increased by 31 percent. The fact that the number of trade unions is rising faster than the increase in unionized workers, unfortunately, weakens the power of the working class. Collective bargaining agreements can be made at the workplace, business, and industry levels for those with worker status. In addition, it is possible to conclude framework agreements that should be evaluated within the scope of social dialogue. Union members who signed the collective bargaining agreement and workers paying solidarity fees benefit from collective bargaining. In addition, the extension of collective bargaining is also legally implemented.

Generally, collective bargaining agreements are drawn up for two years. The number of workers covered by the signed collective bargaining agreements increased until 1991, decreased in 2012, and started to increase again from then to the present. However, although there has been an upward trend in recent years, the scope of collective bargaining has narrowed. From 1963 to 2010, the majority of workers covered by collective bargaining agreements were in the public sector, and from 2010 onward, in the private sector. The increase in the number of workers covered by the collective bargaining agreements in recent years has resulted from the private sector. Considering the ratio of workers covered by collective bargaining agreements among all and unionized workers, 4.97 percent of total workers and 42.1 percent of unionized workers on average since 2013 are within the scope of collective bargaining. The number of those benefiting from the collective bargaining agreement by paying the solidarity fee hasn't been added to this figure.

The collective bargaining agreement is signed between the Public Employers' Board and the Public Servants' Unions Board in the public sector. The Trade Union Board is chaired by the confederation with the highest number of members. Since 2010 Memur-Sen has been the confederation with the highest number of members. The scope of the public collective agreement includes all employees, regardless of union or nonunion discrimination. Collective agreements are usually drawn up for two fiscal years.

The number of mediations in Turkey decreased partially from 1989 to 2014. It peaked from 2014 to 2017 and entered a decreasing trend again. Although the number of workers it covers tended to decline until 2012, it has increased since 2012. Despite this, the rate of those resulting in an agreement has been growing, especially in recent years. Especially in 2016–2017, although the number of mediations peaked, the agreement rates were the lowest. While the number of collective bargaining agreements and workplaces concluded by the Supreme Arbitration Board during the period decreased in the public sector, they increased partially in the private sector. When public officials cannot agree during the collective bargaining process, they must apply directly to the Public Servants Arbitration Board.

In Turkey, we can only use combative means for those with worker status. Public officials do not have the right to strike. The number of strikes in Turkey increased significantly, especially from the mid-1970s to the early 1990s. These years experienced economic and political crises. Since 1992, the number of strikes has decreased tremendously. The number of workers participating in the strike and the number of working days lost during the strike also followed this line. Lockouts are much less common. About 97.8 percent of the lockout applications from 1984 to the present are before 2000.

## NOTES

1. Prof. Dr., Sakarya University, Faculty of Political Sciences, Labour Economics and Industrial Relations Department, eerdogan@sakarya.edu.tr, ORCID: 0000-0002-3480-4758.

2. List of branches of activity: (1) Hunting, fishing, agriculture, and forestry; (2) the food industry; (3) mining and quarries; (4) petroleum, chemical, rubber, plastic, and medicine; (5) Weaving, ready-made clothing, and leather; (6) wood and paper; (7) communication; (8) press, broadcasting, and journalism; (9) banking, finance, and insurance; (10) commerce, office, education, and fine arts; (11) cement, soil, and glass; (12) metal; (13) construction; (14) energy; (15) transportation; (16) shipbuilding and maritime transport, warehouse, and warehousing; (17) health and social services; (18) accommodation and entertainment; (19) defense and security; and (20) general works.

3. For more detailed data, you can refer to the Official Gazette communique on the number of public servants union members between 2002 and 2022.

4. For more detailed data, you can refer to the Official Gazette communique on the number of workers and union members between 2013 and 2022.

5. For more detailed data, you can refer to the Official Gazette communique on the number of public servants union members between 2009 and 2021.

6. For more detailed data, you can look at the Working Life Statistics books in 1989, 1998, 2009, 2010, and 2021 of the Ministry of Labor and Social Security.

7. For more detailed data, you can look at the Working Life Statistics books in 2021 of the Ministry of Labor and Social Security.

8. For more detailed data, you can look at the Working Life Statistics books in between 1989 and 2021 of the Ministry of Labor and Social Security.

9. For more detailed data, you can look at the Working Life Statistics books in between 2006 and 2011 and 2021 of the Ministry of Labor and Social Security.

10. For more detailed data, you can look at the Working Life Statistics books in 1999, 2000 and 2011 and 2021 of the Ministry of Labor and Social Security.

11. For more detailed data, you can look at the Working Life Statistics books in 1999, 2000 and 2011 and 2021 of the Ministry of Labor and Social Security. In 1986, 2001–2002–2007–2009–2013, 2017, 2019, 2020, and 2021, no lockouts were recorded in the statistics.

## REFERENCES

BİRLEŞİK KAMU-İŞ (2022) Birleşik Kamu-İş Tüzüğü, https://www.birlesikkamuis.org.tr/sayfa/detay/Birlesik-Kamu-is-Tuzugu, Erişim Tarihi: February 17, 2022.

ÇGM (2022) Görevlerimiz, https://www.csgb.gov.tr/cgm/genel-mudurluk/gorevlerimiz/, Erişim tarihi: February 9, 2022.

ÇSGB (2022a) Tarihçe, https://www.csgb.gov.tr/bakanlik/hakkinda/tarihce/, Erişim tarihi: February 9, 2022.

ÇSGB (2022b) İsçi Sayıları ve Sendikaların Üye Sayıları Hakkında Tebliğler, https://www.csgb.gov.tr/istatistikler/calisma-hayati-istatistikleri/sendikal-istatistikler/isci-sayilari-ve-sendikalarin-uye-sayilari-hakkinda-tebligler/, Erişim tarihi: April 20, 2022.

ÇSGB (2022c) Çalışma Hayatı İstatistikleri Kitabı, https://www.csgb.gov.tr/istatistikler/calisma-hayati-istatistikleri/resmi-istatistik-programi/calisma-hayati-istatistikleri-kitabi/, Erişim Tarihi: November 9, 2022

ÇSGB (2022d), Kamu Görevlileri Sendika Üye Sayıları Hakkında Tebliğler, https://www.csgb.gov.tr/istatistikler/calisma-hayati-istatistikleri/sendikal-istatistikler/kamu-gorevlileri-sendika-uye-sayilari-hakkinda-tebligler/, Erişim tarihi: April 20, 2022.

ÇSGB (2022e) Kamu Görevlileri Sendikaları ve Bağlı Oldukları Konfederasyonların Tüzükleri, https://www.csgb.gov.tr/sendikalar/kamu/, Erişim Tarihi: September 19, 2022

DİSK (2022) Hakkımızda, http://disk.org.tr/hakkimizda/, Erişim Tarihi: February 17, 2022.

GÜZEL, M. Şehmus (1996) *Turkey'de İşçi Hareketi 1908–1984*, Kaynak Yayınları, 178, İstanbul.

HAK-İŞ (2022) Tarihçe, https://hakis.org.tr/icerik.php?sayfa=3, Erişim Tarihi: February 17, 2022.

İSGM (2022) Kuruluş ve Görevlerimiz, https://www.csgb.gov.tr/isggm/genel-mudurluk/kurulus-ve-gorevlerimiz/, Erişim tarihi: February 10, 2022.

İŞKUR (2022) Tarihçe, https://www.iskur.gov.tr/kurumsal-bilgi/tarihce/, Erişim tarihi: February 11, 2022.

KESK (2022) KESK Hakkında, https://kesk.org.tr/tarihcemiz_kesk/, Erişim Tarihi: February 17, 2022.

KOÇ, Yıldırım (2003) *Turkey İşçi Sınıfı ve Sendikacılık Hareketi Tarihi*, Kaynak Yayınları, İstanbul.

MAHİROĞULLARI, Adnan (2010) Turkey'de Sendikalaşma Evreleri ve Sendikalaşmayı Etkileyen Unsurlar, *C. Ü. İİBF Dergisi*, Cilt 2, Sayı 1, 161–190.

MEMUR-SEN (2022) Tarihçe, https://www.memursen.org.tr/tarihce, Erişim Tarihi: February 17, 2022.

MÜSİAD (2022) Müsiad'la Tanışın, https://www.musiad.org.tr/icerik/musiadla-tanisin-2, Erişim Tarihi: February 23, 2022.

R.G. (1947), İşçi ve İşveren Sendikaları ve Sendika Birlikleri Hakkında Kanun, 26 Şubat 1947 Çarşamba, Sayı: 6542, https://www.resmigazete.gov.tr/arsiv/6542.pdf, Erişim tarihi: February 11, 2022.

R.G. (1951) Teşkilatlanma ve Kolektif Müzakere Hakkı Prensiplerinin Uygulanmasına Müteallik 98 numaralı Milletlerarası Çalışına Sözleşmesinin Onanması Hakkında Kanun, 14 Ağustos 1951, Salı, Sayı: 7884, https://www.resmigazete.gov.tr/arsiv/7884.pdf, Erişim tarihi: February 11, 2022.

R.G. (1961) Turkey Cumhuriyeti Anayasası, Kanun No: 334, Kabul Tarihi: July 9, 1961, 31 Mayıs 1961, Çarşamba, Sayı: 10816, https://www.resmigazete.gov.tr/arsiv/10816.pdf, Erişim Tarihi: February 14, 2022.

R.G. (1963) 274 Sayılı Sendikalar Kanunu ve 275 Sayılı Toplu İş Sözleşmesi, Grev ve Lokavt Kanunu, 24 Temmuz 1963 Çarşamba, Sayı: 11462, https://www.resmigazete.gov.tr/arsiv/11462.pdf, Erişim tarihi: February 11, 2022.

R.G. (1965) 624 Sayılı Devlet Personeli Sendikaları Kanunu, 17 Haziran 1965, Perşembe, Sayı: 12025, https://www.resmigazete.gov.tr/arsiv/12025.pdf, Erişim Tarihi: February 15, 2022.

R.G. (1971) Turkey Cumhuriyeti Anayasasının bazı maddelerinin değiştirilmesi ve geçici maddeler eklenmesi hakkında Anayasa Değişikliği, 22 Eylül 1971 Çarşamba, Sayı: 13964, https://www.resmigazete.gov.tr/arsiv/13964.pdf, Erişim Tarihi: February 15, 2022.

R.G. (1983) 2821 Sayılı Sendikalar Kanunu ve 2822 Sayılı Toplu İş Sözleşmesi, Grev ve Lokavt Kanunu, 7 Mayıs 1983—Sayı: 18040, https://www.resmigazete.gov.tr/arsiv/18040.pdf, Erişim tarihi: February 11, 2022.

R.G. (1993) 87 No'lu Sendika Özgürlüğü ve Sendikalaşma Hakkının Korunması Sözleşmesi, 25 Şubat 1993 / 21507, https://www.resmigazete.gov.tr/arsiv/21507.pdf, Erişim Tarihi: February 14, 2022.

R.G. (2001) 4688 Sayılı Kamu Görevlileri Sendikalar Kanunu, 12 Temmuz 2001, Perşembe, Sayı: 24460, https://www.resmigazete.gov.tr/eskiler/2001/07/20010712.htm#1, Erişim Tarihi: February 15, 2022.

R.G. (2012a) 6356 Sayılı Sendikalar ve Toplu İş Sözleşmesi Kanunu, Tarih: 7/11/2012 Sayı: 28460, https://www.mevzuat.gov.tr/MevzuatMetin/1.5.6356.pdf, Erişim Tarihi: February 14, 2022.

R.G. (2012b) Kamu Görevlileri Sendikaları Kanununda Değişiklik Yapılmasına Dair Kanun, 11 Nisan 2012 Çarşamba, Sayı: 28261, https://www.resmigazete.gov.tr/eskiler/2012/04/20120411-9.htm, Erişim Tarihi: February 15, 2022.

R.G. (2018) Bakanlıklara Bağlı, İlgili, İlişkili Kurum ve Kuruluşlar ile Diğer Kurum ve Kuruluşların Teşkilatı Hakkında Cumhurbaşkanlığı Kararnamesi, Cumhurbaşkanlığı Kararnamesinin Sayısı: 4, Yayımlandığı Resmî Gazetenin Tarihi – Sayısı: July 15, 2018 – 30479.

SGK (2022) Kurumumuz, http://www.sgk.gov.tr/wps/portal/sgk/tr/kurumsal/kurumumuz, Erişim tarihi: February 10, 2022.

TALAS, C., Dilik, S. ve Işıklı, A. (1965) *Turkey'de Sendikacılık Hareketi ve Toplu Sözleşme*, SBF Maliye Enstitüsü yayını, Ankara.

TİCARET BAKANLIĞI (2022) Odaya/Sicile Kayıt İşlemleri, https://ticaret.gov.tr/esnaf-sanatkarlar/sikca-sorulan-sorular, Erişim Tarihi: February 17, 2022.

TİSK (2022) TİSK Hakkında, https://www.tisk.org.tr/hakkimizda, Erişim Tarihi: February 17, 2022.

TİSKO (2022) tüm İşveren Sendikaları Konfederasyonu, http://www.tisko.org.tr/, Erişim Tarihi: September 28, 2022.

TOBB (2022) Kuruluşu / Görevleri / Organları, https://www.tobb.org.tr/Sayfalar/Kurulus_Gorev_Organ.php, Erişim Tarihi: February 17, 2022.

TUNCAY, A. Can (2007) Kamu Görevlilerinin Sendikalaşması ve Toplu Pazarlık Hakkı, *Dokuz Eylül Üniversitesi Hukuk Fakültesi Dergisi,* Cilt: 9, Özel Sayı, s. 157–176.

TÜRK-İŞ (2022) Uzun Tarihçe, https://www.turkis.org.tr/uzun-tarihce/, Erişim Tarihi: February 16, 2022.

TÜRKİYE KAMU-SEN (2022) Turkey Kamu-Sen, https://www.kamusen.org.tr/#, Erişim Tarihi: February 17, 2022.

TÜSİAD (2022) TÜSİAD Hakkında, https://tusiad.org/tr/tusiad/hakkinda, Erişim Tarihi: February 23, 2022.

UİGM (2022) Genel Müdürlük, https://www.csgb.gov.tr/uigm, Erişim tarihi: February 10, 2022.

*Chapter 3*

# Foreign Workers and Migration in Turkey

Eylül Kabakçi Günay[1]

The chapter provides a comprehensive analysis of international migration trends in Turkey, focusing on the Republican period to the present day. It covers the historical context of migration, legal frameworks for work permits, and demographic analysis of foreign workers. Besides the study explores the legal frameworks and policies regarding work permits for foreigners in Türkiye, the distribution of these permits across various demographics such as gender, education level, and nationality, and the different types of work permits available. The study underscores Türkiye dual role in global migration as both a source and a destination country, particularly highlighting the recent influx of Syrian refugees. It offers a comprehensive examination of the types and distribution of work permits issued between 2010 and 2020, along with an in-depth analysis of the educational levels, age groups, and nationalities of the permit holders. The research aims to present a detailed overview of the role and impact of foreign workers in Türkiye's labor markets, examining historical migration patterns and their effects on the nation's demographic, economic, and social landscape. Additionally, it discusses the economic sectors employing foreign workers and proposes policy recommendations for effective labor market management.

## INTRODUCTION

On the threshold of a new world where globalization and technological developments shape the future, new topics of study are emerging. One of these is the changes seen in labor markets and the structure of employment, which are among the main macroeconomic variables. With the increase in regular or irregular migration movements in the globalizing world, the presence of foreign employees has increased in every country. In the literature, a foreigner is defined as a person who does not have citizenship ties with the country where he is located. The conditions for Turkish citizenship in Turkey are regulated by the Turkish Citizenship Law dated June 12, 2009, and numbered 5901. In that case, it can be said that people who have not fulfilled the conditions required to gain Turkish citizenship specified in Turkish Citizenship Law No. 5901 can be considered foreigners. A work permit, on the other hand, is defined as a permit issued by the Ministry of Labor and Social Security in the form of an official document granting the foreigner the right to work and reside in Turkey within the validity period. In this study, information was given about international migration in Turkey from the Republican period to the present day; the legal arrangements created for foreigners to take part in the labor markets in Turkey, the types of work permits, the number of foreigners who have work permits in Turkey, the distribution between genders, their education levels, and the business lines they work in Turkey. The study aims were investigated. In the study, people who are accepted as foreigners refer to refugees, asylum seekers, migrants, and those with temporary protection status. The aim of the study is to reveal the general view of foreigners in the labor markets in Türkiye.

## MIGRATION MOVEMENTS AND FOREIGN LABOR FORCE IN THE REPUBLIC PERIOD

In 1923, the Republic of Turkey was founded following the collapse of the Ottoman Empire. Since then, Turkey has experienced various waves of migration, both as a sending and receiving country. As a sending country, Turkey experienced significant emigration during the twentieth century, particularly to Europe. This began in the 1960s with the signing of a bilateral agreement with West Germany, which allowed Turkish workers to migrate there for employment. The trend continued in subsequent decades, with Turks also migrating to other European countries such as France, the Netherlands, and Belgium. The Turkish migration wave had a significant impact on both Türkiye and the receiving countries. In Turkey, the emigration of large numbers of young and skilled workers resulted in a brain drain, which hindered economic development. However, remittances from Turkish workers abroad also played an important role in Turkey's economy. In the receiving countries, the arrival of Turkish workers sparked debates about integration, identity, and cultural diversity. The Turkish community in Europe has since grown and become an integral part of the social and economic fabric of these countries.

As a receiving country, Turkey has also seen significant immigration, particularly in recent years. In the early 2010s, Turkey became a destination for

Syrian refugees fleeing the civil war in their country. As of 2022, there were over 3.6 million registered Syrian refugees in Turkey. Additionally, Turkey has also received migrants from other countries, including Afghanistan, Iraq, and Iran. Overall, migration has had a significant impact on Turkey, shaping the country's demographics, economy, and society.

Between 1922 and 1938, 384,000 people from Greece;
800,000 people from the Balkans between 1923 and 1945;
800 people from Germany between 1933 and 1945;
51,542 people from Iraq in 1988;
345,000 people from Bulgaria in 1989;
in 1991, after the first Gulf War, 467,489 people from Iraq;
20,000 people from Bosnia between 1992 and 1998;
17,746 people after the events in Kosovo in 1999;
10,500 people from Macedonia in 2001;
and between April 2011 and March 2022, approximately 3.6 million people came to Turkey due to the internal turmoil in Syria.

To reveal the migration movements in Turkey, first of all, the post-Republican period will be examined. The years 1923–1950, a period that can be called the groundbreaking phase of the nation-state building process, included two basic phenomena in terms of population movements in Türkiye: firstly, the migration of the non-Muslim population abroad, and secondly, the migration of the Turkish and Muslim population to Turkey, especially in countries that were outside Turkey's borders and were formerly Ottoman lands. During this period, the proportion of the non-Muslim population in the total population fell from 3 percent to 1 percent: this change is reflected in absolute figures from 350,000 to 225,000. On the other hand, the process that started with the migration of the Turkish and Muslim population from the Balkans to Turkey during the Balkan War, especially in the last period of the Ottoman Empire, continued with the migration movements organized by the planning of a political will of the Turkish and Muslim population to Turkey in the Republican period. In the period 1923–1950, approximately 850,000 people migrated to Turkey from the Balkan countries, mainly from Bulgaria, Greece, Romania, and Yugoslavia (Kirişçi, 2000: 8).

The years between 1950 and 1980, following the early period of the Republic, encompassed the stage of nation-state building in Turkey, gaining a "locally" established dimension. In this period, the homogeneity of the population in the country, which was rapidly urbanized with an intensive rural-urban migration, increased rapidly with the migration of the non-Muslim population to the outside, on the one hand, and the migration of the Turkish and Muslim ones, on the other hand. On the other hand, in this period, for the first time in the history of modern Turkey, the migration of the Turkish and Muslim population out of the country emerged in the form of labor migration, and thousands of Turkish citizens began to go to other countries as migrant workers, especially to European countries. During this period, the ongoing migration of the Turkish and Muslim population to Turkey from the Balkans, especially from Bulgaria and Yugoslavia, enabled more than 800,000 people to come to Turkey between 1950 and 1980, as in the previous period (Kirişçi, 2000: 8).

Another important development is that in the early 1960s, Turkey began to occupy a new position in the international migration market. After the Second World War, when Western countries needed labor force from other countries in the process of reorganizing their economic structures, Turkey-started to export labor to many European countries, especially Germany. For the first time in the history of modern Turkey, this meant that the Turkish and Muslim population was expelled from the country in an intense migration movement. This migration movement, which first started as a short-term temporary labor migration, later became a settlement-based migration in many European countries with family reunification migration. The beginning of an intensive labor migration from Turkeyin the 1960s, especially as reflected in the Five-Year Development Plans, was aimed at: (1) reducing the economic pressures increased by unemployment, (2) bringing the skills gained by the workers returning from abroad to the working life in Turkey, and (3) ensuring the balance of payments with the increase in foreign exchange income. Following the migration to Europe, the 1970s witnessed the beginning of temporary labor migration, first to distant geographies such as Australia and then to the Middle East and North African countries. While the Australian example reflects a migration phenomenon based on settlement, migration to the Middle East and North African countries has developed in the form of Turkish companies taking temporary workers to the contracting works they receive in these countries. When the 1980s began, it was seen that not only did Turkey's identity as a known emigrant country become clearer but also that as a result of migration, immigrant communities of Turkish origin living in different countries emerged.

With the 1980s, Turkey's position in global migration regimes changed. After 1960, Turkey, which joined these migration regimes mostly with mass labor migration and strengthened its identity as a migrant-giving country, began to be a geography that encountered the migration of foreigners for the first time in its recent history and began to acquire the identity of a country that received immigration (Kirişçi, 2003; İçduygu, 2004). The change in Turkey's identity as a receiving country in the period beginning with the 1980s is very important in the following sense: although modern Turkey has always received different migrations since its establishment in the early 1920s, as we mentioned before, this migration was limited to the arrival of "immigrants of Turkish descent and connected to Turkish culture"; in the 1980s, for the first time in the history of modern Turkey, the migration of Turkish and non-Muslim people to Turkeywas witnessed. In short, for the first time, a period has been entered in which the migration of "foreigners" to Turkeycan be mentioned.

In summary, Turkey has welcomed more than 6.5 million people from 1922 to the present day. This number does not include foreigners who come for purposes such as work and education. When the figures regarding the foreigners who came to Turkey for work, education, and other purposes are examined, it is recorded that approximately 3.3 million foreigners have received residence permits in the last fifteen years.[2]

## LEGAL REGULATIONS FOR WORK PERMITS AND EXEMPTIONS OF FOREIGNERS IN TURKEY

The ability of foreigners to work in Turkey is subject to various conditions. The law that determines the types of permits that foreign nationals are subject to work in Türkiye and the criteria according to which these permits are issued is the Law on Foreigners and International Protection No. 6458. The law was published in the Official Gazette No. 28615 on April 11, 2003, and entered into force. Article 27 of this law states that "A valid work permit and a Work Permit Exemption Confirmation Certificate issued pursuant to Article 10 of the Law No. 4817 dated 27/2/2003 on Work Permits of Foreigners shall be deemed to be a residence permit." (LFIP, 2013).[3]

In this context, a foreigner who receives a work permit in Turkeyalso receives a residence permit. Article 89 of the same law Article 4(b) states that "A refugee or holder of subsidiary protection status may work as a dependent or independent from the date of receipt of status. The provisions in other legislation on jobs and professions in which foreigners cannot work are reserved. The identity document to be given to the refugee or temporary protection status holder shall also replace the work permit and this shall be written on the identity document." Here, the expression of jobs and professions that foreigners cannot work in refers to the professions reserved for Turkish citizens. In addition to the fact that foreigners cannot perform any duty in the status of state employees as stated in the Law No. 657 on State Employees in Turkey, Dental Medicine, Dentistry, Nursing Pharmacy, Veterinary, Responsible Directorate in Private Hospitals, Lawyer, Notary, Private Security Officer, Fish, Oyster, Mussel, Sponge, Pearl, Coral Exporter, Diving, Brokerage, Guide, Wheeler, Clerk, Crew, Customs Brokerage, Tourist Guidance they can't do their job either. These professions can only be performed by Turkish citizens (MLSS, 2022).[4] Professions other than these professions can also be performed by foreigners by obtaining a work permit.

## FEATURES OF THE WORK PERMIT GRANTED TO FOREIGNERS IN TURKEY

The nature of the work permit is based on the International Labor Force Law dated Jumly 28, 2016, and numbered 6735 and prepared on the basis of the regulation dated February 2, 2022, and numbered 31738, Article 57. It is regulated by the clause. According to this article:

(1) The work permit or work permit exemption issued by the Ministry shall replace the residence permit as long as it is valid. Without prejudice to the provisions regarding foreigners who are granted refugee or temporary protection status, the foreigner's residence permit for any reason does not provide the foreigner with the right to work.
(2) If the work permit or work permit exemption becomes invalid for any reason, the related right of residence ends.
(3) In the event that the validity of the work permit or work permit exemption granted to the foreigner who has a valid residence permit in Turkeyfor a reason other than the work permit or work permit exemption expires for any reason, the other residence permit held by the foreigner shall not become invalid.
(4) The work permit issued under an employer is valid at the workplace and address where it is issued (ILLIR, 2022).[5] As can be seen, not every residence permit means a work permit, residence permits depending on the work permit end with the disappearance of the permit and the work permit is issued depending on a workplace.

## TYPES OF THE WORK PERMITS ISSUED TO FOREIGNERS

There are several types of work permits issued to foreign nationals working in Türkiye. These are Working Permits for a Definite Period, Renewal of Permit, Unlimited Permit, Renewal of Unlimited Permit, Exceptional Permit, Independent Work Permit, and Turquoise. These types of permits are included in the International Labor Force Law No. 6735, which was published in the Official Gazette dated August 13, 2016, and numbered 29800 and entered into force.

*Temporary Work Permit*: According to the International Labor Force Law No. 6735, which was published in the Official Gazette (OG) dated August

13, 2016, and numbered 29800 and entered into force, the foreigner whose work permit application is evaluated positively is granted a work permit for a maximum of one year in the first application, provided that it does not exceed the duration of the employment or service contract, provided that he works in a certain workplace belonging to a real or legal person or public institution or organization or in the workplaces in the same branch of their business (ILL, 2016).[6]

*Extension*: In the event that the extension application to be made in accordance with Article 7 of the aforementioned law (International Labor Law No. 6735, which was published in the Official Gazette dated August 13, 2016, and numbered 29800) is evaluated positively, the foreigner is granted a work permit for a maximum of two years in the first extension application and up to three years in the subsequent extension applications depending on the same employer. However, applications made to work for a different employer are evaluated within the scope of the first paragraph of this article (ILL, 2016).[7] Article 27 of the International Labor Law implementation regulation published in the Official Gazette dated February 2, 2022, and numbered 31738 states that the regulations regarding the extension of the work permit period are as follows:

(1) The application for the extension of the work permit period is made through the system as of sixty days before the expiry of the work permit period and in any case before the expiry of the work permit.
(2) The work permit period of the foreigner whose work permit extension application made on behalf of the foreigner working under an employer is evaluated positively shall be extended up to a maximum of two years in the case of the first extension application and up to three years in the case of subsequent extension applications depending on the same employer.
(3) In the event that an application for an extension of time is made to work under a different employer, this application shall be considered subject to the procedures and principles of the first application.
(4) In the event that the applications for extension of time to be made for foreigners who are granted an exception in terms of the duration of the independent work permit and the work permit in the fourth section are evaluated positively, the work permit shall be extended for a period of time without being subject to the time limits in the second paragraph.
(5) Foreigners on whose behalf the work permit extension application is made may continue to work as of the date of expiry of the permit period during the evaluation of the application and in any case provided that the work done, and the workplace of work do not change. During this period, the rights and obligations of the foreigner and the employer arising from the work permit continue in the same way.

(6) Those who have completed the work permit extension application within the scope of the fifth paragraph shall be given a work permit extension application certificate that is not subject to any fee or fee and whose form and content are determined by the General Directorate through the system upon request.
(7) If the work permit extension application is evaluated positively, the duration of the extended work permit shall be started as of the day following the day on which the previous period expires.[8]

*Permanent Work Permit*: Foreigners who have a long-term residence permit or a legal work permit for at least eight years in Turkey can apply for an indefinite work permit. However, the fact that the foreigner meets the application requirements does not provide absolute rights to the foreigner (ESG, 2022).

*Exceptional Permission*: How to grant exceptional permission is regulated in Article 16 of the International Labor Law No. 6735. Accordingly, in accordance with the international labor policy determined by the ministry:

a) Evaluated as a qualified workforce in terms of education level, wages, professional experience, contribution to science and technology and similar characteristics,
b) Evaluated as a qualified investor in terms of its contribution to science and technology, investment or export level, size of employment to be provided and similar characteristics,
c) Employed in a project carried out in Turkey by his/her employer for a certain period of time,
ç) Declared to be of Turkish origin by the Ministry of Interior or the Ministry of Foreign Affairs,
d) A citizen of the Turkish Republic of Northern Cyprus,
e) A citizen of a member state of the European Union,
f) An applicant for international protection pursuant to Law No. 6458, a conditional refugee, a victim of human trafficking who is granted temporary protection or who is stateless or who benefits from victim support,
g) Married to a Turkish citizen and living in a marital union with his or her spouse in Turkey,
ğ) Employees working in the representations of foreign states and international organizations in Türkiye without diplomatic immunity,
h) Coming to Turkey for scientific, cultural, artistic or sporting purposes with the success in the field at the international level,
i) Foreigners who are providers of cross-border services may be granted exceptions to the application of Articles 7, 9 and 10 of this Law (ILL, 2016).[9]

*Independent Work Permit*: Foreigners who are members of the professional profession may be granted an independent work permit provided that the special conditions specified in other laws are met (MLSS, 2022).

*Turquoise Card*: It is a document that gives the foreigner the right to work and reside in Turkey indefinitely and gives the right of residence to the relative. There are several characteristics that the foreigner must have to apply for this card. These features are included in Article 5 of the regulation prepared based on Articles 11 and 25 of the International Labor Force Law dated July 28, 2016, and numbered 6735 and published in the Official Gazette No. 30007 on March 14, 2007. According to this regulation:

a) Considered as a highly qualified workforce in terms of education level, wages, professional knowledge and experience, contribution to science and technology and similar qualities,
b) Considered as a highly qualified investor in terms of the level of investment or export, the size of the employment to be provided, the contribution to scientific and technological development and similar characteristics,
c) A scientist or researcher who contributes to scientific and technological development or conducts studies and research in the fields of science, industry and technology that are considered strategic in terms of the interests of the country at the international level,
ç) Are internationally successful in terms of cultural, artistic or sporting activities,
d) It can be given to foreigners who contribute to the international recognition or promotion of Turkey or Turkish culture and who are engaged in activities at the international level in matters related to Türkiye's national interests (TCR, 2017).[10]

## WORK PERMIT EXEMPTIONS GRANTED TO FOREIGNERS IN TURKEY

The work permit exemptions granted to foreigners in Turkey in various cases are regulated by the regulation prepared on the basis of the first paragraph of Article 25 of the International Labor Force Law dated July 28, 2016, and numbered 6735. According to the International Labor Law Implementation Regulation No. 31738 published in the Official Gazette on February 2, 2022, the conditions and periods of Work Permit Exemption to which foreigners in Turkey are subject are 48. Regulated by substance. Accordingly;

(1) Provided that the provisions of special laws and the obligations of the foreigner and the employer arising from other laws are reserved;

a) Foreigners who will work within the scope of scientific, cultural and artistic activities up to one month,

b)Foreigners who will come for the purpose of training on the use of goods and services exported from Turkey or imported into Turkey or for the purpose of assembling, maintaining and repairing, providing training on the use of machinery and equipment imported into Turkey or receiving the equipment or repairing the vehicles that have malfunctioned in Turkey for a total of three months,

c) Foreigners providing cross-border services up to three months,

ç) Members of the board of directors of joint stock companies established in accordance with Law No. 6102 who are not resident in Turkey and the shareholders of other companies who are not directors and foreigners who are not partners in these companies but who are authorized to represent and bind at the highest level will work in Turkey for up to three months,

d) Those who are resident abroad and who are declared to be of Turkish origin by the Ministry of Interior or Foreign Affairs will work in Turkey for up to three months,

e) Foreigners who will work within the scope of sports activities up to four months,

f) Foreigners who will do internship within the scope of student exchange programs between Turkish universities and universities in foreign countries and approved by the Council of Higher Education for up to four months,

g) Foreigners who will work in seasonal agriculture and animal husbandry works determined by the General Directorate up to six months,

ğ) Foreigners who will work in fairs and circuses that will operate outside the boundaries of certified tourism enterprises up to six months,

h) Foreigners who are notified by the relevant public institutions and organizations that they can provide significant services and contributions to Türkiye in economic, socio-cultural and technological fields and education issues up to six months,

ı) Foreigners who will work as tour operator representatives up to eight months,

i) Foreigners who will do internship within the scope of international intern student exchange, newly graduated intern exchange or youth exchange programs approved by the General Directorate up to twelve months,

j) Foreigners who come to universities and public institutions and organizations for the purpose of conducting research or increasing their knowledge and manners are limited to the duration of their education and in any case up to two years,

k) Professional foreign athletes and coaches who come to Turkey with a sportive comprehensive visa provided that they have the appropriate opinion of the Ministry of Youth and Sports or the Turkish Football Federation, and sports physicians, sports physiotherapists, sports mechanics, sports masseuses or masseurs and similar sports personnel during their contracts with foreign sports federations and sports clubs,
l) In accordance with the bilateral protocols made with the states in accordance with Rule I/10 of the International Convention on the Training, Certification and Shift Standards of Seafarers, foreign seafarers who have obtained a Certificate of Conformity Approval from the relevant administration and who are registered in the Turkish International Ship Registry and who work on ships operating outside the cabotage line during the employment or service contract,
m) Foreigners assigned to the programs or projects carried out within the scope of Turkey-European Union Financial Cooperation Programs during their duties,
n) Foreign students enrolled in a formal education program in Turkey who are obliged to do internship with an employer within the scope of vocational education in accordance with the relevant legislation during the compulsory internship period,
o) Foreigners working in schools, cultural institutions and religious institutions operating as subordinate units of diplomatic and consular representations of foreign countries in Turkey during the period of their duties,
ö) Foreigners working in the special service of persons serving as diplomatic staff members, consular officers, administrative and technical staff members and consular servants in diplomatic and consular representations of foreign countries in Turkey, international officers and administrative and technical personnel in international organizations in Turkey during the term of their employment or service contracts,
p) Military factories and shipyards operating under the Ministry of National Defense and foreigners who will work within the Machinery and Chemical Industry Joint Stock Company during the term of their employment or service contracts,
r) Foreign personnel, researchers or managers who will work within the Turkish-Japanese Science and Technology University established by the Law No. 7034 dated 18/6/2017 on the Establishment of the Turkish-Japanese Science and Technology University during their employment contracts,
s) Following the Regulation on Specialty Education in Medicine and Dentistry published in the Official Gazette dated 26/4/2014 and numbered 28983, foreigners who receive specialty education are evaluated within the scope of work permit exemption during their education (UIKU, 2022). [11]

## EVALUATION OF THE NUMBER OF WORK PERMITS ISSUED TO FOREIGNERS IN TURKEY

In this section, the number of work permits granted to foreigners in Turkey between 2010 and 2020 is discussed according to work permit types, education, gender, age, nationality, type of economic activity, and provinces.

Another crucial indicator to dig deeper into the leading situation is the number of work permits granted to foreigners by year and permit types. According to the data announced by the Ministry of Labor and Social Security in Turkey the number of foreigners who received work permits in Turkey between 2010 and 2020; 14,201 foreigners were granted work permits in Turkey in 2010. Till 2020, it was 17,318; 32,191; 45,721; 52,197; 64,402; 73,410; 87,150; 115,826; 145,232; and 123,574, respectively. In 2020, the number of foreigners granted work permits increased to 123,574. When evaluated accordingly, there has been a 770 percent increase in the number of foreigners who received work permits in Turkey between 2010 and 2020. When the distribution of work permits according to their types is examined, it is seen that almost 99 percent of them consist of temporary permits. In the increase in the rate of foreigners obtaining work permits compared to the previous year, 2012 takes the first place. In 2012, the number of foreigners who received work permits increased by 85 percent compared to the previous year.[12]

In Table 3.1, the distribution of the work permits given according to gender is seen. Accordingly, when the rate of work permits between men and women is examined, it is seen that the work permit rates of women were below those of men during 2010 and 2011, but in 2012, the rate of leavıng the job of women exceeded men. This situation continued to exist throughout 2012, 2013–2014, and 2015. However, as seen in Table 3.1, the work permit rate of men exceeded the work permit rate of women for the years 2016, 2017, 2018, 2019, and 2020.

The evaluation of work permits held by foreigners in Turkey according to their level of education is important to make an in-depth evaluation of the subject.

Table 3.1 shows the work permits granted to foreigners according to their level of education in Turkey. According to the data of the Ministry of Labor and Social Security, when the work permits issued between 2010 and 2020 are examined, it is seen that foreigners have a high school and university education. When evaluated according to years, it is seen that 48.9 percent of the foreigners who received a work permit in 2010 were university graduates and 27.7 percent were high school graduates. In 2020, the rate of university graduates is 19.1 percent, while the rate of high school graduates is 29.6 percent. Another noteworthy issue is the increase in the number of foreigners who

**Table 3.1 Number of Work Permits Granted to Foreigners According to Education Level**

| *Years* | *Types of Permits* | *Literate* | *Primary School* | *Secondary School* | *High School* | *College* | *University* | *Graduate* | *Unknown* |
|---|---|---|---|---|---|---|---|---|---|
| 2010 | Definite | NA | 950 | NA | 3,941 | 1,439 | 6,953 | 918 | NA |
| | Indefinite | NA | NA | NA | NA | NA | NA | NA | NA |
| | Independent | NA | NA | NA | NA | NA | NA | NA | NA |
| | Percentage (%) | NA | 6.7 | NA | 27.7 | 10.1 | 48.9 | 6.4 | NA |
| 2011 | Definite | 99 | 159 | 964 | 4,610 | 2,006 | 7,817 | 1,042 | NA |
| | Indefinite | 0 | 0 | 1 | 30 | 8 | 91 | 30 | NA |
| | Independent | 0 | 0 | 0 | 0 | 0 | 22 | 0 | NA |
| | Percentage (%) | 0.5 | 0.91 | 5.5 | 26.3 | 11.4 | 44.7 | 5.9 | NA |
| 2012 | Definite | 670 | 687 | 2,962 | 12,159 | 3,482 | 11,033 | 1,189 | 2 |
| | Indefinite | 1 | 0 | 2 | 13 | 7 | 46 | 9 | 0 |
| | Independent | 0 | 0 | 1 | 0 | 0 | 9 | 0 | 0 |
| | Percentage (%) | 2.0 | 2.1 | 9.1 | 37.6 | 10.7 | 34.1 | 3.6 | 0 |
| 2013 | Definite | 1,060 | 927 | 4,621 | 18,324 | 5,166 | 14,084 | 1,545 | 4 |
| | Indefinite | 0 | 1 | 2 | 25 | 6 | 54 | 6 | 0 |
| | Independent | 0 | 0 | 0 | 1 | 0 | 8 | 0 | 0 |
| | Percentage (%) | 2.3 | 2.0 | 10.0 | 39.9 | 11.2 | 30.7 | 3.3 | 0 |
| 2014 | Definite | 1,553 | 1,195 | 5,464 | 20,515 | 4,851 | 16,974 | 1,646 | 8 |
| | Indefinite | 2 | 0 | 1 | 18 | 6 | 55 | 13 | 0 |
| | Independent | 0 | 0 | 0 | 0 | 0 | 3 | 0 | 0 |
| | Percentage (%) | 2.9 | 2.2 | 10.4 | 39.2 | 9.2 | 32.4 | 3.1 | 0 |
| 2015 | Definite | 3,960 | 1,816 | 6,131 | 24,679 | 5,844 | 20,071 | 1,917 | 8 |
| | Indefinite | 0 | 1 | 3 | 15 | 9 | 72 | 18 | 0 |
| | Independent | 0 | 0 | 1 | 0 | 0 | 3 | 0 | 0 |
| | Percentage (%) | 6.1 | 2.8 | 9.5 | 38.2 | 9.0 | 31.1 | 2.9 | 0 |
| 2016 | Definite | 2,242 | 1,144 | 6,571 | 27,427 | 7,048 | 21,627 | 535 | 6,827 |
| | Indefinite | 0 | 2 | 3 | 15 | 13 | 72 | 5 | 5 |
| | Independent | 0 | 0 | 0 | 0 | 1 | 18 | 0 | 5 |
| | Percentage(%) | 3.4 | 1.5 | 8.9 | 37.2 | 9.5 | 29.4 | 0.7 | 9.2 |

*(Continued)*

**Table 3.1 (Continued)**

| *Years* | *Types of Permits* | *Literate* | *Primary School* | *Secondary School* | *High School* | *College* | *University* | *Graduate* | *Unknown* |
|---|---|---|---|---|---|---|---|---|---|
| 2017 | Definite | 2,796 | 1,127 | 7,486 | 31,480 | 6,646 | 23,881 | 281 | 13,453 |
| | Indefinite | 0 | 0 | 0 | 2 | 3 | 11 | 2 | 1 |
| | Independent | 0 | 0 | 0 | 0 | 0 | 9 | 1 | 3 |
| | Percentage (%) | 3.2 | 1.2 | 8.5 | 36.1 | 7.6 | 27.3 | 0.3 | 15.4 |
| 2018 | Definite | 10,749 | 302 | 8,353 | 38,010 | 1,231 | 27,015 | 420 | 29,746 |
| | Indefinite | 0 | 0 | 0 | 0 | 0 | 2 | 0 | 2 |
| | Independent | 0 | 0 | 0 | 0 | 1 | 4 | 1 | 1 |
| | Percentage (%) | 9.2 | 0.2 | 7.2 | 32.8 | 1.0 | 23.3 | 0.3 | 25.6 |
| 2019 | Definite | 24,625 | 9,286 | 15,478 | 49,095 | 4,857 | 29,530 | 3,670 | 8,691 |
| | Indefinite | 0 | 0 | 0 | 0 | 0 | 0 | 0 | 0 |
| | Independent | 0 | 0 | 0 | 0 | 0 | 0 | 0 | 0 |
| | Percentage (%) | 16.9 | 6.3 | 10.6 | 33.8 | 3.3 | 20.3 | 2.5 | 5.9 |
| 2020 | Definite | 21,676 | 9,369 | 16,721 | 36,582 | 3,021 | 23,721 | 3,347 | 9,137 |
| | Indefinite | 0 | 0 | 0 | 0 | 0 | 0 | 0 | 0 |
| | Independent | 0 | 0 | 0 | 0 | 0 | 0 | 0 | 0 |
| | Percentage(%) | 17.5 | 7.5 | 13.5 | 29.6 | 2.4 | 19.1 | 2.7 | 7.3 |

*Source*: Ministry of Labor and Social Security, https://www.csgb.gov.tr/istatistikler/calisma-hayati-istatistikleri/resmi-istatistik-programi/yabancilarin-calisma-izinleri/. Access Date: May 2, 2023.

have not graduated from any school but have only received a work permit as literate. While this rate was 0.5 percent in 2011, it was 17.5 percent in 2020.

When all years are evaluated, it is seen that the age range in which foreigners have the most intensive work permit is between 20 and 44 years. In this respect, it can be said that foreigners who have a work permit in our country consist of young people. When evaluated according to age ranges, it is seen that the number of foreigners who have a work permit in the 15–19 age range has increased rapidly, especially in 2016 and after.[13]

In table 3.2, the nationalities of foreigners who have received a work permit in Turkey are included. According to the table created according to the data obtained from the Ministry of Labor and Social Security, it is seen that the number of work permits is increasing among the citizens of the countries with which Turkey has geographical and economic proximity. Azerbaijan, Indonesia, Georgia, Iraq, the Islamic Republic of Iran, the Kyrgyz Republic, the Republic of Moldova, Nepal, Uzbekistan, the Russian Federation, Syria, Turkmenistan, and Ukraine were the countries with the highest number of work permits from Turkey. In particular, it is seen that work permits of Syrian origin have increased rapidly with the increasing migration wave due to the civil war and the acceptance policy implemented by Turkey with the granting of temporary protection status to Syrians.

Table 3.3 gives the top five types of economic activity for the years 2010–2020 in which foreigners have the highest rate of work permits. Since the data for 2010 are not shared by the Ministry of Labor and Social Security, the data for this year are not included in table 3.3. When we look at the types of activities in the years between 2011 and 2020, the activities of households as the employers of the most intensive domestic working personnel of foreigners, accommodation, wholesale trade (except motor vehicles and motorcycles), education, building construction, construction of nonbuilding structures, office management, office support and business support activities, clothing manufacturing, textile products manufacturing, creative arts, performing arts and entertainment, it is seen that they operate in areas such as air transport, sports activities, entertainment, and recreational activities.

The top five provinces in Turkeywith the highest number of foreigners who have work permits are Istanbul, Antalya, Izmir, Bursa, and Ankara. Istanbul has been the province with the highest number of foreigners having work permits in each examination year compared to other provinces. In 2020, it was seen that 58,306 foreigners had work permits in Istanbul. This is followed by Bursa with 8,871, Antalya with 8,277, Ankara with 7,781, and Izmir with 4,632.[14] Here, it is necessary to mention the rapid increase in the number of work permits of foreigners in Bursa. From 2010 to 2020, there has been an increase of nearly 1900 percent in the number of work permits for foreigners in Bursa. In the same years, this increase was 650

**Table 3.2 Number of Work Permits Issued to Foreigners According to Nationality**

| | 2011 | 2012 | 2013 | 2014 | 2015 | 2016 | 2017 | 2018 | 2019 | 2020 |
|---|---|---|---|---|---|---|---|---|---|---|
| Afghanistan | NA | NA | 161 | 251 | 305 | 444 | 609 | 894 | 1,466 | 1,921 |
| Germany | 683 | 1,126 | 1,242 | 1,442 | 1,299 | 1,133 | 982 | 895 | 977 | 619 |
| United States | 960 | 936 | 1,108 | 1,199 | 1,232 | 1,164 | 982 | 823 | 857 | 722 |
| Albania | NA | 75 | NA | 109 | 121 | 144 | 160 | 164 | 197 | 174 |
| | 89 | 105 | 133 | 116 | 151 | 180 | 128 | 122 | 103 | NA |
| Australia | | | | | | | | | | |
| | 206 | 191 | NA | 215 | 195 | 180 | 134 | 143 | 143 | 104 |
| Austria | | | | | | | | | | |
| | 459 | 755 | 1,227 | 1,382 | 1,461 | 1,880 | 2,449 | 2,997 | 2,977 | 2,945 |
| Azerbaijan | | | | | | | | | | |
| | 122 | 157 | 195 | 186 | 219 | 195 | 142 | 137 | 128 | NA |
| Belgium | | | | | | | | | | |
| | 97 | 228 | NA | 331 | 339 | 286 | 305 | 335 | 393 | 261 |
| Belarus | | | | | | | | | | |
| | 74 | 117 | 127 | 170 | 250 | 232 | 157 | 174 | 217 | 153 |
| Brazil | | | | | | | | | | |
| | 476 | 447 | 701 | 795 | 839 | 750 | 600 | 415 | 384 | 289 |
| Bulgaria | | | | | | | | | | |
| | NA | 71 | 169 | 328 | 334 | 182 | NA | 111 | 90 | NA |
| Czech Republic | | | | | | | | | | |
| | 1,648 | 2,448 | 3,379 | 2,621 | 2,882 | 4,397 | 4,288 | 2,992 | 2,357 | 1,611 |
| People's Republic of China | | | | | | | | | | |
| | 86 | 72 | 108 | 101 | 106 | NA | NA | NA | NA | NA |
| Denmark | | | | | | | | | | |
| | 528 | 794 | 1,224 | 1,578 | 1,904 | 1,829 | 1,956 | 2,356 | 2,704 | 1,417 |
| Indonesia | | | | | | | | | | |
| Armenia | NA | NA | 160 | 157 | 175 | 148 | 126 | 187 | 189 | 254 |
| | NA | 115 | NA | 172 | 231 | 424 | 476 | 381 | 262 | 170 |
| Ethiopia | | | | | | | | | | |

| | | | | | | | | | | |
|---|---|---|---|---|---|---|---|---|---|---|
| | NA | 132 | 190 | 221 | 324 | 336 | 470 | 614 | 899 | 607 |
| Morocco | | | | | | | | | | |
| | 210 | 369 | 568 | 790 | 1,049 | 1,492 | 1,959 | 2,076 | 1,917 | 1,603 |
| Philippines | | | | | | | | | | |
| Palestine | NA | NA | NA | NA | NA | 220 | 255 | 372 | 547 | 508 |
| | 646 | 677 | 746 | 734 | 791 | 726 | 543 | 544 | 518 | 378 |
| France | | | | | | | | | | |
| Ghana | NA | NA | NA | NA | NA | NA | NA | NA | 406 | 133 |
| South Africa | 70 | NA | NA | NA | 128 | 134 | 141 | 164 | 171 | 136 |
| South Korea (Republic of Korea) | 283 | 305 | 536 | 747 | 952 | 721 | 530 | 531 | 557 | 442 |
| Georgia | 402 | 6,434 | 8,437 | 7,680 | 8,524 | 7,629 | 7,317 | 7,321 | 5,220 | 4,873 |
| India | 243 | 334 | 309 | 369 | 806 | 1970 | 3055 | 1663 | 897 | 850 |
| | 295 | 270 | 405 | 452 | 476 | 481 | 324 | 342 | 294 | 168 |
| Netherlands | | | | | | | | | | |
| | 178 | 209 | 323 | 484 | 692 | 1,031 | 1,137 | 1,365 | 1,947 | 1,794 |
| Iraq | | | | | | | | | | |
| | 699 | 830 | 969 | 1,105 | 1,227 | 1,191 | NA | 1,106 | 1,096 | 795 |
| England | | | | | | | | | | |
| | 410 | 716 | 1,155 | 1,284 | 1,522 | 1,785 | 1,930 | 2,689 | 3,935 | 4,015 |
| Islamic Republic of Iran | | | | | | | | | | |
| | 90 | 75 | NA | NA | NA | NA | NA | NA | NA | NA |
| Ireland | | | | | | | | | | |
| | 243 | 331 | 540 | 479 | 434 | 438 | 304 | 337 | 256 | 202 |
| Spain | | | | | | | | | | |
| | 80 | 141 | 181 | 207 | 200 | 139 | NA | NA | NA | NA |
| Sweden | | | | | | | | | | |
| Italy | 492 | 498 | 686 | 768 | 916 | 888 | 650 | 483 | 421 | 307 |
| | 313 | 286 | 344 | 468 | 536 | 506 | 405 | 397 | 360 | 301 |
| Japan | | | | | | | | | | |
| | 208 | 188 | 225 | 248 | 236 | 234 | 197 | 175 | 194 | 166 |
| Canada | | | | | | | | | | |

*(Continued)*

**Table 3.2 (Continued)**

| | *2011* | *2012* | *2013* | *2014* | *2015* | *2016* | *2017* | *2018* | *2019* | *2020* |
|---|---|---|---|---|---|---|---|---|---|---|
| | 230 | 567 | 899 | 1163 | 1349 | 998 | 1,352 | 1,799 | 2,860 | 961 |
| Kazakhstan | | | | | | | | | | |
| | NA | 74 | 139 | NA | NA | NA | NA | NA | NA | NA |
| Kenya | | | | | | | | | | |
| | 242 | 610 | 1,160 | 2,283 | 4,274 | 3,048 | 6,359 | 13,452 | 11,003 | 3,505 |
| Republic of Kyrgyzstan | | | | | | | | | | |
| Colombia | NA | NA | NA | NA | 295 | 315 | 475 | 495 | 663 | 136 |
| Cuba | NA | NA | 152 | 271 | 435 | 497 | 533 | 648 | 705 | NA |
| Libya | NA | NA | NA | NA | 132 | 191 | 143 | 160 | 211 | 174 |
| Hungary | NA | 80 | NA | 142 | 102 | 124 | NA | NA | NA | NA |
| Macedonia | NA | NA | 156 | 134 | 124 | 132 | 121 | 114 | 146 | 101 |
| Egypt | NA | 75 | 139 | 234 | 287 | 371 | 424 | 1235 | 867 | 630 |
| Mongolia | NA | NA | NA | 102 | 126 | 157 | 166 | 154 | 215 | NA |
| Republic of Moldova | 496 | 889 | 1,825 | 1,907 | 1,778 | 1,481 | 1,236 | 1,370 | 1,386 | 1,240 |
| Nepal | NA | NA | NA | 122 | 170 | 497 | 1,438 | 3,186 | 2,404 | 1,421 |
| | 229 | 829 | 1,708 | 1,993 | 2,319 | 2,436 | 2,465 | 3,969 | 4,480 | 4,383 |
| Uzbekistan | | | | | | | | | | |
| Pakistan | NA | NA | NA | NA | 247 | 269 | 340 | 341 | 369 | 347 |
| Poland | 75 | 138 | 205 | 217 | 264 | NA | 149 | 102 | 169 | 129 |
| Portugal | 103 | 77 | 101 | 104 | NA | NA | NA | NA | NA | NA |
| Romania | 235 | 302 | 473 | 442 | 362 | 260 | 292 | 333 | 249 | 176 |
| Russian Federation | 1,432 | 2,160 | 2,455 | 2,562 | 2,936 | 1,966 | 2,390 | 2,944 | 3,922 | 3124 |
| Syria (Syrian Arab Republic) | 118 | 220 | 794 | 2,541 | 4,019 | 13,290 | 20,966 | 34,573 | 63,789 | 62,369 |
| Tacikistan | NA | NA | NA | NA | NA | NA | 275 | 626 | 726 | 278 |
| | 255 | 262 | 351 | 795 | 1142 | 429 | 402 | 365 | 375 | 243 |
| Thailand | | | | | | | | | | |

| | | | | | | | | | | |
|---|---|---|---|---|---|---|---|---|---|---|
| Tunus | 79 | 184 | 204 | 307 | 363 | 348 | 375 | 420 | 526 | 346 |
| Tunisia | | | | | | | | | | |
| | 143 | 1,422 | 2,714 | 2,635 | 3,323 | 3,471 | 3,847 | 5,547 | 6,128 | 9,721 |
| Turkmenistan | | | | | | | | | | |
| | 1,278 | 2,601 | 3,610 | 4,334 | 6,023 | 5,592 | 5,760 | 6,394 | 6,197 | 2,271 |
| Ukrain | | | | | | | | | | |
| Jordan | NA | NA | NA | NA | 125 | 178 | 195 | 292 | 388 | 327 |
| Vietnam | NA | NA | NA | NA | 487 | 618 | 435 | 146 | 20 | NA |
| Yemen | NA | NA | NA | NA | NA | NA | NA | 146 | 241 | 181 |
| | 358 | 350 | 463 | 483 | 511 | 642 | 521 | 1,908 | 425 | 393 |
| Greece | | | | | | | | | | |
| Other[1] | 1327 | 1,606 | 2,125 | 2,097 | 1,849 | 1,861 | 2,008 | 1,908 | 2,570 | 2340 |

*Source*: Ministry of Labor and Social Security, https://www.csgb.gov.tr/istatistikler/calisma-hayati-istatistikleri/resmi-istatistik-programi/yabancilarin-calisma-izinleri/. Access Date: May 1, 2023.

[1]Nationalities with a presence below 100 work permits are expressed as other.

**Table 3.3 Top Five Types of Economic Activities in Terms of Distribution of the Number of Work Permits Granted to Foreigners**

| *Years* | *1* | *2* | *3* | *4* | *5* |
|---|---|---|---|---|---|
| 2010 | NA | NA | NA | NA | NA |
| 2011 | Education (12.45 percent) | Accommodation (11.8 percent) | Air freight (5.42 percent) | Creative arts, performing arts, and entertainment (5.41 percent) | Wholesale trade (excluding motor vehicles and motorcycles) (5.06 percent) |
| 2012 | As employers of domestic staff, the activities of households (27.4 percent) | Accommodation (15.3 percent) | Education (6 percent) | Creative arts, performing arts, and entertainment (5.6 percent) | Sports activities, leisure and leisure activities (3.9 percent) |
| 2013 | As employers of domestic staff, the activities of households (32.5 percent) | Accommodation (13.6 percent) | Creative arts, performing arts, and entertainment (4.6 percent) | Education (4.4 percent) | Construction of nonbuilding structures (4.4 percent) |
| 2014 | As employers of domestic staff, the activities of households (28.06 percent) | Accommodation (14.9 percent) | Education (4.7 percent) | Creative arts, performing arts, and entertainment (4.3 percent) | Wholesale trade (4.23 percent) |
| 2015 | As employers of domestic staff, the activities of households (26.06 percent) | Accommodation (16.2 percent) | Creative arts, performing arts, and entertainment (4.7 percent) | Wholesale trade (4.4 percent) | Construction of nonbuilding structures (%4.1) |

| | | | | | |
|---|---|---|---|---|---|
| 2016 | As employers of domestic staff, the activities of households (23.1 percent) | Accommodation (8.9 percent) | Construction of nonbuilding structures (6.1 percent) | Wholesale trade (5.9 percent) | Education (4.2 percent) |
| 2017 | As employers of domestic staff, the activities of households (18.2 percent) | Accommodation (12.1 percent) | Wholesale trade (6.3 percent) | Building construction (5.7 percent) | Construction of nonbuilding structures (5.09 percent) |
| 2018 | Accommodation (17.4 percent) | Wholesale trade (7.1 percent) | Office management, Office support, and business support activities (4.9 percent) | Construction of nonbuilding structures (4.5 percent) | As employers of domestic staff, the activities of households (3.05 percent) |
| 2019 | Accommodation (15.9 percent) | As employers of domestic staff, the activities of households (11.5 percent) | Wholesale trade (8.1 percent) | Clothing manufacturing (5.6 percent) | Office management. office support, and business support activities (4.8 percent) |
| 2020 | As employers of domestic staff, the activities of households (19.1 percent) | Wholesale trade (excluding motor vehicles and motorcycles) (7.6 percent) | Clothing manufacturing (6.6 percent) | Accommodation (5.5 percent) | Textile products manufacturing (7.6 percent) |

*Source*: Ministry of Labor and Social Security, https://www.csgb.gov.tr/istatistikler/calisma-hayati-istatistikleri/resmi-istatistik-programi/yabancilarin-calisma-izinleri/. Access Date: May 1, 2023.

percent in Istanbul; this rate was 260 percent in Ankara, 220 percent in Antalya, and 560 percent in Izmir. Considering that these provinces are the largest provinces of Turkey in terms of population and economic activity, the result reached is not surprising.

## CONCLUSIONS AND DISCUSSIONS

In this study, where the types and distributions of the number of work permits of foreigners working in Turkey are evaluated between 2010 and 2020, it is seen that the number of work permits obtained by foreigners in Turkey increased rapidly between 2010 and 2020. In the evaluation, it was seen that this increase rate was over 700 percent. When the foreigners who have work permits in Turkey are evaluated according to gender, it is seen that the work permit rates of women were below those of men during 2010 and 2011, but in 2012, the work permit rate of women exceeded that of men. This situation continued throughout 2012–2015. However, for 2016–2020, the work permit rate of men exceeded the work permit rate of women. When evaluated with the nationalities who have received work permits in Turkey, the main reason for the increase in the work permit rate of men in 2016 can be considered as the participation of men from families who migrated to Turkey due to the civil war in Syria in the labor market in Turkey.

When the education levels of foreigners who have a work permit in Turkey are examined, it is seen that they are generally high school and university graduates. It is seen that more than 80 percent of the foreigners who received a work permit in Turkey between 2011 and 2014 are high school, college, and university graduates. This rate fell below 80 percent in 2015 and beyond. In 2015, the rate of those who had a work permit with high school, college, and university graduation was 78.3 percent; the proportion of illiterate foreigners increased by two times compared to the previous year and increased from 2.9 percent to 6.1 percent. In the years that followed, the proportion of high school, college, and university graduates continued to decline. In 2020, the rate for this group decreased to 51 percent. In 2020, the rate of those who did not graduate from any school and were only literate was 17.5 percent.

In the light of all this information, it is possible to say that there is a decrease in the education levels of foreigners coming to Turkey. Another comment that can be made is that the number of foreigners who have not been able to offer diploma equivalency has increased, and these foreigners have been evaluated in the literacy category.

When the nationalities of foreigners who have work permits in Türkiye are examined, it is seen that the highest number belongs to Syrians. Especially in 2016 and after, it is seen that the work permits of Syrians are dominant in a way that distinguishes them from other nationalities. It can be safely said that the political instability and civil war in Syria have created this situation. Other foreigners who have a weight study permit in Turkeyare seen to be Turkic republics (Azerbaijan, Kyrgyzstan, Uzbekistan, Turkmenistan), Iran, Georgia, and Russia. In this context, it can be considered that foreigners working in Türkiye prefer Türkiye due to reasons such as geographical proximity, cultural proximity, and economic and political instability in their own countries.

In addition, according to the Data on the Types of Economic Activities in terms of the Distribution of the Number of Work Permits Granted to Foreigners, it is mainly within the scope of "As employers of Domestic Staff, the activities of households." In other words, child care, patient care, individuals employed to help with household chores, and so on include foreigners employed by employment methods. It is an undeniable fact that more women are employed in this type of work. In this respect, it can be said that many foreign women working in Turkey are concentrated in a single branch of economic activity. Other weighted types of activities for 2020 are wholesale trade (excluding motor vehicles and motorcycles), clothing manufacturing, accommodation, and textile products manufacturing. It can be said that foreigners are employed in labor-intensive activity branches in Turkey. This situation creates concerns that foreigners who agree to work in labor-intensive sectors at low wages will have a decreasing effect on the wages of Turkish workers who want to operate in the same line of work.

Provinces that host the highest number of foreigners with work permits in Turkey are Istanbul, Ankara, Antalya, Bursa, and Izmir. It is conceivable that the increase in foreigners in these provinces, which already have a high population density, especially in Istanbul, may be a factor that changes the labor market balances.

In this regard, the suggestions that can be supported by the data that emerge as a result of the study are listed below:

1. The Ministry of Interior of the Republic of Turkey Migration Management, and the Turkish Employment Agency should follow the data and records in a coordinated manner and homogeneously direct the unqualified foreign labor force to include other cities.
2. To determine the priority areas that can benefit from the qualified foreign labor force, the Ministry of Labor and Social Security of the Republic of Turkey regularly conducts the necessary research in line with the recommendations to be received from economic stakeholders.

3. As a result of the research to be carried out by the unqualified foreign labor force, vocational training courses and so on are provided for the areas where the need arises within the existing sectors.
4. To prevent illegal wage practices against foreigners (employment below the minimum wage, unregistered wage refund requests, etc.) by tightening employers' controls on employment contracts and thus to prevent the deterioration of the labor supply structure of Turkish workers in the labor markets.

In line with these suggestions, it will be possible for foreigners who have a work permit in Türkiye to benefit from the human capital of foreigners with the highest efficiency without disturbing the structure of the employment markets.

## NOTES

1. Assoc. Prof., Izmir Democracy University, Faculty of Economics and Administrative Sciences, Department of Economics, Izmir, Türkiye, eylul.kabakci@idu.edu.tr.
2. https://www.goc.gov.tr/goc-tarihi. Access Date: May 12, 2022.
3. OG:11/04/2003;28615 1.5.6458.pdf (mevzuat.gov.tr).
4. https://www.csgb.gov.tr/uigm/calisma-izni/turk-vatandaslarina-hasredilen-meslekler/. Access Date: May 1, 2022.
5. OG:02/02/2022;31738.
6. OG:13/08/2016; 29800.
7. OG:13/08/2016; 29800.
8. OG: 02/02/2022;31738.
9. OG: 13/08/2016;29800.
10. OG:14/03/2017;30007.
11. OG: 02/02/2022;31738.
12. Ministry of Labor and Social Security, https://www.csgb.gov.tr/istatistikler/calisma-hayati-istatistikleri/resmi-istatistik-programi/yabancilarin-calisma-izinleri/. Access Date: May 2, 2023.
13. Ministry of Labor and Social Security, https://www.csgb.gov.tr/istatistikler/calisma-hayati-istatistikleri/resmi-istatistik-programi/yabancilarin-calisma-izinleri/, Access Date: May 2, 2022.
14. Ministry of Labor and Social Security, https://www.csgb.gov.tr/istatistikler/calisma-hayati-istatistikleri/resmi-istatistik-programi/yabancilarin-calisma-izinleri/. Access Date: May 1, 2022.

## REFERENCES


ILL, (2016). International Labor Law (6735 SK), Official Gazette, 29800 (August 13, 2016) https://www.resmigazete.gov.tr/eskiler/2016/08/20160813–1.htm

ILLIR, (2022). International Labor Law Implementation Regulation, (6735 SK 1.MD), Official Gazette, 31738 (February 2, 2022)

İçduygu, A., (2004), *Türkiye'de Kaçak Göç. İstanbul Ticaret Odası Yayınları*, Can Ajans ve Matbaacılık, İstanbul

Kirişçi, K., (2000). Disaggregating Turkish Citizenship and Immigration Practices, *Middle Eastern Studies*, 36, 3, 1–22.

Kirişçi, K., (2003). *Türkiye: A Transformation from Emigration to Immigration, Migration Informatİon Source Paper*, Migration Policy Institute, Washington, DC

LFIP, (2013). Law on foreigners and international protection (6458 SK), Official Gazette, 28615 (April 11, 2013) 1.5.6458.pdf (mevzuat.gov.tr)

Ministry of Labor and Social Security, https://www.csgb.gov.tr/istatistikler/calisma-hayati-istatistikleri/resmi-istatistik-programi/yabancilarin-calisma-izinleri/ Access Date: May 1, 2022

Ministry of Labor and Social Security, https://www.csgb.gov.tr/uigm/calisma-izni/turk-vatandaslarina-hasredilen-meslekler/ Access Date: May 1, 2022

MLSS, (2022). Ministry of Labor and Social Security, General Directorate for International Labor Force, https://www.csgb.gov.tr/uigm/calisma-izni/izin-turleri/ Access Date: May 2, 2022

TCR, (2017). Turquoise Card Regulation (6735 SK 11. MD ve 25.MD), Official Gazette, 30007 (March 14, 2017) https://www.resmigazete.gov.tr/eskiler/2017/03/20170314-1.htm

*Chapter 4*

# Information and Communication Sector Labor Market Analysis in Turkey

Hakan Mete[1]

This chapter examines the development of the Information and Communication Technologies (ICT) sector labor market in 100 years starting from 1923, the foundation date of the Republic of Turkey. The main problem of the research is how the ICT sector, in terms of the labor market, has developed from 1923 to the present in Turkey. Answers are sought for the following basic questions: what are the breaking points and significant developments that have occurred in the sub-sector; how have public and private institutions contributed to this development; and, lastly, how has the labour market evolved according to different parameters?

The chapter analyzes the contribution of the sector to the national economy on a macro basis, as well as ICT employment in total employment, ICT employment by gender, R&D employee in ICT employment, ICT employment by education level, wages of ICT workers, labor market development according to the development of the ICT sector, and similar parameters.

In the chapter, analyses were made from different perspectives on the development of ICT in Turkey's 100-year history of the republic, and a detailed picture of the labor market of the sector, which has made significant progress in recent years, has been taken. It aims to record the results of the studies carried out to increase the performance of the ICT sector and the labor market and the results from the macro-collected data in a single document. One of the most important results of the study, in which the general view of the sector's development over 100 years and the quantitative data of the last years were analyzed, is the upward trend of the sector in all aspects. Infrastructure investments made in the communication subsector developed intensely until 1970, and then, with the groundbreaking progress of information technologies, the software sector, which is in the information technologies subsector, showed the greatest development in recent years.

In the field of employment, total sector employment has developed upward and the acceleration of the development has increased exponentially in recent years. The highest increase in employment was realized in the information technologies subsector. While the result of women's employment in the sector followed a horizontal course, it showed an upward momentum in recent years. While a fluctuating graph was observed in the number of higher education graduates in employment, the number of R&D employees generally showed an upward development. Especially after the pandemic period, while the number of ICT employees decreased in small-scale enterprises, the number of employees in large-scale enterprises increased. The wages of the employees were observed in the measured periods, in direct proportion to their educational status and a developmental pattern. All researchers emphasize that the biggest problem faced by the sector in the field of the labor market is the lack of a qualified labor force.

## INTRODUCTION

The development trend of global economies has impacted national economies through international policies and viewpoints. Prioritizing liberal economic policies prior to World War I, statist practices during and after the Great Depression, planned development beginning in the 1960s, and the neoliberal era following 1970, economies endeavoured to undergo constant transformation (Toffler, 1980).

The phenomenon of globalization, which increased its severity in 1970 and after, made the effects of social and political developments more noticeable on the whole world. Due to the fact that information is bought and sold as a commodity in the economy, ICT provides an infrastructure for development by entering all processes in other sectors, and the incredible increase in the daily use of technological tools and devices in social life has accelerated the transformation process into an information society all over the world since 1980 (Masuda, 1990).

The factor determining the historical limit of the research on the ICT sector, which is used as the most basic tool in the transformation process of Turkey into an information society, is the developments experienced within 100 years since 1923, the foundation date of the Republic of Turkey. The research examines the development process that started with infrastructure investments in the field of communication with the first years of the Republic and the information sector that developed with the use of information technology tools in 1960 and later. The study reveals the development trend in the field of labor market in Turkey with its results, based on recent data with statistical information.

As a result of the study examining Turkey's century-old information and communication sector development, many results have emerged regarding the labor market. The most fundamental of the results is that the development trend of the sector is upward in all aspects. The software sector, which is part of the information technologies subsector, showed the greatest improvement proportionally. The software sector was followed by the electronic communication and communication technologies hardware sector in the communication technologies subsector, respectively.

In the section where the data are analyzed, the total sector employment in the field of employment has nearly tripled. The highest increase in employment was in the information technologies subsector with approximately six times. The result about women's employment in the sector, while the development followed a horizontal course in the first years of the period, showed an upward momentum toward the last years. While a fluctuating graph was observed in the number of higher education graduates in employment, the number of R&D employees generally showed an upward development. Especially during the pandemic period, while the number of ICT employees decreased in small-scale enterprises, the number of employees in large-scale enterprises increased. The wages of the employees were observed in the measured periods, directly proportional to their educational status and in a development pattern.

The chapter consists of two parts. The first part discusses the developments in the ICT sector in the 100-year history of the Republic of Turkey and the scope of the data to be used; it examines subsector developments, important breaking points, and the contributions of private and public institutions to development. The second part deals with the data collected in recent years from various sources about the general structure of the sector and the labor market. The chapter provides information about the general picture of the sector by gathering all information about the ICT labor market from a single source in Turkey.

## The Scope and Development of the Information and Communication Technologies Industry

The fact that information and communication tools, which emerged as a technological development, became one of the largest sectors in the world took place in a short time. Computer and network technologies, which started as a military project, were first opened to other public institutions and finally to the private sector, and turned into a product that can be bought and sold economically. With the development of the Internet, this technology, which has penetrated homes and people's pockets, has affected the whole world (Roztocki et al., 2019). Today, eight companies in the list of the ten most valuable companies in the world are in the ICT sector.

## SCOPE OF INFORMATION AND COMMUNICATION TECHNOLOGIES INDUSTRY

The ICT sector, which has important functions in economic and social life, includes all the tools and applications used in the acquisition, processing, storage, transmission, and service of information (United Nations, 2005). The scope of the data to be discussed in the chapter consists of information technologies and communication technologies.

This chapter includes the information technologies and communication technologies subsectors in which the sector is generally differentiated. The research examines hardware, software, and services in the information technologies subfield and hardware and electronic communication technologies in the communication technologies subfield.

Information technologies, with its shortest definition, constitute the computer part of the sector. The scope of the computer concept includes all the tools used in the process of transforming the input, which is defined as data, into information. The concept of information technologies encompasses the systems used in the production, storage, and operation of information (Alter, 2008). The scope of the information technology sector is developing day by day with the use of systems in all activities of society. Information systems are used in technologies such as health, agriculture, the defense industry, space technologies, artificial intelligence, and robotics.

The scope of the study consists of hardware, software, and services subsectors. The concept of hardware in the field of information technologies includes all the devices consisting of electromechanical parts used in the processes of creating and operating information. Information technology equipment is product formed by manufacturing chips, integrated, and other semiconductor materials and combining them in the factory environment. Today, with the development of communication and digital transformation technologies, besides traditional equipment such as computers, printers, and monitors, devices such as refrigerators, CNC benches, virtual reality glasses, and robots are also classified as hardware (WCOE, 2015). The need for intensive capital and R&D investments, the fact that it takes a long time for the investments to turn into products, and a great competitive environment are among the features of the information technology equipment in the sectoral sense. The United States, where technology was first developed in this sector, and the People's Republic of China, which is rich in cheap labor costs and raw material resources, have a significant market share (Bateman, 2022).

Software-defined in the information technology sector refers to applications that enable electronically produced hardware to work in accordance with its intended use. The software industry is the digital codes that are invisible to the naked eye but ensure that the hardware works properly and in accordance with the production purpose and is defined as the spirit of information technologies (Ale, 2022). Within the concept of software, there are embedded software that controls the electronic infrastructure of the hardware, operating systems that enable it to perform its basic functions, programming languages that allow software development on the operating system, application software that allows it to serve special purposes on the hardware, database software that stores data in certain structures, and cyber security software that provides security (Bourgeois, 2014). The software industry, unlike the hardware industry, needs human resource development rather than heavy capital investment. The United States has a significant market share in terms of product diversity and economic development in the world. Countries such as India, Ireland, and Estonia, which have opportunities such as an educated workforce, sectoral infrastructure, and cheap labor in the sector, plan their economic development through the software sector (Salazar-Xirinachs et.al., 2014).

The scope of the sector is expanding day by day due to the development of digital transformation technologies and affecting all sectors such as banking, the defense industry, education, transportation, and production. All processes other than the production of information technology hardware and software development are classified within the services subsector. Information technology consultancy activities, hardware and software maintenance, update and maintenance services, information technologies network installation and management services, web page hosting, cybersecurity services, and server management services are the main services subsector within the information technologies main sector (Kramer et.al., 2007).

The concept of communication in ICT is the electronic transfer of information assets from one source to another. The concept of resource in the definition refers to information and communication technology resources such as computers, mobile phones, servers, and network devices. The concept of information assets consists of all kinds of digital data such as audio, text, image, and video. The development of communication technologies has enabled the transfer of information from the seller to the buyer, allowing it to become tradable in the market. The industry, in which analog voice communication forms the basis, enables the transport of high-dimensional digital data today. The sector generally needs high infrastructure investment. Satellite communication, 5G, 6G, fiber infrastructure, and mobile communication technologies constitute the future of the industry. The most important product of the hardware subsector of the communication technologies sector is the mobile phone. The development of communication technologies and the fact that mobile phones allow data communication instead of only voice communication have made mobile phones an important market player. Devices such as vehicle phones, telegraph, radios, and GPS are other hardware products of communication technologies. In the communication technologies sector, the electronic communication subsector involves the devices, software, and systems used to provide communication. These include satellite, mobile communication, navigation, telephone, and fiber infrastructure and services provided. The weight of public institutions is high in the sector, which has a high importance in terms of national economies and social life (Biddle et al., 2012).

### Development of Turkey's Information and Communication Technologies Sector

The Republic of Turkey, whose entire infrastructure was damaged after the First World War, lost the majority of its population had to pay the debts left by the Ottoman Empire and went through difficult times economically. Having reached 100 years of history, Turkey exports the defense industry to many countries, increases its investments in space technologies, and defines ICT as a priority sector in development.

In this part of the chapter, important developments of the country in ICT, the works of the public and private sectors, and the results of these studies will be discussed.

## THE FIRST PERIOD OF THE REPUBLIC: THE DEVELOPMENT OF COMMUNICATION TECHNOLOGIES—THE PERIOD BETWEEN 1923 AND 1960

The defeat of the Ottoman Empire during the First World War and the subsequent military and political developments resulted in the establishment of the Republic of Turkey. The new state, which was established after the devastating effects of the war, focused on efforts in education, infrastructure, and ultimately economic development, as well as the obligation to pay the debts of the Ottoman Empire (Altıparmak, 1998).

In the words of the founder and first president of the state, Mustafa Kemal Atatürk, the moderate statism economic development model was preferred. In this model, the state fulfills the functions of controlling, directing, and encouraging private sector enterprises. The state makes infrastructure investments and top investments that the private sector cannot enter for various reasons, bringing the business to a profitable position and transferring it back to the private sector (Ulusoy, 2018).

The first targeted infrastructure investments were in railway and road networks, ports, and communication. In the field of communication, the country's first communication technologies investments began to be made. Telephone infrastructure under foreign companies was the first to be nationalized. Along with the nationalized electricity companies, infrastructure investments were made in Anatolian cities where the private sector invested very little. With the Telephone and Telegraph Law No. 406 enacted in 1924, the task of establishing and operating communication means all over the country was given to the General Directorate of Postal Telephone and Telegraph Office (PTT) (Akıl, 2001).

In the previous period, there was a telegraph system established and a manual telephone infrastructure built only in Istanbul. The first communication technology investment of the Republic of Turkey was the establishment of an automatic telephone exchange in Ankara in 1926 as a result of the agreement with the Ericson company. A single-circuit switchboard was established between Istanbul and Ankara for intercity communication. Appropriations were made in the state budget for the improvement of telegraph systems, the supply of new devices after the letter reform, and the training of telegraph operators. Just like the use of radio systems in the world, radio station investments were made in Ankara and Istanbul, and it was possible to establish uninterrupted communication with important centers such as Paris and London (Bengi, 2020).

The human resources working in the communication services had important duties, especially during the war, and worked hard to ensure the active operation of the systems and lines. During the Republican period, the economic, political, and social effects of communication were taken into consideration, and significant wage improvements were made primarily to telephone and telegraph workers. New overtime arrangements were made, and working hours were determined to be eight hours instead of twenty-four hours. Large telegraph centers were established by increasing the number of civil servants (Tekir, 2021).

After a period in which import substitution and state investments were undertaken until the Second World War, there was a period of economic and social decline due to the effect of the war. Infrastructure investments were put into the background by making military expenditures. In the postwar world political and economic history, the period called the Cold War had begun. Significant assistance was received from the United States in line with the objectives of "increasing the general welfare level of Turkey and bringing its defense power to a sufficient level against a possible Soviet attack." Aids made through institutions such as the United Nations, the World Bank, and the IMF brought economic sanctions, and a liberal economic period was experienced between the years 1950 and 1960. The period had consequences such as the encouragement of foreign capital, the development of the agricultural sector instead of large industrial investments, the increase in the importance given to the transportation sector, road and sea transport, and the increase in oil imports. No great progress was made in the field of communication technologies (Şener, 2005).

## PLANNED DEVELOPMENT PERIOD: STARTING THE USE OF INFORMATION TECHNOLOGIES AND SECTORAL DEVELOPMENT—THE PERIOD BETWEEN 1960 AND 2000

Turkey started the planned development process with the 1961 Constitution. Although there had been plans in the field of industry since the establishment of the Republic, the period in which planned development was developed with special laws by taking constitutional guarantees could be realized with the 1961 Constitution. The State Planning Organization, which was established to determine the objectives of the Development Plans and the steps to be taken, assumed the task of coordination between the institutions that would provide the intended development (Bayram, 1994). Development Plans contain important information about the improvements of the sector over the years and the events that are planned.

In the period between 1963 and 1967, the view of communication sector, which was classified as the main transportation sector, should be seen as a public service dominant. According to the data announced in the Development Plan, railways and communication services are monopolized by the state in the transportation and communication sector, which has a share of 7 percent of the national income. Capacity constraints are generally mentioned in communication services. It has been determined that the postal business and telegraph networks meet the needs, but telephone and radio communication need investment.

**Table 4.1 Planned Value Added and Investments of Communication Sector (Million TL)**

| *Years* | *1963* | *1964* | *1965* | *1966* | *1967* |
|---|---|---|---|---|---|
| Value Added | 369 | 451 | 523 | 571 | 659 |
| Investments | 254,5 | 223,3 | 207,7 | 223 | 178 |

*Source*: State Planning Organisation (SPO), 1963.

According to table 4.1, it is seen that the infrastructure investments in the communication subsector were higher in the first years to meet the urgent need, and the investments continued to decrease in the following years. The majority of the allocated budget is planned to be spent on telephone and radio infrastructure.

It was in 1960 that Turkey met with information technologies and computer systems. The 650-Data Processing Machine model computer, imported by the General Directorate of Highways from IBM to make high-level mathematical calculations in road construction works, is the first example. The first informatics education in the country is the training given by American experts on the installation, use, and programming of this computer. Later, information technology training was started to be given in universities, and information system devices were installed and trained in universities. Institutions in Turkey generally work with IBM (Taymaz, 2018).

In the 1967–1972 period, it is emphasized that communication technologies have become an important position for the development of the agricultural sector, universities and other public institutions, commercial and social life, the cooperation of private and public institutions, and the development of health infrastructure. According to the plan, the share of communication in total investments increased to 16.1 percent, together with the transportation sector, where it is classified. It is planned that the communication sector will be opened to private sector investments for the first time and the PTT Directorate will carry out supervisory activities for these institutions. With the partnership agreement signed between the PTT and the British telecommunications company Northern Electric in 1967, NETAŞ company was established and the first R&D investments were made. It is planned to reach the level of export in the field of communication. It is estimated that the imports in the field of wired communication devices will end with a decrease and exports will start from 1972. Another development experienced in Turkey during this period was the establishment of the Turkish Informatics Association in 1971. The aim of the Turkish Informatics Association (TIA), which is the first information technologies association in the country, has been defined as providing development in the sector based on examples from abroad and establishing links between state, university, and industrial organizations. The association has made significant contributions to the informatics sector through conferences, training, and other activities over the years (Bozkurt, 2009).

By 1973, the failure to make the planned investments prevented the development of the telephone infrastructure. In addition, the demand for telephone systems had increased more than anticipated. Although the radio-link lines and telephone infrastructure made significant progress in the wide area network, the bottlenecks could not be eliminated, and the increasing cost of telephone devices and the import rate slowed the progress. Between 1973 and 1977, progress was made in the production of communication technologies, albeit small, and it was planned to start semiconductor and cable production in addition to the devices produced within NETAS. The procurement of information technology devices in the field of electronic calculators was planned for the first time among the import forecasts. Resources were transferred so that public enterprises to be established for the domestic production of electronic technology could lead the sector and make R&D investments. With the satellite earth station commissioned during the plan period, extensive opportunities were provided in international communication (SPO, 1972).

As a result of the expansion of radio link lines at the end of 1978, telephone and television services reached 83 percent of the country. Communication and information flow systems have not developed at the desired level, and no progress has been made in standard studies and material production. In general, the lack of qualified technical personnel has been a general problem of all sectors. The number of technicians per engineer, which should have been at the 2–3 level, decreased to 0.5, and the intermediate staff gap increased. Technology transfer took place in the form of license agreements and know-how imports. Technical skills and qualified human resources have been tried to be developed with these agreements. It is aimed to meet the communication and information flow sector at a speed that does not cause a bottleneck in the industrial and services sector and to integrate it into international systems.

With the development of electrical and electronic technologies, important changes were made in the Fifth Development Plan in order to produce goods and create export channels while imports increased in this direction. It is planned to develop knowledge-intensive technologies by increasing R&D activities. It has been stated that with the increase in demand for the electrical-electronics sector, investments will be made in communication devices, and a significant increase in exports will be achieved with the knowledge produced in terms of laboratories and technical manpower. To improve communication throughout the country, the issues related to the establishment of the second satellite earth station and the extension of the telephone lines to the villages were mentioned.

Within the socioeconomic structure that has evolved into agriculture, industry, and information society, Turkey defined ICT for the first time under the social development section of the Fifth Development Plan, which covers the 1985–1989 period. Efficiency increases with the use of information technologies in other sectors is one of the important targets. In this respect, the plan focused on the contribution of the ICT sector to other sectors rather than its own development (SPO, 1984). In addition to the development of satellite, telephone, radio, and television systems in communication technologies, targets for information flow systems have been determined. Incentives were provided to companies in order to create a data bank of institutions with information technology devices and to train human resources in the computer and especially software sectors.

In the 1990–1994 period, it aimed to use information technologies intensively for the transformation into an information society and gave particular importance to software. In the previous period, incentives given to computer and software technology companies and efforts to create education policies led to the first software export by NETAŞ in 1992. The annual increase in the production of electronic devices, which was 9.5 percent in the Fifth Development Plan, is foreseen as 12.5 percent. It is aimed to increasing the share of R&D expenditures in GNP to 1 percent and above. The quotas in schools were increased by taking measures to increase the supply for manpower trained in the field of computers and communication (Akça et al., 2017).

The Seventh Development Plan, covering the period of 1996–2000, has identified the development of ICT as one of the most important projects that will provide infrastructure for Turkey's transformation into an information society targeted in the twenty-first century. The plan aimed at an internationally competitive structure in the fields of R&D, university-industry cooperation, and information technologies and software. In this period, efforts were made to comply with European Standards as a result of the customs union agreement with the European Union. In this direction, it was planned to increase human resources and budget investments in ICT to close the productivity gaps. It was emphasized that the young population should be directed to science and technological sectors and that education should be developed and disseminated at all levels. One of the features that distinguishes this plan from other plans is its project-based management approach. A transition was made from general statements about development to project management with concrete steps. Under the title of Structural Change in Infrastructure Services, it has been determined that communication technologies are close to the desired level with the investments made, and it is aimed to expand with emphasis on the business world. Steps are planned to transition from the state monopoly model to the free market in telecommunications. For the development of information technologies, the development of the national information network and what needs to be done for its integration into international networks are planned. Afterward, the "Turkey National Information Network Infrastructure Master Plan" was prepared by the Scientific and Technological Research Council of Turkey (TÜBITAK). According to this plan, decisions were taken such as giving priority to the software sector on the way to becoming an information society, strengthening cooperation between the state university and the private sector and making joint projects. It is aimed at increasing structural reforms, education systems, and incentives for the development of the software sector. It is planned to develop a quality certification system and include it in the scope of copyright protection (Avcı et al., 2010).

## TRANSFORMATION INTO THE INFORMATION SOCIETY: THE PERIOD AFTER 2000

As a result of the heavy economic conditions, and political and social events after the establishment of the state, Turkey had a lot of difficulty in reaching the targets set in the published development plans. Turkey has not been able to get rid of the status of a developing country for many years due to the inability to create the desired capital accumulation, the inability to complete industrialization, and the insufficient development of infrastructure and human resources. Although investments were made in the communication infrastructure in the first years, and then, with the development of information technologies, for transformation into an information society, sufficient results could not be obtained (Buyruk, 2016).

In 2001, the development policies were changed and the Long-Term Development Strategy (2001–2023) for the 100th anniversary of the Republic was announced. One of the main objectives of the strategy is to transform into an information society. In 2003, the Turkey E-Transformation Project was initiated as a part of the "e-Europe Initiative" prepared for candidate countries to the European Union.

In the period 2001–2005, the National Academic Network was established to increase the ability of private and public sector R&D institutions and universities to work together. It aimed to increase the share of R&D activities in GDP to 1.5 percent. Priority was given to increasing the competitiveness of the ICT sector, which was defined as a strategic sector, mainly software. With the entry of the private sector into the market in terms of internet infrastructure and services, service quality and information security have increased (SPO, 2000).

With the start of the European Union negotiation process in Turkey, the transformation process has accelerated. Harmonization studies have been carried out based on public order, policies, and laws. Information technology legislation was rearranged within the legal framework, and the transformation process was initiated to cover all segments of the state, private sector, and society. First, the electronic signature law was enacted, and a personal electronic signature infrastructure was established for bureaucratic activities.

In the 2007–2013 period, it was aimed to develop and expand the ICT sector to realize the strategy of increasing competitiveness by the objectives of the "Long Term Strategy (2001–2023)," and the National Science and Technology Policies Strategy Plan was formed (Bayraktutan and Bıdırdı, 2015). Information and communication, R&D, defense, and space technologies sectors were determined as priority areas and were aimed at being supported. In this respect, the plan differs from the others in terms of sector. With the increase in the priority given to ICT in Turkey, important developments have been experienced in the sector during and after the plan period.

Especially after the economic crisis in 2008, important incentives were introduced to the ICT sector, which has a high import rate, to combat the current account deficit. Firms are using ICT incentives, the first concrete steps of which were taken in 2010, and the amount of incentives increases each year. Technology centres, R&D centers, and technopolises opened within universities have been important incentive centers. The export parameters of the sector have improved every year, and the software subsector has experienced a significant leap. The depreciation of the dollarturkish lira exchange rate against the Turkish lira in Turkey, starting in 2013, caused the sector to develop negatively against the dollar (TIA, 2018).

In the early stages of the "Long-Term Strategy" document and at the beginning of the ninth development period, the share of GDP allocated to R&D reached 3 percent, and the number of researchers reached 70,000. Approximately 150 research centers operating in universities and public institutions have become sustainable in cooperation with the private sector. It is aimed at transforming the defence, transportation, and automotive sectors, especially manufacturing, and priority has been given to the development of electronic communication and information technology products for these sectors. The emphasis was placed on efficiency in hardware expenditures and value-added use in software and services sectors. The Cyber Security Board was established for the first time within the ministry, and studies were initiated in the fields of protection of personal data, national information security, and electronic commerce. Within the scope of transformation into information society strategies, it is planned to expand technological developments to increase the efficiency of enterprises, especially SMEs, and to start using smart applications in health, transportation, building, energy, disaster, and water management processes (TÜBİTAK, 2004).

Incentives provided to companies for the development of the software industry for many years have started to yield results since 2000. At the beginning of this period, the number of companies developing web-based software for business such as accounting, human resources, finance, and stock control, especially e-commerce, has increased in the sector where web technologies have developed significantly. In 2010 and later, with the development of digital transformation technologies around concepts, such as cloud computing, the internet of things, artificial intelligence, robotic systems, and material technologies (3D printers, nanotechnology, etc.) and companies' increasing R&D investments, products belonging to these technologies began to emerge. In recent years, when software exports have increased significantly, companies that develop game programming, mobile programming, and other package software have expanded abroad to make a name for themselves in the world markets. Recognition and investment of private enterprises by foreign investment companies have been an incentive in the sector, and the number of software companies has increased.

In the 100th Anniversary Development Plan announced in 2019, a separate chapter was opened for digital transformation and it was aimed to increase productivity by using information and communication devices and applications in all sectors. Targets for domestic product development, training opportunities, development of technological centers, increasing cybersecurity awareness, and using industrial cloud architecture systems have been determined in the manufacturing industry, businesses, and priority sectors. In the field of electronic communication, investments in fiber, satellite, and communication in rural areas, the establishment of a regional data center in the field of information technologies, improvement of the software development sector, production of artificial intelligence technologies, and providing national cybersecurity were given importance.

The sectors aimed to provide efficiency and technological development by using digital transformation technologies are chemistry, pharmaceuticals and medical devices, electronics, machinery-electrical equipment, automotive, rail system vehicles, and other manufacturing industries. It is aimed to develop and use domestic information and communication technology tools for these sectors. To develop in the fields of Agriculture, Defense Industry, and Tourism, R&D opportunities will be increased with the cooperation of the public and private sectors, and added value will be created with the products and services to be produced (Eraslan and Dönmez, 2017).

After the pandemic period that emerged at the end of 2019 and early 2020, the demand for information technology services and products has increased. The sales and trade momentum of the sector increased more than in previous years. Digital transformation technologies have contributed significantly to the development of the industry. New technologies such as artificial intelligence, cloud technologies, big data, cybersecurity, blockchain, virtual reality, and 3D production in the field of hardware and software have started a major change process in the sector (Soylu, 2017).

Public investments in the field of ICT have increased significantly since 2002 within the scope of the e-transformation project. E-government, Equal Opportunity in Education Project (FATIH), investments in satellite technologies (TURKSAT 3-4-5 Satellites), delivery of fiber infrastructure to all regions of the country, R&D investments in TÜBITAK and established Technopolises, incentives provided to information technology companies and privileges, and investments in the regulation of the information technology education structure stand out as important developments (Sevim, 2019).

The biggest development in the field of electronic communication in this period was the privatization of Türk Telekom. As a result of this privatization, the entry of private sector companies to the market was accelerated, and the opportunity for competition emerged by diversifying the service. It has led to an increase in investments in fiber infrastructure and satellite technologies. Turkey, which sent the first communication satellite into space in 1994, commissioned its eighth satellite, TURKSAT 5B, to serve in the middle of 2022, especially in regions where signals in rural and mountainous areas cannot reach and in times of disaster. Studies are continuing to send the observation satellite IMECE developed by Turkish engineers to space in January 2023 and the 6A communication satellite developed in the same way in the middle of 2023 (Kaplan, 2022).

Turkey's increasing interest in the defense industry, space technologies, and smart vehicle and road systems sectors has led to significant progress in the field of hardware and software. Today, Turkey has reached the level of developing its avionics management software, ship-integrated weapon and management software, satellite management software, and software for its vehicles that will start mass production in 2023. In hardware technologies, it develops chip technology under the coordination of TÜBITAK, introduces mobile phone and computer brands to world markets, and produces its satellite.

Turkey's efforts toward the employment of ICT, the regulation of the information education system, the provision of important incentives for the employment of information in the national incentive system, and the employment of public, universities, private sector, and nongovernmental organizations are project-based studies. Especially in the last twenty years, informatics education quotas and education infrastructure have been expanded at all education levels. The level of courses on informatics has been reduced to primary schools, special high schools for software and information technologies have been opened, the quota for informatics has been increased in universities, and quality-enhancing and certificate-winning training programs have begun to be organized by municipalities and nongovernmental organizations (Demirer and Sak, 2015).

## TURKISH INFORMATION AND COMMUNICATION TECHNOLOGIES SECTOR LABOR MARKET

The adventure of the information sector, which started with the electronic communication infrastructure and investments of Turkey in the 100-year-old Republic, continued with the importation of information technology systems, and as a result of long years of efforts, the high-tech products and services produced today have come to a position to be exported to other countries. Although it is still behind the targeted progress, the development continues in an upward direction due to reasons such as giving importance to informatics by determining it as a priority sector, the high rate of young population, increasing educational opportunities, advances in the defense and space technologies industries, and the private sector receiving significant investments.

In this part of the chapter, the ICT sector will be analysed with data collected from various sources, and the development pattern will be examined comparatively over many parameters. Analyses will be made for the sector and the labor market based on total employment, women in employment and R&D workers, and employment by graduation, together with macro data such as the total market size of the sector, subsector components of growth, and export figures. The collected data allow a detailed examination of the outputs before and after the 2007–2013 development plan, in which ICT is defined as the priority sector.

## SECTORAL SIZE, EXPORT DEVELOPMENT, AND DISTRIBUTION OF SUBSECTORS

The macro-level growth of Turkey's ICT sector, the export potential of its products and services by finding buyers in foreign markets, and the contribution of subsectors to this development provide important information about the state of the labor market of the sector. With the young population, the development of quality-enhancing education opportunities, and the increase in investments, the sector has been in development every year and has varied according to the state of technological developments in the world.

According to the ten-year performance of the ICTs sector and its subsectors, the size of the sector has increased from 45.6 million TL to 266 million TL, approximately six times. Although the annual growth of the sector followed a fluctuating pattern, it showed a positive development as a result of the increase in demand with the pandemic period that started in 2018. With the effect of the period, the highest increase in the period was experienced in 2021, with 40 percent. While the performance of the total sector against the dollar remained flat between 2011 and 2017, it showed a negative development as a result of the exchange rate shocks at the end of 2017. After the sectoral development in 2021, the previous development performance was approached again. The annual development in dollar terms has generally been in a fluctuating structure (TUBISAD, 2013–2023).

The size of the information technologies subsector increased ten times and reached 114.5 million TL at the end of 2021. The annual-based development followed a fluctuating pattern parallel to the main sector, and there has been a continuous increase in recent years. In 2021, an annual increase rate of 64 percent was achieved. The share of the information technologies subsector within the main sector increased from 28 percent to 43 percent.

The size of the communication technologies subsector has increased by five times and reached 151.5 million TL at the end of 2021. The annual development of the communication sector decreased after a high level of increase in 2013, and it achieved a high rate of increase after 2017. Its share in the total sector has decreased each year from 71 percent to 56 percent.

In the hardware, software, and services sectors, which are the subsectors of information technologies, the total sector sizes have increased continuously in parallel with the general situation of the sector. The hardware sector has grown from 8.9 million TL to 43.5 million TL at the end of ten years and has grown approximately five times. The sector, which achieved high figures in 2018 and later on an annual basis, followed a fluctuating pattern in previous years. Its share in the IT sector decreased from 67.94 percent to 37.99 percent. In this respect, the development of the hardware sector has been slower than the software and services sectors. The total size of the software, which is the most developed subsector of the main ICT sector, has increased approximately fifty times, from 1.3 million TL to 51 million TL. The size, which rose to double-digit numbers in 2015, made its biggest leap in 2021. Especially the products realized in the field of defense industry have been the locomotive of the development. The game, which received significant investments from foreign companies, bears the fruits of the increase made by desktop programming companies in R&D investments. The annual growth of software was high in 2013, 2017, and 2021. The share in the IT subsector has increased every year and has reached 45 percent from 10 percent at the end of ten years.

The ten-year development in the services sector, where activities such as consultancy, maintenance and repair, and operation in the fields of information technologies, software, hardware, and cybersecurity are carried out, increased from 2.9 million TL to 20 million TL. The annual increase followed a fluctuating course due to sectoral developments and changes in market share. Its share in the IT sector has caused a slight decrease due to the performance of the software sector.

Export performance of the Turkish ICT sector reveals that the software sector has shown great improvement in parallel with the general situation of the sector. The majority of the total exports of 17.641 billion TL were made by the software sector. Although the export volumes of other sectors continue to increase, their share in exports has decreased every year. The hardware sector in total exports increased ten times and reached 1.007 billion TL. For the services sector, this ratio was five times and the total volume was 619 million TL, while the communication sector increased five times to 1.016 billion TL. The software industry has grown approximately forty-five times and reached 14.819 billion TL.

## Information and Communication Sector Employment Development in Turkey

The ICT sector needs highly qualified employees due to the continuous increase in demand for products and services, the leverage effect that contributes to the development of other sectors, and its competitive structure. It is a complex situation to educate the necessary number and quality of employees at every stage of high-technology sectors such as informatics. The developments experienced today show that the ICT sector is growing at a high rate every year. Along with this development, the need for human resources with the qualifications to develop, use, and maintain high technology increases.

Turkey's targeting of technological development in all sectors such as defense, space industry, automotive, and health, especially after the ICT sector has been determined as the priority sector since 2000, has led to an important training effort in all subsectors in the field of software, hardware, and services. Informatics education has been reduced to primary and secondary school levels, only technical and vocational high schools specific to informatics have been opened in high school education, and the number of informatics departments and quotas in higher schools have increased. It has tried to respond to the labor demand of the sector with 1 million jobs, a 2023 vision in Education, and important incentives.

The efforts made have led to an increase in the number of IT companies in Turkey, the execution of important projects at home and abroad, large investments from foreign companies, and high export figures. This development is driven by factors such as a young population, more affordable labor costs than countries that develop high technology and software, and human resources that provide easy integration into the market. With the development of digital transformation technologies such as robots, artificial intelligence, Internet of Things, and virtual reality, it is necessary to make preparations to meet the current needs in the sector as well as to gain the qualifications that will be needed by future employees. In this respect, ICT education should have a constantly developing structure that will produce the number and quality of employees desired by the sector.

After the pandemic period, due to the compliance of the ICT sector with flexible employment methods such as remote working and working from home, IT workers were preferred by foreign companies, causing a decrease in the supply of informatics employment. In addition, the sector is faced with the phenomenon of brain drain, with the effect of foreign companies that want to transfer their workforce, which has become cheaper due to the negative movement in exchange rates.

According to the status of ICT employment between 2004 and 2022, while the total employment created in Turkey has increased by approximately 11 million people and 56 percent, the total employment created in the information and communication sector is approximately 106,000 people and has increased by 73 percent. In this respect, employment in the informatics sector has shown a higher percentage of development than total employment. Except for the negative development of total employment in 2019 and 2020 under the effect of the pandemic, other years showed a positive increase, while employment in the ICT sector followed a fluctuating increase. With an increase of 30 percent in IT employment in 2010, 13 percent in 2012, and 10 percent in 2015, the years with the highest employment difference were these years. About 10 percent of the negative employment gap emerged in 2014 and 2018. The year with the highest number of IT jobs was 2017, with 258,000 people. Employment in the sector, which experienced a great decline after this year, approached the 2017 performance with 257,000 people at the end of 2021. In 2004, total informatics employment was 145,000 people and the share of total employment was 7.39 percent; in the second quarter of 2022, total informatics employment was 251,000 people and the share of total employment was 8.16 percent. The increase in the share of total employment below 1 percent in the last eighteen years indicates that the employment of ICT has not increased at the desired level. The years in which the share taken from the total employment was the highest were the period between 2012 and 2017, which was close to 10 percent.

According to the employment of the ICT sector by gender between 2004 and 2022 in Turkey, the total employment rate of men increased from 119,000 to 184,000, increasing by approximately 54 percent. The total employment rate of women, on the other hand, increased 2.5 times from 26,000 to 66,000. The share of women in total employment in the sector increased from 17.9 percent to 26 percent. In this respect, women have started to be employed in the ICT sector of the Republic of Turkey, showing a proportional increase every year compared to men. The share of men in employment decreased from 82 percent to 73.3 percent. In terms of total employment, the highest number of men was reached with 197,000 people in 2017, and after the high decline, this number was slightly approached at the end of 2021. After reaching the highest number of women employed with 68,000 people in 2013, a decrease was experienced, and this rate was approached with 67,000 people at the end of 2021. When viewed proportionally, it is understood that the percentage of women's employment increased at a high rate between 2004 and 2008, and it showed a positive trend, albeit slowly, by drawing a fluctuating graph in 2008 and after. Despite the decrease in the rate of total employment, it is still seen that the sector is male-dominated.

The number of R&D workers in Turkey has steadily increased despite interruptions, and the number of higher education graduates has fallen after the highest point in 2017, it has remained horizontal and appears to be following a course. The number of employees who graduated from higher education in the sector, which increased to 70 percent in 2017, will be at 57 percent by the end of 2021. The rate of R&D employees, which was 20 percent in 2013, when the measurement was started, reached 40 percent at the end of 2021.

Especially after the sector was defined among the priority sectors and received a significant share from the incentive system, its effects on the defense industry, space technologies, and automotive sector increased and the country's R&D investment grew. The design and development of systems such as sensor technologies, nanotechnology, autonomy, and avionics, which require high expertise and infrastructure, require R&D activities, know-how, and qualified human resources. Despite the disadvantages, such as investment costs and long-term results, strategic progress can only be achieved with such activities. Making technological progress an important target, Turkey's R&D investments in recent years have increased in parallel with these developments.

Turkey's investments in the ICT education system have increased to significant levels. Increasing the quota of information technologies in universities, opening departments for new concepts such as robotics, artificial intelligence, and cybersecurity, developing graduate and doctorate education opportunities, opening vocational high schools in the field of information technologies such as software and cybersecurity, and introducing ICT education to primary school level are some of the important works. Municipalities and nongovernmental organizations also carry out important projects in the fields of certification and vocational training.

According to the ratio of enterprises employing ICT specialists by size group, large enterprises with a large number of employees prefer to employ specialists within their structure. It is understood that the level of employing specialists in the smaller enterprises, where the number of employees has decreased, has also decreased, and they fulfil these processes by taking on consultancy.

As of the end of 2021, 72.6 percent of large enterprises with more than 250 employees employ ICT specialists. The rate of hiring specialists has generally increased steadily, from 53 percent in 2014. Such enterprises usually have their server pool. Alsothe connection processes of those who receive cloud computing services can be provided by their experts. The number of companies that operate the server pool and provide information systems user services and R&D activities by their information units has increased every year. The increase in the use of cloud computing technology has created new expertise, and the server pools have been moved to data center, resulting in a relative reduction in operating costs. In addition, more human resources were needed to sustain processes that require a high level of expertise. In medium-sized enterprises with 50–249 employees, the ratio of informatics employees decreased to 32.3 percent as of 2022. While approximately one-third of such enterprises employ their specialists, the rest perform all their services by consulting. Although the proportional situation has followed a horizontal course until 2020, there has been an upward movement in recent years with the weight of digital transformation technologies. In small businesses with 10–49 employees, the rate of employing specialists in their organisation was 13 percent in 2022. These types of companies outsource their accounting, human resources, finance, and all other services by consulting. In IT services, the server provides the network, system, and human resource costs through external resources.

Workers in the Turkish ICT sector with university and advanced degrees earn much more than other employees when compared to the annual gross salaries that each employee got based on their educational background between 2010 and 2018. Higher education graduates, who are the most employed group in the sector, doubled their annual gross earnings from 52,252 TL in 2010 to 114,515 TL at the end of 2018. Vocational high school graduates are the group whose salaries have increased the most in eight years . The annual income, which was 24,731 TL in 2010, reached 67,880 TL at the end of 2018, and it showed an improvement almost three times. In the graph, it is seen that the wage increase in this group was higher between 2014 and 2018. As the supply of intermediate staff with technical expertise in the sector could not meet the demand, wages increased more than other groups. The wage increase for high school graduates increased from 21,969 TL to 43,126 TL. Unlike employees who graduated from vocational high schools, the rate of increase in wages was higher between 2010 and 2014. Informatics employees who who graduated from primary schools earned 50,270 TL annual gross wage at the end of 2018. In this group, the salary increase was higher between 2014 and 2018. As a result of the increase in recent years, the wages of this group in 2018 were measured to be higher than those of regular high school graduates. The wages of employees who are primary school graduates or have no diplomas increased from 25,688 TL to 40,832 TL. Wages have the least increase among the groups, with an increase of 1.5 percent. According to annual wages and increase rates, while the wages of higher education graduates in the sector are quite high, there are wage differences according to labor force qualifications in lower graduations. Even if they are primary school graduates, they can earn more wages than regular high school graduates. In this respect, it is understood that the sector gives importance to qualifications rather than diplomas in determining wages and salary levels.

In Turkey, managers and experts in the IT sector make more money professionally than members of other occupational groups when it comes to annual salaries. In addition to the difficulty of finding experienced and qualified personnel in the country, it is understood that the need for employees in managerial positions has increased whıle annual salaries of executives increased from 97,966 TL to 238,329 TL. It is seen that technical expertise in the sector has an important role in determining wages, particularly for managers and employees with higher education degrees. The wages of technicians, technicians and assistant professionals, office workers at the operator level, ICT craftsmen, information facility machine operators and assemblers working in the industrial sector, service and sales personnel, and finally nonqualified informatics professionals are listed, respectively. In the eight years, which constitute the statistical period, the profession group whose wages have increased the most is informatics experts. While the average annual wage was 41,846 TL in 2010, their wages nearly tripled in 2018 and reached 114,004 TL. Managers follow the expert profession group in terms of annual increases. The wage increases of technicians, technicians and assistant professionals were particularly high between 2014 and 2018. These statistics show that the need for middle-level workers has increased in recent years at the application level and that the employment supply has difficulty meeting the demand. The increase in the number of IT vocational high schools and vocational training provided by institutions shows that a correct decision has been made regarding the current situation. With the increase in the use of digital transformation technologies in defense, automotive, and other industrial branches, the need for expertise in hardware and software for robots and other devices working in factories has increased, and the wages of employees have increased over the years.

In the ICT sector, especially in recent years, when the concept of digital transformation has gained importance, businesses have difficulty finding specialist employees. The excessive depreciation of the Turkish Lira against the dollar has also considerably reduced the cost of the labor force that foreign companies will find in Turkey. While these companies can outsource the same work to specialists in their own countries for higher wages, they incur much lower costs for skilled workers in Turkey. Brain drain, providing services to foreign companies with remote working, makes it difficult for companies in Turkey to find employees who are experienced in the field of ICT. Nearly half of companies with more than 250 employees and a large IT department have problems finding specialists. Relatively small companies with 50–249 employees have difficulty finding IT specialists at the level of 30–40 percent. It is understood that companies with 10–49 employees have more problems finding IT specialists than medium-level companies due to their low salary levels and limited opportunities in terms of professional development. The difficulty rate of such companies in finding experts is between 36 and 47 percent.

## CONCLUSIONS

The research has examined the development of the Republic of Turkey in the ICT sector in its 100-year history. It analysed recent statistics on the labor market collected from various sources, along with the general situation of the sector and macro data.

The first of the answers to the questions determined in line with the aims of the research stated in the first part is that the sector showed a significant improvement, especially after the year 2000, after it was defined among the priority sectors in development. The adventure of ICT in Turkey started with the investments made in communication technologies in the first years of the republic and the efforts to repair, renew, and develop the communication infrastructure after the First World War. Although the goals in the development plans could not be achieved despite all efforts, Turkey has become a country that exports software, develops its satellite, and develops both hardware and software in the defense, space technologies, and automotive industries.

The establishment of digital telephone exchanges, inter-city connections, telegraph, telephone, radio, and television systems were important investments and improvements made in the early years of the republic. Labor market problems in the sector were tried to be solved by reducing working hours in terms of human resources, salary improvements, and regulations regarding the number of employees. In the field of communication technologies, efforts were made to integrate into international systems by establishing radio links, and significant progress was achieved with the development of satellite technologies. With the development of broadband and internet services, Turkey's fiber infrastructure has been delivered to all cities. Radiolink lines connecting the mountainous regions and the center were established, and the connection was spread throughout the country. It plans the infrastructure to send satellites developed by its engineers into space by 2023.

The information technologies sector, which started with the import of the first information system devices in 1960, continued with the establishment of informatics trainings and laboratories by universities. Universities, banks, and public institutions that train engineers and computer programmers have been pioneers in the sector. In Turkey, in the 1980s, the electronics sector developed and infrastructure was provided to the hardware sector, and there were developments in the definition of ICT as a priority sector after 2000. With the European Union membership process, e-transformation projects were initiated. R&D investments and incentives provided to information technologies enabled companies to take part in the sector.

When the performance of the sector in recent years is analysed, the total sector size has increased six times in ten years and reached 266 million TL. The subsector with the highest development is the software sector in the field of information technologies. The software industry has grown forty-five times in the last ten years, reaching a total volume of 51 million TL. Although the development of the communication technologies sector is less than that of information technologies, it is still the subsector with the highest share in the main sector, with 151 million TL. As a result of Turkey's development of policies encouraging exports in recent years and providing significant incentives for information technology exports, it has enabled businesses to make significant sales in foreign markets. Software exports for games, mobile programming, and defense industry have increased considerably. The software sector provides 85 percent of the main sector exports, which reached 17.5 million TL as of 2022.

Throughout the history of the republic, and especially in the last ten years, important projects have been carried out to improve the informatics education system and the labor market supply of the sector. Projects such as 2023 Vision in Education, 1000 Software Developer Employment by the public education system, quality improvement, and certificate trainings were provided by municipalities and nongovernmental organizations. Although the training efforts carried out provided more informatics employment compared to the general employment increase in the country, the targeted increase in development plans and employment programs could not be achieved. As of 2022, ICT employment in total employment was 8.5 per thousand. Although it is a male-dominated sector in employment, it is evident that the percentage of women has increased in recent years. In 2022, the ratio of male employees was 73 percent, and the ratio of female employees was approximately 27 percent.

In Turkey, especially in recent years, incentives for R&D institutions and companies and increasing university–private sector interaction by establishing technoparks have made significant progress. R&D employees have increased considerably in recent years, in parallel with these studies. Although the number of higher education graduate employees in the sector has followed a fluctuating trend, it has developed in recent years. As of 2022, the rate of R&D employees is 40 percent and the rate of employees with higher education is 65 percent. The vast majority of IT workers are employed by large companies with 250 or more employees. The ratio of companies where services such as server operation, information services, and cybersecurity are carried out by their in-house IT teams has been measured as 75 percent.

According to the statistics on the wages of IT workers in Turkey, the highest earnings are achieved by graduates of higher education. The earnings of managers and professional informatics professionals are quite high compared to other informatics professions. It is observed that the salaries of technicians and technicians with vocational high school and associate degree who work in the sector on an application basis have increased considerably after 2014.

One of the biggest problems experienced by the IT companies operating in Turkey in this sector is that they have difficulty finding experienced and qualified employees. In line with its growth performance, the sector, which cannot catch a sufficient number of jobs, cannot meet the demand for labor force. After the depreciation of the Turkish Lira, the labor force, which became cheaper, is in demand by foreign companies, and with the brain drain, the labor supply is further reduced. About half of large companies with more than 250 employees cannot reach the IT workforce they need.

The literature review and statistical information collected and created from many sources show that the overall size of the Turkish ICT sector is increasing and approaching the targeted figures, while the labor market cannot provide a sufficient number and quality of employee supply. To get a share of the groundbreaking innovations of digital transformation technologies, it should be in a position to produce services and products in technologies such as virtual reality, blockchain, metaverse, data science, and artificial intelligence. In this regard, it is necessary to increase R&D investments in ICT, which is determined as the priority sector in development, to develop the infrastructure that will improve the application skills of project-based students, and to increase the capacity of the education system quantitatively and qualitatively.

## NOTE

1. Dr., Sakarya University, Faculty of Political Sciences, Department of Labor Economics and Industrial Relations, Sakarya, Türkiye, hakanmete8@gmail.com

## REFERENCES


Akça, Y., Şahan, G., and Tural, A. (2017) "Türkiye'nin Kalkınma Planlarında Eğitim Politikalarının Değerlendirilmesi" *International Journal of Cultural and Social Studies,* 3 (Special Issue), s. 394–403.

Akıl, S. (2001) "PTT'nin Yönetiminde Bir Yeniden Yapılanma Çalışması" Unpublished Master Thesis. Sakarya University.

Ale, F. (2022) *Computer Hardware.* Noun Press, Nigeria.

Alter, S. (2008) "Defining Information Systems as a Work Systems: Implications for the IS field" *European Journal of Information Systems,* 17, s. 448–469.

Altıparmak, A. (1998) "Türkiye'de Cumhuriyetin İlk Yıllarında Müteşebbis Sınıfının Gelişimi" *Erciyes University Journal of Economics and Administrative Sciences (ERUFEAS),* 13, s. 169–181.

Avcı, Ü., Kurtoğlu, M., ve Seferoğlu, S.S. (2010) "Türkiye'de Planlı Kalkınma ve Teknoloji Politikaları." Proceedings of the 10th Academic Informatics Conference, Muğla, Turkey.

Bateman, J. (2022) *U.S.-China Technological Decoupling: A Strategy and Policy Framework.* Carnegie Endowment for International Peace Publications, Washington.

Bayraktutan, Y., and Bıdırdı, H. (2015) "Türkiye'de Teknolojiye Dair Politika Perspektifi ve Kalkınma Planları" *Kocaeli University Journal of Social Sciences,* 29, s. 37–55.

Bayram, M.E. (1994) "Türkiye'de Planlama Teşkilatının (Türk Plancılığının) Hukuki ve İdari Yapısı ile İlgili Sorunları ve Çözüm Önerileri." Master thesis, State Planning Organization Publications, Ankara, Turkey.

Bengi, H. (2020) "Anadolu Ajansının Türk Radyoculuğuna Katkıları" *Kırıkkale University Journal of Social Sciences,* 11(1), s. 113–134.

Biddle, B., Curci, F.X., Haslach, T.F., Marchant, G.E., Askland, A., ve Gaudet, L. (2012) "The Expanding Role and Importance of Standards in the Information and Communication Technology Industry" *Jurimetrics Journal,* 52(2), s. 177–208.

Bourgeois, D. (2014) *Information Systems for Business and Beyond.* Saylor Foundation Publications, CA.

Bozkurt, A. (2009) "Bilişimin Gelişmesine 38 Yıldır Katkı Veren Sivil Toplum Kuruluşu: Türkiye Bilişim Derneği" *Journal of Turkish Librarianship,* 23(4), p. 902–906.

Buyruk, H. (2016) "Ekonomik Kalkınma Hedefinden Bin Yıl Kalkınma Hedeflerine: Eğitim-Kalkınma İlişkisine Dair Bir Çözümleme" *Mülkiye Dergisi,* 40(1), s. 11–142.

Demirer, V., ve Sak, N. (2015) "Türkiye'de Bilişim Teknolojileri (BT) Eğitimi ve BT Öğretmenlerinin Değişen Rolleri" *International Journal of Educational Sciences,* 2(5), s. 434–448.

Eraslan, İ.H., ve Dönmez, C.Ç. (2017) "Endüstriyel Kümelenme Uygulamalarının Türkiye Genelinde İncelenmesi: Sanayi, Tarım ve Hizmet Sektörleri Açısından Bir Değerlendirme" *Electronic Journal of Social Sciences,* 16(61), s. 325–368.

Kaplan, S. (2022) "Cumhuriyetin 100. Yılında İMECE ve TÜRKSAT 6A Uyduları Fırlatılacak." https://www.defenceturk.net/cumhuriyetin-100-yilinda-imce-ve-turksat-6a-uydulari-firlatilacak Date of access: August 6, 2022

Kramer, W.J., Jenkins, B., and Katz, R.B. (2007) "The Role of the Information and Communication Technology Sector in Expanding Economic Opportunity." Corporate Social Responsibility Initiative Report No: 22, Harvard University Publications, Cambridge.

Masuda, Y. (1990) *Managing in the Information Society.* Blackwell Publishers Inc, Cambridge, MA.

Okur, M. (2007) "Yazılım Endüstrisinin Geleceği: Gelişmekte Olan Ülkeler ve Türkiye" *Yaşar University Journal,* 2(7), s. 651–660.

Roztocki, N., Soja, P., ve Weistroffer, H.R. (2019) "The Role of Information and Communication Technologies in Socioeconomic Development: Towards a Multi-Dimensional Framework," *Information Technology for Development Journal,* 25(2), s. 171–183.

Salazar-Xirinachs, H.M., Irmgard, N., ve Kozul-Wright, R. (2014) *Transforming Economies: Making Industrial Policy Work for Growth, Jobs and Development.* International Labour Office Publication. Geneva, Switzerland.

Şener, S. (2005) "Türkiye Ekonomisinde İkinci Dönem Liberal İktisat Politikaları," *Journal of Management Sciences,* 3(1), s. 141–148.

Sevim, M.F. (2019) "Bilgi ve İletişim Teknolojilerinin Ekonomik Kalkınma Üzerindeki Etkileri: Türkiye Örneği" Unpublished Master Thesis. Sivas Cumhuriyet University.

Soylu, A. (2017) *Endüstri 4.0 ve Girişimcilikte Yeni Yaklaşımlar.* Pamukkale University Journal of Social Sciences Institute, Denizli. Turkey. 32 s. 43–57.

State Planning Organization (2000) *Long-Term Strategy and Eighth Five-Year (2001–2005) Development Plan.* SPO Publications, Ankara.

Taymaz, E. (2018) "Dijital Türkiye ve Ekonomik Büyüme: Dijital Teknoloji Sektörlerinde Türkiye'nin Konumu Fırsatları, Seçenekleri" TUSIAD Publications. Publication Number: TÜSİAD-T/2018,10-600. İstanbul.

Tekir, S. (2021) "Erken Cumhuriyet Yıllarında Türkiye'de İletişim Araçları: Posta, Telefon, Telgraf ve Telsiz (1925–1930)" *Vanakuvis-International Journal of Historical Studies*, 6 (Prof. Dr. Süleyman Büyükkarcı Special Issue) s. 270–285.

Toffler, A. (1980) *The Third Wave*. Pan Books, Great Britain.

The Scientific and Technological Research Council of Türkiye (TÜBİTAK) (2004) *Science and Technology Policies Implementation Plan (BTP-UP).* TÜBİTAK Science and Technology High Council Report. TÜBITAK Publications, Ankara.

Turkish Informatics Association (2018) *Küresel Gelişmeler Raporu.* Turkish Informatics Association Publications, Ankara.

Turkish Informatics Industry Association (TUBISAD) (2013–2023) *Information and Communication Technologies Market Data 2012–2022 Reports.* Informatics Industry Association Publications, Istanbul.

Ulusoy, İ. (2018) "Atatürk Dönemi İktisadi Kalkınma Modeli (1923–1983)" *Journal of Akdeniz University Institute of Social Sciences*, 1(2), s. 111–124.

United Nations (UN) (2005) *Measuring ICT: The Global Status of ICT Indıcators.* United Nations Information ve Communication Technologies Task Force Publications, New York.

Wroclaw Centre of Excellence (WCOE) (2015) "Report on Major Research Areas of the Largest Growth Potential and Competition" Project Report. Wroclaw Centre of Excellence Publications, Poland.

## *Chapter 5*

# Vocational Education and Training Active Labor Market Policy in Turkey

## *A Historical Overview*

Ufuk Bingöl[1]

Unemployment is a major problem in Turkey as well as in the whole world. The causes of the unemployment problem vary from state to state. Macroeconomic infrastructure, sociocultural structure of society, and political and geopolitical factors affect countries' struggle against unemployment. Particularly with the effect of technological advancements, the quality problem required by labor markets turns unemployment into a structural problem. Providing long-term success in Active Labor Market Policies (ALMPs) to be implemented with the aim of reducing unemployment involves supplying the labor force quality that markets demand. In this sense, the capacity development and interest in vocational training, which is an important practitioner of ALMP, is increasing.

Vocational education and training (VET) is the main formula for ensuring sustainable employment of those who do or could not have a profession despite being in the labor market or cannot meet the qualification criteria created by technological developments. Thus, it will be possible to increase employment and decrease unemployment rates.

VET is being handled by governments in order to gain knowledge, skills, and behaviors to individuals related to any profession. In this sense, starting from secondary education, all training activities implemented by Turkish Employment Agency (İŞKUR) located in the concept of vocational training. Thanks to vocational training, it provides a positive contribution for those who leave the labor market for various reasons or new entrants to the labor force. On the other hand, it enables the disadvantageous groups of the society to be included in the labor market. However, vocational training is the costliest policy element of ALMP. Therefore, the key education model for sustainable success in employment will be a sustainable and cost-effective vocational training model that can meet the requirements of the labor markets. Otherwise, question marks will arise at the point of effectiveness of vocational education.

The Ministry of National Education (MoNE) has been handling and troubleshooting the whole issues till the early republic period. Turkish Employment Agency (TEA) has also been providing appropriate services and policies for nearly seventy years to improve the quality of labor and increase employment in Turkey. This study aims to scrutinize vocational training enhancements, policies, and applications, which were performed in Turkey primarily by the MoNE and TEA over the last decade toward the objective of increasing employment capacity. At the end of the introduction, the theoretical framework of the concept of vocational training will be articulated in historical perspective based on literature. The third section provides an analysis of the effectiveness of vocational trainings over the last decades in terms of legal infrastructure and types of activities, activities and responsibilities of the agencies, and perspectives in Turkey. This study will be concluded with theoretical discussions related to the assessment of the future of vocational training in Turkey.

This chapter provides an overview of the use of vocational training as an active labor market policy (ALMP) in Turkey. The chapter first reviews the current state of the labor market in Turkey, including trends in employment and unemployment rates, and the characteristics of the labor force. It then discusses the rationale for using vocational training as an ALMP tool, including its potential to enhance the skills and employability of workers and its ability to reduce the duration of unemployment spells.

The chapter then examines the different forms of vocational training programs that are currently available in Turkey, including programs offered by the public sector, private sector, and civil society organizations. The chapter analyzes the strengths and weaknesses of these programs and identifies the factors that determine their effectiveness.

The chapter also discusses the challenges that vocational training programs face in Turkey, including issues related to program design, program delivery, and the quality of training. It highlights the need for a more coordinated and comprehensive approach to vocational training policy in Turkey, one that takes into account the needs of different groups of workers and the requirements of different sectors of the economy.

Finally, the chapter concludes by outlining several policy recommendations to enhance the effectiveness of vocational training programs in Turkey. These recommendations include strengthening the institutional capacity of vocational training providers, expanding the coverage of vocational training programs, improving the quality of training, and promoting greater collaboration between vocational training providers and employers.

In summary, this chapter provides a comprehensive overview of the use of vocational training as an ALMP tool in Turkey. The chapter highlights the importance of vocational training for enhancing the skills and employability of workers and identifies the challenges that must be addressed to ensure the effectiveness of vocational training programs. The chapter concludes by outlining several policy recommendations to enhance the effectiveness of vocational training programs in Turkey and to ensure that they contribute to the broader goals of economic development and social inclusion.

## INTRODUCTION

VET is a crucial component of ALMP in many countries, including Turkey. In the early years of the Turkish Republic, vocational education was seen as an important means of transforming the country's economic structure and modernizing its society. The first vocational schools were established in the 1920s, and by the 1930s, VET had become an integral part of the country's educational system in separate branches (Çapa, 2012; Sarıkaya, 2016). However, the quality of vocational education remained low until the 1980s, when the government began to implement a series of reforms aimed at improving the system. These reforms included the establishment of vocational high schools and the introduction of vocational courses in general high schools.

In the 1990s, Turkey began to experience a shift toward a more market-oriented economy, which led to changes in the labor market. As a result, there was an increased demand for skilled workers, which highlighted the need for further improvements in vocational education. The government responded by implementing a series of policies aimed at strengthening the vocational education system and increasing the number of students enrolled in vocational schools. In recent years, Turkey has continued to invest in vocational education, with a particular focus on aligning the system with the needs of the labor market. The government has introduced new vocational programs and increased funding for vocational schools, as well as providing incentives for businesses to offer apprenticeships and on-the-job training. These efforts have led to an increase in the number of students enrolled in vocational education and have helped to improve the quality of the system.

This chapter states that while there have been improvements in the vocational education system, challenges remain. One of the main challenges is the perception of vocational education as a secondary option for students who are not able to succeed in academic education. This perception has led to a lack of interest in vocational education among students and has contributed to a shortage of skilled workers in certain sectors of the economy. In addition, there is a need for further reforms to improve the quality and relevance of vocational education and to ensure that graduates can meet the demands of the labor market.

Overall, vocational training programs aim to provide job seekers with the necessary skills and knowledge to secure employment or advance in their careers. In Turkey, the government has implemented several vocational training programs to address the high unemployment rate and the skills mismatch in the labor market. One of the primary vocational training programs in Turkey is the Vocational Qualification Institution (VQI), which provides VET to individuals in various fields, such as construction, health care, and tourism. The VQI also offers certification for individuals who have acquired the necessary skills and knowledge in their respective fields. Another program, the Vocational Training Centers (VTCs), provides vocational training to individuals who have dropped out of school or have limited education. The VTCs offer a wide range of courses, including computer skills, language courses, and technical training. Despite the efforts to improve vocational training in Turkey, challenges persist. The quality of vocational training programs is often criticized, and many employers do not perceive the training as relevant to their needs. Furthermore, the low participation rates in vocational training programs and the high dropout rates remain significant challenges for the effective implementation of these programs. To address these challenges, it is crucial to examine the effectiveness of vocational training programs in Turkey and identify the factors that affect participation and completion rates. This chapter aims to provide a comprehensive analysis of vocational training as an ALMP in Turkey, exploring the strengths and weaknesses of existing programs and the potential for future improvements. Using a literature review and empirical data, this chapter will assess the impact of vocational training on employment and career advancement, identify the key factors that affect participation and completion rates, and recommend policy implications for the effective implementation of vocational training programs in Turkey.

## LABOR MARKET TRENDS IN TURKEY

Turkey is a rapidly growing economy with a labor force of over 30 million people (TURKSTAT). The country has undergone significant changes in its labor market in recent years, including shifts in employment patterns, education and training, and government policies. This section will examine some of the key labor market trends in Turkey.

One major trend in Turkey's labor market is the shift from traditional industries to service-based sectors. This shift has been fueled by the growth of the country's urban centers and a rise in consumer demand for services such as banking, health care, and tourism. As a result, employment in service-based sectors has grown significantly, while the manufacturing sector has experienced a decline in employment. Another trend in Turkey's labor market is the increasing importance of education and training. The government has implemented several policies to improve education and increase access to training programs to meet the demands of a more modern, service-based economy. This has resulted in a higher percentage of workers with tertiary education degrees and an increased emphasis on vocational training programs. However, despite the government's efforts to improve education and training, Turkey still faces significant challenges in its labor market. One of these challenges is the high rate of informality in the workforce, with a large percentage of workers employed in informal jobs without social security or labor protections. This has a negative impact on workers' wages, job security, and access to benefits such as health care and pensions. In addition to informality, Turkey's labor market is also characterized by a high rate of youth unemployment, particularly among those with lower levels of education. This highlights the need for continued investment in education and training programs, as well as policies aimed at reducing the barriers to entry for young people in the labor market. Overall, Turkey's labor market is undergoing significant changes as the country continues to develop and modernize. While the shift to service-based sectors and the emphasis on education and training are positive developments, there remain significant challenges, such as informality and youth unemployment, that must be addressed to ensure a more inclusive and equitable labor market for all workers.

The Turkish labor market has undergone significant changes in recent years, with shifts in employment trends, unemployment rates, and skill mismatches. In this section, we will explore each of these topics in more detail. In recent years, Turkey has experienced a rise in employment rates. According to data from the Turkish Statistical Institute (TUIK), the country's employment rate stood at 46.4 percent in 2020, up from 44.5 percent in 2019. This increase in employment is driven in part by the growth of the service sector, which has become a major employer in Turkey. The service sector accounted for 62.5 percent of total employment in 2020, up from 61.8 percent in 2019. Additionally, the government has launched various initiatives to promote entrepreneurship and create new jobs, such as the Youth Employment Support Program and the Industrial Zones Development Program. Despite the rise in employment rates, Turkey still faces challenges in reducing unemployment. In 2020, the country's unemployment rate was 12.7 percent, down from 13.7 percent in 2019. This is partly due to the COVID-19 pandemic, which has had a significant impact on the Turkish economy. The pandemic has led to job losses in industries such as tourism and hospitality, which are important sources of employment in Turkey. Furthermore, the country has a relatively young population, which means that more people are entering the labor market than leaving it. This puts pressure on the government to create more jobs to meet the demands of the growing labor force. Another challenge facing the Turkish labor market is skill mismatches. This refers to a situation where the skills possessed by workers do not match the requirements of the jobs available. In Turkey, there is a shortage of workers with high-level skills, particularly in the fields of science, technology, engineering, and mathematics (STEM). This has led to a situation where many companies struggle to find workers with the skills they need. On the other hand, there is also a surplus of workers with low-level skills, particularly in the service sector. This mismatch between skills and jobs is a significant barrier to economic growth and development in Turkey. In conclusion, the Turkish labor market has seen significant changes in recent years, with shifts in employment trends, unemployment rates, and skill mismatches. While there has been a rise in employment rates, the country still faces challenges in reducing unemployment and addressing skill mismatches. These challenges will require sustained efforts from the government and other stakeholders to create more jobs, develop the skills of the workforce, and promote economic growth and development.

## VOCATIONAL EDUCATION AND TRAINING IN TURKEY

### Chronological Review of Vocational Education and Training in Turkey

The responsibility for vocational tasks and education was under the jurisdiction of Provincial and Municipal Administrations until the start of the 1930s. However, in 1927, the task of providing funds for these kinds of education and schools' programs, equipment, teacher training, and employment was assigned to the MoNE (2023). During the early republican period, as the institutional framework for vocational education was being established under the MoNE, Male and Female Art Schools, as well as Trade Schools, began to receive academic and technical support. The foundation of vocational education in the early years of the Turkish Republic was established through the contributions of foreign experts like John Dewey, Alfred Kühne, and Ömer Buysse, alongside the research conducted by Turkish educators such as İsmail Hakkı Tonguç and Mehmet Rüştü Uzel. This effort aimed to cultivate a skilled workforce in alignment with the state-led industrialization initiatives (Gemici, 1993; Yildirim & Şahin, 2015). The foundation of this infrastructure lies in the *Vocational Education Development Plan*, which envisions the establishment of Apprentice Schools, Art and Middle Art Schools, Evening Art Schools, Technician Schools, Engineer Schools, and Mobile Village Courses. These institutions will form the cornerstone of the Industry-Production-Education triangle, with the collaboration of various ministries. In addition to Trade Schools and Evening Art Schools operating in numerous cities across Turkey, there were also Village and City Yacht Schools in various provinces. Industrial Schools were established in Aydın and Diyarbakır, a Hat and Clothing School in Istanbul, and the Courthouse Vocational School in Ankara. Additionally, there were Land Registry Cadastre Schools, Girls' Institutes, and Art Schools founded in Istanbul and Kastamonu. Furthermore, a Fishing School was established in Balıkesir's Marmara Island, while Construction Master Schools were located in Ankara, Istanbul, and Erzurum. Lastly, Nursing and Village Midwife Schools can be found in Istanbul, Ankara, Balıkesir, and Konya (MoNE, 2019).

After the management and planning responsibilities of vocational education were transferred to the MoNE, the reports of relevant domestic and foreign field experts, as mentioned earlier, were implemented in the planning and programs of both existing and newly established vocational schools. Within this context, considerations were made to account for socioeconomic and geographical regional differences in school types and curricula. The objectives also included aligning the durations of education and integrating practical training with the industry. To achieve these goals, the training of educators in relevant fields was prioritized. To ensure the preparation of teachers in the field of technical and vocational education, approximately 250 or more prospective teachers were sent abroad for education, primarily to European countries and the United States, covering a wide range of areas from textiles to heavy industry. This practice continued until the Second World War (Gemici, 1993). In subsequent years, the demand for technical educators was fulfilled through the training of these teachers, alongside the establishment of teacher schools in various cities across the country. By the culmination of the period leading up to the outbreak of the Second World War, there was a concerted effort to formulate a vocational education policy aimed at regional competency in line with socioeconomic capabilities. As a tangible manifestation of the collaboration between education and industry, apprentice schools were established as a notable example. These apprentice schools represented the formal alignment of educational institutions and sectoral cooperation in the training of the workforce, as Turkey was taking its initial steps toward industrialization. Furthermore, alongside the apprentice schools, the inception of Public Education Centers in 1953 marked an initiative aimed at aiding and guiding all segments of society toward social, cultural, and economic development through education, particularly within the scope of lifelong learning.

From the inception of the Republic until the conclusion of the Second World War, the primary objective was the institutionalization of vocational education. This endeavor began with a comprehensive analysis of the existing landscape of technical and vocational education infrastructure in Turkey. Subsequently, vocational schools were established at various levels, spanning nearly all cities in the country. Following this phase, a clear demarcation was made between formal educational institutions and nonformal educational opportunities, as part of a strategic plan to expand the reach of vocational education across society. However, in alignment with the planned developmental trajectory of the nation, vocational education became an integral component of the secondary education system. The initial recognition of the country's sustained demand for a skilled workforce came to the forefront of the First Development Plan. It sought to channel a substantial portion of the youth within the secondary education age group into vocational education programs. Consequently, throughout subsequent development plans, there was a gradual escalation in the allocation of investments directed toward vocational education (Aslan & Yilmaz, 2021). Furthermore, since the inception of the First Development Plan, there has been a concerted effort to shift away from the educational model of women's technical education, which primarily aimed to prepare women for domestic roles as housewives. Instead, the focus has shifted toward technical education that emphasizes sectoral equality and inclusivity (Argün, 2003). In this context, various types of vocational high schools were established, but the demand for vocational and technical high schools remained somewhat constrained. Consequently, the advancement of vocational education within secondary education was hindered by the inclination of high school students toward general education. Although there was an upswing in demand for vocational education, particularly through the redesign of Technical High Schools into a two-tier system during the fourth five-year development program, progress was constrained due to limitations in capacity and teacher resources. It was only with the initiation of the fifth five-year development plan that private schools were actively encouraged. Thus, during the period leading up to the 1990s, there was a targeted goal to achieve an enrollment rate of approximately 20 percent in vocational education.

Alongside the resource allocation and program objectives outlined in the development plans, institutions were established to facilitate on-the-job training within various industries. In addition to these on-the-job training centers, there was a strategic initiative to incorporate the military into the vocational training system to enhance the vocational and qualification training of conscripted soldiers during their mandatory military service. The vocational training model driven by education-industry collaboration, which was a focal point in the initial three five-year development plans, materialized with the enactment of the 1977 Apprenticeship Law. Subsequently, the objective became the preparation of a workforce aligned with market demands, achieved through a robust partnership between the industry and Apprenticeship Training Centers. In preparation for the 1990s, various regulations were introduced concerning the mandatory provision of practical and skills training by enterprises to vocational high school students, as well as outlining wage structures, social security benefits, and leave entitlements for these students and prospective apprentices. In this context, the objective of cultivating a skilled workforce in alignment with the industry's demands, which had been advocated by various stakeholders during the Republican era and further integrated during the planned development period, was systematically restructured and consolidated with the enactment of the Vocational Education Law in 1986 (Özsoy, 2007). Under this law, a systematic framework for vocational education was established, encompassing formal, apprenticeship, and nonformal education categories. Table 1 presents data on student and teacher figures within the domains of General Education and Vocational Education in ten-year intervals up to the present day.

As illustrated in table 5.1, a notable quantitative expansion in the student and teacher population within formal vocational education, particularly during the 2000s, is evident. However, during the 2010s, while the number of students in vocational education continued to rise, there was a substantial increase in the student-to-teacher ratio. Nevertheless, in recent years, there appears to be a shift back toward a greater emphasis on general education. The demand for vocational education has predominantly been met at the higher education level, while there has been a consistent decline in the academic performance of vocational education at the secondary level in recent years. Consequently, the vocational education landscape exhibits significant challenges both in terms of accessibility and quality (MoNE, 2021). However, it is noteworthy that labor force participation and employment rates

**Table 5.1 General Education and Vocational Education Student and Teacher Information**

| | *General Secondary Education* | | | *Vocational and Technical Secondary Education* | | |
|---|---|---|---|---|---|---|
| *Year* | *Students (000)* | *Teacher* | *Students per Teacher* | *Students (000)* | *Teacher* | *Students per Teacher* |
| 1950–1951 | 22 | 1954 | 11 | 53 | 4488 | 12 |
| 1960–1961 | 76 | 4219 | 18 | 108 | 8333 | 13 |
| 1970–1971 | 245 | 11219 | 22 | 235 | 15021 | 16 |
| 1980–1981 | 535 | 41334 | 13 | 355 | 33690 | 11 |
| 1990–1991 | 799 | 63858 | 13 | 627 | 48917 | 13 |
| 2000–2001 | 1.704 | 71.594 | 24 | 903 | 69847 | 13 |
| 2010–2011 | 2.676 | 118.378 | 23 | 2.072 | 104327 | 20 |
| 2021–2022 | 4.092 | 193.589 | 21 | 1.833 | 143953 | 13 |

*Source*: MoNE (2011, 2021); Özsoy (2007).

among graduates of vocational secondary education programs are relatively higher compared to those from general high schools, and they stand on par with graduates from higher education programs, as indicated by TURKSTAT statistics (Özer, 2020). Contrary to prevailing perceptions, graduates of vocational education programs may possess a distinct advantage in labor markets. However, factors such as the initial salary levels and instances of employment outside their field of study have sustained the demand for higher education among vocational education students. This phenomenon has also fueled a growing interest in pursuing advanced technical education for enhanced qualifications (Ozer, 2019). As part of the Education 2023 vision, released by the MoNE, project-based vocational high schools have been established in collaboration with the nation's leading technology firms, and technical research universities, to bolster interest in secondary vocational education and deliver high-quality vocational training in cutting-edge technologies (Eren SUNA & Özer, 2019). The integration of vocational secondary education with the industry also signifies a commitment to eroding long-term employment policy continuity.

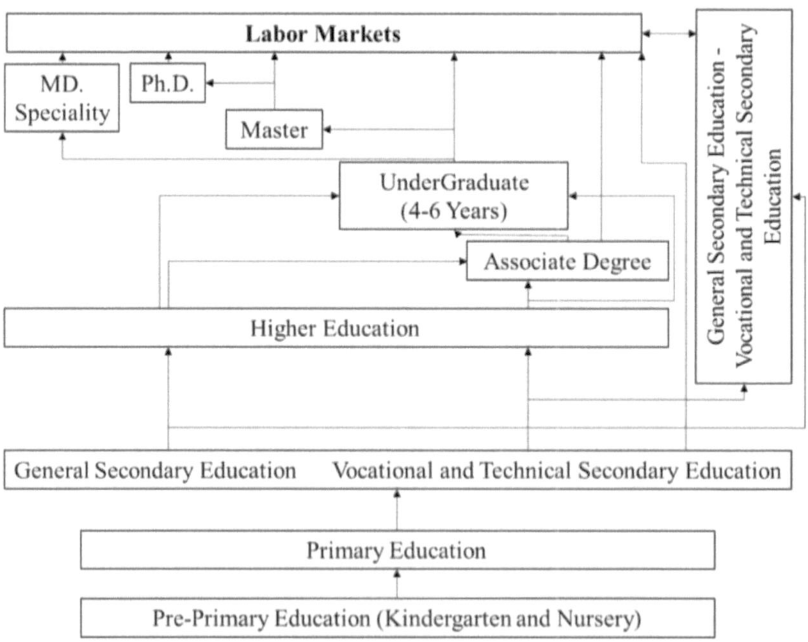


**Figure 5.1 Turkish Educational System and Transition Diagram to Labor Markets.** *Source*: Summarized from MoNE (2021).

## Vocational Education and Training as Active Labor Market Policy in Turkey

Vocational training holds a prominent position as a vital component of active employment policies in Turkey, akin to practices worldwide. In alignment with the objectives of nurturing a skilled workforce to fuel economic growth and diminishing unemployment rates, vocational education institutions and programs endeavor to prepare individuals who are job ready and qualified for the labor market. Particularly noteworthy is Turkey's distinction as the European country with the youngest population, which underscores the imperative of enhancing the vocational skill development of its youth for effective integration into the workforce. While vocational education might not exhibit a substantial impact on employment rates in Turkey, those who undergo vocational training tend to experience reduced career uncertainty, owing to their acquired qualifications (Hirshleifer et al., 2016; Torun & Tumen, 2017). Hence, vocational training plays a pivotal role in easing entry into labor markets. To illustrate this point, according to TEA's research as of 2023, conducted within the framework of the Turkish labor market outlook, it is evident that there are presently 387,490 vacant positions across over one and a half million enterprises. Furthermore, in more than 130,000 enterprises, there exists a shortage of nearly 380,000 employees across various sectors, highlighting significant challenges in labor supply (TEA, 2023b). As indicated in the same report, the most substantial deficit in employee skills pertains to the insufficiency of vocational and technical knowledge and experience. Consequently, enhancing the vocational and technical competencies of the workforce required by enterprises should serve as the cornerstone of active employment policies to be enacted. It is only through a comprehensive education policy focused on quality that the workforce can acquire the skills necessary to facilitate their employability.

To utilize vocational training as a policy instrument within Active Employment Policies, the establishment of standards is a crucial initial step. These standards are formally established by the Vocational Qualifications Authority, which was founded in 2006 with the primary objective of defining the essential norms and competencies requisite for the practice of any profession. Presently, Turkey has 901 occupational standards that have been published in the Official Gazette and are in effect. In parallel with the evolution of professions, relevant boards continuously develop new standards while also revising existing professional and vocational standards to accommodate changes. In addition to standardization, vocational accreditation stands as a significant component of vocational education policies. The Vocational Qualifications Authority has granted authorization to 315 certification bodies responsible for assessing and certifying vocational qualifications. These organizations carry out the requisite examinations and certification procedures by the established occupational standards.

The harmonization of vocational education with vocational qualifications should represent the second phase of active employment policies. Nevertheless, students enrolled in vocational education high schools often face challenges in gaining practical experience related to their curriculum and establishing effective industry-school collaborations, thereby limiting their exposure to real-world applications of their education up to the twelfth grade (MoDev, 2019). Due to students' hesitancy in opting for vocational high schools, which continue to be a fundamental component of vocational education, academic performance among students attending these institutions tends to be subpar. This trend is further substantiated by the outcomes of PISA studies. Notably, in the PISA assessments encompassing reading comprehension, science, and mathematics, scores attained by vocational high school students consistently fall below those achieved by their counterparts in general high schools (OECD, 2019). PISA tests, which assess the ability of students receiving vocational education to apply development and skills they acquire in school to real-life situations, also indicate that vocational education is inadequate in meeting the demands of the current labor market. The follow-up to PISA, the Survey of Adult Skills (PIAAC), exhibits a similar trend. Consequently, the results indicate that the outcomes of higher education do not significantly differ from those of individuals with a high school education. Furthermore, the survey highlights that individuals are often reluctant to invest in their skill development, largely due to inadequate rewards in the labor market (Kavuncu & Polat, 2020). Hence, to incorporate vocational education into active policies aimed at boosting employment, several developments have unfolded in recent years, aligning with evolving development objectives and the national education vision.

In 2016, apprenticeship training, categorized as nonformal education, was incorporated into the framework of the twelve-year compulsory education system. As a result, Vocational Training Centers affiliated with the National Education system started issuing certificates of mastery and diplomas from Vocational and Technical Anatolian High Schools. During the apprenticeship training period, students receive a salary, equivalent to 30 percent of the minimum wage during the first three years and at least 50 percent of the minimum wage in the final year. They also benefit from occupational insurance coverage, which begins in the ninth grade. Furthermore, the government provides period and incentive advantages for entrepreneurial projects. This policy reform, as reported by the MoNE, has led to an employment rate reaching as high as 88 percent within the respective field of study (MoNE, 2023). To align vocational education with sectoral expectations and facilitate collaboration on matters such as modernizing vocational fields, enhancing school infrastructure and capabilities, tailoring programs to regional demands, and promoting on-the-job training, Vocational and Technical Education School Management Boards have been established in all municipalities. Furthermore, the implementation of School Report Cards in recent years has provided valuable data for mapping Vocational and Technical Education and for monitoring school performance and annual progress, as well as for assessing the success levels and sectoral engagement of educational institutions, thus facilitating the transition from education to employment. On the nonformal education front, programs guaranteeing employment outcomes through İŞKUR (Turkish Employment Agency) aim to integrate disadvantageous demographic segments into the labor market. Over the years, these training programs have witnessed increased participation rates, and nonformal education has been instrumental in developing vocational qualifications tailored to industry needs (TEA, 2023a).

## CONCLUSION

Vocational education has emerged as a significant contributor to labor transition challenges in Turkey. The literature highlights several key factors contributing to this phenomenon. Firstly, vocational education programs have often lagged in adapting and updating to meet the evolving demands of the labor market. Secondly, Vocational Education Institutions have faced inadequacies in terms of equipment, teacher qualifications, and curriculum development. Additionally, historical practices such as the unfair coefficient application, which was once imposed on vocational high school students, have substantially limited their opportunities for higher education, leading to a decline in the prestige associated with vocational high schools. As a result, there exists a prevailing perception among vocational education students that they face disadvantages in the job market. Furthermore, students who have transitioned to secondary education have frequently been guided toward general education programs instead of vocational ones.

Inheriting a legacy from the Ottoman Empire, the early years of the Turkish Republic witnessed significant institutionalization efforts aimed at establishing vocational education, thereby addressing the demand for a skilled workforce in the nascent nation. Leading up to the Second World War, substantial strides were taken in institutionalization, along with the training of vocational education teachers. During this period, numerous vocational schools were founded, fostering the development of a qualified labor force. Following this phase, particularly during the Planned Development era, the relationship between vocational education and industry was forged. The infrastructure for nonformal vocational education was established through entities such as Public Education Centers, TEA, NGOs, and Local Governments. Moreover, high schools offering vocational education, particularly those under the MoNE, have attracted high-achieving students through collaborations with leading companies in Turkey. Additionally, involving industrial organizations at the regional level in the governance and management processes of vocational education can further facilitate the transition from education to employment.

In the forthcoming period, achieving the objectives outlined in the existing literature on vocational education is undeniably crucial. These objectives include enhancing the physical infrastructure, augmenting the quantity and quality of teachers, and allocating greater budgetary resources to vocational education. Beyond these recommendations, proactive initiatives are equally imperative. These encompass the establishment of policymaking processes rooted in the Vocational Education data system, fostering effective governance of vocational education, perpetually evolving the curriculum, formulating incentive policies to counter the prevailing negative perception of vocational education within society, and implementing early talent screening to identify individuals' compatibility with specific occupations. These multifaceted actions collectively develop position vocational education as a potent instrument for active employment policy.

## NOTE

1. Assoc. Prof., Bandırma Onyedi Eylül University, Manyas Vocational School, Balıkesir-Türkiye, ubingol@gmail.com.

## REFERENCES

Argün, H. (2003). *Vocational and Technical Education in the Planned Development Eriod (1963–2002) (Developments, Applications and Problems)* [Master]. Gazi University.

Aslan, O., & Yilmaz, M. (2021). Turkey Cumhuriyeti Kalkınma Planları Kapsamında Eğitim Yapılarının Analizi. *Turkish Scientific Researches Journal*, 6(1), 114–132.

Çapa, M. (2012). Trabzon Ticaret Mektebi. *Karadeniz İncelemeleri Dergisi*, 12(12), 133–142.

Eren SUNA, H., & Özer, M. (2019). Future of Vocational and Technical Education in Turkey: Solid Steps Taken After Education Vision 2023. *Journal of Education and Humanities*, 10(20), 166–192. www.dergipark.gov.tr/eibd

Gemici, N. (1993). *Turkey'de Mesleki Eğitimin Gelişimi ve Endüstri Meslek Liselerinin Durumu*. İstanbul University.

Hirshleifer, S., McKenzie, D., Almeida, R., & Ridao-Cano, C. (2016). The Impact of Vocational Training for the Unemployed: Experimental Evidence from Turkey. *The Economic Journal*, 126(597), 2115–2146. https://doi.org/10.1111/ecoj.12211

Kavuncu, F., & Polat, S. (2020). *A Brief Assessment of Adults' Skills in Turkey: Results from Survey of Adult Skills (PIAAC)* Ekonomi-tek, 9(1): 25–57.

MoDev. (2019). *Onbirinci Kalkınma Planı (2019–2023) Mesleki Eğitimde Niteliğin Artırılması Çalışma Grubu Raporu*. MoDev.

MoNE. (2011). *National Education Statistics 2011*. MoNE.

MoNE. (2019). *Vocational and Technical Education with Photos: From Past to Present*. MoNE.

MONE (2021). Ministry of National Education Regulation on Pre-school Education and Primary Education Institutions https://www.mevzuat.gov.tr/File/GeneratePdf?mevzuatNo=19942&mevzuatTur=KurumVeKu rulusYonetmeligi&mevzuatTertip=5 MoNE. (2023). Vocational Training Centers. https://meslegimhayatim.meb.gov.tr/egitim/mesleki-egitim

OECD. (2019). *Programme for International Student Assessment (PISA)—2018*. OECD.

Ozer, M. (2019). Reconsidering the Fundamental Problems of Vocational Education and Training in Turkey and Proposed Solutions for Restructuring. *İstanbul Üniversitesi Sosyoloji Dergisi*, 39(2). https://doi.org/10.26650/sj.2019.39.2.0098

Özer, M. (2020). *Mesleki eğitimde paradigma değişimi : Türkiye'nin mesleki eğitim ile imtihanı*. Maltepe University Press.

Özsoy, C. (2007). *The Role and the Importance of Vocational and Technical Education in the Economic Development of Turkey* [Ph.D.]. Anadolu University.

Sarıkaya, M. (2016). Ziraat Mektepleri. *Kafdağı*, 1(1), 24–37.

TEA. (2023a). *Report for Provincial Boards of Employment and Vocational Training 2022*. TEA.

TEA. (2023b). *Turkish Labor Market Research Results-2022*. TEA.

Torun, H., & Tumen, S. (2017). Do Vocational High School Graduates Have Better Employment Outcomes than General High School Graduates? www.iza.org

Yildirim, K., & Şahin, L. (2015). Osmanlı'dan Günümüze Mesleki Eğitimin Gelişimi. Çalışma ve Toplum, 2015(1), 77–112.

Çapa, M. (2012). Trabzon Ticaret Mektebi (1924–1927). Karadeniz İncelemeleri Dergisi, 12(12), 133–142.

Ministry of National Education. (2022). Vocational Qualification Institution (VQI). Retrieved from https://www.meb.gov.tr/meb_iys_dosyalar/2016_01/15153403_vqi_eng.pdf

OECD. (2021). Getting skills right in Turkey: Skills for jobs indicators. Retrieved from https://www.oecd.org/skills/piaac/Country%20note%20-%20Turkey.pdf

MoNE (2018). Outlook of vocational and technical education in Turkey. Education, Analysis and Evaluation Report Series No:1. Ankara: MoNE Publications. http://mtegm.meb.gov.tr/meb_iys_dosyalar/2018_11/12134429_No1_Turkiyede_Mesleki_ve_Teknik_Egitimin_Gorunumu.pdf

Tansel, A., & Gungor, N. D. (2017). Vocational education and training in Turkey: A labor market perspective on supply and demand. In R. Maclean, D. Wilson, & L. E. Price (Eds.), Post-Globalization of Higher Education (pp. 299–318). Springer.

*Chapter 6*

# Employment and Unemployment in Turkey

M. Çağlar Özdemir[1]

Employment and price stability are among the most important economic problems in the world. Price stability is of great importance for the cyclical sustainability of the economy, as employment shows the production potential. The situation of the Turkish labor market provides important clues in terms of showing its economic structure. This section provides information about Turkey's employment and unemployment adventure. A general evaluation was made from the period when the Republic was declared to 2010, and the labor market situation was revealed with detailed analyses between 2011 and 2020. The data used in the study were obtained from the Turkish Statistical Institute. It is understood that the Turkish labor market is in a worse situation than it was at the beginning of the 100th year of the Republic. Employment and labor force participation rates decreased compared to the Republic's first years, and unemployment rates increased. For a healthy economic restructuring, there is a need for qualified policies in the labor market as soon as possible.

## INTRODUCTION

A country's labor market analysis provides essential information about the structure and state of its economy. A healthy labor market constitutes the central dynamic of production and growth potential (Roa, Saura and Vázquez, 2011). The labor market has a multi-component, intricate structure that, on the one hand, wants to move freely with a liberal approach and, on the other hand, strives for intervention with an institutional approach(Duval and Loungani, 2019). In any case, a well-functioning labor market means a well-functioning economy (Haddad, 2002).

Two critical concepts integrated into the labor market are employment and unemployment. Although they are often perceived as opposite concepts, employment and unemployment are not opposites. Employment generally means the effective use of the factors of production (Brennerand Brenner-Golomb, 2000). In this context, natural resources, capital, entrepreneurs, and labour are employed when they are used economically and effectively (Falkinger, and Grossman, 2005). Unemployment is only the result of the ineffective use of labor, which is a factor of production (Tsaliki, 2009). In addition, it is only sometimes possible to claim that the unemployed, the subject of official statistics, are economically inactive(Yfanti, Michalopoulou and Zachariou, 2019). However, since the purpose of this section is not to discuss the concepts of employment or unemployment at the theoretical level, it is helpful to focus on the subject.

This study aims to reveal the situation of employment and unemployment in the Turkish labor market in the 100th year of the Republic. Due diligence assessments are usually carried out at external and internal levels. The scope of this study is not intended to show Turkey's position relative to international or nearby countries. The scope is limited to evaluating the developments in Turkey itself. In the study, the employment and unemployment process since the proclamation of the Republic in 1923 has been examined at a level where statistics can be found. The period 2011–2020, covering ten years, was examined in detail, and more up-to-date information about the current situation was presented to the reader.

## A BRIEF HISTORY OF EMPLOYMENT AND UNEMPLOYMENT IN TURKEY

The Republic was proclaimed in 1923(Alpkaya, 1998). The State Institute of Statistics (now the Turkish Statistical Institute—TUIK) was established on February 26, 1926(TUIK, Officialwebsite). Since labor market statistics are sometimes recorded at different levels due to current conditions and the effects of the Second World War, achieving precise stability seems complicated (Ergene, 1986). Despite this, we have information on employment and unemployment. The 1925 census shows that Turkey had a population of approximately 13 million. In the same year, it is understood that there was approximately a 6 million labor force, 5.6 million employed and 3.1 million unemployed. Unemployment continued to decline in 1935 and 1945. In 1950, with the transition to the multiparty system, the economy was expanded. It is observed that the number of unemployed has increased since this period.

It is understood that the labor market situation was relatively stable in the first thirty years after the Proclamation of the Republic. However, it is understood

**Table 6.1 Labor Market Indicators by Year: 1927–2010 (Thousand)**

| *Year* | *Total Population* | *15+ Population* | *Labor Force* | *Labor Force Participation Rate (%)* | *Employment* | *Unemployment* | *Unemployment Rate (%)* |
|---|---|---|---|---|---|---|---|
| **1927** | 13.103 | 8.020 | 5.922 | 73.8 | 5.606 | 316 | 5.3 |
| **1935** | 16.158 | 9.495 | 7.284 | 76.7 | 7.045 | 239 | 3.3 |
| | | 11.369 | | | | | |
| **1945** | 18.790 | 11.369 | 8.420 | 74.1 | 8.159 | 261 | 3.1 |
| **1955** | 24.064 | 14.589 | 11.427 | 78.3 | 11.077 | 350 | 3.1 |
| | | 18.242 | | | | | |
| **1965** | 31.391 | 18.242 | 13.175 | 72.2 | 12.694 | 481 | 3.7 |
| **1975** | 40.347 | 24.017 | 16.330 | 68.0 | 15.089 | 1.241 | 7.6 |
| **1985** | 50.664 | 31.654 | 18.382 | 58.1 | 17.445 | 937 | 5.1 |
| **1995** | 60.380 | 36.728 | 22.446 | 61.1 | 20.833 | 1.613 | 7.2 |
| **2005** | 70.586 | 51.944 | 22.454 | 43.2 | 20.066 | 2.388 | 10.6 |
| **2010** | 73.722 | 54.843 | 25.641 | 46.8 | 22.594 | 3.047 | 11.8 |
| **2015** | 78.741 | 59.855 | 29.741 | 49.7 | 26.610 | 3.130 | 10.5 |
| **2020** | 83.614 | 64.546 | 30.873 | 47.8 | 26.812 | 4.061 | 13.2 |

*Source*: TURKSTAT (Turkish Statistical Institution). * approximate estimated calculation

that there has been a significant deterioration in the labor market, especially after the period following 1970 (Bulutay, 1996; Mütevellioğlu and Isık,2009). In Turkey, which met in 2010 with an unemployment rate of approximately 12 percent, fluctuating unemployment rates were seen again in the following years (Zaim, 1992).

Changes in statistical calculations do not allow a very healthy interpretation of the relevant data. TURKSTAT revised its calculation methods with the changes it made in 1988 (Zaim, 1992). The second significant change dates back to 2000 and beyond. Over the years, revisions have been made at different levels within the framework of EU harmonization laws.

A high positive correlation exists between population growth and labor force and employment growth ($r = 0.9$). However, a moderate negative correlation exists between population and labor force increase and unemployment increase ($r = -0.3$)(Calculations from years' statistics).

## OUTLOOK AND FEATURES OF EMPLOYMENT

In 2020, 69 percent of the employment of 26,812,000 people in Turkey is men (18,506,000), and 31 percent is women (8,306,000). The highest employment is in the services sector with 15,060,000 people (56.2 percent). A total of 5,497,000 people are employed in the industry sector (20.5 percent). A total of 4,716,000 people are employed (17.6 percent) in the agricultural sector, which ranks third in employment density. The construction sector is in the last place (5.7 percent) with 1,538,000 jobs (TUIK, years statistics).

The most employed group in 2020 is salaried or casual workers (18,719,000, 69.8 percent). Self-employed people totaling 4,421,000 are second (16.5 percent). Unpaid family workers take the third place with 9.2 percent (2,473,000). Employers, defined as those who employ at least one person, constitute the least employed group with 1,199,000 people (4.5 percent).

Total employment in Turkey has been increasing over the years. However, it started to decrease from 2018 to 2020. It is observed that total employment contracted by approximately 6.7 percent from 2018 to 2020.

In 2020, Turkey's average working time was 43 hours per week. Those with a single job work 42.7 hours, while those with additional job work 51.9 hours. Men work more than women (39.2 hours), with an average of 45.7 hours of work per week. While men with additional job work 53.9 hours a week, women work 46.2 hours.

Women's employment in Turkey is low compared to men. In the ten years, the analysis covers, this rate has changed in favor of women. As of 2020, it is understood that the most intense employment of both men and women is in the 35–39 age group (in 2011, the highest employment was in the 30–34 age group. Employees are also getting older). However, there are similar movements between the employment of men and women by age groups; a low negative relationship is found if a simple correlation is made regarding employment intensities. The 35–39 age group rate in male employment (14.7 percent) is lower than the rate of women employed in the same age group (15.2 percent). This shows that women are employed more than men in the 35–39 age group. At 65 and above, 3 percent of men continue to work, while 2.4 percent of women continue to work.

## Employment by Sectors (2011–2020)

Sectoral distribution of employment in Turkey is listed as Services (56.2 percent), Industry (20.5 percent), Agriculture (17.6 percent), and Construction (5.7 percent). It is seen that the highest employment loss from 2018 to 2020 is in the construction sector (approximately 23 percent). However, employment in the construction sector increased rapidly from 2011 to 2017 (approximately 25 percent). However, it has lost this pace since 2018. In 2018–2020, employment in the agricultural sector decreased by approximately 11 percent, employment in the industrial sector by approximately 3 percent, and employment in the services sector by approximately 4.5 percent.

A total of 4,792,000 of the employment in Turkey is in the public sector, of which 2,970,000 are permanent civil servants and 1,162,000 workers work in the public sector. Contracted personnel are around 503,000; temporary workers are around 50,000 (temporary workers should be distinct from subcontracted workers defined as temporary personnel. Since the second quarter of 2018, temporary personnel have not been employed in the public sector). The remaining nearly 107,000 people are employed in other jobs in the public sector.

When evaluated in terms of occupations, it is seen that the most intense employment is composed of service and sales personnel (5,190,000—19.4 percent). In the second place are those who work in jobs that do not require qualifications (3,858,000—14.4 percent). Those working in qualified agriculture, forestry, and aquaculture take third place, and their number is 3,647,000 (13.6 percent). Artisans and those working in related jobs are fourth (3,378,000—12.6 percent). A total of 3,297,000 people are employed in professional occupational groups (12.3 percent). Plant and machine operators and assemblers have a size of 9 percent with 2,424,000 people. The office and customer services staff are 1,642,000 people and have a 7th employment weight. The last employment was created in the manager's profession with 1,502,000 people (5.6 percent).

## Employment by Status at Work

Of those employed in Turkey in 2020, 69.8 percent are paid, salaried, or casual wage earners, 16.5 percent are self-employed, 9.2 percent are unpaid family workers, and 4.5 percent are employers. In the analysis period, it is understood that the ratio of the wage, the salaried, or casual group increased, while those of employers decreased. In addition, 70 percent of approximately 18.5 million total male employment (12,991,000) and approximately 8.3 million female employment (5,728,000) are wage or salaried workers.

In Turkey, there is an intense labor migration to specific regions, especially during the summer seasons. Significant numbers of employment are created in the form of casual or seasonal work. Seasonal employees, who are not looking for a job and are not ready to start work due to their seasonal work, generally work with a daily wage. In the questionnaire that has been used in statistics for the workforce since 2009, wage earners and casual wage earners have been combined, and after this date, casual workers are also evaluated in the "paid or salaried" category.

## Agricultural/Nonagricultural and Regional Employment (2011–2020)

Employment in Turkey mainly occurs in nonagricultural fields. From 2011 to 2020, nonfarm employment increased by 70 percent. It is observed that agricultural employment contracted by 55 percent in the same period. When the 2020 distribution is examined, it is seen that 82.5 percent of employment in Turkey is outside of agriculture, and 17.5 percent is in agriculture.

In Turkey, regional employment analyses are carried out at two levels within the scope of statistical region classification. These regions are divided into Level 1 and Level 2. In comparison, there are twelve regions in the first-level classification and twenty-six regions in the second-level classification. All provinces in Turkey are distributed within the level region classification. For example, although Istanbul is geographically located in the Marmara region, it is considered a stand-alone region in TUIK statistical classification at Level 1. At Level 1, the Marmara region is divided into West and East, excluding Istanbul. For example, eight provinces in the Eastern Marmara (TR4) region (Bursa, Eskişehir, Bilecik, Kocaeli, Sakarya, Düzce, Bolu, and Yalova).

The most intense employment in Turkey is in the Istanbul region (TR1), together with the West and East Marmara. Bursa, Kocaeli, and Sakarya provinces in the Eastern Marmara region stand out as critical industrial regions. A significant part of the automotive production in Turkey is carried out in these three provinces.

Capital Ankara constitutes an integral part of the employment. In addition, Eskişehir is one of the centers where employment is concentrated. The provinces with the highest employment rate in 2020 are in the TR21 region west of the country (Tekirdağ, Edirne, and Kırklareli) (50.9 percent). The provinces with the lowest employment rate are in the TRC3 region in the country's Southeast (Mardin, Batman, Şırnak, Siirt) (26 percent).

## Underemployment

*Underemployment* is when the employed workforce in an economy cannot reach the job required by their education, skills, and experience, despite their desire (Feldman, 1996). The underemployed person is not unemployed and has a job. However, he states that he wants to change his current job or is looking for a second one, alleging that he needs more income from his current job or is not employed in a field suitable for his qualifications. Those who are forced to work part-time because they cannot find a full-time job but who are looking to work for more hours are also underemployed (ILO and TUIK Definations).

While the number of underemployed was approximately 617,000 in 2011, it doubled to 1,251,000 in 2020. While the underemployment rate was 2.6 percent in 2011, when employment was 24,110,000 people, the underemployment rate increased to 4.7 percent in 2020, when the employment was 26,812,000 people.

## Education–Employment Relationship (2011–2020)

The education group that receives the highest share of employment in Turkey is primary school graduates. To put it more clearly, the highest employment is among primary school graduates. When we add primary education (eight-year education) and secondary school or equivalent vocational schools to this, it is seen that more than half (65 percent) of employment is created by those in the low education group. Moreover, this situation has continued similarly for years. Low-educated employment is due to the intensity of agriculture and jobs that do not require qualifications.

The second group that weighs employment is college or faculty graduates (27.6 percent). The employability of the education level in between is lower than the others. The need for intermediate staff, which is often mentioned in Turkey, is expected to be met by high school and/or vocational high school graduates. However, the total employment of these two groups cannot reach the employment of either primary or college graduates. The increase in employment among university graduates reveals an economic structure that needs qualified personnel, and the increase in employment among high school graduates reveals an economic structure that needs intermediate personnel. In labor markets with structural problems, it is sometimes seen that unqualified (or qualified) university graduates start to work as intermediate staff. This situation, common in Turkey, can be considered an extension of a well-regulated labor market or an immature economic structure.

According to the calculations, in 2020, 2.6 percent of total employment are illiterate, 2.8 percent are literate but have not completed a school, 27.1 percent are only primary school graduates (five-year primary school), 11.2 percent of them are secondary school or equivalent vocational school graduates (three-year secondary school graduates), 10.4 percent are generally high school graduates, 11.2 percent are high school equivalent vocational school graduates (vocational high school), and 27 percent of them are college or faculty graduates. The weight of primary education graduates, which is structured with the four plus four systems and includes secondary school, in total employment is 7.1 percent.

### Child Employment

In 2020, there were 3,682,420 children in the age group of 15–17 who are of working age in Turkey. The working-age child population is 16.2 percent of the total child population. Our noninstitutional child population is 3,660,000. There is a 593,000 child labor force in Turkey. Of this, 501,000 are employed, and 92,000 are unemployed (TÜİK, 2020). While 19.5 percent of boys are employed, 7.5 percent of girls are employed. A total of 3,067,000 children are not included in the labor force. When evaluated in terms of the total number of children, the child labor force participation rate is 16.2 percent. The employment rate is 13.7 percent; the unemployment rate is 15.6 percent. Moreover, only 17.2 percent of working children between the ages of 15 and 17 are in decent work, defined as stable, inclusive, and productive work. The rest are employed in jobs unworthy of human dignity.

The proportion of children aged 15–17 who are neither in education nor employment (NEET) is 11 percent. In 2020 Turkey, approximately 1,850,000 children's fathers, mothers, or household heads are unemployed (TUIK Child Statistics, 2020 and Statistics on Child in Türkiye 2020).

## OUTLOOK AND FEATURES OF UNEMPLOYMENT

Unemployment rates fluctuated between 9 percent and 13.7 percent in the ten years from 2011–2020 in Turkey. During this period, the highest unemployment was in 2019, with 13.7 percent. Unemployment was at its highest level since the post-2008 economic crisis period (the unemployment rate climbed to 16 percent in February 2009 and averaged 14 percent in 2009).

In 2020, there were 4,061,000 registered unemployed in Turkey. The annual average unemployment rate was 13.2 percent. The nonagricultural unemployment rate was 15.3 percent; the youth unemployment rate in the 15–24 age range was 25.3 percent. Including seasonal effects, the combined rate of unemployed and potential workforce in Turkey was 24.6 percent. In 2020, the unemployment rate among the male workforce was 12.3 percent, while the unemployment rate among the female workforce was 15 percent. The integrated ratio is calculated by dividing the total of the unemployed and potential labor force by the sum of the labor force and potential labor force. In Turkey, the rate of the idle labor force at the end of 2020 was 29 percent. As will be remembered from the previous section, the idle labor force ratio is the ratio of the time-related underemployment, unemployed and potential labor force to the total labor force and potential labor force.

Long-term unemployment (Mueller and Spinnewjin, 2023), which generally grew numerically between 2011 and 2020, appears to decrease in 2020 for job seekers between one and three years. However, it can be said that more people have been looking for a job for more than three years, and they are probably losing their hopes (in 2020, approximately 1,369,000 people reported that they were not looking for a job because they were hopeless but ready to work).

It is understood that approximately 1,300,000 people had been looking for a job for one to two months in 2020. This number, lower than the previous year, may have decreased due to job seekers transferring to the following year. In general, most of the 4,061,000 unemployed people formed in 2020 had been looking for a job for one to two months.

In Turkey, they primarily seek a job through their peers (88.9 percent). It is followed by a direct application to the employer (60 percent). Approximately 48 percent of job seekers said they applied for a job and were waiting for news. While those waiting for an answer to İŞKUR's application constitute 26 percent of the unemployed, those who take the exam opened by state institutions and wait for the result are around 5 percent. Loans, licenses, etc., with those who are looking for a place or equipment to start their own business is around 7.8 percent.

As of 2020, the unemployment rate is high among young people in Turkey. When the young population is examined in subgroups, it is seen that unemployment between the ages of twenty and twenty-four is more intense. There is also a particular group among the young population. The number of this group conceptualized as NEET (Neither in Education, Employment or Training) and its proportion in the workforce is significant (Holte, 2018). The NEET rate between the ages of fifteen and twenty-four in Turkey in 2020 is 28.3 percent. (This rate was 26 percent in 2019.) Over the years, unemployment has always been intense among this group. As age increases, the unemployment rate decreases.

## Unemployment by Sectors and Growth (2011–2020)

A total of 54.5 percent of the unemployed who had worked in a job before worked in "services," 22 percent in "industry," 12.1 percent in "construction," 5.2 percent in "agriculture," and 3.5 percent of them left their jobs before eight years (TUIK, Household Labor Force Statistics).). About 8.1 percent of the unemployed are looking for a job for the first time (91.9 percent of the job seekers have had a job before).

A fluctuating decline is observed in growth rates in the 2011–2020 period in Turkey. The growth rate of 11.1 percent in 2011 declined to 0.5 percent in 2019. Although 2020 is the year of the pandemic, the country grew by 1.8 percent, according to TUIK statistics. When unemployment rates in the same period are analyzed, a fluctuating increase is observed. By the theory, unemployment increases as the growth rate decreases. When evaluated within the framework of years (or lagged years), it is seen that there are no equal negative changes between growth rates and unemployment rates. Of course, it is impossible to attribute unemployment only to growth rates. As mentioned earlier, unemployment has many structural causes. Productivity gains can also lead to growth that does not create jobs (Hull, 2009). In addition, many other factors, such as the high growth rate of the working-age population, technology, regional imbalances, and informal employment, are related to growth, employment, and unemployment (Ok, 2008).

When we make a simple correlation calculation between Turkey's growth and unemployment rates over the years, the high negative relationship can be easily seen ($r = -0.7479$). As it is known, when the correlation ($r$) coefficient is $-1$, it indicates a perfect negative relationship; when it is $+1$, it indicates a perfect positive relationship. In Turkey, as predicted by the neoclassical theory, there is a high negative relationship between growth and unemployment rates.

## Agricultural/Nonagricultural and Regional Unemployment (2011–2020)

Unemployment in Turkey can be seen to decrease to the lowest level of 8.4 percent during the analysis period. The nonagricultural unemployment rate is 2–3 percent higher than the general unemployment rate. The nonagricultural unemployment rate was the lowest at 10.3 percent. While the average unemployment rate in Turkey was around 9.67 percent in 2011–2020, the nonagricultural unemployment average was 11.55 percent.

In Turkey, employment density is increasing in cities. Employment in urban areas (nonagricultural employment) in 2020 was approximately 3.7 times that in rural areas (agricultural employment). According to the intensity of employment, it can be seen that unemployment is naturally lower in rural areas. In 2020, nonagricultural unemployment was approximately 14.9 percent, and agricultural unemployment was 4.4 percent.

As of the end of 2020, the region with the highest unemployment was Southeastern Anatolia (TRC3) (20.7 percent). This is followed by Middle East Anatolia (TRB) (17.4 percent) and Istanbul (TR1) (14.7 percent). The Southeast Anatolian Region has always been the region with the highest unemployment rate over the years. The lowest unemployment in 2020 was in the West Black Sea (TR8) region (8.2 percent). By 2018, the Eastern Black Sea (TR9) would generally have the lowest unemployment rate. However, unemployment rates in the Western Black Sea Region were lower in 2019–2020. West Marmara (TR2) is one region with low unemployment rates.

The Western Black Sea (TR8) Region, where unemployment was low in the 2020 average, consists of ten provinces, TR81-82 and 83. TR81: Zonguldak, Karabuk, Bartin; TR82: Kastamonu, Çankırı, Sinop; TR83: it consists of Amasya, Çorum, Samsun, and Tokat provinces. TR82 region covers the provinces with the lowest unemployment in Turkey (6.6 percent). The highest unemployment is in the region of TR81 (9.3 percent), with the effect of population density. The provinces with the highest unemployment rate are Mardin, Batman, Şırnak, and Siirt, which are in the TRC3 regional classification, and the lowest are Kastamonu, Çankırı, and Sinop, which are in the TR82 regional classification.

## Education–Unemployment Relationship (2011–2020)

It is seen that the lowest unemployment rate in Turkey is among the illiterate. It is known that this segment is employed in secondary labor markets and mainly in jobs without job security or social security. In addition, they can find a job quickly because they work in jobs that do not require qualifications. Most of them work in agriculture and partly in the construction sector.

When the educational levels come into play, it is seen that the highest unemployment is among the primary school graduates who are "combined" (employment was also highest in this group). General high school graduates have the second highest unemployment rate. However, it was also measured that those who did not finish school despite being literate in 2020 were unemployed at the level of general high school graduates. The unemployment rate of college or faculty graduates is low compared to other education levels, except for the unemployment rate of illiterate students.

The rapid increase in university graduates has replaced high school (or vocational high school) graduates, who are expressed as intermediate staff, with university graduates. This situation has narrowed the employment opportunities for those with lower education, and the need for intermediate staff has now begun to be met among university graduates with low wages. Unemployment is now an essential risk for every education level in Turkey.

### Those Who Are Not in the Labor Force

The population that is not usually included in the labor force is seasonal workers, those who are busy with housework, students in education, retirees, and those who cannot work (ILOSTAT, 2019).When we add to these the "disappointed" who are not looking for a job but are ready to work, and the other group who is not looking for a job for different reasons and is ready to work, a significant mass remains out of the workforce.

Those who lost hope of finding a job doubled in 2020 compared to the average of previous years. There is also a general increase in the group ready to work without looking for a job. Not being included in the labor force in Turkey is being busy with housework. The majority (or almost all) of them are women. Retirees, those unable to work, and those in education are also among the population not included in the labor force.

## CONCLUSION

Turkey has not achieved a remarkable success story in the labor market in the last hundred years, which it has spent integrating with the international market. Unemployment rates are gradually increasing, and the expected increase in labor force participation rates cannot be achieved. Female labor force participation rates are still meager (around 30 percent). Most women do not participate in the workforce because they are busy with housework.

Although agriculture and service sector employment has been replaced by industry and service sector, sufficient employment level has not been reached yet. The most intense employment is in the Marmara (including Istanbul) region. About 70 percent of the employed people throughout the country work for wages and daily wages. The ratio of employers in total employment does not reach 5 percent (4.47 percent).

There is an increase in the risk of underemployment in Turkey. This situation, which is supported by the education–employment conflict, causes an increase in unemployment, especially among higher education graduates. This also feeds NEET.

Child employment accounts for approximately 16.2 percent of total employment. Boys (19.5 percent) are employed more than girls (7.5 percent).

The unemployment rate in Turkey is more than twice the world average (13.2 percent). Agricultural unemployment rates can reach 15 percent. The highest unemployment rates are among primary school graduates or illiterates (18 percent). This is followed by public high school and higher education graduates (approximately 14.5 percent).

It is understood that there is a need for urgent and radical revisions in Turkey's labor market institutional structuring. In particular, it is crucial to produce stable solutions to meet the rapidly changing and developing labor market needs. Although Turkey has a robust institutional infrastructure, the system's working dynamics need to be updated and fast, and current problem-solving priorities, instead of holistic solution proposals, lock the system. Considering Turkey's unique labor market dynamics, taking advantage of international experiences and embarking on a new institutional setup is necessary.

## NOTE

1. Prof. Dr., Sakarya University, Faculty of Economics and Administrative Sciences, Department of Labour Economics and Industrial Relations, Sakarya, Turkey, cozdemir@sakarya.edu.tr

## REFERENCES

Alpkaya, F. (1998). *Türkiye Cumhuriyetinin Kuruluşu*, 3th edition, İletişim Yay. İstanbul.

Brenner, Y.S. and Brenner-Golomb, N. (2000). *A Theory of Full Employment*, Second Edition, Taylor&Francis.

Bulutay, T. (1996). *Employment, Unemployment and Wages in Turkey*, Ankara: ILO/ State Institute of Statistics. ISBN: 9221091937.

Duval, R.A. and Loungani, P. (2019). Designing Labor Market Institutions in Emerging and Developing Economies: Evidence and Policy Options, SDN/19/4, International Monetary Fund.

ERGENE, C. (1986). Devlet İstatistik Enstitüsü'nde Demografik İstatistiklerin Tarihçesi. *İstanbul Üniversitesi İktisat Fakültesi Mecmuası*, *42*(1–4). Erişim: https://dergipark.org.tr/tr/pub/iuifm/issue/833

Falkinger, J. and Grossmann, V. (2005). "Distribution of Natural Resources, Entrepreneurship, and Economic Development: Growth Dynamics with Two Elites," IZA Discussion Paper No. 1756, CESifo Working Paper Series No. 1562, Available at SSRN: https://ssrn.com/abstract=822766 or http://dx.doi.org/10.2139/ssrn.822766

Feldman, D.C. (1996). "The nature, antecedents and consequences of underemployment".

Haddad, L. (2002). *Towards a Well-functioning Economy: The Evolution of Economic Systems and Decision-making*, Edward Elgar, Cheltenham, UK.

Holte, B. H. (2018). "Counting and Meeting NEET Young People: Methodology, Perspective and Meaning in Research on Marginalized Youth," *YOUNG*, 26(1), 1-16.

Hull, K. (2009). "Understanding the Relationship between Economic Growth, Employment and Poverty Reduction," Promoting Pro-Poor Growth: Employment – OECD, 69-94.

ILOSTAT (2019). "Persons outside the labour force: How inavdive are they really?," https://ilostat.ilo.org/persons-outside-the-labour-force-how-inactive-are-they-really/Journal of Management, 22/3, (385-407).

Mueller, A. I. and Spinnewijn, J. (2023), "The Nature of Long-Term Unemployment: Predictability, Heterogeneity and Selection," NBER, Working Paper: 30979.

Mütevellioğlu, N., and Işık, S. (2009). "Türkiye emek piyasasında neoliberal dönüşüm," Küreselleşme, kriz ve Türkiye'de neoliberal dönüşüm, 159-204. Editors Nergis Mütevellioğlu-Sinan Sönmez, İstanbul Bilgi Universitesi Yay.

Roa, M.J., Saura, D. and Vázquez, F.J. (2011). "Economic growth, labor market and demographic patterns," Structural Change and Economic Dynamics, 22/1, 81-91. Statastics on Child 2020, TÜİK, https://www.tuik.gov.tr/media/announcements/istatistiklerle_cocuk_2020.pdf

Taş, B. (2006), "AB Uyum Sürecinde Türkiye İçin Yeni Bir Bölge Kavramı: İstatistiki Bölge Birimleri Sınıflandırması(İBBS)," Sosyal Bilimler Der., 8/2, (85-197)

Tsaliki, P.V. (2009). "Economic development and unemployment: do they connect?," *International Journal of Social Economics*, 36/7, 773-781.

Yfanti, A., Michalopoulou, C. and Zachariou, S. (2019). "The impact of definitions in classifying the employed, unemployed and inactive when comparing measurements from different sources," Communications in Statistics: Case Studies, Data Analysis and Applications, 5/1, 46-58.

Yiğit, Ö. (2023), "Türkiye'de Sektörler Arası Yayılma Etkileri: Global VAR Yaklaşımı," Business and Economics Research Journal, 14/2, 173-189.

Zaim, S. (1992). *Çalışma Ekonomisi, 5.Bası*, Filiz Kitabevi, İstanbul.

## *Chapter 7*

# Informal Employment in Turkey

Hülya Yilmaz[1]

Informal employment is the failure to reflect the employment activities in official documents or the underreporting to the official authorities the duration of employment and the amount of wages received. Informal employment is an important problem that arises with the reflection of the informal economy on working life. The problem of informal employment began to spread rapidly throughout the world in the 1950s and in Turkey in the 1980s. The phenomenon of informal employment in Turkey has become a structural problem, especially after 1980. It has reached 50 percent since the 1990s, and this level lasted until the early 2000s. With the measures taken, the informal employment rate, which was as high as 50 percent, decreased to 43 percent in 2008 and 33 percent in 2015. However, the aforementioned problem is still at a high level and continues to exist as a structural employment problem. The size of informal employment differs depending on the social and economic development levels of the countries. In general, however, the underlying causes of the informal employment problem are generally sociocultural and economic, such as population growth, unemployment, inflation, migration from rural to urban areas, and lack of education. Informal employment has many positive and negative effects. In terms of its results, it also affects workers, employers, and the state in the formal economy. Therefore, it is important to reduce the size of the informal economy and informal employment.

This study discusses the problem of informal employment in the 100th anniversary of the Republic of Turkey. The general status of informal employment in the last ten years (in terms of gender, sector, age, education, etc.) has been revealed through the statistical data of the Turkish Statistical Institute (TurkStat). In addition, the programs, projects, and prevention strategies implemented to reduce the problem were also analyzed. It can be said that the implemented policies are insufficient to solve the problem of informal employment but have effects on its reduction.

## INTRODUCTION

Informal employment is the reflection of the informal economy to the labor market. The concepts of informal employment and the informal sector are often confused with each other. While the informal sector and the formal sector indicate the characteristics of the sector, informal employment activity refers to being registered with a social security institution or not. While the concept of informal economy includes all unregistered activities in a country's economy, informal employment is only used to express informality in labor force employment.

The concept of informal employment is frequently used in the Kenya Report prepared within the scope of the World Employment Program organized by the International Labour Organization (ILO) in 1970. The informal sector has been defined by the ILO as "small-scale units which produce goods and services with an undeveloped organizational identity, that are formed by one person or several persons without the element of continuity, and whose primary purpose is to provide employment and income to individuals" (ILO, 1972; TOBB, 1994). The European Commission defines informal employment as "taking into account the differences in the regulatory systems of the Member States, any paid activity that is legal in nature but is not reported to public authorities" (EC, 1998). OECD made the definition in 1987 as "activities that are legal in nature but not reported to one or more institutions" (Mateman and Renooy, 2001).

Within the framework of ILO's report in 1972, it is possible to list the main features of informal employment as follows: unregistered work, easy access to the system, irregular and flexible work, difficulty in measurement, labor-intensive work usually with unskilled workers, and generally being common in small-scale enterprises (ILO, 1972).

Although the first thing that comes to mind about informal employment is the forms of employment that are not covered or documented within the social security framework, informal employment emerges in many different ways. Informal employment is classified as those whose work is not reported in any way, those whose work is underreported in terms of days or wages, and works that are excluded from the registry by the legislation (SGK, 2021). The problem of informal employment may originate from employees or from employers.

Although the causes of informal employment differ from country to country, the factors that have a greater effect on the emergence of informal employment in Turkey may be listed as: poverty, income inequality, high unemployment and inflation, high labor costs (social security deductions and tax burden), the majority of the enterprises in the country being small- and medium-sized enterprises, rapid population growth, migration from rural to urban areas, new forms of work, low level of education of the workforce and low awareness of social security, bureaucratic procedures related to establishing a business and employing workers being excessive and complicated, lack of coordination between public institutions and organizations, and insufficient supervision.

Although it has some positive effects, informal employment has many negative consequences for employees, employers, and the state. Some of those consequences are employees who are not registered with any public institution and therefore also their families not having any social security rights, deterioration in income distribution, increase in unfair competition, decrease in public trust, and loss of taxes and premiums. Considering all these negative effects, it is of great importance to reduce the size of the informal economy and informal employment.

Informal employment is higher in underdeveloped and developing countries than in developed countries, but it continues to be an important problem for developed countries as well. The problem of informal employment began to spread throughout the world in the 1950s and in Turkey in the 1980s. The phenomenon of informal employment in Turkey has become a structural problem, increasing especially after 1980. It has reached 50 percent since the 1990s, and this level lasted until the early 2000s. With the measures taken, the informal employment rate, which was as high as 50 percent, decreased to 43 percent in 2008 and to 33 percent in 2015. However, the aforementioned problem is still at a high level and continues to exist as a structural employment problem. The fact that the informal employment rate in Turkey is between 30 and 40 percent in the last ten years, which constitutes almost half of the employment rate, indicates that it is one of the priority problems that needs to be resolved.

In this study, Turkey's informal employment is discussed. The general view (in terms of gender, sector, age, education, etc.) of informal employment in the last ten years (2011–2020) has been examined in detail. The data were obtained from the Turkish Statistical Institute (TurkStat). Since it was reported by TurkStat that a comprehensive revision study was carried out on the 2021 data on informal employment, the 2021 statistics could not be included in this study. In addition, the programs, projects, and prevention strategies implemented to reduce the problem were also analyzed. It is understood that the implemented policies are insufficient to solve the informal employment problem completely, but they have a decreasing effect on the informal employment rate.

## UNREGISTERED PROCESS IN TURKEY

The concept of informal employment, especially after the high inflation that emerged with the 1973 Oil Crisis, and the economic recession that became evident with unemployment, has been among the problems of the working life of developed and developing countries. In addition to high inflation and unemployment factors, factors such as increasing international competition caused by globalization after 1980, the decrease in the employer role of the state with the adoption of neoliberal policies, and illegal labor due to external migration have also been effective in the increase in the importance of the informal employment problem. As in many developing countries of the world, informality is not a new phenomenon in Turkey. It has become a structural problem by increasing especially after 1980; since the early 1990s, when statistics on informal employment began to be kept, it became more evident and attracted attention.

While informal employment was one of the most important problems during the Republican period in Turkey, it is seen that the legal regulations regarding informal employment gained momentum with the establishment of the Social Insurance Institution. The development process of the Republican period in the field of social security is closely related to the development of the political regime and slow progress has been made. Although the first Labor Law of the Republic of Turkey, dated 1936, foresees the establishment of a social insurance institution for workers within one year from the effective date, the social security institution for dependent workers in the private sector was established only in 1946 under the name of "Workers Insurance Institution." In 1965, the Workers Insurance Institution was transformed into the "Social Insurance Institution" (SII). With the Retirement Fund Law No. 5434, which entered into force in 1950, the private pension funds previously established for public sector employees were abolished and social protection was provided to civil servants under a single roof. The legal regulation on the social security of independent workers was completed with the 1971 Social Security Organization for Artisans and Self-Employed. This differentiation based on employment status came to an end with the Social Security Institution Law No. 5502 dated 2006, and the

"Social Security Reform" brought the Social Insurance Institution, Social Security Organization for Artisans and Self-Employed, and Retirement Fund under one roof. Comprehensive arrangements have been made in the fight against informal employment with the social security reform. In the fight against informal employment, it is not possible to be successful only with the efforts of the Social Security Institution; it has been adopted that this problem can be eliminated by cooperating with public institutions and organizations, nongovernmental organizations, banks, and other relevant segments of the society.

Informal employment, which is the reflection of the informal economy on working life, has tended to increase due to reasons such as the increase in taxes and social security premiums after 1980, excessive regulations in the labor market, early retirement, and unemployment. The unequal distribution of income and poverty, the low level of education of the workforce, and the reasons stemming from the public and social security system have been influential in people's unregistered work. The prevalence of small businesses makes monitoring and auditing difficult, and these businesses are excluded from many legal regulations—tax, employment, social security, and so on. Laws on these matters generally do not cover such small businesses. With the effect of the economic crisis in Turkey, informal employment has reached significant dimensions. Turkey experienced the biggest crisis in the history of the Republic in 2001. The labor-intensive sector was more affected by the crisis environment and turned to an informal economy. The decrease in national income and real wages, the decrease in the bargaining power of workers and unions, the change in the production structure of the real sector, and the hardships in the labor market (severance pay, high minimum wages, high social security premium payments) have affected the labor markets and led to informality. Unemployment figures rising in the crisis environment forced them to agree to work without social security. After the 2001 crisis, informal employment increased, especially in the nonagricultural field. It has reached 50 percent since the 1990s; this level lasted until the early 2000s. Within the framework of the measures taken, the informal employment rate as high as 50 percent decreased to 43 percent in 2008; It decreased to 33 percent in 2015. However, the aforementioned problem is still at a high level and continues to exist as a structural employment problem. The fact that the informal employment rate in Turkey has been between 30 and 40 percent in the last ten years, and almost half of the employment rate, indicates that it is one of the priority problems to be solved.

**Table 7.1. Labor Market Indicators by Year: 1927–2010 (Thousand)**

| *Year* | *Total Population* | *15+ Population* | *Labor Force* | *Labor Force Participation Rate (%)* | *Employment* | *Unemployment* | *Unemployment Rate (%)* |
|---|---|---|---|---|---|---|---|
| **1927** | 13.103 | 8.020 | 5.922 | 73.8 | 5.606 | 316 | 5.3 |
| **1935** | 16.158 | 9.495 | 7.284 | 76.7 | 7.045 | 239 | 3.3 |
| **1945** | 18.790 | 11.369 | 8.420 | 74.1 | 8.159 | 261 | 3.1 |
| **1955** | 24.064 | 14.589 | 11.427 | 78.3 | 11.077 | 350 | 3.1 |
| **1965** | 31.391 | 18.242 | 13.175 | 72.2 | 12.694 | 481 | 3.7 |
| **1975** | 40.347 | 24.017 | 16.330 | 68.0 | 15.089 | 1.241 | 7.6 |
| **1985** | 50.664 | 31.654 | 18.382 | 58.1 | 17.445 | 937 | 5.1 |
| **1995** | 60.380 | 36.728 | 22.446 | 61.1 | 20.833 | 1.613 | 7.2 |
| **2005** | 70.586 | 51.944 | 22.454 | 43.2 | 20.066 | 2.388 | 10.6 |
| **2010** | 73.722 | 54.843 | 25.641 | 46.8 | 22.594 | 3.047 | 11.8 |
| **2015** | 78.741 | 59.855 | 29.741 | 49.7 | 26.610 | 3.130 | 10.5 |
| **2020** | 83.614 | 64.546 | 30.873 | 47.8 | 26.812 | 4.061 | 13.2 |

*Source*: TURKSTAT (Turkish Statistical Institution)

## STATUS OF INFORMAL EMPLOYMENT IN TURKEY

The problem of the informal economy, which has been experienced for many years in Turkey, naturally increases informal employment. As seen in the results of the informal economy, informal employment deprives the state of an important income, and those who are employed in this way have to work in precarious and unhealthy conditions. Employees who are deprived of social security are also deprived of many benefits such as health, work injury compensations, or other compensations within the scope of social security. The fact that individuals in the labor market continue their lives without social security does not only have negative consequences for individuals but also family members are affected by the situation. In particular, children cannot benefit from other services and assistance provided by the social security system, especially access to health services, due to the informal work of their dependent parents.

Labor demand and labor supply are effective together in informal employment. To compete with prices in global markets, employers try to reduce product costs by employing informal workers. Employers who want to avoid social security premium payments and tax liabilities have turned to informal employment.

According to the Tax Burden on Wages Report published by the Organization for Economic Cooperation and Development (OECD) in 2020, the tax burden on the wages of a married man with two children and an unemployed wife is (38.2 percent) well above the OECD average (13.8 percent) (OECD, 2021). The high financial burden of tax and insurance obligations on the employer has a great impact on the emergence of informal employment. Due to the rigidity of the labor market in Turkey, employers tend to employ informal workers to reduce the cost of dismissal and other costs arising from the legislation. According to TurkStat data, in the fourth quarter of 2020, the hourly labor cost increased by 3.7 percent compared to the previous quarter. Considering this indicator, which is very important in terms of informal employment, from a sectoral point of view, it is seen that there was an increase of 4.5 percent in the industry sector, 1.8 percent in the construction sector, and 3.6 percent in the trade services sector. From the perspective of the employee, informality occurs mostly as members of the unqualified labor force, who have a low level of education and migrate from the rural areas to the cities and settle for the low level of wages offered to them in order not to be unemployed.

In this part of the study, the evolution of informal employment in Turkey is discussed in terms of sectors, status of the workforce, gender, education, age, work types, workplace size, occupational groups, and regions under this heading. The review period was discontinued in 2020, as a comprehensive revision study was made in the informal employment 2021 data.

## Informal Employment by Years

Due to the structural characteristics of the economy, the size of informal employment in Turkey cannot be calculated distinctly, and this ratio is tried to be calculated approximately with the studies carried out by TurkStat and OECD.

Informal employment, which has become a structural problem of working life in Turkey, is at a high level. When the results of December 2020 are examined, 30.6 percent (8,202,000) of the total employment 26,812,000 are employed without being registered with the social security institution as seen in figure 7.1. With this ratio, it is understood that three out of every ten employed people in Turkey work informally. Considering the course of the informal employment rate in the last ten years, a decrease of around 12 percent is observed. The informal employment rate, which was approximately 42 percent in 2011, decreased to approximately 30 percent in 2020. The decrease in the informal employment rate can be attributed to the economic policies followed, the projects and measures implemented, the development of the awareness of the employees to be insured, and the effective use of information technologies in the audit process. Although important steps have been taken to reduce informal employment, the informal employment rate in Turkey is far above both the EU and OECD countries. The size of the informal economy, which has been decreasing, albeit slowly, since 2009 in European and OECD countries was estimated at an average of 16.7 percent of GDP in 2015 (ILO & SGK, 2020).

| | 2011 | 2012 | 2013 | 2014 | 2015 | 2016 | 2017 | 2018 | 2019 | 2020 |
|---|---|---|---|---|---|---|---|---|---|---|
| Total employment (Thousand people) | 24.110 | 24.820 | 25.524 | 25.933 | 26.621 | 27.205 | 28.189 | 28.738 | 28.080 | 26.812 |
| Registered (Thousand people) | 13.971 | 15.134 | 16.145 | 16.864 | 17.684 | 18.094 | 18.614 | 19.134 | 18.388 | 18.610 |
| Informal (Thousand people) | 10.139 | 9.686 | 9.379 | 9.069 | 8.937 | 9.111 | 9.575 | 9.604 | 9.692 | 8.202 |
| Rate of Informal Employment (%) | 42,1 | 39,0 | 36,7 | 35,0 | 33,6 | 33,5 | 34,0 | 33,4 | 34,5 | 30,6 |

**Figure 7.1 Registered and Informal Employment in Total Employment (Thousand People).** *Source*: TurkStat Labour Force Statistics.

## Informal Employment by Sector

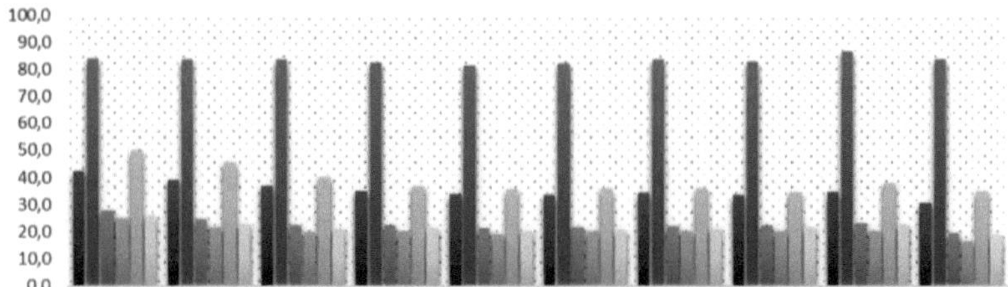


| | 2011 | 2012 | 2013 | 2014 | 2015 | 2016 | 2017 | 2018 | 2019 | 2020 |
|---|---|---|---|---|---|---|---|---|---|---|
| Total | 42,1 | 39,0 | 36,7 | 35,0 | 33,6 | 33,5 | 34,0 | 33,4 | 34,5 | 30,6 |
| Agriculture | 83,8 | 83,6 | 83,3 | 82,3 | 81,2 | 82,1 | 83,3 | 82,7 | 86,6 | 83,5 |
| Outside Agriculture | 27,8 | 24,5 | 22,4 | 22,3 | 21,2 | 21,7 | 22,1 | 22,3 | 23,0 | 19,3 |
| Industry | 25,0 | 21,6 | 19,9 | 20,3 | 19,1 | 20,2 | 20,0 | 20,3 | 20,0 | 16,5 |
| Construction | 49,9 | 45,4 | 40,1 | 36,6 | 35,6 | 35,8 | 35,8 | 34,4 | 37,7 | 34,7 |
| Service | 25,7 | 22,7 | 20,9 | 21,1 | 20,1 | 20,4 | 20,9 | 21,5 | 22,5 | 18,8 |

**Figure 7.2 Informal Employment Rates by Sectors (%).** *Source*: TurkStat Labour Force Statistics.

The sectoral distribution of the informal employment rate shows that informal employment in Turkey is mostly seen in the agricultural sector, which provides job opportunities to a significant part of the country's population. Reasons such as unskilled labour, the employment of people with low education levels, and seasonal jobs that do not provide continuity cause an increase in informal employment in the agricultural sector. Most of the workers in the agricultural sector are unpaid family workers working informally. In terms of the size of informal employment, the industry and service sector comes after the agriculture sector. When we look at the development of the size of informal employment in figure 7.2, it is seen that informal employment tends to decrease in all sectors between 2011 and 2020. It is possible to say that the employment mobilization initiated and continued between February and March 2017, the incentives brought for women, youth, and the disabled, and the coverage of the SSI and income tax burden by the state within the scope of this mobilization are very effective in reducing informal employment.

## Informal Employment by Labor Force Status

Informal employment mostly affects the poor segments of society with low incomes or living below the subsistence level. When we look at the distribution of those who are employed informally in terms of their status at work, at the beginning of these are unpaid family workers, self-employed, and wage earners.

According to TÜİK data, in 2020, 34 percent of those employed informally in Turkey were paid or casual workers, 34.6 percent were self-employed, 27.4 percent were unpaid family workers, and 4 percent were employers. (In 2011, these rates were 36.9 percent, 30.3 percent, 30 percent, and 2.7 percent, respectively.) As it can be understood from these data, while employers rarely work informally, all other employee groups other than the employers are employed informally. Considering the agricultural and nonagricultural distinction, informality rates are quite high among unpaid family workers and the self-employed. One factor that proportionally increases the total informality in Turkey is largely the informal work of unpaid family workers and self-employed workers. When the data for the period of 2011–2020 are examined, it is seen that the informality rate of these two groups, especially the nonagricultural informality, has decreased significantly (figure 7.2) ; the rate of informality of the self-employed in total informal employment is 64.2 percent by the end of 2020, and it is seen that unpaid family workers still have a high rate of 91 percent (TurkStat).

## Informal Employment by Sector and Gender

Considering the distribution of informal employment rates by gender in Turkey, it is seen that there are significant differences between women and men. The tendency of informal employment is higher for women than for men.

As can be seen from figure 7.3, according to TurkStat 2020 end-of-the-year data, 37.1 percent of women were unregistered, while 27.7 percent of men were unregistered. (In 2011, these rates were 57.8 percent and 35.6 percent, respectively.) It can be attributed to reasons such as the high rate of informality in women's employment, the inconsistency of women's qualifications with the requirements of the labor market, low labor force participation rate and low level of education, gender perception, and women working as unpaid family workers, especially in the agricultural sector. The perception of women's income as "additional income," the idea that the family's livelihood is primarily under the responsibility of the man, and the fact that the insured spouse, mother, father, and child can have social security rights, especially in terms of health, pave the way for women to work in the labor market for low wages informally. In addition to unpaid family labor in the agricultural sector, women work informally by becoming a part of contract manufacturing in small workshops or homes in cities. Women working/employed informally do not have the guarantees provided by the social security system, and they do not have protection against occupational accidents. Working hours are long and wages are low. Working for their "own account" and as "unpaid family worker" are the forms of work among women in which informality is highest.

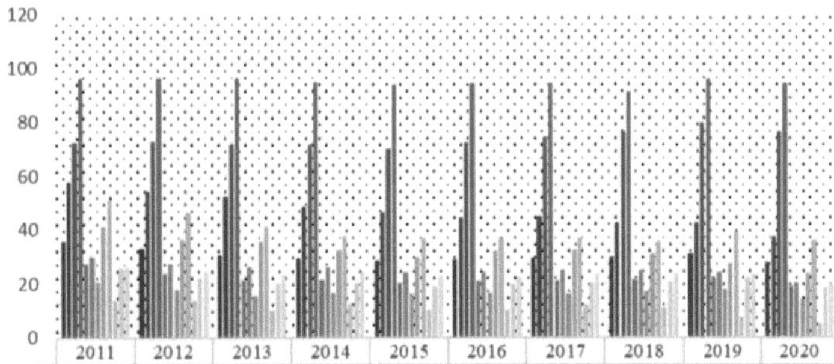


| | 2011 | 2012 | 2013 | 2014 | 2015 | 2016 | 2017 | 2018 | 2019 | 2020 |
|---|---|---|---|---|---|---|---|---|---|---|
| Total Male | 35.6 | 32.7 | 30.2 | 29.3 | 28.2 | 28.8 | 29.2 | 29.4 | 30.9 | 27.7 |
| Total Female | 57.8 | 54.2 | 52 | 48.4 | 46.1 | 44.3 | 44.6 | 42.1 | 42.2 | 37.1 |
| Agriculture Male | 72.5 | 72.6 | 71.8 | 71.8 | 70.2 | 72.2 | 74.4 | 76.2 | 79.5 | 76.2 |
| Agriculture Female | 96.2 | 96 | 96.3 | 94.4 | 94 | 94.2 | 94.2 | 90.9 | 95.7 | 94.3 |
| Outside Agriculture Male | 27.2 | 23.7 | 21.2 | 21.1 | 20.2 | 20.8 | 21 | 21.2 | 22.4 | 18.9 |
| Outside Agriculture Female | 29.7 | 27.1 | 26 | 25.9 | 24.1 | 24.2 | 25 | 24.9 | 24.2 | 20.2 |
| Industry Male | 20.6 | 17.6 | 15.4 | 16.6 | 16 | 16.6 | 16.2 | 16.9 | 17.8 | 14.2 |
| Industry Female | 41.1 | 36.2 | 35.6 | 32.3 | 29.7 | 32 | 32.3 | 30.9 | 27.1 | 23.5 |
| Construction Male | 51.1 | 46.4 | 41.2 | 37.6 | 36.6 | 36.9 | 36.8 | 35.4 | 39.1 | 36.1 |
| Construction Female | 13.6 | 13.9 | 10.2 | 12.7 | 10 | 10.3 | 12.2 | 11.1 | 7.5 | 5.2 |
| Service Male | 25.5 | 22.1 | 19.9 | 19.9 | 18.9 | 19.5 | 19.9 | 20.4 | 22 | 18.4 |
| Service Female | 26.2 | 24.5 | 23.4 | 24.1 | 22.8 | 22.3 | 23.2 | 23.6 | 23.7 | 19.6 |

**Figure 7.3 Distribution of Informal Employment Rates in Turkey by Sector and Gender (%).** *Source*: TurkStat Labour Force Statistics.

Looking at the sectoral distribution by gender, it is seen that women are mostly employed informally in the agricultural sector. The high rate of female employment in unpaid family work also increases the informal employment rate of women in the agricultural sector. While the rate of women working informally in the agricultural sector is 94.3 percent, this rate is 76.2 percent for men. The informal employment rate of women working in the industry and service sector is lower than in the agriculture sector. While the informal employment rate for women in the industry sector is 23.5 percent, it is 19.6 percent in the service sector (figure 7.3). Education level is also the most important factor that determines the share of women in informal employment. The majority of women who are deprived of social security and work informally are illiterate or primary or secondary school graduates.

## Informal Employment by Educational Status

The inadequacy of the education level of the employees and the resulting lack of qualifications directly affect informal employment. In Turkey, as the level of education increases, informality decreases.

, The informal employment rate of illiterate people was 86.7 percent in 2020, while this rate was 44.6 percent for those with less than a high school education, it was 20.9 percent for high school or equivalent vocational school. The rate of informal employment among college and faculty graduates was 8.4 percent. (In 2011, these rates were 91.9 percent, 54 percent, 23.2 percent, and 7.7 percent, respectively.) As can be seen, as the level of education increases, the rate of informal employment decreases. Informal employment is highest among the illiterate and least among college and university graduates (TurkStat, 2021).

## Informal Employment by Age Groups

It is observed that the tendency to work/employ informally is higher in the young age groups that will enter the labor market for the first time and in those who are retired, especially those over the age of sixty-five.

Informal work/employment is quite high in the retired sixty-five and over age groups. Individuals who retire at an early age have an old-age pension but can work; thus, they continue to work actively in the labor market. Those in this group tend to work informally due to the decrease in their income levels during the retirement period. Employers hiring this age group with high qualifications and experience generally prefer not to pay premiums to the social security system. The informal employment rate, which is 68.9 percent for employees over the age of fifty-five, is 87.7 percent for those over the age of sixty-five.

Apart from the relatively elderly population, the other age group with high informality is young people between fifteen and twenty-four. The reason for the prevalence of informal employment among young people is that they enter the labor market for the first time and therefore lack work experience. The fifteen to twenty-four age group is the group that feels the pressure of unemployment the most today. In this age group, the unemployment rate for December 2020 was 25.3 percent. The young population, who cannot find a demand corresponding to the labor supply in the formal sector, are willing to work in precarious jobs in the informal sector in order not to be unemployed. According to 2020 data, 41.4 percent (1,414,000) of the total youth employment was working informally.

## Informal Employment by Work Types

Part-time workers are more affected by informal employment than full-time workers. The rate of informal employment among full-time workers is quite low compared to part-time workers.

According to TUIK data, in 2011, the informal employment rate for full-time workers was 36.3 percent, while the informal employment rate for part-time workers was 84.5 percent. In 2020, these rates were 24.6 percent and 72.5 percent, respectively (seven of ten part-time workers were unregistered).

### Informal Employment by Workplace Size

An important problem in preventing informal employment is the size of the workplaces. In small-scale workplaces, workers are employed informally to avoid legal obligations and tax applications. Due to the lack of supervision, informal employment is seen in enterprises where ten or fewer workers are employed at the most.

According to TUIK data, in 2011, informal employment was 60.7 percent in enterprises employing ten or fewer people, while informal employment was 5.4 percent in enterprises employing fifty or more people. In 2020, unregistered employment was 53.9 percent in enterprises employing ten or fewer people, while informal employment was 1.9 percent in enterprises employing fifty or more people. It is understood that informal employment is more common in the informal sector, which employs less than ten people.

Considering that workplaces employing fifty or fewer workers have a very high rate of 56 percent, it is observed that informal employment is common in Turkey (TurkStat, Small and Medium Enterprise Statistics, 2019).

### Informal Employment by Occupational Groups

The prevalence of informal employment in the agricultural sector and the inability to benefit from educational opportunities also affect the distribution of occupations.

When looking at the occupational distribution of informal employment, it is mostly concentrated among qualified agricultural, forestry, and aquaculture workers with 81.3 percent. In the second place, with 45.3 percent, some work in jobs with a low level of education and which do not require qualifications. Again, informality among artisans and service and sales personnel working in small businesses is around 28–30 percent. According to the occupational distribution, the jobs with the lowest informality are in office services at 4.4 percent and in professional occupation groups at 5.1 percent.

## INFORMAL EMPLOYMENT BY REGION

There are also differences between provinces regarding informal employment. The provinces with the highest informal employment are Eastern Anatolia, Southeastern Anatolia, and Black Sea regions. Informality in the region covering Ağrı, Kars, Iğdır, and Ardahan was 57 percent in 2020. In the provinces where the industry is developed, the size of enterprises and the number of people benefiting from qualified education opportunities increase while informal employment decreases. For example, the informal employment rate in Ankara is 15.4 percent, in Istanbul 18.6 percent, in İzmir 22.5 percent, and in Bursa, Eskişehir, and Bilecik 22.8 percent (figure 7.1).

It is seen that the decrease in informal employment is higher in Adana and Hatay provinces, which receive a higher rate of immigration compared to their population. In the meantime, it should be noted that most of the Syrians who took refuge in Turkey work in the informal sector. For this reason, there are doubts about the reliability of the statistical decreases in informality rates.

## MEASURES TAKEN TO FIGHT INFORMAL EMPLOYMENT IN TURKEY

Increasing labor costs due to high insurance premiums and taxes in Turkey lead employers to employ informal workers. This situation causes the rate of informal employment to increase day by day. For this reason, many regulations have been made to prevent informal employment such as insurance premium incentives, incentives for additional employment, regulations for women's work, and regulations to prevent child labor.

Although the scope of the study consists of the last ten-year period (2011–2020), it is useful to briefly introduce the basis of developments that took place in this period. For this reason, the measures taken within the scope of combating informal employment in Turkey are discussed under two headings: the developments in 2010 and before and the developments in the period of 2011–2020.

### 2010 and before Period

Under this title, the legislation, activities, and projects enacted before 2010 in the fight against informality were examined.

#### *Legislation Arrangements*

With Law No. 3910, which was published in the Official Gazette on May 12, 1993, the low fines for employing illegal workers were equated to the minimum wage and thus, the effectiveness of the penalties was increased.

Law No. 4306, which came into force in 1998, indirectly contributed to the fight against informal work by increasing the duration of compulsory basic education from five to eight years and reducing the employment of children under the age of fourteen.

Unemployment Insurance Law No. 4447 dated 1999 and Social Insurance Law No. 506 amended some articles to prevent informal work. This law is also known as the first unemployment insurance law in Turkey. In the detail of the law:

> – With Law No. 4447, the unemployment insurance application, which partially eliminates the temporary income loss during the period of unemployment, was introduced. Unemployment insurance benefits prevent the insured from turning to informal employment during the period of unemployment. Insurance, which is a prerequisite for benefiting from unemployment benefits, is another factor that encourages people to work formally.
>
> – With the amendment made in Article 9 of Law No. 506 with Law No. 4447, the employer is obliged to notify the Social Security Institution (SSI) of the persons to be employed before starting to work; with the amendment made in Article 79, the employer is obliged to certify that the insurance holders, who are declared not to have worked on certain working days during the month and are not paid, have worked less than thirty days.
>
> – With the amendment made in Article 61 of Law No. 506 with Law No. 4447, the coefficient indicator system was abolished in the calculation of pensions, and the amount of earnings subject to premium, which was updated according to the growth rates of inflation and gross national product, was introduced. The lower limit of the premium-based earnings is equal to the minimum wage. Thus, the premium burden on the employer arising from the difference between the minimum wage and the income based on the insurance premium was removed and employment costs were reduced.
>
> – It has been attempted to encourage formal employment by providing premium incentives to employers by covering a certain part of the premiums belonging to the employer's share from the Unemployment Insurance Fund in case of employment (art.50/5) and additional employment (provisional article.9).
>
> – To promote the formal employment of young people and women over the age of 18 and under the age of 29, and women over the age of 18—regardless of age, who meet the necessary conditions, and are recruited and employed within two years; it has been made possible to cover a certain part of the employer's share of the insurance premium, which will be calculated over the lower limit of the income based on the insurance premium, from the Unemployment Insurance Fund (Temporary article 7).

In addition, a regulation made in 2000 covering the period until December 31, 2002, also indirectly contributed to the reduction of informality by stipulating that the employer's share of the social insurance premiums of the workers to be employed in the investments made in the provinces considered within the State of Emergency Region will be covered by the Treasury.

With Law No. 4817, which came into force in 2003, the work permits of foreigners were bound to certain principles and it was stated that they had to get permission before starting to work. Heavy sanctions were envisaged for those who employ foreign workers without permission; penal measures have been introduced, such as accommodation expenses of the foreigner's spouse and children, if any, return expenses, payment of health expenses by the employer, increasing the penalty by onefold in case of repetition of the act, and closing the workplace (Art. 21).

With Labour Law No. 4857, which entered into force in 2003, concepts such as part-time work, on-call work, temporary (borrowed) employment relationship, compensatory work, fixed-term work, indefinite-term work, and short-term work were introduced into working life and important steps had been taken for the flexibility of the labor market. With the flexibility of the Labour Law, formal work and registered workforce were encouraged.

With Law No. 4958 enacted in 2003, with the amendment made in Article 79 of the Social Security Law No. 506, in case the documents of the insured persons, which are determined by their actual employment, or by the workplace records are not submitted to the social security institution or are incomplete, these documents will be issued by the institution ex officio and insurance premiums will be determined by the institution and notified to the employer. With the same law, it is obligatory to submit the documents requested by the institution, within one month by the public institutions to the social security institution.

With the regulation made in the temporary Article 90 added to Law No. 506 with Law No. 5073 dated 2004 on the Contribution of the State to the Employers in terms of Insurance Premiums, the state encouraged registered employment by providing a certain amount of contribution to the employers for each insured person working for the minimum wage.

With the incentive measures implemented within the scope of Law No. 5084, which came into force in 2004, the financial liabilities of employers in thirty-six provinces were reduced. This regulation, which covers the provinces that are underdeveloped in terms of development level, it is aimed to increase investments and employment by applying tax and insurance premium incentives, providing energy support, and providing free plots and land for investments (Article 2). With Law No. 5350, the number of provinces benefiting from the law increased to forty-nine.

With the Social Security Institution Law No. 5502 published in the Official Gazette dated May 20, 2006, three social security institutions (Social Insurance Institution, Social Security Organization for Artisans and The Self-Employed, the General Directorate of Retirement Fund) were combined under one roof. Thus, it was aimed to eliminate the differences in the provision of services to the citizens, ensure equality and uniformity, and register informal employment with the audit structure strengthened as a result of merging these institutions.

In paragraph (f) of Article 4 of the Vocational Qualifications Authority Law No. 5544, which entered into force on October 7, 2006, the task of "determining the accuracy of the vocational qualification certificates held by foreigners who want to work in Turkey" is given to the aforementioned institution. In this way, it was aimed to prevent the illegal work of foreigners informally.

In 2007, with Law No. 3395 and the amendment made to Article 79 of Social Security Law No. 506, employers were obliged to display the lists showing the names of the insured employees and the hours worked in a visible place in the workplace.

With Law No. 5615 on Income Tax and Amendments to Some Laws of 2007, a minimum living allowance was introduced (Article 32). A minimum living allowance encourages formal employment by reducing employment costs.

With the Social Insurance and General Health Insurance Law No. 5510, which came into force in 2008, all public administrations are assigned to inspection and control, to determine whether the employed people are insured to prevent informal employment, during the research, investigation, audit, and examination they will carry out in their workplaces under their legislation (Article 59). According to subparagraph (i) of Article 81 of the Law, employers who meet the conditions are provided with a five-point discount on their insurance premium shares.

In addition to employment and premium incentives, making wages, premiums, bonuses, and all kinds of payments of this nature through banks is important for the follow-up of registered employment. With the regulation introduced in Article 10 of the mentioned regulation, which entered into force on January 1, 2009, private sector employers with at least five employees are obliged to make all kinds of payments to their employees through banks.

### *Activities Conducted*

There are measures in national development plans, medium-term programs, government actions, and action plans to combat informality. Accordingly;

> In the Seventh (1996–2000) and Eighth (2001–2005) Five-Year Development Plans and the Ninth (2007–2013) Development Plan, the concepts of informal economy and informal employment were included and the importance of combating informal employment was emphasized (SBB, 2021).

> In the five Medium-Term Programs prepared in 2010 and before, the issue of combating informal employment was emphasized and was among the main targets (SBB, 2021)

> In the 58th Government Program presented to the Grand National Assembly of Turkey on 23.11.2002 and the 60th Government Program presented to the Grand National Assembly on 31.08.2007, it was stated that the fight against informal employment was one of the priority targets.

Within the scope of combating the informal economy in Turkey, the Strategy Action Plan for Combating Informal Economy for the period 2008–2010 was prepared and implemented. In the Action Plan, it was stated that the fight against the informal economy should be adopted as a state policy, cooperation and coordination between institutions should be ensured, and an effective monitoring and evaluation system should be established to achieve success in the fight against the informal economy and reduce informality (SBB, 2021).

### *Projects*

Two projects that stood out in Turkey before 2010 in the fight against informal employment can be introduced as follows:

*Project on Combating Informal Employment*: One of the important steps taken in the fight against informality in Turkey is the Project on Combating Informal Employment. The project, prepared by the Ministry of Family, Labour and Social Services, entered into force by being published in the Official Gazette dated October 4, 2006, and numbered 26309 with the Prime Ministry Circular No. 2006/28. This project aims to contribute to the transition to formal employment by eliminating the factors that cause informal employment and employment of illegal foreign workers in Turkey. In the project, four activities were carried out under the headings of effective and deterrent implementation of supervision, information and awareness-raising activities, making legislative changes, and removing bureaucratic obstacles. With these activities, it was aimed to register informal workers and to minimize illegal foreign labor (MOLSS, 2006).

*Registered Employment Incentive and Technical Support Projects (KITUP I-KITUP II)*: KITUP I (June 2012) and KITUP II (October 2016) Projects, which were implemented in 2010 and co-financed by the European Union and the Republic of Turkey, were completed. The KITUP I Project aimed to increase the capacity of the parties related to the Social Security Institution within the scope of combating informal employment and to raise awareness in the public about social security and informal employment. On the other hand, the KITUP II Project aimed to increase the number of people employed by increasing the labor force participation rate especially women and youth (SSI, 2021)

## Period of 2011–2020

The developments between 2011 and 2020, which cover the main period of the study, can be analyzed similarly.

*Regulations Made by Law*

***Arrangements Made by Law No. 4447***
With the arrangements made in the Unemployment Law No. 4447 in 2011 (Provisional Article 10), 2015 (Provisional Article 15), and 2018 (Provisional Article 19), in case of additional employment to private sector employers, the employers were provided with premium incentives by covering the entire share of the employer in the insurance premium calculated over their earnings based on the insurance premium from the Unemployment Insurance Fund, and formal employment was tried to be encouraged.

***Arrangements Made by Law No. 5510***
With the regulation made in 2013 in the Social Insurance and General Health Insurance Law No. 5510, by providing a reduction in the employer's share in insurance premiums (Article 81/1(ı)), Article 81/2); also, with the regulation made in 2020, it was attempted to encourage registered employment by providing minimum wage premium support to employers meeting certain conditions (Provisional Article 80).

***Social Services Law No. 2828***
With the regulation made in the Social Services Law No. 2828 in 2018, the insurance premium and unemployment insurance premium calculated over the lower limit of the income subject to premium by the private sector employers of the persons covered by the Additional Article 1 of the Law, provided that the share of the insured and the employer is fully covered by the Ministry of Treasury and Finance, in case of employment of beneficiary children, premium incentives were provided to employers to encourage registered employment.

***Social Assistance and Solidarity Encouragement Law No. 3294***
The regulation made in Law No. 3294 in 2016, has tried to encourage registered employment by reducing employment costs by covering all of the insurance premium share calculated over the lower limit of earnings subject to the premium of employers employing social assistance recipients by the Ministry of Family, Labour and Social Services (Annex Article 5).

***Occupational Health and Safety Law No. 6331***

With the Occupational Health and Safety Law No. 6331 dated 2012, to support occupational health and safety services in workplaces with less than ten employees in the dangerous and very dangerous class, employment support has been provided and registered employment has been encouraged by paying a certain part of the daily gross minimum wage per insured person to the hazard class of the workplaces (Article 7).

### *The Activities Conducted*

In the Tenth (2014–2018) and Eleventh Development Plans (2019–2023), combating the informal economy and informal employment was among the priority targets and basic targets were set for its reduction (SBB, 2021)

In the ten Medium-Term Programs prepared in 2011 and after, combating the informal economy and informal employment was among the primary objectives, and it was stated that measures would be taken to prevent informal employment and encourage additional employment (SBB, 2021).

In the 61st, 62nd, 64th, and 65th Government Programs prepared by the governments established between 2011 and 2020, it is stated that combating informal employment and reducing informal employment are among the priority targets.

Within the scope of combating the informal economy in Turkey, Action Plans for the Fight Against Informal Economy Strategy for 2011–2013, Action Plan for Reducing the Informal Economy Program (2015–2017), and Strategy for Combating Informal Economy (2019–2021) were prepared and implemented. In general, these action plans were aimed at increasing the level of voluntary compliance, strengthening the audit capacity, reviewing the legislation and making regulations, improving data sharing between institutions, and raising awareness for all segments of society (SBB, 2021).

### *. Projects*

Three projects that stand out in the fight against informality in 2011 and beyond can be defined as follows:

*Supporting Registered Employment Project (KİDEP*): To reduce the informal employment rates, strengthen the process of combating informal employment, and increase the contribution of registered worker employment to the Turkish economy, the Support for Registered Employment Project was implemented by the SSI on May 25, 2017. During the implementation of visual materials and activities within the scope of the project, priority was given to the principles of preventing child labour, supporting the employment of disadvantaged groups, strengthening gender equality in working life, and complying with occupational health and safety rules (SSI, 2021).

*Transition to Registered Employment Project (KİGEP)*:It is a program that was implemented between February 1, 2018, and July 31, 2020, in cooperation with three institutions (International Labour Office, Ministry of Family, Labour and Social Services-Directorate General of International Labour, and Social Security Institution) and covers five provinces (Adana, Bursa, Hatay, Istanbul, and Konya). The program aims to to improve and protect employment and job opportunities to contribute to raising the living standards of Syrians under temporary protection and Turkish citizens living in the regions they migrated. The strategic aim of the program is to gain a "registered work culture" through the employment support method (ILO, 2020).

*Supporting Registered Women Entrepreneurship and Registered Women Employment Project (Women UP)*: Due to the high rate of informal employment among women and being in last place compared to other countries, to support women entrepreneurs, to make them more resistant to competition, and to raise Turkey to better levels in terms of women entrepreneurs and employed women, "Project for Increasing and Maintaining Registered Women's Entrepreneurship and Registered Women's Employment" was built. Project signatures were signed on March 5, 2020, but were delayed within the scope of Covid-19 measures (SSI, 2021).

## Conclusion

Informal employment has become a structural problem of the Turkish economy, especially after the 1980s, and has gradually increased after 1990. The following factors had a significant effect in the increasing rate of informal employment: internal and external factors such as high unemployment rates, poverty, rapid population growth, rapid increase in migration from rural to urban areas and the continuation of internal migration due to terrorism, unplanned urbanization, high inflation rates, international competition gaining a global dimension, high insurance premiums and taxes on the workforce, economic crises, inadequate workplace control, and illegal foreign labor. Jobs could not be created to meet the increasing labor supply. The low-skilled or unskilled workforce who migrated to urban areas could not find a job, and they turned to informal employment and work informally.

Informality in the agricultural sector in Turkey is higher than in all other sectors. Since it changes all the averages, studies on informality are mostly done by separating the agricultural sector. Informality is also high in the services sector. Here, as in agriculture, difficulties in monitoring and auditing increase informality. In addition, the prevalence of small businesses across the country also complicates monitoring and auditing.

Informal employment in Turkey is more common among the unemployed, unskilled people with low education levels, child workers, women, illegal foreign national workers, retirees, and self-employed tradesmen and craftsmen. In addition, unregistered work is common among the fifteen to twenty-four young age group and fifty-five and over age groups, within the illiterate group, and among those who have not completed a degree even if they are literate.

The economic conjuncture is a phenomenon that can affect the level of informal employment. In periods of economic crisis, unemployed masses tend to seek employment opportunities in informal employment, which they cannot find in the formal economy. Likewise, employers consider reducing production costs by employing informal workers to reduce the negative effects of the crisis. The effects of the global financial crisis experienced in 2008 were also strongly felt by our country's economy. It is observed that the shrinkage in demand due to the global financial crisis and the decrease in production levels in the majority of sectors cause an increase in informal employment levels while reducing total employment. In addition to rapid population growth and internal migration, factors such as the rise of unemployment in Turkey due to the global financial crisis and the decrease in family income caused workers to work in precarious jobs informally and it has led employers to employ some workers informally in order not to lose their competitiveness in global markets and to reduce production costs. As a result of the reflection of the 2008 global financial crisis, it is seen that the informal employment rate, which was 43.3 percent in 2010, decreased to 30.6 percent by 2020. While there was a general decrease in the informal employment rates in the 2010–2020 period, the rate which decreased to 33.4 percent in 2018 increased to 34.5 percent in 2019. After the economic fragility experienced in Turkey in 2018, the increase in the exchange rate and the decrease in the income levels of the people due to the increase in debts are important factors in the increase of informality.

The Turkish Lira depreciated significantly, and the growth rate of the economy slowed down, after the increase in inflation created by the exchange rate increase, a serious decline occurred in domestic demand and therefore in production, unemployment reached its highest level in recent years (13.7 percent), and real disposable income of people decreased. Despite all this, the decrease in the total informal employment rate from a level as high as 50 percent to 30 percent in Turkey is the result of reducing insurance premium incentives and tightening controls, the increase in the average level of education in employment, the concentration of employment in the service and industry sectors where informality is relatively lower, and insurance premium incentives that reduce nonwage labor costs.

In addition, the legal regulations, in particular the Unemployment Insurance Law No. 4447, came into effect in 2002, the Anti-Informal Employment Project (KADİM), which was initiated at two-year intervals as of 2006, and the Registered Employment Incentive and Technical Support Project, which was put into effect since 2010 (KİTUP), and awareness-raising activities to prevent informal employment have a great role.

The positive and negative effects of the informal employment of millions of immigrants who came to Turkey after the Syrian civil war on the economy are observed. In Turkey, positive effects such as creating employment, efficient distribution of resources, and increasing competitiveness were observed in addition to negative effects such as reducing tax revenues and eliminating tax justice, adversely affecting resource distribution, causing unfair competition, exploiting child labour, and deteriorating the social security system.

According to the data of the Directorate of Migration Management, many legal and administrative regulations have been implemented in Turkey in 2016 to bring Syrians under temporary protection into registered employment. However, only a very small percentage of Syrians in Turkey can work as registered, insured, and minimum-wage earners. Syrian refugees, who cannot apply for a work permit because they cannot obtain a residence permit, cause informal employment to grow in sectors such as agriculture and construction. Statistics on employment in Turkey are calculated over the citizen labor force. For this reason, although it is not possible to determine the effect of the refugee workforce on informal employment, it is possible to say that it has a significant effect on informal employment. Refugees close the labor gap in low-paid, temporary/seasonal, insecure lines of work where local people do not want to work and the employment effect it creates, it makes the informal employment figures seem lower than they are.

The structural transformation in the economy, which will enable production and employment to shift from agriculture to nonagricultural sectors, has not yet been completed in Turkey. It is possible to say that the shift of people who leave agriculture, which is predominantly done by self-employed and unpaid family workers, to nonagricultural sectors has a limited effect on the reduction of informality. Today, both the effective employment policies of the state and the administrative fines applied in cases of employing uninsured workers play a major role in the gradual decrease in informal employment. Thanks to the systematic and determined policies to prevent informal employment, significant decreases were realized in the informal employment rate. Despite these developments, the informal employment of one out of every three people on average is an important problem in terms of the labor market. Although important steps have been taken to reduce informal employment, informality in Turkey is far above both the EU and OECD countries. To further reduce informal employment, it is necessary to continue the sustainable battle. Although it is not a problem that can be solved in the short term, in order for the activities carried out within the scope of combating informal employment to yield effective results, in addition to the legal and administrative arrangements, social consensus of public institutions and organizations, social partners, and nongovernmental organizations is required within the framework of these activities.

## NOTE

1. Dr., Ministry of Treasury and Finance, Ankara, Turkey, hly_ylmz@yahoo.com.

## REFERENCES

ÇSGB (2006). Kayıt Dışı İstihdamla Mücadele (KADİM) Projesi, http://docplayer.biz.tr/736434- Kayit-disi-istihdamla-mucadele-kadim-projesi.html

Çalışma ve Sosyal Güvenlik Bakanlığı, Dış İlişkiler ve Avrupa Birliği Genel Müdürlüğü. Kayıtlı İstihdamın Yenilikçi Yollarla Teşviki Operasyonu, http://www.ikg.gov.tr/kayitli-istihdamin-yenilikci-yollarla-tesviki-operasyonu/ (February, 2022).

European Commission; Communication (COM98-219). (EC, 1998).

Hazine ve Maliye Bakanlığı, Gelir İdaresi Başkanlığı. Kayıt dışı Ekonomiyle Mücadele Stratejisi Eylem Planı (2019–2021), https://www.alomaliye.com/2019/06/10/kayit-disi-ekonomiyle-mucadele-2019-2021/ (September, 2021).

ILO (1972). *Employment, Incomes and Equality a Strategy for Increasing Productive Employment in Kenya*, Internatıonal Labour Offıce Geneva.

Kayıtlı İstihdama Geçiş Programı Birinci Faz Etki Analizi Çalışması, https://www.ilo.org/wcmsp5/groups/public/---europe/---ro-geneva/---ilo-ankara/documents/publication/wcms_764,195.pdf (ILO, 2020).

Mateman, S. ve Renooy, P. (2001). *Undeclared Labour in Europe, Towards an Integrated Approach of Combatting Undeclared Labour*, Regioplan Research Advice and Information.

Mülteciler Derneği. Türkiye'deki Suriyeli Sayısı, https://multeciler.org.tr/turkiyedeki-suriyeli-sayisi-aralik-2020 (April, 2021).

OECD, Taxing Wages 2021, https://www.oecd-ilibrary.org/sites/83a87978-en/index.html?itemId=/content/publication/83a87978-en (OECD, 2021).

Resmi Gazete. Eylem Planı (2008–2010), https://www.resmigazete.gov.tr/eskiler/2009/02/20090205-4.htm (April, 2021).

Sosyal Güvenlik Kurumu, Kayıt dışı istihdam, http://www.sgk.gov.tr/wps/portal/sgk/tr/calisan/kayitdisi_istihdam (October, 2021).

Sosyal Güvenlik Kurumu, KİTUP Projesi, http://www.sgk.gov.tr/wps/portal/sgk/tr/kurumsal/projelerimiz/kitup_projesi (January, 2022).

Türkiye Cumhuriyeti Cumhurbaşkanlığı, Strateji ve Bütçe Başkanlığı. Kalkınma Planları, https://www.sbb.gov.tr (May, 2021).

Türkiye Odalar ve Borsalar Birliği (TOBB), Ekonomik Rapor 1993, Ankara, 1994.

## *Chapter 8*

# Hundred Years of History of Women's Employment in Turkey

## *Obstacles and Solutions*

Meltem İnce Yenilmez[1]

Gender inequality in the labor sector remains a concern, with negative economic repercussions such as disparities in welfare and unequal resource allocation. The literature frequently gives examples of the "feminization of poverty," demonstrating that economically insecure women, particularly single moms and retirees, account for a larger share of the world's poor. Eliminating barriers to women's labor force participation is a vital step toward strengthening women's empowerment, particularly in developing nations like Turkey. Turkish society, including its culture, geopolitical position, and government policies, has not (could not) aided in increasing both fertility and female labor force participation. State-funded in vitro fertilization treatments for the sole child, employment protection during pregnancy, and wage replacement rates equal to 80 percent of the wage during fourteen weeks of paid maternity leave were not adopted. Given this circumstance, support for working moms in Turkey lags well below that offered in OECD nations. This research also examines the labor market status of women and the amount of education, which is a significant determinant in Turkey.

## INTRODUCTION

One of the prominent features of the labor market in Turkey is that women's labor force participation rates are consistently low compared to other countries. Despite economic growth and significant developments in women's educational achievement, internal and external economic crises, consequent shrinkage in employment, rapid urbanization due to migration to cities, unqualified labor seeking, unregistered or inflexible working style, and/or low higher education completion rate by more women are prevelant. Rural women still work as unpaid family workers due to agricultural activities. Labor force participation rates of women in rural areas have been declining, especially in the last decade due to internal migration and rapid urbanization. Women's participation rates in cities are likewise exceedingly low and stagnating. Since the early 2010s, there has been a minor improvement in urban participation rates. This, however, was insufficient to halt the decreasing trend in women's labor force participation rates.

Women's labor force involvement impacts not just the conceptions of work and family but also has social, cultural, and economic consequences. Women's employment has a significant influence on a country's growth. This scenario was highlighted in the studies, and many views on how the woman development connection could be built arose. Women are individuals of society who are often overlooked yet have a significant impact on progress/empowerment. The more industrious and productive a woman is, the more developed a community becomes. Women's engagement in the labor force is critical to gaining the value of their labor in the process of social and economic development. At the same time, women must labor in order to improve their social standing and acquire economic independence.

Sustainable growth is one of any country's primary objectives. Economic growth, effective use of scarce resources, technology, capital rise, and other comparable goals are critical for all governments. To attain these goals, it is vital to invest in human resources, and women are critical members of the economic development team in this regard. Women's education and labor force participation are critical issues that must be addressed. Education, which is a requirement for a contemporary society, adapts to the world's quick change and growth process. As a result, the quality of education that should be provided to individuals in a community is critical in terms of covering all parts of society.

The majority of the present literature on women's labor market involvement in Turkey is based on neoclassical labor supply models. Women's low participation rates are often explained by human capital characteristics, with the impact of traditional beliefs and culture being overlooked. However, because patriarchal ideals continue to dominate Turkey, it is critical to evaluate societal values, culture, and patriarchal structure. Because of a combination of these factors, the majority of women in Turkey either work informally or are compelled to exit the labor market. The simultaneous rise of demand and supply-side variables is the most fundamental cause of the growth of the informal labor market in Turkey. Turkey's increased integration into global markets has resulted in unregistered employment on the demand side, driven by price rivalry in tradable industries and production cost pressure. On the supply side, rapid migration from rural to urban regions, along with privatization and a diminishing percentage of public sector employment, provides a sizable workforce willing to work in the informal sector (Elgin and Oyvat, 2013).

In the early 2010s, unemployment in Turkey averaged 11.9 percent. The rise in employment that began in 2011 and the country's resilience to the crisis have altered the labor market's outlook. Furthermore, foreign investment expanded the labor market (Şengül, 2012). While the employment rate achieved its greatest level in 2019, the unemployment rate was 13.4 percent, the highest level in the prior ten years. However, there are numerous flaws in this positive/negative image. Despite recent increases in pay growth, the labor force's proportion of national income remains low (ILO, 2021). Job quality is also an issue as a result of the labor market impact of temporary contracts. Because of the shrinking working-age population, labor force participation will drop in the future years, resulting in a reduction in the workforce.

The goal to protect the present workforce by deferring retirement appears to have been effective as a result of the measures enacted in 2008. However, the consequence of these policies, which increased engagement and employment among comparatively older employees, generated a new problem area with the rise in retirement age. Wage growth has risen since 2000, thanks to the labor market expansion in 2011 (OECD, 2018; Street and Ní Léime, 2020). The goal of increasing the minimum wage is to alleviate inequality. However, policymakers have not adequately addressed the growing proportion of transitory work. Furthermore, labor force participation remained lower than predicted, and the aging population that is still working threatened to diminish the availability of fresh workers. As a result, policy solutions should include enhancing employment protection for all workers, lowering the tax burden on low-wage workers, and regulating the retirement age once again.

## WOMEN'S EMPLOYMENT IN THE REPUBLICAN PERIOD

After the proclamation of the Republic in 1923, critical preparations commenced being made under the management of Mustafa Kemal Atatürk for Turkish people to be more active both economically and socially and to be frequent in society (Önder, 2013). The 1927 Industrial Census data, which cover all industrial firms and consider the distribution of the team of workers via gender and solely employ four workers, are the first necessary supply of records on female employees in the Republican era. According to the results, 29,533 out of 124,444 employees working over the age of fourteen are girls (24 percent), and 8,107 out of 22,684 people under the age of fourteen are women (36 percent). In total, 37,640 out of 147,128 people are female (26 percent). Out of a total of 7,817 civil servants, only 1,609 (21 percent) are women. When girls with company reputations are examined, only 14 percent of 10,941 commercial enterprise owners are female enterprise owners (Makal, 2010). All over Turkey, women's three days off of the month, eight weeks of paid depart earlier than and after the birth, and breastfeeding go-away provisions have been taken at the Turkish Economy Congress held in 1923 (Önder, 2013). Regarding the regulations related to the training of women with the Education Union Law (Tevhid-i Tedrisat Law) and the Teşkilat-ı Esasiye Law made in 1924, training was given a secular structure and primary training used to be made obligatory for female and boys with equal rights (Çakmak, 2001). The implementation of the General Health Protection Law (Public Health Protection Law) on April 24, 1930, ensured that the difficulty of the job, the period of leave, the working age, and different working prerequisites have been put into impact for adult workers as nicely as female plus child people in all industrial businesses in the United States (Önder, 2013). In addition, the criminal safety of the rights of all working individuals, in particular female employees, used to be realized with Law No. 394, which started to be carried out in 1925, and Law No. 2739, which was once adopted in 1935 (Kocacık and Gökkaya, 2005). The Labor Law No. 3008, permitted in 1936, was once evaluated as the most essential step in the working existence of woman employees, and the working stipulations of men, women, and children had been regulated from scratch employing this regulation (Yaşar, 2007). In 1937, the first outcomes of worldwide rules in the use of commenced to be viewed with the ratification of the ILO Convention No. 45 on the Prevention of Women Working in Mines and Underground (Şenol and Mazman, 2013). Women employees have been taken below social safety with the Law on Occupational Accidents, Occupational Diseases, and Maternity Insurance, which was once first accepted in 1945 (Atıl-Yörü, 2009). Gender-based wage differences continued in the Republican administration as well. According to the first job data made in 1937, 1943, and 1947, the number of female personnel employed in places of work challenged by the Labor Law was 50,131, while the fee used to be 19 percent; In 1943, the number of employees rose to 56,937 and the price rose to 21 percent, ensuing in an increase of about 12 percent in women's employment. In 1947, the total number of employees was once 289,147; the number of female personnel in this total was 50,851, and the price was once 18 percent (Makal, 2010). The improvement of the rules on the safety of women was made with the 1961 Constitution. Labor Law No. 1475 started to be applied in 1971 and was carried out for many years till the new Labor Law No. 4857 came under pressure on June 10, 2003, primarily based on the principle of equality between men and women (Atıl-Yörü, 2009). The principle of equal pay for equal work, which began to be applied in 1971, was once enacted with Labor Law No. 1475 (Önder, 2013). With Law No. 4857, it was once emphasized that woman personnel must be given paid leave for ordinary check-ups at some point of pregnancy, related to the safety of female employees for the duration of and after being pregnant (Kartal and Çoban, 2018). The Convention on the Political Rights of Women, ratified in 1952, and the Beijing Declaration and Platform for Action conventions, ratified in 1995, contributed to the improvement of women's rights and their extraactive function in the political platform (Demirtaş and Yayla, 2017). With the impact of industrialization, urbanization, and financial development, the casual area has expanded since the 1970s. The expansion in the range of women in the informal sector emerged because of the structural adjustment plans that began to be carried out in Turkey in the 1980s. In the method of growing industrialization, females who have simply migrated to the metropolis and whose training stage is low can't be economically active, and they have begun to work in casual piecework, such as stitching and embroidery, in small organizations and domestically (Dedeoğlu, 2002). The neoliberal insurance policies that were dominant in Turkey in the 1980s, which had been superb no longer solely in the financial but also in the social and cultural fields, induced modifications in phrases of women.

With the decisions of January 24, 1980, Turkey left the mixed economic system and switched to the market economy. The employment rate of women in sectors other than agriculture has increased, and they have received greater monetary freedom in contrast to the past (Gürol, 2007). Increases in women's employment, specialization, and management-related profession quotas have been documented in the post-1980 period (İzgi-Balcı and Akdeniz, 2011). In 1985, the United Nations Convention on the Elimination of All Forms of Discrimination Against Women (CEDAW) was once ratified with the aid of our country to abolish the legal guidelines and traditional initiatives that avoid the crucial rights and freedoms of females in the political, economic, social, and cultural fields (Mercanlıoğlu, 2009). Vocational education, work, social security, acquiring equal employment opportunities as men, equal pay, and fertility safety rights have been received by women through CEDAW (Demirtaş and Yayla, 2017). In 1990, the General Directorate of the Status of Women, affiliated with the Prime Ministry, was established; it is aimed at protecting the rights of women in many economic, social, political, and cultural fields (Mercanlıoğlu, 2009). It was mentioned in the Decisions of the World Conference on Women that the household unit must be bolstered and that women acquire a very necessary position in the family, which is an important aspect of the social structure. In Turkey, When there was a significant shift in the social, political, and economic spheres; public participation in the financial system decreased; and agriculture began to lose its value in the post-2000 era. Unemployment increased rapidly due to these structural adjustments and transformations in the economic system and the insurance policies observed were inadequate to reduce this problem. Women have been the section most affected by the growing unemployment and employment trouble (Karabıyık 2012b; Hüseyinli, 2015). When the statistics are examined, one out of every three females joined the labor market in Turkey in the 1990s, while in the 2000s, one out of every four women in Turkey joined the labor market. Among the reasons for the reduction in employment rates of females in the labor market are the increase in migration to cities, the limit in the number of women working in the agricultural sector, and unregistered employment (Erdoğan and Yaşar, 2018).

## Women's Employment in Turkey after the 2000s

The popular and social motives for this have been a financial system primarily based totally on agricultural manufacturing till the end of the 1950s, social cost judgments, gender-based division of labor, migration from the village to the city, disintegration within the agricultural structure, family structure, low monetary employment volume, low demand for women's labor, marriage, and having children. Lack of mechanisms to grant women admission into the labor market, low wages, inadequate training, women and families, and painting balance are all contributing factors to the inability to institutionalize senior care and housekeeping (Ince and Demir, 2006; Uraz et al., 2010).

Table 8.1 indicates the labor force participation, general employment, and general unemployment costs in Turkey. In the 2010–2020 period, there may be a boom in the labor force participation of females and a decline in the labor force participation of men. There is a comparable image when looking at the employment rate within the same period. Although there has been a boom in female employment and female labor force participation rates over the final ten years, the rate of girls continues to be very low compared to both women and men operating in other countries. In addition, with the pandemic that began in the first quarter of 2020, the female labor force participation rate, which may be multiplied by 4.4 percent within side the last 10 years,

**Table 8.1 Labor Force Statistics**

| | *Labor Force Participation Rate* | | *Employment Rate* | | *Total Unemployment Rate* | |
|---|---|---|---|---|---|---|
| | *2010* | *2020* | *2010* | *2020* | *2010* | *2020* |
| Women (15+) | 27.6 | 32 | 24 | 26.3 | 13 | 45.3 |
| Men (15+) | 72.4 | 68.2 | 70.1 | 58.9 | 9.5 | 13.2 |

*Source*: TUIK Labour Force Statistics, 2021.

decreased (Grekou and Lu, 2021). The fact that women are the first group to be sacrificed in times of crisis has a significant impact.

Unregistered employment is one of the most significant variables influencing women's employment. Cities' unemployment has risen because of factors such as regional backwardness, internal migration, and fast population expansion. This condition, which happened in cities, limited the unemployed's job options and forced them to work without insurance (OECD, 2018). Those who are unable to work in the formal sector due to a lack of employment opportunities, particularly in recent years, work without insurance in the informal sector, where entry and exit to the market are simple, no training or expertise is required, and some jobs, such as housework, peddling, and marketing, do not require a large amount of capital. Unregistered employment is rising due to all these factors (Tunç, 2007). To study unregistered employment, Şahinli and Şahbaz (2013) analyzed whether women working in Turkey's agricultural sector were registered with the Social Security Organization between 2004 and 2011. Because of their research, they discovered that the number of people registered with a social security organization has grown in most areas in recent years.

## BARRIERS TO FEMALE EMPLOYMENT IN TURKEY

Women's labor force involvement is inextricably related to their status in larger societies, and their greater labor force participation is inextricably linked to economic development. While the female employment rate in Turkey is low (32 percent as of 2020), an examination of the labor market reveals that there are significantly more challenges. Informal employment continues to be a big issue for working women in Turkey, owing to a lack of social protection and poor working conditions. Women's informal employment rate decreased from 43.25 percent in 2010 to 35.5 percent in 2020 (ILO, 2021). On the other hand, there are several barriers to working for women with advanced degrees and education. In Turkey, women hold just 15.1 percent of management posts, while 40.7 percent of highly educated women are unemployed. It implies a significant loss of human capital because of women's poor labor force participation due to the exclusion of educated women from male-dominated occupations. In summary, even though women are educated and/or come from specific socioeconomic situations, there remain barriers to women's employment caused mostly by comparable determinants.

Gender inequality and discrimination in the Turkish labor market can be attributed to a variety of factors. Women relocating from rural regions to cities lack the qualities necessary for the urban job market, including (1) a low level of education; (2) maintaining the notion that women are responsible for domestic work and unpaid family work; (3) an insufficient low-cost institutional framework to address the childcare problem; (4) on the job market, because jobs are divided into women's and men's labor, the system is monopolistic; (5) low salary level, wage disparity between male and female employees, and the widespread informal economy; (6) the phenomena of unemployment; (7) employers' and society's opinions on female employees; (8) women's perspectives on women; (9) the constraints of safe workplaces; (10) the fact that flexible working methods are not widely used in Turkey; (11) sexual harassment in the workplace; and (12) communication challenges encountered by women on their way to work. These can be identified as the primary factors (ILO, 2021).

The most serious issue with women's employment, when examined at the micro level, is that the home division of work is inequitable. In other words, women have a double load because of their household obligations and their expectations in a paid job. In 2020, 55 percent of economically inactive women cited "being a housewife" as a reason for not working in a paid job. Unsurprisingly, Turkey has the lowest mother labor force participation rate among OECD nations. According to the Turkish Statistical Institute (2021), mothers shoulder 86 percent of all obligations for children aged zero to five, grandmothers 7.4 percent, and paid nursery/kindergarten 2.8 percent and 1 percent. It is followed by nannies/babysitters, who have a rate of 0.5 percent. For dads, the rate is 0 percent, which is quite concerning. This incident also throws light on the issues surrounding moms' work. As a result, one of the most visible and persistent challenges in terms of gender disparity in the labor market is the micro-level impediments to female employment. This demonstrates that social policy support for women may be enhanced by acknowledging home obligations and childcare as a family issue rather than a woman's responsibility as well as by fostering gender-based political discourse.

At a modest level, statistical discrimination continues to be a substantial obstacle to entrance, especially for women in prominent occupations. Prejudices against women taking time away from their work, mostly owing to productivity and family/child duties, cause women to be barred from specific positions. Statistical discrimination based on gender, which investigates this scenario, highlights that women face a "glass door" in their labor market advancement rather than a "glass ceiling," and their recruiting procedures suffer as a result. Gender discrimination may be reduced at the institutional level by providing gender equality training to businesses and monitoring recruiting procedures. Furthermore, positive discrimination practices and gender quotas are required in relatively more prestigious professions to prevent exclusion until a certain level of gender equality is achieved in all segments of the labor market, and vertical and horizontal gender segregation in the workplace is reduced to a satisfactory level.

Gender, family, and work-related social policy formulation are the primary macro-level problems affecting women's labor force participation. In Turkey, there are social measures that favor women's employment to some extent. The major issue, however, is that males are excluded from the process of forming a family while determining the social policy agenda. Given that women's work and family responsibilities are key barriers to employment, it is critical to emphasize the necessity of supporting men's roles at home as well as women's positions in the labor market to guarantee that women can participate in the labor market.

While social policies can be tailored to the existing situation, they can also be socially reconstructed and modified to effect change. Furthermore, despite rejecting the sexist roles assigned to men and women in the family and society, it is critical to positively transform men's responsibilities as husbands and fathers at home.

Policies to enhance vertical and horizontal education are vital at the macro level for both men and women. Not only should the labor market and/or equal educational opportunities be considered, but so should the good influence of education on both men and women. Men's gender awareness and sensitivity levels are critical in breaking the vicious loop of women who are deficient in particular job positions, increasing the number of female role models in all sections of the labor market, and assisting in the creation of a support network in accessing professions.

In Turkey, traditionalism has dominated the legal and institutional framework, particularly in gender roles and the norm of the man and woman who contribute to the household's livelihood. Women choose to stay at home due to a shortage of inexpensive childcare facilities and the fact that their rates are frequently lower than booking fees. This percentage has risen even more, owing mostly to the rising expense of daycare services, which has bolstered this notion. Furthermore, rather than enhancing access to public institutional care facilities, current policies such as cash transfers to low-income families and financial aid for home care of the aged and disabled have tended to boost home care services and entrench this notion. Traditional or conservative societal norms and cultural beliefs, as well as community-specific variables, strengthen the gendered division of work at home and in the job market in Turkey, while also demonstrating that gender equality is restricted. The conventional family structure in which women are housewives has begun to alter as a result of the structural revolution that will let women move toward and work in the professions they wish to work in.

## GLASS CEILING SYNDROME

The term "glass ceiling" refers to the portrayal of 1970s America. In an unusual approach to this notion, it may also be employed for local physical problems (Lockwood, 2004). The glass ceiling is another phenomenon that keeps the invisible and women from their top levels without considering their growth and achievement (Cotter et al., 2001; Bingöl et al., 2011). Women in their careers have likewise encountered a glass barrier in their respective eras. "Women are top executives," as used in one practice, is a categorical refusal. They can prepare for what they can prepare for, in collaboration with those who are preparing for people who are linked to them and those who are preparing for their senior management (Irmak, 2010). However, in this context, their lack of prejudices and insensitivity leads them to typically accept women's responsibilities and place their positions in the workplace on the second plan (Kocacık and Gökkaya, 2005). Therefore, when a used asset is not measured, it appears to be a barrier.

## CONCLUSION

Adam Smith's Wealth of Nations serves as the foundation for modern theory, which was inspired by the notion of human capital developed by Chicago School economists Gary Becker, Jacob Mincer, and Theodore Schultz in the late 1950s and early 1960s. It is based on the research of human capital investment. These ideas explain how an increase in education level raises wage rates and, as a result, influences labor force participation. If leisure is considered a typical good, as the worker's income rises, he desires more leisure time and works fewer hours. If the wage rate changes, for example, a worker's working hours will increase but his leisure time will decrease. Human capital investment theory, on the other hand, highlights how resources invested in persons boost their future production and revenues. This rise in income tends to boost labor force participation. Although the active engagement of women in the labor field, which has been referenced several times in development plans or different policy papers in Turkey, began in the 1950s, it remains a significant issue. Unlike in many other nations, female labor force participation in Turkey is low.

In industrialized economies, female employment in agriculture is low, whereas it is high in industry and services. The same is true for men in the labor force. This tendency is a development indicator as well as a predicted outcome for developed countries. In developing nations, unlike in industrialized countries, the proportion of women employed in agriculture is high, while the proportion of women employed in manufacturing and service sectors is low. Although the sectoral distribution of male labor in developing nations is comparable to that of the female workforce, males have a greater employment rate than women. Women make up a sizable proportion of wage employees in industrialized economies.

However, in high-income nations, the share of women working as employers is higher than the global average. Women are concentrated in the first status group in the agriculture sector and the second status group in the industry and service sectors in the Turkish labor market. The number of female employees in this sector is low because the business lines in the industrial sector are not conducive to women entering and remaining in the industry for legal and social reasons. Although the services industry is more favorable for women, it is possible to argue that it does not offer enough job opportunities for women. Women who are unable to obtain work may be directed to "informal sector positions, where labor demand is the most uneven, the most unstable, disorganized, and leading to the highest level of exploitation."

Education is the most essential component in determining women's roles in economic growth and facilitating their full involvement in the labor force. Education boosts labor productivity, raises family income, decreases poverty, improves health and nutrition, and lowers fertility, all of which have an impact on a country's social and political growth. Women participate in the labor sector at a high rate in rural regions, yet the majority of them work as unpaid household workers.

Women are underrepresented in the labor force in metropolitan regions, and as education levels rise, so does their proclivity to work. Other reasons for low labor force participation include women with young children having to care for themselves alone, women working more in daily household and care activities than men and putting in more effort, low education levels, high population growth rate, new employment opportunities in the market, and a new female population entering the labor market. Inadequate work, the fall in closely related girl-centerd agricultural employment, an extension of the common schooling period, early retirement, casual economy lifestyles, inadequate capital accumulation, leaving the industry, additional supply due to activity search by individuals who have lost hope in finding an activity, immaturity of market conditions, inadequate qualifications, low salary offers, shortcomings in criminal laws governing business life, and migration. In this regard, while women's hard work-pressure participation has increased in the previous ten years, it's miles obvious that women must be engaged in the labor market more to avoid and empower their disadvantaged conditions. First and foremost, social security must be provided for women who work as informal and unpaid family workers. It is critical to make and execute provisions for equitable division of household obligations among family members, equal chances in business life, and equal remuneration for similar labor to expand women's involvement in the workforce to expected levels.

## NOTE

1. Professor at Dept. of Economics, Izmir Democracy University, Izmir, Turkey; Visiting Professor at Graduate Studies of Business and Economics, Tohoku University. E-mail: melteminceyenilmez@gmail.com.

## REFERENCES


Atıl-Yörü, H. (2009). Türkiye'deki Üniversite Kütüphanelerinde Kadın İşgücü. *Türk Kütüphaneciliği*, 23(2): 351–366.

Becker, G. S. (1957). *The Economics of Discrimination*. University of Chicago Press.

Bingöl, D., Aydoğan, E., Şenel, G. ve Erden, P. (2011). Cam Tavan Sendromu ve Kadınların Hiyerarşik Yükselmelerindeki Engeller. *Dokuz Eylül Üniversitesi İşletme Fakültesi Dergisi*, 12(1): 115–132.

Cotter, A. D., Hermsen, M. J., Ovadia, S. and Vanneman, R. (2001). The Glass Ceiling Effect. *Social Forces,* 80(2): 655–681.

Çakmak, R. (2001). *Kadın İş Gücü ve Yönetim Kadrolarında Kadın İstihdamı. İstanbul Üniversitesi,* Sosyal Bilimler Enstitüsü Çalışma Ekonomisi ve Endüstri İlişkileri Ana Bilim Dalı, Endüstri İlişkileri ve İnsan Kaynakları Bilim Dalı, Yüksek Lisans Tezi, İstanbul.

Dedeoğlu, S. (2002). Toplumsal Cinsiyet Rolleri Açısından Türkiye'de Aile ve Kadın Emeği. *Toplum ve Bilim,* 86: 139–170.

Demirtaş, G. ve Yayla, N. (2017). Küresel Entegrasyonun Kadın İstihdamı Üzerine Etkisi: Ampirik Bir İnceleme. *Journal of Yasar University,* 12(48): 339–349.

Elgin, C. and Oyvat, C. (2013). Lurking in the Cties: Urbanization and the Informal Economy. *Structural Change and Economic Dynamics,* 27: 36–47.

Erdoğan, S. ve Yaşar, S. (2018). Türkiye'de Kadın İstihdamının Gelişimi: Konya-Karaman Örneği. *KMÜ Sosyal ve Ekonomik Araştırmalar Dergisi,* 20(34): 18–28.

Grekou, D. and Lu, Y. (2021). Gender Differences in Employment One Year into the COVID-19 Pandemic: An Analysis by Industrial Sector and Firm Size. *Economic and Social Reports*, 1(5): 1–13.

Gürol, M.A. (2007). Türkiye'de İş Yaşamındaki Kent Kadınının Açmazı: Kariyer-Aile İkilemi. Selçuk Üniversitesi Karaman İ.İ.B.F. Dergisi Yerel Ekonomiler Özel Sayısı, 144–150.

Hüseyinli, N. (2015). Uluslararası Sözleşmeler Işığında Aile ve Çalışma Yaşamının Uzlaştırılması Kapsamında Ebeveyn İzninin Uygulamadaki Yeri. *Selçuk Üniversitesi Hukuk Fakültesi Dergisi,* 23(1): 271–311.

ILO (2021a). *ILO Monitor: COVID-19 and the World of Work: Updated Estimates and Analysis*. 7th edition. ILO.

ILO (2021b). *Working to Eliminate Gender Wage Gap in the World of Work at Country Level, ILO Embarks on Achieving Equal Pay at Enterprise Level*. ILO.

Ince, M. and Demir, M. (2006). The Determinants of Female Labor Force: Empirical Evidence from Turkey. *Eskisehir Osmangazi University Journal of Faculty of Economics and Administrative Sciences*, 1(1): 71–90.

Irmak, R. (2010). *Cam Tavan Sendromu- Bir Hastane Uygulaması, Yüksek Lisans Tezi*. Dokuz Eylül Üniversitesi, Sosyal Bilimler Enstitüsü.

İzgi Balcı, B. ve Akdeniz, S. (2011). Kadın İstihdamı Sorunsalı Nereden Doğuyor? EconAnadolu 2011: Anadolu International Conference in Economic II. Eskişehir, 1–26.

Karabıyık, İ. (2012b). Türkiye'de Çalışma Hayatında Kadın İstihdamı. *Marmara Üniversitesi İ.İ.B.F. Dergisi*, 32(1): 231–260.

Kartal, M. ve Çoban, O. (2018). Emek Piyasasında Kadın Çalışanlara Yönelik Cinsiyet Ayrımcılığı: Kahramanmaraş Tekstil Sektörü Örneği. *Selçuk Üniversitesi Sosyal Bilimler Enstitüsü Dergisi*, 39: 67–81.

Kocacık, F. ve Bilican Gökkaya, V. (2005). Türkiye'de Çalışan Kadınlar ve Sorunları. *Cumhuriyet Üniversitesi İktisadi ve İdari Bilimler Dergisi*, 6(1): 195–289.

Lockwood, N. (2004) The Glass Ceiling: Domestic and International Perspectives. *Human Resource Magazine Research Quarterly*, 49(6): 1–49.

Makal, A. (2010). Türkiye'de Erken Cumhuriyet Döneminde Kadın Emeği. *Çalışma ve Toplum*, 2(25): 13–40.

Mercanlıoğlu, Ç. (2009). Cinsiyete Dayalı Eşitsizlik; Kadın Yöneticilerin İş ve Özel Hayatlarını Dengeleme Zorlukları Ve Bedelleri. *Uluslararası Disiplinlerarası Kadın Çalışmaları Kongresi*. Sakarya: Sakarya Üniversitesi, ISBN: 978-975-7988-45-8 35–44.

Mincer, J. (1958). Investment in Human Capital and Personal Income Distribution. *The Journal of Political Economy, 66*: 28.

OECD (2018). *Key policies to promote longer working lives in Denmark*. OECD.

Önder, N. (2013). Türkiye'de Kadın İş Gücünün Görünümü. *ÇSGB Çalışma Dünyası Dergisi*, 1(1): 35–61.

Şahinli, M. A. and Şahbaz, N. (2013). Tarımda Kadın İstihdamı: Sosyal Güvenlik Kurumuna Kayıtlılık Durumu. *Karamanoğlu Mehmetbey Üniversitesi Sosyal ve Ekonomik Araştırmalar Dergisi*, 2013(2): 85–103.

Schultz, T. W. (1959). Investment in Man: An Economist View. *The Social Service Review*, 33(2): 109–117.

Şengül, G. (2012). *Ins and Outs of Unemployment in Turkey*. Central Bank of the Republic of Turkey.

Şenol, D. ve Mazman, İ. (2013). Tarihi Bir Bakışla Çalışma Hayatında Kadın. *Aile ve Kadın Sempozyumu Bildiri Kitabı*. Kırıkkale: Kırıkkale Üniversitesi Yayınları. 151–162.

Street, D. and Ní Léime, Á. (2020). Problems and Prospects for Current Policies to Extend Working Lives. In: Ní Léime Á. et al. (eds.) *Extended Working Life Policies*. Springer.

TUIK (2021). *Labor Force Statistics*. TUIK.

Tunç, M. (2007). Kayıt Dışı İstihdamla Mücadelede Geliştirilen Stratejiler Uygulanan Politikalar ve Gelişmiş Ülke Örnekleri. Uzmanlık Tezi, ÇSGB, Türkiye İş Kurumu, Ankara.

Uraz, A.; Aran, M. A.; Hüsamoğlu, M.; Okkalı Şanalmış, D. and Capar, S. (2010). *Recent trends in female labor force participation in Turkey*. State Planning Organization of the Republic of Turkey and World Bank Welfare and Social Policy Analytical Work Program Working Paper (2).

Yaşar, O. (2007). Türkiye'de kadın Eğitimi, Kadınlara Ait Diğer Göstergeler ve Çanakkale İli Örneği. *Uluslararası İnsan Bilimleri Dergisi,* 4(1): 1–35.

# Chapter 9

# Not in Education, Employment, or Training (NEET) in Turkey

Menekşe Şahin[1]

Compared to traditional workforce indicators, NEET is a relatively new concept. After 2000, the rate of growth in youth unemployment in EU nations has led to its use as an indicator of the situation facing young people without any formal training, education, or employment in the labor market. Since 2014, NEET has been utilized in the Turkish labor market. Eurostat data are used in this section to provide a general evaluation of NEET youth in Turkey. Between 2011 and 2020, NEET youth were categorized by age, gender, education level, and employment status. According to the classification, women and young people who drop out of tertiary education are more at risk.

This study analyzes the current situation, policies, and practices of young people not in employment, education, or training in Turkey, which has the highest NEET rates compared to EU and OECD member countries. Using Eurostat and OECD data, NEET status profiles for Turkey are presented with ten-year cross-sectional data. Age, gender, educational attainment, and employment status of NEET youth between 2011 and 2020 are categorized using Eurostat data in this section, which provides a general assessment of NEET youth in Turkey. The need for a coordinated study focused specifically on this population is made clear by the fact that women and young people who drop out of school pose a higher risk in the classification.

## INTRODUCTION

The sharp rise in youth unemployment rates, particularly in EU countries, has led to widespread concern about the situation of young people in the labor market across all nations, especially since the global crisis of 2007 (Bell and Blanchflower, 2022: 245). Traditional labor market indicators cannot be used to track the situation of young people because their transition from school to work involves more complicated procedures, takes longer, and they leave and reenter the workforce more frequently. Indicators of youth unemployment were insufficient to fully explain how vulnerable young people they were as entered the workforce. To better understand the economic and social vulnerabilities, labor market participation, and social exclusion risks of these young people who drop out of both work and school, new indicators are required (Eurofound, 2012: 19). In this regard, the term "NEET," which refers to young people who are neither in school nor employed, has begun to be used as a second indicator of the unemployment rate for the state of young people in the labor market.

The term "NEET" was first used to describe young people under the age of eighteen who did not engage in any form of education, employment, or training in England in 1988, following the implementation of the social assistance regime (Furlong, 2006: 553). It was used to describe young people between the ages of fifteen and twenty-four who were not enrolled in employment, education, or training in almost all EU member states in the early 2000s. In a short period, the idea began to gain acceptance in nations like Japan, New Zealand, Hong Kong, and South Korea (Eurofound, 2012: 20).

The concept of NEET is a term that encompasses more than just youth unemployment and youth who aren't working because they are in school. The concept includes young people who are not economically active due to a disability or care obligations like housework as well as the resentful young workforce who leave the labor market because they have lost hope of finding a job and are not included in unemployment rates (Tamesberger and Bacher, 2014: 1239; ILO, 2013: 38; Yates and Payne, 2006: 333; Furlong, 2006: 554). It can also draw attention to young people who have the potential to enter the labor market because the concept of NEET includes young people who have either voluntarily or involuntarily left the labor force and the educational system (Arabacı, 2020: 104). The concept of NEET has also been frequently criticized due to the heterogeneity of this group (Furlong, 2006; Cuzzocrea, 2014; Holte, 2018; Sergi, Cefalo, and Kazepov, 2018).

To comprehend the situation of young people, particularly their inactivity and vulnerability in the labor market, there is no broadly agreed definition for the term NEET. Being outside of the educational system and unemployed is the fundamental qualification for the NEET category. The selection of an age range is a symptom. Individuals in the sixteen to eighteen age range are referred to as NEETs, for instance, in the United Kingdom and New Zealand (Eurofound, 2012:1). The age range of sixteen to eighteen marks the end of compulsory schooling (Coles et al., 2002: 1). In Japan, those between the ages of fifteen and thirty-four who are single, not enrolled in school, employed, or looking for work now qualify as NEETs (Ykji, 2007: 23). In South Korea, it is a general term used to describe people aged fifteen to thirty-four who are not married, not in employment, not in school or job training, not looking for a job, and not taking care of family obligations (OECD, 2007: 3). Initially used in EU member countries for the fifteen to twenty-four age range, it has since been extended to include the fifteen to twenty-nine age range (Eurofound, 2012: 20). According to the ILO concept, it refers to young people between the ages of fifteen and twenty-four who are neither employed nor enrolled in any type of formal or informal education. It is used by the OECD to cover young people who are not enrolled in school, employment, or training. Indicators and breakdowns for the fifteen to twenty-nine age group are available in the OECD database. It is very challenging to recognize global trends or draw comparisons because there is no accepted definition for how the NEET concept is used.

Youth NEET status is maintained by a variety of factors, including supply and demand levels for restraint (Pemberton, 2008: 243), educational attainment and content, peer reactions, the burden of family caregiving, safety, and the presence of disabilities, delinquency, and substance use (Hutchinson, Beck, and Hooley, 2016: 7) in structures and profiles. NEET has numerous flaws in terms of social, economic, and individual aspects. It may have detrimental effects on young people's socioeconomic, psychological, and emotional health (Dickens and Marx, 2016: 707), including chronic unemployment, poverty, and incarceration (Backman and Nilsson, 2016: 136). Additionally, youth who spend a long time out of school and employment run the risk of social exclusion (Yates and Payne, 2006: 334). NEETs are defined by the OECD and ILO as people with incomes below the poverty line who lack the skills necessary to improve their economic circumstances. It is emphasized in the research report by Eurofound (2012) that NEETs in Europe are a huge burden on society, the economy, and labor resources. In addition to improving NEETs' employability and personal gain, the identification and reintegration of NEETs into the labor market or education also benefit the social and economic well-being of society as a whole. Being a NEET has numerous negative effects, so addressing it has also risen in importance on the list of priorities for employment and youth unemployment policies.

Although Turkey has one of the highest NEET rates in the EU and OECD, this problem is still relatively new to the Turkish labor market. Since 1945, Turkey has had a high proportion of people between the ages of fifteen and twenty-four. As we approach the 100th anniversary of the Turkish Republic, the rate of the young population, which was 29 percent in 1945, has decreased somewhat since the 2000s but is still higher than the EU member countries with a ratio of 15.3 percent (EU average: 10.6 percent). The youth workforce has always been more likely to be unemployed than adults due to the high proportion of young people in the population of working age. Furthermore, the youth unemployment rate continues to rise despite the rise in the educational levels of young people. The youth unemployment rate rose from 13.1 percent in the 2000s to 18.4 percent in 2011 and 22.6 percent in 2021, according to TURKSTAT data. These rates demonstrate how underutilized Turkey's young population is. Youth unemployment is a significant issue, particularly for the young population with higher education, according to numerous studies on the Turkish labor market (Yalçıntaş and Akkaya, 2019; Mütevellioğlu, Zanbak, and Mert, 2010; Çakır and Kellevezir, 2020). The transition from education to employment is said to be problematic (Erdayı, 2009: 145; Sayın, 2011: 39; Özaydın, 2013; Bayraktar ve İncekara, 2013; Arpat, 2018). Due to this circumstance, young people who have finished school are unable to participate in the labor market and fall into the NEET category.

The inclusion of young people in social and economic life has been a part of employment and youth unemployment policies in Turkey, which benefits from having a young population. Indicators for the NEET group have been included in the national statistical data (Turkstat) since 2014, according to the literature review conducted as part of this study's analysis of the state of labor markets for the 100th anniversary of the Republic. NEET is defined as "the young population who is unemployed and not included in the labor force but does not attend education (formal education, non-formal education, apprenticeship training) at the same time" by the Turkish Statistical Institute (TUIK).

TUIK did not give a range for the age symptom in NEET status but instead used the term "young population." The population between the ages of fifteen and twenty-four is referred to as the young population in the TUIK dataset about the young workforce. In this instance, it can be said that the NEET status as defined by TUIK includes youths between the ages of fifteen and twenty-four who are not currently enrolled in school, do not attend any formal education, or are not employed. Since 2014, annual cross-sectional data have been used to present NEET rates in Turkstat data. However, there is a dearth of information in Turkstat about the current state of NEET youth. Only breakdowns by educational level are made available for NEETs. There was no information on NEET profiles broken down by age, gender, or employment status. Because of this, descriptive statistics about young people in Turkey who are not engaged in education or employment were based on Eurostat data.

## STATUS OF NEETS IN TURKEY

Turkey has one of the highest NEET rates among OECD and EU nations. After South Africa and Brazil, Turkey has the highest NEET rate among

OECD members for young people, young men, and young women. Data from the OECD for 2021 show that Turkey's NEET rate for people aged fifteen to twenty-nine is 28.7 percent, double the average for OECD members (14.5 percent). The very high NEET rate among women is the primary cause of Turkey's high rate. The NEET rate in the relevant age group is 18.4 percent for men and 39.5 percent for women. For OECD member countries, the gender gap in NEET rates is 3.7 points on average. Turkey, however, has a much wider gap (21 points). Turkey is only better than Mexico at this level (OECD data, 2023).

NEETs are a significant issue in EU nations. The NEET rate is lower than the EU average in nations like the Netherlands, Germany, Denmark, Sweden, and Austria, despite variations among EU member states. It is higher than average in some nations, like Italy, Bulgaria, Spain, Poland, and Romania. According to the most recent Eurostat data, figure 9.1 depicts the NEET rate in Turkey and EU member states for people aged fifteen to twenty-four. According to Eurostat data, NEETs aged fifteen to twenty-four make up 10.5 percent of the EU average. The NEET rate in Turkey is 27.7 percent, which is higher than the average for the EU and higher than the rate in all other member states. Young people aged fifteen to twenty-nine are also affected by Turkey's high NEET rates. Nearly 2.5 times higher than the EU average (13.6 percent), Turkey's rate of NEET youth aged fifteen to twenty-nine is 31.5 percent.

Figure 9.2 shows the ten-year course of NEET rates in Turkey and EU member states. Turkey has a young population. The young population constitutes 15.3 percent of Turkey's population. The high proportion of the young population in the total population contributes to the high NEET rates. The NEET rate in Turkey has been well above the EU average in every year during the 2011–2020 period. The NEET prevalence of young people aged

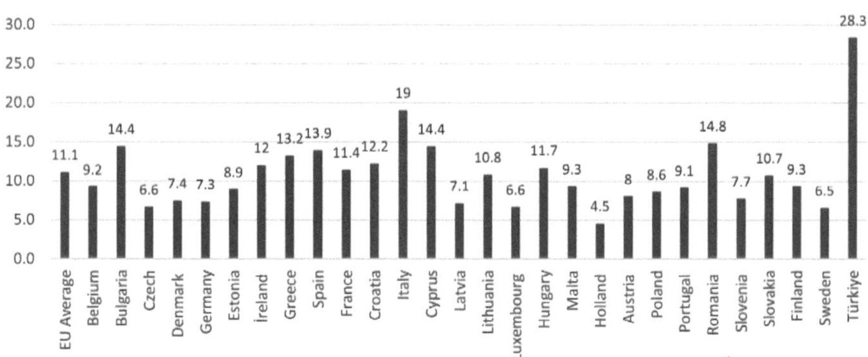


**Figure 9.1 NEET Rate between the Ages of Fifteen to Twenty-Four in EU Countries and Turkey (2020).** *Source*: Eurostat.

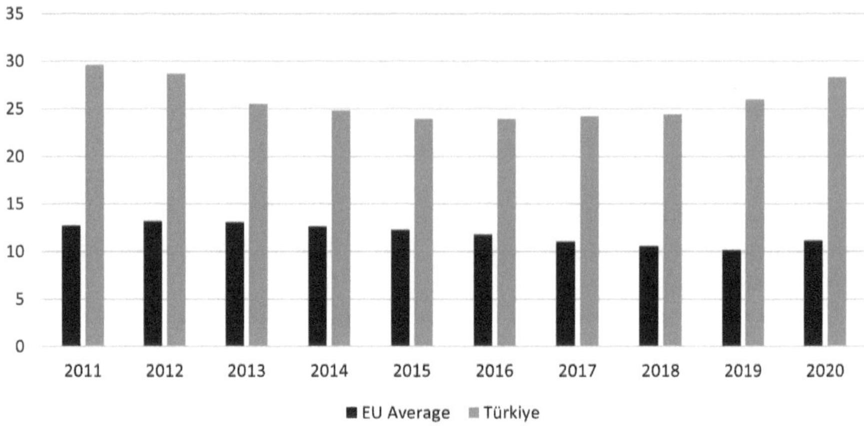


**Figure 9.2 Trends in NEET Rates for Fifteen- to Twenty-Four-Year-Olds (2011–2020).** Source: *Eurostat.*

fifteen to twenty-four in Turkey decreased from 28.7 percent to 28.3 percent between 2011 and 2020. After a relative decline in 2012–2013, there was stagnation between 2014 and 2017. After the stagnation, growth in NEET rates resumed in 2018. The share of the young population in the fifteen to twenty-four age group in the total population (from 16.8 percent in 2011 to 15.4 percent in 2020) declined over the decade. Despite the declining youth share in the total population, high NEET rates persist.

It is noteworthy that the highest decline in NEET rates in the last decade was between 2012 and 2013. This decline can be associated with the regulation on the extension of compulsory education in the same period. With Law No. 6287, compulsory education in Turkey was extended from eight to twelve years as of the 2012–2013 academic year. After Law No. 6287, the net enrollment rate in secondary education increased from 66.07 percent in 2010–2011 to 85.01 percent in 2019–2020 (TUIK, Education Indicators). The extension of the compulsory education period had an impact on NEET rates. The inclusion of the fifteen to seventeen age group in compulsory education was also reflected in the NEET rates of this age group. Eurostat data show that the rate of NEET youth aged fifteen to seventeen in Turkey has decreased compared to the general age group. The rate of NEET youth aged fifteen to seventeen decreased to 16.6 percent in 2011, 12.7 percent in 2013, and 11.1 percent in 2020. In general, extending the time spent in education can contribute to a decrease in the NEET rate. There has been an increase in the number of universities in Turkey since 2000, when the government started implementing a "one university per province" policy. The number of public and foundation universities, 71 in 2000, reached 156 in 2011 and

207 in 2020. The higher education enrollment rate increased from 33 percent in 2010–2011 to 44.4 percent in 2020–2021. The rate of NEET youth aged eighteen to twenty-four, mainly covering the time spent in higher education, decreased from 36 percent to 30.7 percent between 2011 and 2018. However, it rose again after 2018 and reached 36 percent in 2020. Figure 9.3 shows the ten-year course of the age group distribution of NEET youth. The proportion of NEET youth increases with age. According to the latest available data, the proportion of NEET youth in 2020 is 11.1 percent for fifteen- to seven-year-olds, 19.7 percent for fifteen- to nineteen-year-olds, 28.3 percent for fifteen- to twenty-four-year-olds and 32 percent for fifteen- to twenty-nine-year-olds.

NEET rates differ significantly by gender. The NEET rate among women in Turkey is 35.7 percent, more than three times higher than the EU average (11.7 percent). High NEET rates among women make Turkey the country with the highest NEET rate compared to EU countries. Notably, the NEET rate of women in Turkey has gradually decreased over the last decade. From 2011 to 2020, the female NEET rate decreased from 41.5 percent to 35.7 percent. NEET rates show a decrease for young women (−5.8 points) and an increase for young men (+4.1 points). This can be explained by the increase in women's labor force participation and the decreased unemployment rate over the decade. However, despite this decline, Turkey still has one out of every three young women neither in education nor in employment. The high NEET rate for women indicates that they are busy with household chores and/or that there are substantial institutional barriers limiting women's participation in labor markets (ILO, 2013: 38).

Women's low educational attainment, labor force participation rates, and employment rates are significant problems in the Turkish labor market. Studies focusing on women's employment in Turkey agree that women's

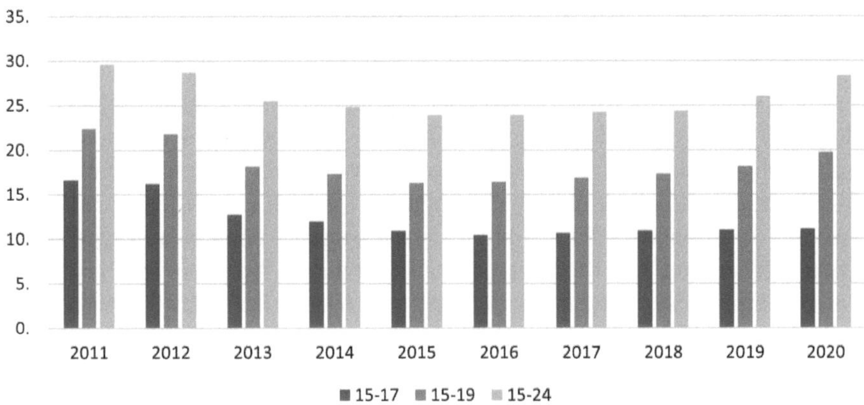


**Figure 9.3 NEET Rates by Age Groups in Türkiye (2011–2020).** *Source*: Eurostat.

underrepresentation in employment is a result of traditional gender representation and specific labor market characteristics. Family care activities are still primarily the responsibility of women (Aşkın, 2018; Durmaz, 2016; Öz and Peri, 2019). Gender differentiation among NEETs in Turkey is significantly high. While there was a 0.5 percentage point difference between the NEET rates of men and women in the EU average in 2011, this difference decreased to 0.1 percentage point in 2020. Gender differentiation in NEET rates is relatively high in Turkey. Although the gender gap in NEET rates shows a decreasing trend between 2011 and 2020 (from 24 points to 14 points), it is still more prominent than in all European countries. The reason for such a high gender gap is gender-based discrimination, which is one of the consequences of a malfunctioning labor market (Işık, 2016: 134). Policies, programs, and strategies on gender equality over the last decade have had a noticeable impact on reducing NEET rates among women. However, it is significantly higher compared to both EU and OECD countries.

TurkStat data on the number of young people who are NEET in Turkey have been available since 2014. In Turkey, it is noteworthy that NEET rates increase as educational attainment increases, except for illiterates. The distribution of NEETs by education level is 81.4 percent for illiterates, 23.1 percent for those with less than high school education, 26.7 percent for high school, 34.2 percent for vocational or technical high school, and 41.7 percent for higher education. In the study by Uysal and Acar (2019) analyzing the situation of NEET youth in the fifteen to nineteen age group, it is argued that although compulsory education has increased to twelve years, one-third of young people remain outside the education system and do not continue their high school education. According to TUIK data, it is noteworthy that the highest increase in NEET rates between 2014 and 2020 was in higher education graduates, with 13.9 points. It increased by 11.6 points for vocational and technical high school graduates, 7 points for high school graduates, and 3.8 points for illiterates. It decreased by 0.7 points for graduates below high school.

NEET rates are higher for women than men according to the level of education completed. When the NEET rates by educational attainment are analyzed by gender, it is 75.7 percent for illiterate, 16.3 percent for those with less than high school education, 21.6 percent for high school level, 26.3 percent for vocational or technical high school, and 35.8 percent for higher education. For women, it is 85.3 percent for illiterate, 30.8 percent for those with less than high school education, 31.8 percent in high school, 43.1 percent in vocational or technical high school, and 45.7 percent in higher education.

Just like the highest unemployment rate in Turkey, the highest NEET rates are also observed among higher education graduates. As of 2020, the unemployment rate among young higher education graduates is 35.8 percent, and the NEET rate is 41.7 percent. Many researchers suggest that the higher NEET rate, especially among higher education graduates, may indicate significant discouragement and skills mismatch (ILO, 2013; Caroleo et al., 2018). In Turkey, the number of universities has increased since the 2000s, and participation in higher education has increased. However, the ineffective transition from education to employment is an essential reason for youth unemployment.

Eurostat data show that most of the NEET youth in Türkiye are inactive youth who are not looking for a job for various reasons. According to labor force status, 21 percent of NEETs are out of the inactive workforce, and 7 percent are unemployed young people. From 2011 to 2020, the rate of NEET out of the labor force decreased by only 3.3 points. However, NEET young women are less active in the labor market compared to men. The majority of NEET men and women are inactive young people who are not looking for a job. These young people are considered "at risk" as they are unemployed and/or inactive and do not have access to learning opportunities. They are also at risk of disengagement from the labor market and society in general (Maguire, 2015: 123).

According to TurkStat data, the reasons why young people do not participate in the labor force for young men are: not finding a job suitable for their skills despite having previously searched for a job, attending classes or courses, and continuing education or training. Among young women, family-child-patient care responsibilities stand out as the reason for not participating in the labor force.

## POLITICAL INTERVENTIONS AND PRACTICES

NEET and youth unemployment are related concepts. However, there are essential differences between the two. Interventions to reduce youth unemployment will contribute to reducing the number of NEETs by preventing young people from potentially becoming NEETs. However, this will not be a sufficient intervention to manage NEET (Furlong 2006: 559; Eurofound 2012: 19). While there is no doubt that policies focused on reducing NEET rates are important, the heterogeneity of this group requires specific policy interventions.

In Turkey, policies and practices aimed at combating unemployment have been expanded over the last decade. In these practices, particular interventions have been included for the high youth unemployment rate. Turkish Employment Agency (ISKUR) has increased the number and variety of active employment programs. Within the scope of active employment programs, many programs such as vocational and skills training, internship and workplace practices to support the transition from school to employment, job and vocational counseling, career training and guidance, promotion of entrepreneurship, and financial incentives for employers have been implemented (Baykal and Bayat, 2020: 84; Şahin, 2020: 139). Although these programs do not directly target NEETs, they can be seen as practices that reduce their potential to become NEETs. However, policy interventions that directly target NEETs and aim to manage the existing NEET potential will be encountered after 2020.

The most important top policy documents for Turkish labor markets and employment policies are considered to be the Development Plans and the National Employment Strategy (2014–2023). The first top policy document in Turkey that emphasizes this group by using the concept of NEET is the 10th Development Plan (2014–2018). One of the priority transformation plans defined by the 10th Development Plan was the "Basic and Vocational Skills Development Program." The objectives of the program are: (1) increasing the weight of basic skills in education levels, (2) developing lifelong learning programs that provide basic skills, (3) Strengthening the link between the labor market and the education system, and (4) reducing the number of young people not in employment and education. For the first time, the program sets a target for NEETs. However, there is no indicator in the program to directly monitor the performance of the policies and implementations to be put forward to realize this target. The performance indicators of the program are determined as the transition time from school to work, the number of people working in a job suitable for their skill level, the number of young people receiving basic skills training, and the long-term unemployment rate among young people. Within the scope of the "Priority Transformation Program for Basic and Vocational Skills Development" of the Development Plan, it aims to improve young people's basic skills. TEA is responsible for the necessary practices for this target. ISKUR's responsibilities include: expanding contact points at universities, providing job search skills training for secondary education and senior university students, preparing materials and a website on job search and occupation, and revising active labor force programs to provide basic skills. There are no direct targets for NEETs in the program components. However, the program components, making the young workforce more attractive to employers and improving the primary and personal skills of young people in the education system, will contribute to reducing the number of NEETs.

The most important policy document that sets priorities and targets in the labor market in Turkey is the National Employment Strategy. However, NEETs are not directly addressed in the National Employment Strategy. The 2023 targets of the National Employment Strategy include reducing the unemployment rate to 5 percent, increasing the employment rate to 55 percent, and reducing the informal employment rate for nonagricultural sectors to below 15 percent. The policy axis of strengthening the education-employment relationship has been identified to address these objectives. The strategy sees unemployment more as an education problem. It gave more space to interventions aimed at preventing young people who are currently going through the education system from becoming unemployed. These interventions include making young people more attractive to employers, trying to raise their achievements/skills in school, and promoting lifelong learning to acquire basic and vocational skills. Such interventions to orient young people toward education or employment are important to prevent young people from becoming potential NEETs. They are measures that can effectively reduce the number of NEETs in the long term.

It took until 2021 to prepare a strategic plan to manage or reduce the current NEET population in line with the National Employment Strategy targets. The only intervention in Turkey that explicitly targets NEETs by directly emphasizing the concept of NEETs is the "National Youth Employment Strategy 2021–2023 (UGIS)." UGIS was prepared in line with the objectives and policies of the National Employment Strategy. The measures, targets, and policies for young people under the main policy axes of the National Employment Strategy, namely Strengthening the Education-Employment Relationship and Increasing the Employment of Groups in Need of Special Policies, are monitored in this document.

In addition to reducing youth unemployment and increasing youth participation in the labor force, the UGIS aims to reduce the NEET rate. The NEET rate is targeted to be reduced to 20 percent in 2023. The UGIS document emphasizes the development of special policy measures due to the high NEET rates in Turkey and includes the following targets:

- Increasing research, orientation, and promotion activities to increase the employment of NEETs.
- Prioritizing Turkish Employment Agency services for young people identified as potential NEETs.
- Increasing infrastructure and training activities to increase the employment of NEETs.

NGIS can be seen as an essential step toward managing NEETs, apart from preventing NEETs. The NGIS is important for the management of NEETs in two ways. It is the recognition of the heterogeneous nature of this group and the need for specific policy interventions different from youth unemployment. The UGIS envisages researching the profiles of existing NEETs and the reasons for their nonparticipation in education and employment as the first strategic action. In line with the results of the profile study, it is aimed that

ISKUR will implement the necessary programs and practices by considering why young people become NEET. It also envisages the integration of the institutions of the Ministry of Labor and Social Security, Ministry of National Education, Higher Education Institution, ISKUR, and TurkStat for policy measures specific to NEETs. The Ministry of Labor and Social Security has been identified as responsible for the action.

## CONCLUSION

This analysis investigates young people in the fifteen to twenty-four age group who are not involved in any education, training, or employment process, a new Turkish labor market term called NEET. NEET, a new concept in the Turkish labor market, has been included in national employment and labor force indicators since 2014. The current situation of NEET youth in Turkey for ten years is analyzed. NEET youth in Turkey who are not in education and employment are analyzed in terms of gender, age, labor market status, and educational attainment. The rate of NEET youth in Turkey has been considerably higher than the averages of EU and OECD countries in all periods of the decade. This high trend applies to NEETs among both young women and young men. Over the decade, NEET rates decreased by only one percentage point, from 29 percent to 28 percent. The highest decline (−3.2 points) between 2011 and 2020 was observed in 2013. The increase in the duration of compulsory education to twelve years was effective in this decrease.

Higher than in all EU member states, the NEET rate among young men increased from 17.1 percent to 21.2 percent over the decade. In Turkey, young men are NEET because they could not find a job suitable to their skills despite having looked for a job before and because they were attending classes or courses. For young women, being busy with housework and family and childcare responsibilities are the main reasons for being NEET.

In Turkey, the NEET rate (excluding illiterates) increases as the level of education increases. There is a continuous increase in the NEET rate of higher education graduates. From 2011 to 2020, the NEET rate of higher education graduates increased from 27.8 percent to 41.7 percent. Despite the increase in the compulsory duration of education, the expansion of higher education, and the widening of participation, the NEET rate of educated graduates has continued to rise in Turkey over the last decade. Education is the key element of the transition to employment. Extending the time spent on education contributes to a decrease in the NEET rate. This is because the time spent in education is expected to improve the skill level. Therefore, higher education is considered to have a protective effect against becoming NEET. Increasing the number of educational institutions alone has been insufficient to contribute to the decrease in NEET rates. It is necessary to ensure the sustainability of opportunity spaces where young people can use the vocational knowledge they receive from educational institutions.

The problem of NEET youth is addressed through policies and programs with specific targets at the EU and member state levels. It is monitored as an important indicator of the labor market. Despite the high NEET rates in Turkey, no policy documents (within this study's reference period) directly target this group. In the decade-long process, NEET youth have not been seen as a particular group that should be evaluated separately from youth unemployment. The first top policy document to emphasize this group using the NEET concept was the 10th Development Plan. The Plan aims to reduce the number of NEET youth by addressing them under the Priority Transformation Program for Basic and Vocational Skills Development. However, there is no indicator to monitor this target or a strategic plan within the Plan period. However, NEET youth are a heterogeneous group. There are differences between NEET and unemployed youth. Programs to prevent youth unemployment can prevent young people currently in education from becoming NEET.

Moreover, this can contribute to reducing the number of NEETs. However, this will not be a sufficient intervention to manage NEET. The distinction between policies and practices that seek to prevent young people from becoming NEET and those that seek to reengage with those who are NEET seems to have been overlooked.

NEET is a much newer concept in Turkey than in Europe. The fact that discussions and policies for young people in Turkey have mainly focused on unemployment has postponed addressing the problems of young people not being employed or educated. The first policy document in which NEET youth are considered differently from the unemployed youth is the National Youth Employment Strategy 2021–2031, issued in 2021. The goal of "reducing the number of NEET youth" in the National Youth Employment Strategy can be considered as a step toward researching the profiles and characteristics of this group, identifying their needs, generating relevant data, developing comprehensive policies and programs to solve the problem, and establishing indicators to ensure monitoring. In addition to the existing approaches to develop policies against rapidly increasing levels of youth unemployment, it is crucial to consider NEET youth separately. A fundamental need for policy interventions on NEETs is descriptive, inclusive research focusing on needs analysis. NEETs can be managed and attracted to education or employment through policies addressing the identified problems.

## NOTE

1. Assoc. Prof. Dr., Hitit University, Faculty of Health Sciences, Department of Social, Çorum, Turkey, meneksesahin@hitit.edu.tr.

## REFERENCES


Arabacı, R. Y. (2020). The Socio-Demographic Structure of Young People Neither in Education nor in Employment in Turkey and Its Connection with the Labor Market. *Journal of Amme Administration, 53*(3), 103–130.

Arpat, B. (2018). The Role and Importance of On-the-Job Training Applied in Vocational Schools in Combating Youth Unemployment in Turkey: Honaz Vocational School Case. *Çalışma ve Toplum, 2018*(4), 2193–2229.

Aşkın, E. Ö. (2018). Factors Affecting Women's Position in the Labor Market. *Gaziosmanpaşa University Journal of Social Sciences Research,* 10(1), 100–120.

Backman, O. and Nilsson, A. (2016). Long-term Consequences of Being Not in Employment, Education or Training as a Young Adult. Stability and Change in Three Swedish Birth Cohorts. *European Societies*, 136–157.

Baykal, B. and Bayat, İ. K. (2020). The Outlook of Youth Unemployment in Turkey and Measures to Prevent Youth Unemployment within the Framework of the National Employment Strategy. *İş, Güç Journal of Industrial Relations and Human Resources, 22*(3), 81–102.

Bayraktar, S. and İncekara, A. (2013). Turkey'nin Genç İşsizlik Profili. *Çalışma İlişkileri Degisi, 4*(1), 15–38.

Bell, D. and Blanchflower, D. (2022). Young People and the Great Recession. *Oxford Review of Economic Policy, 27*(2), 241–267.

Çakır, Ö. and Kellevezir, I. (2020). The Phenomenon of Unemployment and Qualification Mismatch in Higher Education Graduates: An Evaluation in the Light of Uni-Veri Research Results. *Journal of Labor Relations, 1*(Special Issue), 1–7.

Caroleo, F., Demidova, O., Marelli, E. and Signorelli, M. (2018). *Young People and the Labour Market.* Oxford: A Comparative Perspective: Routledge.

Coles, B., Hutton, S., Bradshaw, J., Craig, G., Godfrey, C. and Johnson, J. (2002). *Literature Review of the Costs of Being "Not in Education, Employment or Training" at age 16–18.* Department for Education and Skills Research Report, Colegate: Norwich, NR3 1BQ..

Cuzzocrea, V. (2014). *Projecting the Category of NEET into the Future. In Perspectives on Youth.* Strasbourg Cedex: Council of Europe.

Dickens, L. and Marx, P. (2016). NEET as an Outcome for Care Leavers in South Africa: The Case of Girls and Boys Town. *Emerging Adulthood, 8*(1), 64–72.

Durmaz, Ş. (2016). Women in the Labor Market and the Barriers They Face. *Ahi Evran University Journal of Institute of Social Sciences, 2*(3), 37–60.

Eurofound. (2012). *NEETs Young People not in Employment, Education or Training: Characteristics, Costs and Policy Responses in Europe.* Luxembourg: Publications Office of the European Union.

Eurostat. (2022). Retrieved July 20, 2022 from https://ec.europa.eu/eurostat/databrowser/view/LFSI_NEET_Q/default/table?lang=en&category=educ.educ_outc.edatt.edatt0.edatt0_https://ec.europa.eu/eurostat/databrowser/view/LFSI_NEET_Q/default/table?lang=en&category=educ.educ_outc.edatt.edatt0.edatt0_

Furlong, A. (2006). Not a Very NEET Solution: Representing Problematic Labour Market Transitions among Early School-leavers. *Work, Employment and Society, 20*(3), 553–569.

Holte, B. H. (2018). Counting and Meeting NEET Young People: Methodology, Perspective and Meaning in Research on Marginalized Youth. *Young, 26*, 1–16. doi:10.1177/1103308816677618

Hutchinson, J., Beck, V. and Hooley, T. (2016). Delivering NEET Policy Packages? A Decade of NEET Policy in England. *Journal of Education and Work, 29*(6), 707–727.

ILO (2013). *Global Employment Trends for Youth 2013: A Generation at Risk.* Geneva: International Labour Organization.

Işık, V. (2016). Youth Unemployment and Inertia in the Young Population in Turkey. *Labor and Society, 5*(11), 130–146.

Maguire, S. (2015). NEET, Unemployed, Inactive or Unknown—Why Does It Matter?. *Educational Research, 57*(2), 121–132.

Mütevellioğlu, N., Zanbak, M. and Mert, M. (2010). Unemployment, University Youth and the Future: Findings of a Field Research. *Cumhuriyer University, Journal of Faculty of Economics and Administrative Sciences, 11*(1), 207–229.

OECD. (2007). *Jobs for Youth/Des emplois pour les jeunes: Korea 2007.* Paris: OECD Publishing.

OECD Data. (2022). OECD 2022 Youth Not in Employment, Education or Training (NEET) Indicatör. Retrieved May 12, 2022, from https://data.oecd.org/youthinac/youth-not-in-employment-education-or-training-neet.htm

Öz, C. S. and Peri, D. (2019). Women's Employment in Turkey and the European Union: A Comparison in the Context of Welfare Regimes. *Journal of Labor Relations, 10*(2), 1–26.

Pemberton, S. (2008). Tackling the NEET Generation and the Ability of Policy to Generate a NEET Solution - Evidence from the UK. *Government and Policy, 26*(1), 243–259.

Şahin, I. F. (2020). Youth Unemployment and Fighting Methods. *Journal of Youth Research,* 8(20), 135–153.

Sergi, V., Cefalo, S. and Kazepov, Y. (2018). Young People's Disadvantages on the Labour Market in Italy: Reframing the NEET Category, 23(1): 41–60.

Tamesberger, D. and Bacher, J. (2014). NEET Youth in Austria: A Typology Including Socio- demography, Labour Market Behaviour and Permanence. *Journal of Youth Studies, 17*(9), 1239–1259. doi: 10.1080/13676261.2014.901492

Uysal, G. and Acar, U. (2019). 1.3 Million 15–19 Year Olds Neither in Education nor in Employment. Research Note, 19/242. BETAM-Bahçeşehir University.

Yalçıntaş, A. and Akkaya, B. (2019). Academic Inflation in Turkey: The Turkish Higher Education System after the "One University for Each Province Policy". *Ankara University SBF Journal, 74*(3), 789–810.

Yates, S. and Payne, M. (2006). Not so NEET? A Critique of the Use of "NEET" in Setting Targets for Interventions with Young People. *Journal of Youth Studies, 9*, 329–344. doi: 10.1080/13676260600805671

Ykji, G. (2007). Jobless youths and the NEET problem in Japan. *Social Science Japan Journal, 10*(1), 23–40.

# *Chapter 10*

# Working Poor in Turkey

Suheyla Erikli Selek[1]

In almost every slice of history, one of the important problem areas of working life is the group that cannot get rid of poverty despite working. This problem was also addressed in the work titled *Capital* written by Karl Marx in the 1860s. It has been stated that wages play an important role in the well-being of the individual for the group that has no income other than their labor. The neoliberal understanding of the economy and the policies implemented throughout the world in the 1980s led to the widening of the scope of the problem by covering almost every group in employment as well as the working poor group. The production of data on the related problem since the 2000s has increased the visibility of the problem.

This study aims to determine the current situation by revealing the dimensions and causes of working poverty in Turkey in the last century. The last ten-year period has been examined in more detail based on data. In the study, secondary data from various institutions, especially the data of the Turkish Statistical Institute (TUIK) and the European Union Statistical Office (Eurostat), were used. When the Turkish labor market is analyzed, it is seen that the people employed in the agricultural sector from the 1920s to the 2010s are more dominant than the people employed in other sectors. In the data after 2010, it is seen that the risk of working poverty in the agricultural sector is higher than in other sectors. Based on these two pieces of information, it can be stated that the risk of working poverty in the Turkish labor market between 1920 and 2010 is at a significant level. As a result of the secondary data in the study, it has been determined that the factors of the individual's age, education level, household structure, working styles, and quality of work are effective on the risk of working poverty in Turkey. In light of current data, it is seen that working poverty in Turkey is considerably higher than the EU average, but over the years, this ratio has decreased by about five points to

13 percent. The risk of working poor is higher in men than in women, those with a low level of education, those who work in a permanent job, those who work for less than one year, those who work for one year, and those who work part-time than those who work full-time.

## INTRODUCTION

The Industrial Revolution led to the expansion of the wage-working population. This situation has made it necessary for countries to make regulations regarding working life, such as determining the duration of work and right to leave. Thus, modern labor relations emerged (Castel, 2017: 107). But, this period also brought many problems related to working life. One of these problems is the emergence of a group defined as the working poor. The starting point of the working poor concept is the labor–wage relationship. This group describes people who, despite their work, cannot earn enough wages to lift themselves out of poverty (LegCo, 2006). In Marx's words, wages are the most important determinant of the poverty problem for the group that has no income other than their labor.

The neoliberal policies implemented after 1980 and the globalization process throughout the world played a major role in the development of working poverty (Gilbert, 2002; van Kersbergen, 2000; Visser, 2005; Western, 1995; O'Higgins & Moscariello, 2017).

In this period, states made regulations in many areas to adapt to international competition. Social welfare practices have been restricted, mechanisms supporting the free market have been put into practice, and the labor market has been flexible (flexibility in wages, jobs, employment, and qualifications). If labor markets are not flexible, labor costs will increase and companies will shift their production to countries with lower costs. This will prevent investment in countries with high labor costs (Standing, 2014: 19).

Standing explains the impact of globalization on the labor market with "Prekarya," which he defines as the child of globalization (Standing, 2014: 22). The precariat is closely related to the concept of insecurity working. Working conditions become "precarious" when the standard employment relationship based on full-time, permanent employment with a single employer is replaced by temporary contracts. Precarious work has become widespread throughout the world, and employment conditions that offer limited rights and provide limited protection against risks have become the norm (Goldring & Landolt, 2012). The precariatization process causes the destabilization of stable jobs and deforms jobs within the scope of social protection. At the same time, it causes newly created jobs to be temporary and insecure (Castel, 2017: 366–373).

This transformation resulting from the globalization process and economic policies have created a dual structure in the labor market. While primary jobs are jobs that employ fewer people, are open to career development, employ qualified workers, and have a high wage level, secondary jobs consist of jobs that have low wages, high turnover rate, and include a large part of the workforce. Therefore, while the globalization process suppresses the wages and social rights of unskilled labor, it raises the wages of high-level labor to a very high level. While highly skilled people can find a job in the global market, unskilled labor has to make do with the conditions of the domestic market (Kazgan, 2009: 270).

It should be noted that the epidemic, which was detected in Wuhan, China, in 2019, is another process that negatively affected the labor market and led to the expansion of the working poor group. It is stated that the COVID-19 epidemic is the most severe crisis after the Great Depression in the 1930s (ILO, 2021: 1). According to the International Labor Organization (ILO), in 2020, around 200 million people lost their jobs in the COVID-19 pandemic worldwide. Additionally, it has been determined that there has been a decrease of approximately 50 percent in working hours of those in employment. This situation creates great downward pressure on the wages of those in employment. Thus, according to the ILO, 108 million people worldwide joined the working poor or extremely poor group in 2020, compared to the previous year, due to the COVID-19 epidemic.

In Turkey, as in the rest of the world, the measures taken within the scope of combating COVID-19 have led to losses in employment and working time in many sectors, especially services, in the labor market. In the February–August period of 2020, the decrease in employment rates is estimated to be 7 percent. In the accommodation sector, where the most employment loss is experienced, this decrease has reached 30 percent. It is observed that employment losses are higher for youth and women than for adults and men. In addition, this process prevented the increase in employment. In the study conducted by the ILO, it was stated that the general employment level would have exceeded 29 million without COVID-19, while this number remained at the level of 27 million due to the effect of COVID-19 (ILO, 2020).

In this study, the working poor is examined through Eurostat data by comparing Turkey and the EU average between 2010 and 2020, which we accept as the starting limit of a new world. According to Eurostat, a person with a disposable income below 60 percent of the national average income despite working more than half of the year is at risk of poverty (Eurofound, 2018). The work is structured around three parts. First of all, the concept of working poverty and its causes are examined and a conceptual framework is formed. Then, the developments in the labor market in the development of the working poor problem in Turkey are examined. In the last part of the study, the working poverty data of Eurostat are used to compare Turkey and the EU country average.

## WORKING POVERTY

Until the sixteenth century, the problem of poverty was explained by relating it to the characteristics of the individual, natural conditions, epidemics, and factors such as war. In the agricultural society of medieval Europe, the poor who lived on charity were not disturbed; on the contrary, they attributed a positive function to their existence. In this period, the rich believed that they gave peace to their souls by giving alms (Buğra, 2010: 36). However, in the seventeenth century, poverty was associated with individual causes. In this process, it is seen that institutions were opened especially in France for individuals who prefer to beg despite having the ability to work. These institutions also constitute the basic building blocks of social policy (Jütte, 2011: 141–142). This is related to the fact that "labor" is at the center of the (capitalist) economic order that has been valid since the emergence of European capitalism. It is seen that the way to increase the wealth of a nation is to increase the use of labor and in this process, labor is considered as a production factor that should not be wasted. This perspective has led to the evaluation of the poor as the "labor force." Thus, the cause of poverty was seen as the result of the individual's unwillingness to work due to his incompetence or laziness (Buğra, 2010: 36–42).

However, on the other hand, many thinkers before the nineteenth century, including Adam Smith, defended the idea that a person's income by working may not be able to make a living due to reasons such as work irregularity or low wages. The Speenhamland Act, which came into force in England in 1795, was built on this understanding. The judges meeting in Speenhamland, near Newbury, decided that the poor should be given a minimum income regardless of their earnings. Accordingly, the difference that arises when the wages fall below a minimum subsistence limit determined according to the price of bread has been completed by using public resources. Thus, it was foreseen that the working poor could be prevented from falling into misery (Polanyi, 2014: 126; Buğra, 2010: 44).

The idea that an individual could not escape from poverty even if he took part in employment came to the fore again in the 1970s. The concept was used for the first time in the United States to describe the problems of families working in poor conditions and low wages were seen as the main determinant of working poverty (Gündoğan, 2007; Bennet, 2014). Low wages are closely related to nonstandard forms of work such as part-time work and temporary employment contracts. Low work intensity, which is more common in nonstandard forms of work, significantly increases the risk of working poverty (Gautie & Ponthieux, 2016; Horemans & Marx, 2013; Marx & Nolan, 2014; Korpi, 2003; Pierson, 2001).

The European Union's "European Employment Strategy," published in 2003, aimed to reduce the number of working poor in the fight against poverty and exclusion. For this purpose, in the same year, indicators were added to the "Income and Living Conditions Research" to detect working poverty. The working poverty outlook of countries has been monitored in terms of various variables since 2003.

When the literature is examined, it is seen that working poverty is measured in different scopes and methods. In terms of scope, it is divided into two approaches based on the individual and the household. In terms of method, some studies are based on the wage income of the individual, while in some studies it is calculated over the wage and nonwage total income. Accordingly, the working poverty data are obtained by dividing the total income of the household where the working individual lives by the number of people living in the household. Therefore, the working poor can be defined as a situation where the total net income of the working individual's household is insufficient to meet the needs (Hick & Lanau, 2017: 5).

In approaches based on the individual, if the individual's income falls below the absolute poverty line, working poverty occurs. For example, the ILO defines individuals with an income below $3.20 a day as the working poor and those who earn less than $1.90 as the overworked poor. Worldwide, extreme poverty among working people decreased from 31.6 percent in 1994 to 7.1 percent in 2019. Moderate working poverty fell from 21.2 percent to 12.2 percent. However, despite this, one out of every five workers is in the working poor group today (ILO, 2020: 37).

Eurostat data used in this study, on the other hand, are a measure based on household income. According to Eurostat, a person with a disposable income below 60 percent of the national average income level despite working more than half of the year is at risk of poverty (Eurofound, 2018). Since the Eurostat definition is based on household income, it is closely related to social transfers and thus to the welfare regime of the country.

## CAUSES OF EMPLOYEE POVERTY

The concept of working poverty is related to both employment and poverty. This makes it difficult to determine the causes of the problem. However, in general, it is possible to consider the cause of working poverty in three categories: micro, mezzo, and macro (Spannegel, 2013: 13).

Micro approaches focus on low wages (Cooke & Lawton, 2008). When the reasons for the low wage of the individual are examined, the low level of education, lack of qualifications and skills, inexperience, taking part in nonstandard forms of employment (part-time work, etc.), being an immigrant, and being young or a woman are effective. Most of these factors also constitute factors that increase the risk of poverty (Lohmann & Andreß, 2008: 304). The ILO explains the problem of working poverty at a micro level. According to the ILO, working poverty arises as a result of a lack of "decent work" in the labor market. The importance of decent work policies (adequate earnings, job security, and a safe working environment) is emphasized in tackling the problem.

Mezzo approaches focus on household composition. In this approach, the total income of the household, the size of the household, the number of dependent people in the household (children, the elderly, the disabled), the number of unemployed in the household, the single earner, and/or single-parent family structure are effective.

Macro approaches focus on the welfare practices/policies of countries. According to this approach, the fact that the problem of working poverty is related to nonwage incomes and household structure shows that there is a relationship between working poverty and welfare policies (Lohmann & Marx, 2008; Lohmann, 2009, 2010). As the welfare practices of the countries will increase the welfare of the households, it will reduce the rate of working poverty. For example, child benefit in Germany represents one of the most important transfers in reducing working poverty (Lohmann & Marx, 2008: 19).

In addition to the causal explanation, by some researchers working poverty is defined through three elements (Goerne, 2011: 5). These are job quality (remuneration levels), amount of work (household member's participation in the labor market), and household expenditures (cost of dependents) (Hick & Lanau, 2017: 7).

- Work quality (remuneration levels): The ILO defines work quality as three elements: adequate earnings, work safety, and a safe working environment. When the concept is analyzed in terms of working poverty, "wage level" is meant. In other words, being in employment alone is not enough to protect against poverty. The wage level must be at a level that will protect against poverty.
- The amount of work (the participation of household members in the labor market): Since the working base onculated on the basis of the household, the number of employees in the household plays a decisive role.

- Household expenses (cost of dependents): As the number of children increases, household expenditures increase. In this case, even if individuals are employed, they can be working in poverty.

## OVERVIEW OF WORKING POVERTY IN TURKEY

This section consists of the titles Overview of Employee Poverty from 2002 to 2009, Individual and Demographic Factors Effective in Employee Poverty: 2011–2020, and The Effect of Labor Market Structure on Employee Poverty.

### Overview of Employee Poverty from 2002 to 2009

When Turkey's labor relations history is examined in general, it is seen that the Second World War, economic crises, and coups cause the wage level to decrease and increase the risk of working poverty. It is possible to state that the regulations made to protect employees, especially the Labor Laws, the Union and Collective Bargaining Law, and the Minimum Wage Regulation since the 1930s, have a positive effect on wages and reduce the risk of working poverty. However, these regulations have provided a partial improvement, and it has been emphasized since the Second Development Plan (1968–1972) that the welfare of the employees should be increased and that the wages should be at a level that would ensure the livelihood and welfare of the individual.

On the other hand, until the 1980s, the rural population (56 percent) was higher than the urban population (44 percent), and there was a labor market structure predominantly based on the agricultural sector. Due to the higher risk of poverty in the agricultural sector compared to other sectors, it can be stated that the risk of working poverty and unregistered employment was high until the 1980s.

Since the 1980s, the decrease in the role of the state in the economy, the transition to a free market economy, and the increase in privatizations have reduced the welfare level of the working group (Gül, 2006: 303–304). As a reflection of the globalization process and liberal economic policies, the gaining of flexible working styles has had a downward effect on wage levels. In addition, the state's restrictions on the services it provides in the fields of social assistance, education, and health caused a decline in the welfare level of the households. These factors increase the risk of working poverty.

Data on working poverty in Turkey began to be created in the 2010s. The Household Budget survey, which was started to be implemented by TURKSTAT in 2002 and ended in 2009, does not include direct data on "working poverty" but within the scope of poverty data; it is possible to evaluate it within the scope of the study because it provides data on those who are in employment and work below the poverty line.

**Table 10.1 Poverty Rates of Individuals by Employment Status and Sector (%), 2002–2009**

| | *2002* | *2003* | *2004* | *2005* | *2006* | *2007* | *2008* | *2009* |
|---|---|---|---|---|---|---|---|---|
| Status at work | | | | | | | | |
| Paid, salaried | 13.64 | 15.28 | 10.35 | 6.57 | 6.00 | 5.82 | 5.93 | 6.05 |
| Jobber | 45.01 | 43.09 | 37.52 | 32.12 | 28.63 | 26.71 | 28.56 | 26.86 |
| Self-employed | 29.91 | 32.38 | 30.48 | 26.22 | 22.06 | 22.89 | 24.10 | 22.49 |
| Employer | 8.99 | 8.84 | 6.94 | 4.80 | 3.75 | 3.15 | 1.87 | 2.33 |
| Unpaid family worker | | | | | | | | |
| Sector | | | | | | | | |
| Agriculture | 36.42 | 39.89 | 40.88 | 37.24 | 33.86 | 32.05 | 37.97 | 33.01 |
| Industry | 20.89 | 21.34 | 15.64 | 9.85 | 10.12 | 9.70 | 9.71 | 9.63 |
| Service | 25.82 | 16.76 | 12.36 | 8.68 | 7.23 | 7.35 | 6.82 | 7.16 |

*Source*: TURKSTAT, 2009 Poverty Survey Results.

Between 2002 and 2009, it is seen that poverty rates have decreased in terms of the status of individuals at work and the sector they work in. It is thought that this situation is due to the increase in social assistance and transfer expenditures and wage levels. According to the situation at work, the poverty rate of those in the employer group is at the lowest level. The most impoverished group is casual and unpaid family workers. When examined from a sectoral point of view, it is seen that the poverty rate among the workers in the agricultural sector is quite high compared to the industry and service sectors. The sector with the lowest number of working poor is service.

## Individual and Demographic Factors Effective on Working Poverty in Turkey: 2011–2020

In the Turkish labor market, as of 2020, approximately 24 million people are actively insured and 12 million are paid workers (industry, construction, trade, and service) (SGK, 2020). Half of those who are actively insured under the Social Security Institution (SGK) are paid employees. In this section, working poverty in Turkey for the period 2010–2019 has been examined in terms of individual, demographic, and labor market (accordıng to table 10.1).

There has been a significant decrease in the risk of working poverty in Turkey in the last ten years. Working poverty decreased from 18 percent in 2011 to 13.1 percent in 2019 with a decrease of about five percentage points. Despite this, it has a rate above the EU average. While working poverty fluctuated between 8 percent and 9 percent in the EU average in the years examined, this rate is about 4–5 points higher in Turkey.

There has been a significant improvement in working poverty in the 18–24 age group compared to other age groups in Turkey. While the risk of

**Table 10.2 Working Poverty Risk by Age Groups, Gender, Education Level, and Household Structure (%), 2011–2019**

| | | *2011* | *2012* | *2013* | *2014* | *2014* | *2016* | *2017* | *2018* | *2019* |
|---|---|---|---|---|---|---|---|---|---|---|
| Working poverty | AB-28 | 8.3 | 8.8 | 8.9 | 9.0 | 9.5 | 9.5 | 9.6 | 9.4 | 9.4 |
| | TR | 18.0 | 16.0 | 15.3 | 14.9 | 14.4 | 13.7 | 13.5 | 12.8 | 13.1 |
| Age | | | | | | | | | | |
| 18–24 | AB-28 | 11.2 | 11.7 | 11.2 | 12.9 | 12.3 | 12.1 | 10.9 | 12.1 | 11.6 |
| | TR | 17.0 | 15.7 | 17.4 | 16.4 | 14.3 | 14.3 | 11.4 | 11.2 | 12.2 |
| 18–64 | AB-28 | 8.8 | 8.9 | 9.0 | 9.5 | 9.5 | 9.6 | 9.4 | 9.4 | 9.2 |
| | TR | 15.9 | 15.3 | 14.9 | 14.4 | 13.7 | 13.5 | 12.8 | 13.1 | 13.2 |
| Gender | | | | | | | | | | |
| Women (18–64) | AB-28 | 8.3 | 8.3 | 8.4 | 9.1 | 8.7 | 9.0 | 9.0 | 8.9 | 8.8 |
| | TR | 17.3 | 15.7 | 13.9 | 12.8 | 11.3 | 9.8 | 9.0 | 10.0 | 9.8 |
| Man (18–64) | AB-28 | 9.2 | 9.4 | 9.4 | 9.9 | 10.2 | 10.1 | 9.8 | 9.8 | 9.6 |
| | TR | 15.3 | 15.1 | 15.4 | 15.4 | 14.7 | 15.1 | 14.4 | 14.5 | 14.7 |
| Education | | | | | | | | | | |
| Less than primary, primary and lower secondary education | AB-28 | 17.3 | 17.3 | 17.8 | 18.6 | 18.9 | 19.3 | 20.2 | 19.3 | 19.0 |
| | TR | 20.1 | 19.3 | 18.8 | 20.8 | 20.4 | 20.3 | 19.5 | 19.7 | 20.1 |
| Tertiary education | AB-28 | 4.0 | 4.1 | 4.2 | 4.5 | 4.6 | 4.8 | 4.6 | 4.8 | 4.9 |
| | TR | 0.6 | 0.9 | 1.0 | 1.2 | 1.0 | 1.3 | 1.0 | 1.6 | 1.9 |
| Household structure | | | | | | | | | | |
| Households without dependent children | AB-28 | 7.1 | 7.4 | 7.5 | 8.0 | 8.0 | 8.2 | 7.9 | 7.9 | 7.7 |
| | TR | 7.6 | 6.4 | 5.6 | 5.7 | 5.2 | 4.5 | 4.4 | 4.5 | 4.7 |
| Single person | AB-28 | 12.2 | 12.6 | 13.1 | 13.5 | 13.2 | 13.9 | 13.5 | 13.1 | 12.9 |
| | TR | 5.9 | 6.0 | 4.1 | 4.4 | 3.3 | 5.6 | 3.9 | 3.3 | 3.7 |
| Single person with dependent children | AB-28 | 19.6 | 19.8 | 20.2 | 20.0 | 19.9 | 21.6 | 21.8 | 23.3 | 22.2 |
| | TR | 17.8 | 14.8 | 12.0 | 15.5 | 10.9 | 13.5 | 7.2 | 10.9 | 11.9 |
| Two or more adults with dependent children | AB-28 | 10.1 | 10.1 | 10.0 | 10.5 | 10.6 | 10.4 | 10.2 | 10.1 | 9.2 |
| | TR | 19.5 | 19.4 | 19.3 | 18.6 | 18.1 | 18.2 | 17.5 | 18.0 | 18.1 |

*Source:* https://ec.europa.eu/eurostat.

working poverty in the 18–24 age group was 17 percent in 2011, it decreased to approximately 12 percent in 2019. In this age group, the gap between the EU average and Turkey has almost closed. It can be thought that the improvement experienced in this group is due to the increase in the participation rates of young people in higher education and therefore their higher wages in the labor market.

The risk of working poverty in the 18–64 age group in Turkey decreased from 15.9 percent in 2011 to 13.2 percent in 2019. The decrease in this age group may be due to the change in the household structure. The replacement of the single-earning family structure with the double-earning family structure will increase the household income, thus reducing the risk of the working poor. On the other hand, when this age group is compared with the EU average, it is seen that the difference of about four points has not closed over the years.

When the working poverty of the 18–64 age group in Turkey is analyzed in terms of gender, it is seen that there has been an improvement of approximately eight points in the last eight years for women. Positive momentum has been recorded in reducing the risk of female working poverty. This may be due to the increase in the tendency to work in higher-paid jobs due to the increase in the education level of women over the years. However, it is noteworthy that the working poverty among men remained almost constant in this process (14–15 percent).

Educational status is an important factor determining the risk of working poverty. As the education level increases, the risk of working poverty decreases as the income earned by the individual in return for his/her work increases. In Turkey, one out of every five workers with less than tertiary education is at risk of working poverty over the years examined. The risk of working poverty among higher education graduates is between 1 percent and 1.5 percent. However, while the risk of working poverty remained constant for those with a high school or lower education, there was an increase of up to three times at the level of higher education. This situation can be explained by the decrease in the wages of higher education graduates in the labor market in parallel with the increase in higher education participation rates. When a comparison is made, it is seen that the risk of working poverty with higher education graduates in Turkey is less than half of the EU average (table 10.2).

When household structures in Turkey are examined, it is seen that working poverty is high in "households with two or more adults with dependent children" and "single-parent households with dependent children." The risk of working poor is low in "one person living" or "household with no dependent children." While the risk of working poor was 19.5 percent in "households with two or more adults with dependent children" in 2011, this rate was

17.8 percent in "single-parent families with dependent children." It is only 5.9 percent in families live alone. Therefore, the risk of working poverty in "single-parent households with dependent children" and "households with two or more adults with dependent children" is approximately three times higher than in "single-person living" families (table 10.2)

It is seen that the highest decrease in the risk of working poor among different household structures is in "single-parent households with dependent children." In this group, there was a decrease of approximately six points between 2011 and 2019, and the risk of working poor was determined as 11.9 percent in 2019.

Again in this period, it is observed that the risk of working poverty in households without children has decreased in Turkey. While the risk of working poverty in this group was 7.6 percent in 2011, it decreased to 4.7 percent in 2019. This may be related to the participation of women in working life and the increase in household income.

In table 10.2 it is seen that there is a difference between Turkey and the EU average in terms of the working poor ratio in "households with one person" and "households with two or more adults with dependent children." While the risk of working poverty in "single-person households" was 12.2 percent in the EU in 2011, this rate is 5.9 percent in Turkey. While there has been an improvement in this household structure in the eight years examined in Turkey, the EU average has remained stable. Therefore, the difference between them has widened even more. While the EU average is 13 percent in 2019, this rate is 3.7 percent in Turkey.

When the ratio of working poverty risk in households with two or more adults with dependent children is examined, it is seen that Turkey is nearly twice as high as the EU average. This situation can be associated with the fact that the family has an important role in the provision of care services in Turkey. Providing care for the elderly, children, and disabled in the household increases the dependent population and thus the working poverty ratio.

## Employee Poverty by Working Time and Contract Type

For individuals who have no income other than wages, working time determines working poverty to a large extent. Accordingly, long-term work reduces the risk of poverty, while full-time work reduces the risk compared to part-time work.

The risk of poverty decreases as the working time increases for one year or more. In Turkey, between 2011 and 2019, the poverty rate for those who worked for less than one year in general was approximately eight points higher than for those who worked for one year (table 10.3).

**Table 10.3 Working Poverty Risk by Working Time, Time-Based Contract Type, Qualification-Based Contract Type (%), 2011–2019**

| | | *2011* | *2012* | *2013* | *2014* | *2014* | *2016* | *2017* | *2018* | *2019* |
|---|---|---|---|---|---|---|---|---|---|---|
| Working time | | | | | | | | | | |
| One year | Ab-28 | 8.3 | 8.4 | 8.5 | 9.0 | 9.0 | 9.1 | 9.0 | 9.0 | 8.8 |
| | TR | 15.2 | 14.2 | 14.3 | 13.5 | 12.8 | 12.5 | 12.0 | 12.2 | 12.4 |
| Less than one Year | Ab-28 | 16.7 | 17.2 | 16.3 | 18.1 | 17.5 | 18.3 | 16.7 | 17.1 | 16.4 |
| | TR | 21.0 | 23.1 | 19.0 | 20.6 | 20.4 | 21.4 | 19.8 | 20.4 | 20.4 |
| Time-based contract type | | | | | | | | | | |
| Part-time workers | Ab-28 | 13.5 | 13.7 | 14.7 | 15.7 | 15.3 | 15.8 | 15.6 | 15.6 | 15.1 |
| | TR | 23.8 | 23.5 | 20.9 | 19.8 | 17.8 | 15.3 | 16.2 | 16.4 | 16.6 |
| Full-time workers | Ab-28 | 7.4 | 7.4 | 7.2 | 7.7 | 7.7 | 7.8 | 7.7 | 7.6 | 7.5 |
| | TR | 14.8 | 14.3 | 14.2 | 13.8 | 13.2 | 13.2 | 12.5 | 12.6 | 12.8 |
| Qualification-based contract type | | | | | | | | | | |
| Permanent job | Ab-28 | 5.5 | 5.5 | 5.5 | 5.8 | 5.7 | 5.8 | 5.8 | 6.0 | 9.2 |
| | TR | 7.2 | 7.7 | 8.6 | 9.0 | 8.8 | 9.4 | 8.4 | 8.7 | 13.2 |
| Temporary job | Ab-28 | 13.8 | 14.2 | 14.9 | 15.7 | 15.6 | 16.2 | 16.1 | 16.1 | 16.2 |
| | TR | 26.3 | 27.4 | 26.9 | 26.3 | 25.5 | 27.6 | 22.6 | 23.7 | 22.5 |

*Source*: www.ec.europa.eu/eurostat

The rate of working poverty for one year decreased, albeit limitedly, and became 12.4 percent in 2019. For those working less than one year, the rate remained almost constant.

It is seen that the risk of working poverty in Turkey is higher than the EU average for both one-year and shorter-term workers. However, it is understood that the difference between the EU average and the Turkey average has decreased as a result of the decrease in Turkey's data, especially among those who work for one year.

In Turkey, about three out of ten people working part-time in 2010 are at risk of working in poverty. In 2019, this group decreased by about twelve points to 16.6 percent. While the risk of working poor among full-time workers in Turkey was 16.7 percent in 2010, it was determined as 12.8 percent in 2019.

Turkey's risk of working poverty among part-time workers in 2010 was more than double the EU average. However, over the years, it is seen that there has been an increase in the EU average and a decrease in Turkey. The risk of part-time working poverty between the EU average and Turkey is gradually closing. When the risk of poverty among full-time workers is examined, it is seen that while there is a decrease from 16 percent to 12 percent in Turkey, the EU average (7–8 percent) remains constant.

The type of employment contract is another important factor in determining working poverty. In Turkey, while the risk of poverty was 7.2 percent for those working with a permanent employment contract in 2011, it was 26.3 percent for those working with a temporary contract. Until 2018, the rate of working poverty continued to be more than three times among those working with temporary employment contracts compared to those working with permanent employment contracts. This is important in terms of showing that the permanent employment contract is a protective mechanism for the individual against the risk of the working poverty.

It is seen that the risk of poverty for those who work with both permanent and temporary employment contracts in Turkey is above the EU average. The poverty rate is considerably higher than the EU average, especially for those working with temporary employment contracts. In 2019, it is observed that the rate of working poor among those working with permanent employment contracts in Turkey, as well as the EU average, increased significantly compared to the previous year. This may be due to the downward movement in wages caused by the shortening of working hours within the scope of the measures taken during the COVID-19 period.

## The Effect of Turkish Labor Market Structure on Employee Poverty

It is seen that those who are not registered with the Social Security Institution (informal work) in the Turkish labor market have a significant role influencing the risk of working poverty. While unregistered employment was 43 percent in 2010, this rate decreased by about fourteen points over the ten years and was determined as 30.5 percent in 2020 (www.sgk.gov.tr). Despite the significant decrease in informal employment, it is still not uncommon for at least three out of ten workers to be unregistered. Many reasons stemming from labor market regulations such as high unemployment rates, severance pay, insurance premiums, financial, administrative, and legal systems, and lack of supervision are effective in the formation of unregistered employment. Informal employment, where the labor force turnover rate is high, the wage level is low, and social protection is not provided against various risks, increases the rate of the "working poor."

The low rate of female labor force participation has been an important structural problem in the Turkish labor market for years. When the data of the Turkish Statistical Institute (TUIK) are analyzed, it is seen that female employment (28 percent) is approximately half of male employment (57 percent). Also, high unemployment rates increase the risk of working poverty. Unemployment rates in Turkey have been above the world average for years. This situation both prevents new workforce from entering the labor market and causes wages to decrease due to a significant amount of new workforce waiting at the door. Low wages naturally increase the risk of working poverty.

The number of employees in the household is one of the determinants of working poverty, and in Turkey, the risk of working poverty increases due to the low participation of women in employment. The fact that care work (services for children, the elderly, the disabled, and the sick) is mostly provided by women in Turkey is one of the factors that prevent women from taking part in employment. This situation causes the formation of a single-earning family structure and an increase in the risk of working poverty.

The low level of real wages is also an important factor in working poverty. Even though nominal minimum wages are constantly increasing in the Turkish labor market, rapid decreases can be experienced in purchasing power against the general level of prices. Low purchasing power is one of the chronic problems of theTurkish labor market. This situation reduces the chance of reaching welfare by working and increases the risk of working poverty.

## EVALUATION AND CONCLUSION

The problem of the working poor is related to both the working status of the individual and the structure of the household in which he lives. According to these criteria, working poverty is the situation where the income per capita is below the poverty line as a result of dividing the total income of the household in which the working individual lives by the number of people living in the household.

In the working poverty, in an individual context, while factors such as low education level, low qualification, low wage, age, and gender are effective, in the labor market context, the prevalence of atypical employment patterns, low-wage policies, and low union density affect the working poor rate. In terms of household, single-earning family structure, the high number of children, elderly, or unemployed in the household, and therefore having a dependent population, increase the risk of working poverty.

In Turkey, from the 1920s to the 2010s, the number of people employed in the agricultural sector was higher than in the other sectors. In the data after 2010, the risk of working poverty was found to be higher in the agricultural sector compared to other sectors. Based on these two pieces of information, it is possible to state that the risk of working poverty in the Turkish labor market between 1920 and 2010 was at a significant level.

Data on working poverty in Turkey have started to be produced since the 2010s. Therefore, when the data after 2010 are examined, it is seen that there is a significant decrease in working poverty. In the last ten years, the working poverty rate has decreased from 18 percent to 13 percent, with a decrease of approximately five percentage points. It is thought that the change in the household structure is important here. In other words, the risk of working poor decreases as the increase in women's participation in employment increases household income. On the other hand, families with children constitute the segment where the risk of working poor is high due to the dependent population. However, while the rate of these families was around 55 percent at the beginning of the 2010s, there was a decrease of twelve points until 2020 and decreased to 42 percent. Therefore, the radical change in households has reduced the risk of working poor.

However, it is observed that the risk of poverty in single-person households has increased more than two times compared to other types of households in the years examined. This may be an indication that wages are not sufficient to protect individuals from poverty.

It is seen that education level is more determinant than gender and age factors in the risk of working poverty in Turkey. In other words, the risk ratio of working poor for men and women aged 18–24 and 18–64 is close to each other. However, when the education level is examined, it is seen that the risk of working poverty is approximately ten times higher among those who graduate below the higher education level. Therefore, it is understood that the level of education is an important factor that protects the individual from the risk of the working poor. When the risk of working poverty is analyzed in terms of household structure, it is seen that the dependent population and the number of parents are determinants. In the years examined, the risk of working poverty was approximately four times higher in single-parent families with a dependent population than in families with only one person and no children.

As in the rest of the world, the neoliberal policies implemented after 1980 and the globalization process in Turkey have caused the effect of the state on the labor market to be replaced by the free market. Along with this process, different forms of atypical employment became widespread and wages moved downward. In the period examined in the study, the risk of poverty is quite high in part-time employees compared to full-time employees, in those who work less than one year compared to those who work for one year, and in those who work on a temporary contract compared to those who work on a permanent contract. In addition, the prevalence of unregistered employment in the labor market and the low participation of women in employment lead to a limited level of household income.

## NOTE

1. Assoc. Prof. Dr. Social Service, Ankara Yildirim Beyazit University, Ankara, Turkey, suheylaerikli@aybu.edu.tr.

## REFERENCES

Bennett, F. (2014). "The 'Living Wage', Low Pay and in Work Poverty: Rethinking The Relationships". *Critical Social Policy*, 34(1), pp. 46–65.

Boratav, K. (2015). *Tu̇rkiye Iktisat Tarihi*, Imge Yayınevi, Ankara,

Boratav, K. (2016). *1980'li Yıllarda Türkiye'de Sosyal Sınıflar ve Bölüşüm*, İmge Kitabevi, 3. Baskı, Ankara.

Buğra, A. (2010). *Kapitalizm, Yoksulluk ve Türkiye'de Sosyal Politika*, İletişim Yayınları, 4. Baskı, İstanbul.

Buğra, A., and Savaşkan, O. (2015). *Türkiye'de Yeni Kapitalizm Siyaset, Din ve İş Dünyası, (çev) Bülent Doğan*, İletişim Yayınları, 2. Baskı, Ankara.

Castel, R. (2017). *Ücretli Çalışmanın Tarihçesi Sosyal Sorunun Dönüşümü, çev. Işık Ergüden*, İletişim yayınları, İstanbul.

Eurofound (2021). Working Poor. erişim, https://www.eurofound.europa.eu/tr/topic/working-poor

Gautie, J., and Ponthieux, S. (2016). Employment and working poor. In D. Brady and L. M. Burton (Eds). Oxford Handbook of the Social Science of Poverty, Oxford: Oxford University Press.

Goldring, L., and Landolt, P. (2012). Caught in the work-citizenship matrix: The lasting effects of precarious legal status on work for Toronto immigrants. In R. Munck, C. Schierup and R. D. Wise (Eds). *Migration, Work and Citizenship in the New Global Order*, Edward Elgar Publications, Cheltenham, MA, 77–94.

Gündoğan, N. (2007). *Yoksulluğun Değişen Yüzü Çalışan Yoksullar*, Anadolu Üni Yayınları, Eskişehir.

Hausermann, S., and Schwander, H. (2012). Varieties of dualization? Labor market segmentation and insider-outsider divides across regimes. In P. Emmenegger, S. Hausermann and B. Palier (Eds). *The Age Dualization: The Changing Face Of inequality in Deindustrializing Societies*, Oxford University Press, New York, 27–51.

Hick, R., and Lanau, A. (2017). *In-Work Poverty in the UK: Problem, Policy Analysis and Platform for Action*, Nuffield Foundation Final Report, Cardiff: Cardiff University.

Horemans, J., and Marx, I. (2013). Should we care about part time work from a poverty perspective? An analysis of the EU15 Countries. In M. Koch and M. Fritz (Eds). *Non-Standard Employment in Europe,* Palgrave Macmillan, Basingstoke, 169–189.

ILO. (2019). The Working Poor or How a Job Is No Guarantee of Decent Living Conditions, a Study Based on ILO's Global Estimates of Employment By Economic Class- April 2019.

Jütte, R. (2011). *Erken Modern Avrupa'da Yoksulluk ve Sapkınlık, (çev) Bengu Kurtege-Sefer*, Boğaziçi Üniversitesi Yayınevi, İstanbul.

Kazgan, G. (2009). *Küreselleşme ve Ulus Devlet Yeni Ekonomik Düzen*, İstanbul Bilgi Üniversitesi yayınları, 5. Baskı, İstanbul.

Kuruç, B. (2006). *"Ücretler ve Karlar Üzerine İktisat üzerine Yazılar 2", İktisadi Kalkınma Kriz ve İstikrar Oktar Türel'e Armağan Kitabı içinde*, (der) A.H. Köse, F. Şenses, E.Yeldan, , 3. Baskı, İletişim Yayınları, Ankara, 31–69.

Loakimoglou, E., and Soumeli, E. (2002). Low-wage workers and the working poor, erişim, https://www.eurofound.europa.eu/publications/report/2002/low-wage-workers-and-the-working-poor

Lohmann, H. (2009). Welfare states, labour market institutions and the working poor: A comparative analysis of 20 European countries. *European Sociological Review* 25(4): 489–504.

Lohmann, H. (2010). Armut von Erwerbstätigen im europäischen Vergleich. Erwerbseinkommen und Umverteilung. In *Kölner Zeitschrift für Soziologie und Sozialpsychologie,* Discussion Papers, No. 887, Deutsches Institut für Wirtschaftsforschung (DIW): Berlin, 621–630.

Lohmann, H., and Andreß, H.-J. (2008). Explaining in-work poverty within and across countries. In H.-J. Andreß and H. Lohmann (Eds). *The Working Poor in Europe. Employment, Poverty and Globalization*, Edward Elgar Publishing, Bodmin, Cornwall.

Lohmann, H., and Marx, I. (2008). The different faces of in-work poverty across european welfare state regimes. In H.-J. Andreß and H. Lohmann (Eds). *The Working Poor in Europe. Employment, Poverty and Globalization,* Edward Elgar Publishing, Bodmin, Cornwall.

Marx, I., and Nolan, B. (2014). In work poverty. In B. Cantillon and F. Vandenbroucke (Eds). *Reconciling Work and Poverty Reduction: How Successful Are European Welfare States?* Oxford: Oxford University Press, 134–156.

O'Higgins, N., and Moscariello, V. (2017). *Labor Market Institutions and Youth Labor Markets: Minimum Wages and Youth Employment Revisited.* Genève: ILO Employment Working Paper No. 223

Polanyi, K. (1986). *Büyük Dönüşüm Çağımızın Siyasal ve Ekonomik Kökenleri, çev. Ayşe Buğra*, İletişim yayınları, 14. Baskı, İstanbul.
Şenses, F. (2009). *Küreselleşmenin Öteki Yüzü Yoksulluk*, İletişim Yayınları, 5. Baskı, İstanbul.
Spannagel, D. (2013). *In Work Poverty in Europe Extent, Structure and Casual Mechanisms*, COPE Combating Poverty in Europe, Oldenburg: Germany.

## *Chapter 11*

# Hundred Years of Social Work in Turkey

## *From the Republic to the Present Day*

Volkan Işık[1]

This study focuses on the social work and social workers in the Turkish labor market in the 100 years since 1923. It aims to understand the scope of social work and evaluate the related vocational training fields together in Turkey to put forward a perspective for the future of social work. There is limited data on the field of "social service" workers at the national level because it is classified together with "Human Health" in the branches of economic activity of Turkish Statistical Institute Nace Rev.2. This situation statistically pushes social work to a limited area that is handled together with human health. In this study, a comprehensive dataset was used by availing from the extended scope of social work related to social policy. In this context, this study gives an outlook for social work, which cannot be revealed due to its classification and the field of human health in Turkey. Moreover, this study ends with assessing the future of social work in Turkey by taking advantage of the extensive literature on social entrepreneurship, workforce trends, social services, and so on.

## INTRODUCTION

In parallel with the prevailing global transformations, liberal policies were tried to be adopted in 1923 and after the establishment of the republic in Turkey, and development efforts by the private sector could not be realized due to insufficient capital. Although it was aimed that the newly established republic would develop and implement economic policies in line with the investment objectives of the private sector, and that the state monopolies in consumer and investment goods would gradually be abolished and private investments would be encouraged instead, these objectives could not be realized due to the 1929 Depression (Great Depression). After the Great Depression, the pure liberal policies, which started to be abandoned all over the world, were replaced by the state's tools of intervention, and similarly, in Turkey, the development policies evolved toward development by the state. During the guided period when the state entered the market as a capitalist, five-year state development plans were prepared, and finally, the "social state" identity was given to the state with the 1961 Constitution and lasted until the 1980s. This fifty-year period has also been a period in which nongovernmental organizations gained legitimacy by establishing their legal infrastructures.

It is possible to come across some regulations that paved the way for the development of social work in Turkey in the early periods of the republic. The Turkish Himaye-i Etfal Society, which would later become an indicator of the Republic of Turkey's public obligation as a social state (Çengelci, 1998, s.111), fulfilled the goals and activities of the Turkish state, which was reorganized and restructured with all its institutions just before the proclamation of the republic, by fulfilling the social service understanding and understanding of the state.

The sustainability of this period, in which the state mostly assumed responsibilities alone and was not only limited to the public sphere but also assumed the identity of a capitalist, came to an end due to the Oil Crisis in the 1970s and the increase in costs. Subsequently, a new approach to the sustainability of capitalism came to the fore, and neoliberalism replaced the weakened welfare state in the 1980s.

In the neoliberal era, nongovernmental organizations that assumed responsibility with the state to combat social problems began to come to the fore. In the twenty-first century, where states assume limited responsibility due to the neoliberal understanding, however, social issues are globalized, nongovernmental organizations have become increasingly widespread, social responsibility and awareness increase, philanthropy comes to the fore, individual initiatives that develop innovative solutions in the fight against social problems make a difference, and corporate social responsibility is special. It has been the beginning of a century in which it has affected the brand value in the sector. In this century, concepts such as social innovation, social business and social entrepreneurship have also become frequently discussed topics within the broad scope of social work.

The activities of nongovernmental organizations based on the principles of solidarity, cooperation, and self-help have expanded with the increase in the awareness of individual responsibility. The popularity of social work in the modern sense is an extension of this process. Social work is carried out in almost all areas of society. It shows its existence in many areas such as the fight against unemployment, poverty, health, education, housing, and even environmental policies and the fight against crime, which are directly in the area of interest and influence of social policy. The changing social needs with urbanization and the transformation of flexibility in working life are among the dynamics affecting social work's spread. As individuals' level of education and social awareness increased with urbanization, sensitivity toward social problems increased. Flexibility in working life after the 1990s, with the widespread use of information and communication technologies, caused a shortening of the time allocated to working and allowed people to find time to do social work.

Since social work includes all work activities focused on social benefit, it can refer to all work done for a fee or voluntarily. The difference between social work and employment is not whether a wage is paid for the work done but the fact that the output necessarily provides social benefits. The social benefit in question can be a social service activity such as elderly, disabled, or childcare, or it can be a social entrepreneur's fight against poverty or a nongovernmental organization's work for sustainable food production or zero waste.

This study has assessed the social work field's 100-year journey from the republic to the present, which is becoming more and more significant in Turkey within the context of social work, employment in the third sector, and social entrepreneurship. In the study conducted using secondary data, it can be understood how social work in Turkey is at the beginning of the digital new world.

## THEORETICAL BACKGROUND OF SOCIAL WORK

The development of welfare states, which emerged as a complement to the Keynesian era, made possible the transformation of the political environment, including social policy. Thus, the understanding of the social state, which sees the struggle against social problems as one of the main duties of the state, has been shaped. However, the effects of the 1973 crisis and the features that determined the social policy environment of the 1980s caused deviations from the protectionist state understanding. Especially since the 1990s, the "welfare governance" model, which envisages the sharing of authority in the responsibility of providing welfare, has started to come to the fore (Buğra, 2016:77).

While the process of globalization and the spread of neoliberalism has led to some fundamental debates about the functions of the state and therefore its social duties, the social dimension of the state, which is already inadequate in many countries, has become more controversial in recent years with the rhetoric of the necessity of reducing the state in terms of powers and responsibilities. In the understanding of the welfare mix that came to the fore in the axis of these discussions, it is aimed to benefit from private and nongovernmental sectors and even family, religion, and individual philanthropy without disabling the state in ensuring welfare, and philanthropy come to the fore. There are frequent discussions that philanthropy has become an important feature that defines the social sphere in today's societies and that the twenty-first century will be the century of philanthropy (Economist, 2006:44).

The break with an understanding of the welfare state, welfare governance, and welfare mix discourses and philanthropy debates suggests a new formula in the fight against social problems instead of the state producing services alone. In the neoliberal period, it is desired that social services and thus the fight against social problems should be carried out jointly by the public, private, and third sectors. Thestate should provide financial support to these segments and be responsible for the regulation of services (Özdemir, 2004:347–348). After these conversations, the following are discussed: Gilbert and Terrell's social welfare institutions; the civic sector, which includes family, friends, and the person's social circle; religious institutions; the third sector, which includes nongovernmental organizations and is made up of public and private sectors, local and federal governments (Gilbert and Terrell, 1998:3).

The increasing adoption of the welfare mix approach has brought the public, private, and civil society sectors closer together and has led to the emergence of new means of struggle within these sectors. As of the beginning of the twenty-first century, corporate social responsibility investments are gaining importance in the private sector, the understanding of social municipality is becoming widespread, and membership in nongovernmental organizations is gradually increasing. In addition, innovative and creative initiatives are developing within nongovernmental organizations; philanthropic/individual initiatives sensitive to social issues have shaped social entrepreneurship with the innovative solutions they have developed.

It is known that nongovernmental organizations, which are expressed as nonprofit organizations, have played a major role in the provision of social welfare services throughout history until the state intervened in the social field. However, the gradual development of societies, the emergence of industrialization, the emergence of new classes (employee-employer), the development of technology and the increase in its effectiveness in the production process, and the growing social problems beyond the reach of nongovernmental organizations have led to the intervention of the state as a large and powerful institution in this field. In the recent past, when the Keynesian welfare state began to be questioned, nongovernmental organizations started to attract attention again as a new method alongside the state in providing social policy (Özdemir, 2004:374).

The increasing importance of nongovernmental organizations and the fact that the concept of corporate social responsibility has started to be carried out based on entrepreneurship have led to the requestioning of the concept of work in its traditional sense. Today, in nongovernmental organizations and social profit enterprises, it is mentioned that income is not the primary purpose, the social purpose-oriented working style (Işık, 2016:36). Authors such as Ulrich Beck, Andre Gorz, and Zygmunt Bauman argue that we have now reached a stage of capitalist development where it is clear that it must be transcended and replaced by a more humane and ethical system. For example, Gorz states that it is possible to provide "work improvement" by doing social work to prevent people from alienating from constantly boring and repetitive work (Gorz, 2007). The approach of rewarding social work also suggests seeing the work as a result of an effort to color it with another work (Strangleman and Warren, 2008).

Unlike in the past, employees no longer evaluate their work only according to their financial gains but also pay attention to how meaningful and beneficial their work is to society. In other words, they also attach importance to the moral gains that their work brings to them.

Mohammed Yunus, based on the desire of employees to achieve this moral gain, the motivation behind working in social-purpose jobs/social entrepreneurship, connects it to the idealism and hope ingrained in the essence of all human beings (Yunus, 2012:50).

It can also be mentioned the flexible transformation process based on information and communication technologies in urbanization and working life within the dynamics that direct individuals to social work. First of all, the shift of working life from rural areas to cities, together with economic development and industrialization, changes the consumption patterns of societies and raises the standard of living (Biçerli, 2019:63). Working life in cities is shaped around the industry and service sector. Individuals who have higher wages and welfare levels in urban areas compared to rural agricultural production and unpaid family labor increase their work-leisure preference in favor of working together with the substitution effect. This situation, which increases labor force participation rates and working hours, raises the standard of living and changes social needs. Especially with the participation of women in the workforce, the need for social services has emerged for the care of children, the elderly, and the disabled, which was previously carried out through family relations.

Another effect of urbanization on the field of social work can be shown as the increase in social sensitivity toward social problems with the increasing level of education. The education levels required by the labor demand for vacant jobs in cities cause the labor supply to increase human capital investments in education. The awareness and sensitivity of individuals with increasing education levels toward social problems increase. Thissituation has a two-way effect: direct participation in social work and indirect effect. Firstly, individuals directly participate in social work activities by establishing various nongovernmental organizations or through the voluntary activities of these organizations on issues such as the environment, health, poverty, gender, discrimination, and so on. The rise of third-sector organizations from the 1970s can be interpreted as the result of this influence. Increased social consciousness also has the unintended consequence of making for-profit businesses more environmentally conscious. In this respect, it is seen that the importance of corporate social responsibility has increased since the last quarter of the twentieth century.

## OVERVIEW OF WORKING IN THE THIRD SECTOR

The development of the third sector, which is a completely different structure from the private sector in terms of purpose and activity in combating social problems, has led to the emergence of a new field of work and therefore a new need for manpower to be used in this field. This manpower, unlike private sector employees, will work to achieve a social purpose, and its primary purpose will not be to generate income but to contribute to the realization of the social purpose in parallel with the objectives of the organization it works for. For this reason, those working in third-sector organizations can be evaluated within the broad scope of social work.

The most important human resource of the third sector consists of members and volunteers. Therefore, the power and effectiveness of nonprofit organizations operating in the third sector are directly proportional to the number and effectiveness of their members and volunteers directly or indirectly involved in social work activities (Şenkal, 2003:8).

The spread of the third sector, which has been experienced more intensely in recent years as a part of the paradigm shift in developed countries, reflects the change in the basic structure of societies (Işık, 2013:102–132). Indeed, twenty years ago, individuals who said "*I want to work in a nongovernmental organization*" were not very common in Turkey, but now it has become commonplace, especially among young people, to work in NGOs. This situation also provides the opportunity for young people to be in a position that will provide them with real authority and responsibility in the early stages of their careers, rather than being unemployed until they choose the social work profession and find the organization they will be employed in (Güler, 2010:106).

## FOUNDATIONS

The Republic of Turkey, founded in 1923, took over the social service organizations that existed in the Ottoman Empire, both as an institution and as a cultural heritage. Foundations are one of them. Ottoman foundations are called *Mülhak foundations* in our current laws. *Mülhak* is an Arabic word that means added or joined. It comes from the word "annexation." To annex also means to add. *Mülhak Foundation* was established according to the Law on Foundations No. 5737, before the first Turkish Civil Code (Turkish Civil Code No. 743) enacted after the republic (i.e., during the Ottoman Empire), and its management was "conditional" (Art. 3). It refers to the foundations left to the ownership of the descendants of the donors.

In the last twenty years, there has been an increase in the number of foundations that show effective activities in the field of social work in Turkey. Besides, cooperative unions are also important. However, the numbers of these structures are kept separately for the cooperative unions under the Ministry of Food, Agriculture and Livestock, the Ministry of Environment and Urbanization, and the Ministry of Customs and Trade. A retrospective view of cooperatives cannot be presented due to the insufficient statistics of the relevant ministry and the dispersion of data.

Foundations in Turkey are classified as *Mülhak foundations*, *Community foundations*, *Artisan foundations,* and *New foundations* according to the classification of the General Directorate of Foundations. Among these, *New Foundations* constitute almost all of the total foundations (94 percent). Although the data on foundations are included in the statistics of the General Directorate of Foundations, the oldest data every year go back to 2001 in new foundations. For other types of foundations, data are not available until 2015. For this reason, while only the number of new foundations is given for the period 2001–2014, the total number of foundations, including other foundations, is given for 2015 and beyond.

The decrease in the number of new foundations in the ten years between 2001 and 2011 is remarkable. Accordingly, the number of foundations, which was 4,566 in 2001, dropped to 4,504 in 2010 with a steady decline. As of 2011, an increase is observed in the number of foundations. However, since other foundations were added to the total number as of 2015, it is necessary to state in which foundation type the increase occurred. While there were 271 *Mülhak foundations* in 2015, this number decreased to 251 in 2021. There was no increase or decrease in the number of 167 community and artisan foundations. Therefore, the increase is in *New Foundations.*

When the number of employees at foundations is examined, it is seen that there is no data on the number of employees of new foundations. Still, there is data on the number of *Mülhak* and *Community Foundation* employees for the last five years. Accordingly, it is understood that the number of personnel working in foundations tends to decrease over time. The number of volunteers has also decreased over time.

Similar to the data on the number of foundations, the oldest data on the number of associations belong to the year 2000. Therefore, an evaluation can be made for the last twenty-two years.

## ASSOCIATIONS

Associations, like foundations, have a deep-rooted historical background in Turkey. Toward the end of the 1860s, the emergence of societies (associations) similar to the nongovernmental organizations in the West increased in the Ottoman Empire. These developments are similar to the development process of nongovernmental organizations in the West, which is parallel to the development of constitutional freedoms and the parliamentary representation system (Tosun, T. 2008:10–17). Although its history dates back to the Ottoman period at the end of the nineteenth century, it was only in 1946 that civil society began to take shape in Turkey due to the bans on associations and other nongovernmental organizations. In other words, it is the period when the civil society, whose foundations were laid during the Tanzimat, Constitutional Monarchy, and One Party periods but could not develop sufficiently due to the pressures of the state, began to take shape again (Akçeşme, 2013:212–213). Although steps were taken toward democratization with the transition to a multiparty system in the 1950s, the Democratic Party government turned its direction more toward economic development. However, religious groups, employers, labor unions, media, and villagers, which were restricted during the single-party period, reemerged. With the Law on Associations adopted in 1946, it became possible to establish associations completely independently, and the administrative permission required to establish an association was no longer required. This paved the way for civil society development, albeit limited (Akçeşme, 2013:213).

The 1961 Constitution expanded the freedom of association. The organization, which was under the control of the public in the first years of the republic, left its place to a free organization with the Constitution. The number of associations increased from 205 in 1938 to 41,000 in 1961 (Lale ve Mert, 2019, s.6395).

The appearance of the number of associations from the past to the present can only be revealed for the period 2000–2022 due to the insufficiency of the available data. When the twenty-two-year numerical change of the associations discussed is examined, it is seen that there has been a continuous increase in the number of active associations for 2004 and beyond. On the other hand, the number of associations, which was 78,771 in 2003, decreased to 69,753 in one year and increased to 121,087 in 2021, continuing its steady increase after 2004. Contrary to the increasing trend in the number of associations, the decrease in the relevant year may be due to data correction (https://www.siviltoplum.gov.tr/dernek-sayilari).

According to the years, the number of members of the associations goes back to 2012 at most. It is seen that there has been a steady increase in the number of members in the last ten-year period between 2012 and 2021 (https://www.siviltoplum.gov.tr/dernek-sayilari).

The oldest official data on the number of voluntary and professional (paid) employees in associations is from 2004. While the total number of voluntary employees in associations was 160 in 2004, this number increased to 32,941 in 2021. Particularly in 2008 and 2013, the sudden increase in the number of volunteers draws attention. The fact that these two increases occurred soon with the 2007/2008 and 2012 global economic crises shows that there may be a relationship between the increased unemployment due to the crisis and the tendency to volunteer work.

Although there is a fluctuating appearance in the number of paid employees in associations, the general trend is toward an increase. While there were sixty-five paid professional employees in associations in 2004, it reached the highest level with 39,625 people in 2019. The number of professional employees has continued to increase over the years.

It is possible to classify the employees of the association as full-time, part-time, and project-based, as well as voluntary and professional classification. In figure 11.1, the outlook for the last eighteen years regarding the status of employees in associations is discussed.

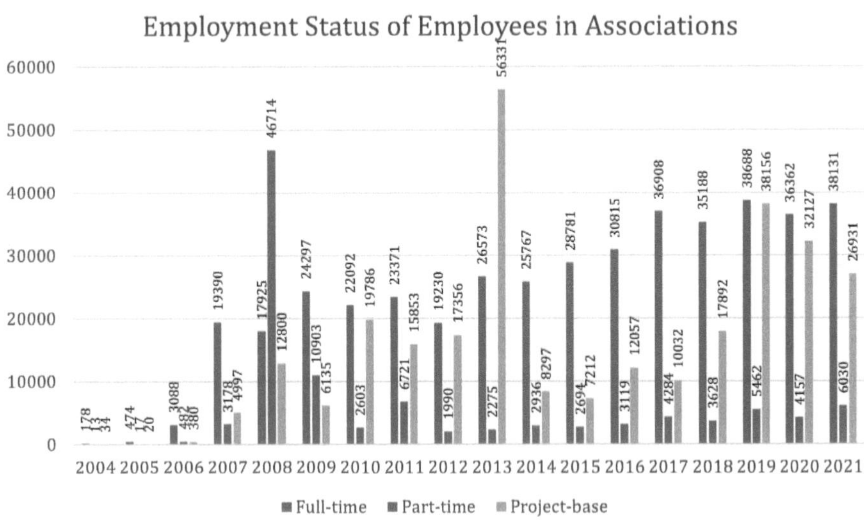


**Figure 11.1 Employment Status of Employees in Associations in Turkey (2004–2021).** *Source*: Republic of Turkiye Ministry of the Interior, https://siviltoplum.gov.tr/illere-gore-derneklerdeki-calisan-sayilari.

According to this, in 2021, there were 38,131 full-time, 6,030 part-time, and 26,931 project-based employees in associations. Except for 2008, there was no significant change in the number of part-time employees. On the other hand, it is observed that there is a regular increase in the number of full-time employees. While there are periodic changes in the number of project-based employees, an increase of approximately five times outside the normal trend in 2013 draws attention.

## COOPERATIVES

It is accepted that the first practice of cooperatives in Turkey, which has an important place among nongovernmental organizations, started with the "hometown funds," a structure similar to the agricultural credit cooperatives established by the state in 1863. However, the first fundamental development in terms of contemporary cooperatives coincides with the Republican period. The development of cooperatives has been with the Turkish Cooperative Association, which was established in 1931 at the request of Mustafa Kemal Atatürk. In this context, it is possible to say that the first important developments in the field of cooperatives took place in the Republican period between 1920 and 1938 under the leadership of Atatürk. For the first time, in the 51st article of the 1961 Constitution, the state was given the task of taking measures to ensure the development of cooperatives, and cooperatives became an important national social policy tool as an aid movement.

Initially, due to the density of the agricultural sector in GDP and the prevalence of life in rural areas, cooperatives emerged in agricultural areas and concentrated in agricultural areas for many years. Later, due to the new needs that emerged with the changes in the economic and social structure, especially industrialization and urbanization, it became widespread in areas such as housing/workplace construction, transportation, consumption, and credit guarantee.

Although it has a long history, there is not enough data on the appearance of cooperatives every year. As of the end of 2021, there are 53,259 cooperatives of thirty different types operating in the field of duty and responsibility of the Ministry of Food, Agriculture and Livestock, the Ministry of Environment and Urbanization, and the Ministry of Customs and Trade, and the total number of their members is 7,422,994 (https://ticaret.gov.tr/kooperatifcilik/bilgi-bankasi/kooperatifler-hakkinda/turkiyede-kooperatifcilik).

There are limited data on foundations, associations, and cooperatives in Turkey. If we need to put forward a view for the end of 2021 by making use of the current statistics, a total of 57,000 paid employees are employed, of which 38,000 are in associations and 19,000 in foundations, in a total of

215,000 nongovernmental organizations. According to TURKSTAT's 2021 household workforce survey data, the workforce in Turkey is 33,298,000. Therefore, it can be said that the total employment rate in foundations and associations is at the level of 0.2 percent. The number of volunteers is 32,941 in associations and 361,071 in foundations. The total number of volunteers corresponds to 0.6 percent of the working-age population aged fifteen and over.

The rate of nongovernmental organizations per 10,000 people in Turkey is low, as in most developing countries.

In response to Turkey's population of over 82 million, when nongovernmental organizations are examined according to their status, it is seen that there are 6,004 foundations, 121,087 associations, 53,259 cooperatives, 2,998 trade associations, and 640 trade unions, and there are 183,998 nongovernmental organizations in total as of 2021. The number of foundations per 10,000 people is 0.7, the number of associations is 14.6, and the number of cooperatives is 6.3 (https://ticaret.gov.tr/kooperatifcilik/bilgi-bankasi/kooperatifler-hakkinda/turkiyede-kooperatifcilik).

## COMPARISON OF SOCIAL WORK IN THE THIRD SECTOR IN TURKEY WITH SELECTED EUROPEAN COUNTRIES

In terms of the prevalence of third-sector organizations, it is important to compare the current view in Turkey with examples of good practices at the global level, in terms of the current view of social work in Turkey. In this context, especially in the United Kingdom, Scandinavian countries, where the culture of membership in nongovernmental organizations and active participation in social work activities is developed, and Italy, France, and Germany, where the cooperative mechanism is strong with a tradition from the past, can be considered as examples of good practice.

There are over 167,000 registered nongovernmental organizations in England and Wales. The donation industry across the United Kingdom has a total revenue of £75 billion. Nearly 76,000 charities earn less than £10,000 per year, representing 0.35 percent of industry revenue. Nearly 2,000 charities have revenues of over £5 million, representing 71 percent of industry revenue. About 900,000 people work in the charity sector. There are more than three million volunteers who regularly participate in civil society relief efforts every year. Charities benefit from over £4 billion in tax exemptions and rebates each year. According to the official figures of September 30, 2018, there are a total of 168,186 NGOs registered with the Charity Commission.

The number of people who volunteer at least once a month in England and Wales is 11 million. In 2016/17, 24 percent of the general male population volunteered at least once a month. These numbers are 30 percent of the female population. The proportion of the male population who volunteered at least once a year was 49 percent; the female population ratio is 55 percent. The number of paid employees in the NGO sector is 880,556, according to 2017 figures. (Women are 63 percent of this workforce with 558,929 people, and men are 37 percent with 312,626 people.) (https://data.ncvo.org.uk/workforce/).

According to the census conducted in 2016, there are 106,382 registered associations and 2,830 registered foundations in the Republic of Finland, which has a population of more than 5 million (https://www.prh.fi/en/uutis-listaus/2015/P_6954.html). Accordingly, approximately 75 percent of the population has been a member of an association at some point in their lives. The role of NGOs in Finland is mainly to complement the range of public services available. In addition, NGOs have duties such as service delivery and development, volunteer work, expert knowledge, and mutual support. In this context, 17 percent of social services and 5 percent of health services are provided by NGOs in the country. NGOs in Finland act as a catalyst to mobilize people to take part in social work roles in their communities. In this respect, NGOs are seen as a factor that activates society.

In the Netherlands, where the population is approximately 17 million, there are approximately 250,000 nongovernmental organizations, and approximately 130,000 of them have association status. There is a very developed awareness of volunteering and participation in civil society in the Netherlands. The number of volunteers nationwide is over 6,500,000, which corresponds to approximately 40 percent of the total population. No record is kept of the member information of nongovernmental organizations, and therefore there is no data on the number of people who are members of nongovernmental organizations (https://dafne-çevrim içi.eu/country-profiles/#netherlands).

According to current statistics, the number of registered NGOs in Italy is 336,275. NGOs employ approximately 800,000 people, and it is estimated that there are approximately 5,500,000 volunteers. Associations constitute 85.3 percent of nonprofit structures across the country. More than half (52.8 percent) of total employment is social cooperatives (4.8 percent of all establishments). It is stated that this number has increased by 5 percent in the last eight years compared to 2011 (Public-NGO Cooperation Project Report Study Visits Report, 2019).

The number of citizens who are members of NGOs in France is 24 percent of the population. The number of paid employees in NGOs is 1.8 million, and the number of volunteers reaches 16 million. The total number of NGOs is

1,367,180 (as of March 25, 2019) (http://www.journalofficiel.gov.fr/association/index.php).

The population of Germany is more than 86 million. In the Federal Republic of Germany, which has a similar appearance to Turkey in terms of population density, there are over 660,000 registered associations as of the end of 2020. A total of 17.5 million German citizens, who make up about 20 percent of the population, are members of the association. However, there are over 18,000 foundations. Although it is not known for certain, approximately 52 percent of the members of the association are women and 48 percent are men. The number of volunteers is over 25,000,000 (approximately 36 percent of the country's population).

## SOCIAL SERVICE WORKERS

. Social service; the accepted definitions in the literature that embrace that society has a duty and responsibility to protect groups that are deemed to fall under the purview of social policy, specifically individuals who are socioeconomically weak and in particular need of protection, also support this perspective. Accordingly, social work—these are systematic, regular, and continuous activity developed for the solution of individual and social problems that people cannot solve without help through formal, semiformal, and voluntary activities (Tomanbay, 1999:237). Social workers press for fair and responsive social policies that benefit all persons and advocate changes in policies affecting disenfranchised and oppressed groups whose dignity has been diminished by injustice (Miley, O'Melia, and DuBois, 2017:10, Danış, 2007:58).

Social policy has been of great importance in terms of social work since it emerged as a discipline (Pearman, 1973:19). Social policy's goals, such as social development, social peace, social justice, social balance, social integration, and social democracy, are also shared by social work.

At the national level, there are limited data on the field of "social work" workers, since it is classified together with "Human Health" within the economic activity branches of TURKSTAT Nace Rev.2. This situation statistically pushes the field of social work to a limited area that is considered together with human health.

The confusion regarding the field of social work in Turkey is primarily seen in the definition of social workers. Professionals who are considered social workers within the scope of social work are also defined as social workers/social service workers in the field. The concept debate on naming creates uncertainty about the scope of social work in both academic and practical fields (Canbulut, 2021:166).

Professionals working in social work are not only social work graduates. Many professional groups, such as sociologists, labor economists/social politicians, psychologists, teachers, child development specialists, and pedagogues, can also be social workers. However, Article 3 of the Child Protection Law No. 5395 is defined as "Social worker: It refers to the professionals who graduated from institutions providing education in the fields of psychological counselling and guidance, psychology, sociology, child development, teaching, family and consumer sciences and social work." On the other hand, Article 16 of the Regulation on Day Care and Home Care Services to be Provided in Elderly Service Centers, which regulates the duties and authorities of the social worker, states, "They are personnel who have received at least four years of training in the departments of universities that provide education in the field of social work."

The confusion regarding the definition and scope of social worker and social work dates back to the 1960s. Professional social work education in Turkey started with the establishment of the Social Services Academy in 1961, and the first graduates were given the title of social worker in 1965. In 1967, the School of Social Work was established within the body of Hacettepe University, then the School was transformed into the Department of Social Work, and it gave diplomas to its graduates with the title of Social Worker within the Faculty of Social and Administrative Sciences. After the Social Services Academy was transferred to Hacettepe University in 1982, it has been continuous to graduate students with a title in social work.

Statistical Classification of Economic Activities of the European Community (NACERev 2) is taken as a basis for the classification of the sector of social work in Turkey. According to the relevant classification, within the main category of human health and social work (Q), there are three main subcategories: human health services (86), residential care activities (87), and social services provided without accommodation (88). According to this classification, there are no data specifically related to the field of social work, and the field of social work is evaluated together with human health activities.

The results of the Turkish Employment Agency (İŞKUR) Labor Market Research (IPA) can be used for the last ten-year outlook of the field of human health and social work in Turkey. Accordingly, when compared to Turkey in general, the share of human health and social work activities in the total number of workplaces with two or more employees constitutes 1.8 percent and 3.2 percent of the workplaces with twenty or more employees.

About three out of every five workplaces with more than two employees in the sector are younger than ten years old. The ratio of workplaces aged 0–4 is 32.1 percent, while the rate of workplaces operating between the ages of 5 and 9 is 24.7 percent. About 19.3 percent of the workplaces has been operating for twenty years or more. Since approximately one-third of the workplaces in Turkey are in the 0–4 age group, the rate of "young" workplaces in the sector is high.

The rate of workplaces with part-time employees in the sector was determined to be 13.5 percent. As the size of the workplace increases, the proportion of workplaces with part-time employees also tends to increase. While this rate was 7.5 percent for workplaces with two to nine employees, it was 27.4 percent for businesses with ten to nineteen employees and 41.8 percent for businesses with more than twenty employees. Compared to Turkey in general, the rate of workplaces with part-time employees is higher in the sector. In Turkey, this rate is 7 percent.

From past to present, the number of workplaces in the field of human health and social work activities can only reveal a view of the last fourteen years within the existing data. When the annual data of the İŞKUR labor market research are examined, it is seen that the number of workplaces in the human health and social services sector has a share of 2.9 percent in the total workplaces in 2020. In terms of the change in the last fourteen years, the sectoral weight ranged between 1.7 percent and 3.8 percent; it decreased to 1.7 percent in the 2017–2019 period and increased to 2.9 percent in 2020.

The last annual outlook on social workers is also evaluated together with the field of human health, similar to the number of workplaces. In table 11.1, the ratio of those employed in the field of human health and social work in Turkey is given in comparison with the gender distribution and Turkey in general.

**Table 11.1 Human Health and Social Work Employment Rate by Gender (2007–2020)**

| | *Human Health and Social Work Employment (%)* | | | *Total Employment TR (%)* | |
|---|---|---|---|---|---|
| *Years* | *Male* | *Female* | *Total* | *Male* | *Female* |
| 2007 | 45.5 | 54.5 | 3.0 | 76.2 | 23.8 |
| 2008 | 47.3 | 52.7 | 2.1 | 74.3 | 25.7 |
| 2009 | 47.3 | 52.7 | 3.5 | 73.3 | 26.7 |
| 2010 | 46.6 | 53.4 | 3.5 | 75.5 | 24.5 |
| 2011 | 39.6 | 60.4 | 3.2 | 75.6 | 24.4 |
| 2012 | 38.9 | 61.1 | 4.3 | 74.8 | 25.2 |
| 2013 | 39.2 | 60.8 | 2.7 | 75.3 | 24.7 |
| 2014 | 40.5 | 59.5 | 2.7 | 74.0 | 26.0 |
| 2015 | 31.8 | 68.2 | 1.5 | 76.9 | 23.1 |
| 2016 | 39.3 | 60.7 | 2.7 | 74.8 | 25.2 |
| 2017 | 35.9 | 64.1 | 2.5 | 74.8 | 25.2 |
| 2018 | 36.9 | 63.1 | 2.6 | 74.3 | 25.7 |
| 2019 | 36.0 | 64.0 | 2.7 | 72.6 | 27.4 |
| 2020 | 38.3 | 61.7 | 3.6 | 69.2 | 30.8 |

*Source*: Turkish Employment Agency Labor Market Research Reports, https://www.iskur.gov.tr/kurumsal-bilgi/raporlar/.

The Human Health and Social Work Activities sector stands out as the sector with the highest rate of female employees. While one out of every four people working in Turkey is a woman, six out of ten people working in the Human Health and Social Services sector are women. In addition, the fact that women work in qualified jobs in this sector increases the importance of the sector in terms of women's employment.

Particularly, part-time work has a positive effect on women's entry into the labor market. Part-time work is of great importance both in the employment of women who do not have sufficient work experience in the labor market and in increasing the employment of women who are out of the labor market due to family obligations. Part-time work also acts as a bridge for the transition to full-time work and can even lead to permanent employment from temporary employment. The rate of female employment in workplaces that work part-time in Turkey is higher than in other workplaces.

According to the results of the research, while the rate of female employees in workplaces with part-time employees is 32.6 percent, it is 24.2 percent in workplaces without part-time employees. However, this situation may differ between sectors.

Part-time work in workplaces in the Human Health and Social Work Activities sector is not seen as a factor that significantly affects women's employment. While female employment in the workplaces operating in the sector with part-time work was 63.1 percent of the total employment, this rate was determined at the same level in workplaces that do not work part-time. As can be seen, whether or not part-time work is done in this sector does not affect women's employment.

## SOCIAL ENTREPRENEURSHIP

The concept of social entrepreneurship, which found its place in the social change literature in the world in the 1970s, became known in Turkey in the early 2000s. When evaluated historically, it is possible to take the examples of social entrepreneurship in Turkey as far as Darüşşafaka, which was founded in 1873. Darüşşafaka, which was founded during the Ottoman Empire and means "the nest of compassion," aims to provide equal opportunities in education and provides boarding education to children whose fathers are dead and whose financial situation is insufficient. Similarly, Zeynep Kamil Hospital, which was built by Yusuf Kamil Pasha and his wife Zeynep Hanım in 1862 to provide free service to patients on their private property, is also expressed as another long-term example of social entrepreneurship in our country. However, although similar initiatives organized as foundations, associations, and cooperatives have existed in the past, most of them are not called "social entrepreneurship" (Yaraç, 2013:93). Therefore, it would not be wrong to say that the concept of social entrepreneurship in today's sense came to Turkey with Ashoka in the early 2000s and that it is a new concept.

In Turkey, nongovernmental organizations (NGOs) include organizations such as associations, foundations, trade unions, chambers/social unions, professional organizations, and cooperatives at the legal level (Akbaş, 2014:7). In this context, legal status comes first among the defining elements for NGOs in Turkey. However, both the legal status and the daily use of the concept of NGOs are not enough to understand and define this phenomenon in depth.

In our world, where public-sourced solutions are dominant in the resolution of social problems, social entrepreneurship that can be considered new in the world, apart from foundations, unions, cooperatives, associations, and similar institutions, which have been considered classical social policy institutions for a quarter of a century, are emerging as a new tool in the struggle against social problems.

Social entrepreneurs who stand out with their innovative solutions to social problems have started to become important civil society actors due to their contribution to social welfare increase. On the other hand, they are not legally recognized in Turkey. Types of commercial companies in Turkey, according to Article 124 of the Turkish Commercial Code, include collective, limited, joint stock, limited, and cooperative companies. Foundations and associations have their special laws. Since there is no legal regulation that directly expresses or covers social entrepreneurship, social entrepreneurs also position themselves within the legal status of foundations, associations, cooperatives, or profit-oriented companies.

However, unlike traditional nongovernmental organizations that mostly depend on donations, they ensure their sustainability by making a profit with their income-generating activities. Unlike traditional for-profit entrepreneurship, it stands out as a different model because they use their profits in socially beneficial businesses.

Social entrepreneurship— is expressed as private/for-profit entrepreneurship that try to achieve a social purpose and that provide commercial income (both from the equity capital of their founders and public and private/for-profit entrepreneurshipentrepreneurship) as well as the traditional income sources of nonprofit organizations (donations and voluntary participation) (Mair and Marti, 2006:36–44).

Social entrepreneurship, which are the combination of the aims of being social and engaging in entrepreneurial activities, are established to combat social problems. They carry out their struggles using innovative, creative, and sustainable models. The social problems they struggle with manifest in a wide range from child labor to education, from gender-based discrimination to unemployment, and from environmental problems to poverty. In this context, social entrepreneurs, individuals employed in these initiatives, and even volunteers should be included in the broad scope of the concept of social work.

Despite the legal and institutional obstacles, social entrepreneurship in Turkey has shown significant development, especially in the last twenty years. The influence of the Ottoman foundation culture in the historical background is undeniable in this development. However, it can be said that the organization of Ashoka in Turkey in the early 2000s played an important role.

Since social entrepreneurship are not yet legally recognized in Turkey, they are mostly established as foundations, associations, cooperatives, or private/for-profit entrepreneurship; therefore, they operate by the legislation of these structures. For this reason, it would be appropriate to say that it is difficult to talk about full social entrepreneurship structuring in Turkey. Structures are described as social entrepreneurship in Turkey due to both the lack of legal infrastructure for social entrepreneurship and the inadequacy of institutional structuring. Foundations cannot go beyond the framework of associations or cooperatives and therefore cannot use their current potential. Many social entrepreneurships that can be established in the form of foundations, associations, and cooperatives in Turkey do not operate as a foundation/association, cooperative, or company in the classical sense. They often find themselves trying to stretch their existing institutional structures and adapt them to their goals. When the legal status of entrepreneurs who define thementrepreneurshipentrepreneurships in Turkey is examined, most of the social entrepreneurship in Turkey are registered as cooperatives (28.7 percent), limited liability companies (18.6 percent), and sole proprietorships (18.6 percent). While a significant number of entrepreneurship (14 percent) preferred the association structure, 3.1 percent of the entrepreneurship preferred to be established as foundations. Social entrepreneurships established as joint-stock companies correspond to 13.2 percent of the respondents (British Council, 2019:54).

The fact that social entrepreneurship is not yet legally recognized in Turkey plays an important role in the fact that a separate statistical database on social entrepreneurs has not been established. In this context, the results of the research conducted by the British Council on the status of social entrepreneurship in Turkey between October 2018 and May 2019 contain the most up-to-date data revealing the current outlook. The data in the report were obtained through consultation meetings with relevant institutions, semi-structured interviews in twelve provinces, an online survey, focus group discussions, roundtable meetings, feedback and information from experts, and desk research (British Council, 2019:26).

It is very difficult to calculate the number of social entrepreneurship in Turkey due to the lack of both a legal status defining social entrepreneurship and sufficient data on the field. However, to better understand the size of the area for the report, a rough calculation was made, and NGOs, cooperatives, and micro, small, and medium-sized enterprises with the characteristics of being social entrepreneurship were examined. In this context, it is estimated that there are approximately 9,000 social entrepreneurships organized in different statuses today.

Based on the data on the "*Status of Social Entrepreneurship in Turkey Report*" published by the British Council in 2019, when the tendency to the voluntary sector and the tendency to be a social entrepreneur in Turkey are analyzed demographically, compared to traditional entrepreneurship, prevalence is observed in the young population. While 21.4 percent of leaders in traditional entrepreneurship are under the age of thirty-five, this rate is 47.3 percent in social entrepreneurship (British Council, 2019:6).

It is seen that the majority of social entrepreneurs are women (55 percent). On the other hand, according to TÜİK Entrepreneurship statistics, the ratio of female managers among total entrepreneurs is 18.9 percent (TÜİK, 2017). Women's participation in civil society is also low. About 10.4 percent of nongovernmental organization members are women, and only 14 percent of nongovernmental organizations' leaders are women (TÜSEV, 2011). According to these data, it can be said that glass ceilings do not exist in social entrepreneurship (Özdemir, 2009:135), which is associated with the fact that women are not equally empowered with men in working life and are not equally included in decision-making, management, and policy-making processes.

When the education levels of social entrepreneurs are examined, it is seen that 84 percent of them have at least an associate's degree and/or undergraduate degree. In 2017, this rate was recorded as 27.7 percent among commercial enterprises. As can be seen, the education level of social entrepreneurs is higher when compared to commercial enterprises in Turkey. In addition, let's also state that 20 percent of the founders and managers of social entrepreneurship have a master's or doctorate.

A large number of individuals who carry out social work activities together with social entrepreneurs are employed in these entrepreneurships. Social entrepreneurship operating in Turkey employ more female employees than male employees, both full-time and part-time. The increasing number of full-time and part-time employees in social entrepreneurship shows that employment is created in this field.

**Table 11.2 Employed in Social Entrepreneurship (2019)**

| *Workers* | *Average (2018)* | *Average (2019)* |
|---|---|---|
| Full-time male employee | 1.3 | 1.5 |
| Full-time female employee | 2.9 | 1.9 |
| Total number of full-time employees (female + male) | 4.2 | 3.4 |
| Part-time male employee | 0.9 | 0.9 |
| Part-time female employee | 4.4 | 6 |
| Total part-time employees (female + male) | 5.3 | 6.9 |
| Total male employees (part + full time) | 2.2 | 2.4 |
| Total female employees (part + full time) | 7.2 | 7.9 |
| Total employee | 9.4 | 10.4 |

*Source*: British Council (2019). The State of Social Enterprise in Türkiye. https://www.britishcouncil.org.tr/sites/default/files/20190702_se_research_report_the_state_of_social_enterprise_in_turkey_eng_single_page.pdf.

In countries where social entrepreneurship is developed, employment has a significant share in the socioeconomic added value created by social entrepreneurs. For example, in the United Kingdom according to table 11.2, where social entrepreneurship is legally and institutionally recognized, 9 percent of small businesses are social businesses, according to 2017 statistics. This rate corresponds to approximately 471,000 social entrepreneurship. While there are no employees in 371,000 of these entrepreneurship, approximately 1.44 million people are employed in the remaining 100,000 social entrepreneurships (UK, 2017:8). Similarly, data published in 2015 in Italy, where the social economy has a significant size, it was stated that nearly 100,000 social entrepreneurships created around 850,000 jobs (Italiangoodnews, 2015). Social cooperatives, which represent the basic form of social entrepreneurship in Italy, have grown rapidly with the adoption of Law No. 381 of 1991, and the annual growth rate of social entrepreneurship in the country has increased from 15 percent to 30 percent (UNDP, 2008:21).

## CONCLUSION

This study has focused on the position of the social work field in the labor market in Turkey since 1923. In this process, the understanding of social work in Turkey has been evaluated from a broad perspective.

At the national level, there are limited data on the field of "social work" workers, since it is classified together with "Human Health" within the economic activity branches of TURKSTAT Nace Rev.2. On the other hand, the dataset has been enriched with statistics on the employees in the relevant nongovernmental organizations, especially in social entrepreneurship, by making use of the scope of the social work field. In this context, the study is structured over three main sections. The first part examined social workers in third-sector organizations in terms of foundations, associations, and cooperatives. Due to the inadequacy of available data for those working in nongovernmental organizations, the outlook for foundations and associations for the last twenty-two years has been presented. Due to the lack of data for cooperatives, only the current outlook could be emphasized. In the second part, social workers, who express the legal equivalent of the social work profession, are handled by using the data of İŞKUR IPA, and the view of the last fourteen years from 2007, when the IPA reports began to be published and presented. In the third part, social entrepreneurship as a popular and recognized social work field in Turkey in the last twenty years is discussed. The fact that social entrepreneurship are not legally recognized is a factor in the absence of a statistical database. For this reason, the situation of employees in social entrepreneurship. The outlook of social entrepreneurship in Turkey, published by the British Council in 2019, has been interpreted through the results of the research.

Within the scope of the relevant three sections, the current appearance of the social work field in Turkey and its appearance from the past to the present, to the extent allowed by the data, have been revealed in comparison with international country examples.

Although the is associated with the field of social work, it constitutes a wide area that includes the activities of nongovernmental organizations and social entrepreneurship activities. In Turkey, there is no detailed data on these three fields that will make the social work field visible in a broad sense. The social work field is defined within the Nace-Rev2 economic activity branches, but it is classified together with the human health field. Data for the last twenty-two years for foundations and associations are partially available. However, there are no such data available for cooperatives. Social entrepreneurship, on the other hand, constitutes an area where the definition is problematic along with the data shortage. Social entrepreneurship in Turkey is intertwined with foundations, associations, cooperatives, and sometimes company activities.

In conclusion, social work is a developing field in Turkey. When evaluated at the international level, it is seen that the social work field is behind the EU countries, where it has a legal equivalent in different aspects. Although the Ottoman foundations have an important place in the historical origin of the Republic of Turkey, it can be said that their social equivalent has weakened over time. Turkey is making great efforts to return to the culture of cooperation and unpaid work that has been destroyed by capitalism. However, it is still seen that the ratio of the number of foundations, associations, and cooperatives to the population is very low, and membership in these organizations remains at very low levels compared to EU countries. However, awareness of social problems in the digital world is gradually increasing in society, which leads individuals to the field of social work. Information, which becomes accessible at any time thanks to social media platforms and information technologies, increases social awareness and sensitivity. For this reason, in Western countries where social work is developed, especially at the level of socioeconomic development, the orientation to voluntary and professional social work areas is increasing day by day.

## NOTE

1. Assoc. Prof. Dr., University of Hacettepe, Department of Vocational School of Social Sciences, Ankara/Turkey, volkani@hacettepe.edu.tr.

## REFERENCES

Akbaş, K. (2014). *Nonprofit law in Turkey*. Working Papers of the Johns Hopkins Comparative Nonprofit Sector Project, No. 51. Baltimore, MD: Johns Hopkins University Center for Civil Society Studies. at ccss.jhu.edu.

Akçeşme, F. (2013). Sivil Toplum ve Türkiye Cumhuriyeti'ndeki Yeri. *HAK-İŞ Uluslararası Emek ve Toplum Dergisi*, 2(4): 202–225.

Biçerli, K. (2019). *Çalışma Ekonomisi*. İstanbul: Beta Yayınlar.

British Council (2019). The State of Social Enterprise in Turkey, https://www.britishcouncil.org.tr/sites/default/files/20190702_se_research_report_the_state_of_social_enterprise_in_turkey_eng_single_page.pdf

Buğra, A., ve Keyder, Ç. (2003). Yeni yoksulluk ve Türkiye'nin değişen refah rejimi. (BM Kalkınma Programı Proje Raporu), http://www.tr.undp.org/content/dam/turkey/docs/povreddoc/UNDP-TR-new_poverty.pdf

Canbulut, T. (2021). A Qualitative Study: Who Are The Social Workers? *Ankara Üniversitesi Sosyal Bilimler Dergisi*, 12(1), 165–173.

Çengelci, E. (1998). *Sosyal Hizmetler ve Çocuk Esirgeme Kurumu*. Ankara: Aydınlar Matbaacılık.

Danış, M. Z. (2007). Sosyal Hizmet Mesleği ve Disiplininde Sosyal Politikanın Yeri ve Önemi. *Toplum ve Sosyal Hizmet*, 18(2), 51–64.

Gilbert, N., ve Terrell, P. (1998). *Dimensions of Social Welfare Policy*. MA: Allyn-Bacon Publication, Fourth Edition 3. Pearson: Allyn and Bacon.

Gorz, A. (2007). *İktisadi Aklın Eleştirisi: Çalışmanın Dönüşümleri Anlam Arayışı* (çev. I. Ergüden). 2. Baskı. İstanbul Ayrıntı Yayınları. (Eserin orjinali 1988'de yayımlandı), 27–39.

Güler, B. Kümbül. (2010). *Sosyal Girişimcilik*. İstanbul: Elif Yayınevi, 3.

International Social Work Federation. (2021). https://www.ifsw.org/what-is-social-work/ (accessed March 2, 2021).
Işık, V. (2013). Kurumsal Sosyal Sorumluluğun Değiştirdiği Çalışma Kavramı ve Yeni Bir Çalışma Alanı Olarak Sosyal Girişimler. *Sosyal Güvenlik Dergisi*, 3(1), 115.
Lale, A. and Mert, K. Melek. (2019). Türk Sivil Toplumunun Tarihi Gelişimi: Osmanlı Devleti'nden Cumhuriyet'e Mukayeseli Bir Analiz (1839). *International Social Sciences Studies Journal*, 5(49), 6390–6399.
Mair, J. and Marti, I. (2006). Social Entrepreneurship Research: A Source of Explanation, Prediction, and Delight. *Journal of World Business*, 41, 36–44.
Miley, K. K., O'Melia, M. W., ve Dubois, B. L. (2017). *Generalist Social Work Practice: An Empowering Approach*, Eighth Edition. Pearson: Boston.
Özdemir, M. Ç. (2009). Kapitalizm Kadın ve Cam Tavanlar. *Uluslararası Disiplinlerarası Kadın Çalışmaları Kongre Bildirileri*, 1, 126–137.
Özdemir, Süleyman. (2004). *Küreselleşme sürecinde refah devleti*. İstanbul: İstanbul Üniversitesi.
Pearman, R. J. (1973). *Social Science and Social Work*. The Scarecrow Press: New Jersey.
Republic of Turkiye Ministry of the Interior, https://siviltoplum.gov.tr/illere-gore-derneklerdeki-calisan-sayilari
Şenkal, A. (2003). *Küreselleşme, Sosyal Politikanın Dönüşümü ve Sivil Toplum Örgütleri*. İstanbul: Sosyal Siyaset Konferansları Dergisi: 45.Kitap, 8.
Strangleman, T., and Warren, T. (2015). *Çalışma ve Toplum: Sosyolojik Yaklaşımlar, Temalar ve Yöntemler. Çev: Fuat Man*. Ankara: Nobel Yayınları, 270.
Tomanbay, İ. (1999). *Sosyal Çalışma Sözlüğü*. Ankara: Selvi Yayınevi.
Tomanbay, İ. (2012). *Sosyal Hizmet Mevzuatı*. Eskişehir: Anadolu Üniversitesi Yayınları.
"The Fight Over a Big Idea," Economist, July 22–28, 2006, s.44.
Turkish Employment Agency Labour Market Research Reports, https://www.iskur.gov.tr/kurumsal-bilgi/raporlar/
UK Government Report, Government for Digital, Culture Media & Sport; Department for Business, Energy & Industrial Strategy. Social Enterprise Market Trends 2017, September 2017.
UNDP. (2008). *Social Enterprise: A New Model for Poverty Reduction and Employment Generation*. UNDP, 21. Türkiye, ISBN: 978-92-9504-278-0
Yaraç, N. (2013). Paris'in Arı Kovanı. *Optimist Dergisi,* ss. 21–28.
Yunus, M., and Weber, K. (2012). *Sosyal İşletme Kurmak*. İstanbul: Doğan Kitap Yayınları, 51–52.
ZiviZ-Survey 2017: Vielfalt verstehen. Zusammenhalt stärken. (2017). 1st ed. ZIVIZ
http://www.italiangoodnews.com/social-entrepreneurs-rise-in-italy/, erişim: August 23, 2021.

## *Chapter 12*

# Social Dialogue in Turkey

Cihan Durmuşkaya[1]

Social dialogue is a central concept in employment relations and economic development. In this context, they can be seen as the relations or mechanisms between the actors of working life (workers, employers and organizations representing them, and the specialized institutions of the state related to working life). Established mechanisms are shaped at the micro (workplace, public institution) and macro (sector, national) levels. There are about thirty social dialogue mechanisms, including micro and macro, in Turkey. Within the scope of this study, macro-social dialogue mechanisms such as the Economic and Social Council, the Tripartite Advisory Board, the Minimum Wage Determination Commission, and the Labor Council were discussed. In addition, chapters related to social dialogue in Turkey were examined in the EU progress/country reports. A qualitative research methodology was adopted in this study. The reports of social dialogue mechanisms were evaluated by content analysis. As a result, although there are many mechanisms with a legal basis in Turkey, most of them are seen as "showcase" mechanisms.

## INTRODUCTION

Social dialogue is key in ensuring industrial peace in employment relations and taking action against crises and opportunities in coordination with employment relations actors. Especially during the COVID-19 pandemic, the importance of working life actors in responding quickly to the challenges of working life in coordination has been understood.

Social dialogue can be seen as a mechanism realized with the participation of bilateral, tripartite, or more actors at all levels of employment relations (workplace, industry, national, international). This perspective means that countries or sectors with different employment relations characteristics use these mechanisms at different levels of effectiveness. For this reason, an ideal social dialogue mechanism differs from society to society and even from sector to sector. The International Labor Organization (ILO) proposes ideal mechanisms to member countries. However, the effective functioning of these mechanisms depends on the characteristics of the working relations of the countries and the dimensions of the interaction between the actors. For this reason, member countries' efficiency in using social dialogue mechanisms varies.

Turkey has accepted ILO conventions on social dialogue because of being a member of the ILO. However, Turkey's history of social dialogue dates back to the first Republic years. For this reason, it can be said that social dialogue mechanisms have a history of more than 100 years. Working life actors create many social dialogue mechanisms with different goals and objectives in Turkey. These mechanisms are generally classified as macro- and micro-mechanisms. While macro-mechanisms refer to the national level, micro-mechanisms are used to achieve the institutional or sectoral goals and objectives of working life actors. This study examines macro-social dialogue mechanisms implemented at the national level in Turkey. The study consists of three parts:

In the first part, the perspective of the ILO on social dialogue is discussed. The ILO's recommendations to countries on social dialogue are examined. The structure for social dialogue mechanisms, which is called ideal according to the ILO, has been discussed.

In the second part, the historical background of social dialogue in Turkey is discussed. Social dialogue mechanisms have been introduced in Turkey. In addition, studies on the effective functioning of mechanisms in Turkey are discussed.

In the third part, the functioning of social dialogue mechanisms such as the Minimum Wage Determination Commission, Tripartite Advisory Board, Economic and Social Council, and Labor Council was analyzed and discussed in the context of macro-mechanisms. In addition, the evaluations related to social dialogue in Chapter 19 of the European Union progress/ country reports were discussed.

## PERSPECTIVE OF THE INTERNATIONAL LABOR ORGANIZATION ON SOCIAL DIALOGUE

Social dialogue is one of the most critical factors in achieving the ILO's goal of inclusive social justice through decent work in stable and democratic societies. Social dialogue is understood to include any negotiation, consultation, or simply the exchange of information between governments, employers, and workers on issues of common interest related to economic and social policy (ILO, 1999:46).

The ILO recognizes that the definition of social dialogue varies from country to country and over time. Information exchange is the most basic process of social dialogue. It does not imply real discussion or action on relevant issues but is a fundamental starting point for broader social dialogue. Negotiation is a tool where social partners share information and engage in a more in-depth dialogue about the issues raised. While the negotiation does not have decision-making powers, it can be part of such a process. Collective bargaining and policy cohesion can be interpreted as the two dominant types of negotiation. Collective bargaining is one of the most common forms of social dialogue and has been institutionalized in many countries. It consists of negotiations between an employer, a group of employers, or employers' representatives and workers' representatives to determine wage and working conditions issues. Successful collective bargaining results in collective agreements. Collective bargaining can be centralized at the national level or decentralized at the sectoral, regional, business, or bargaining unit level (Ishikawa, 2003:3).

According to Compston (2002:4), policy cohesion is defined as "the joint determination of public policy by governments, employers' organisations and trade union confederations." Tripartite policy cohesion or "social cohesion" can be considered the "ideal structure" of social dialogue. Employers, workers' representatives, and governments can develop coherent and multifaceted behavior to address all important national economic and social policies. This is only possible when the government fully acknowledges the legitimacy and constructive functions of the social partners' participation in the national policymaking process. The consequences of successful tripartite policy alignment are sometimes manifested in social contracts.

The ILO's International Labour Conference adopted three important international labor standards supporting the tripartite structure. These are the Tripartite Consultation (International Labor Standards) Convention, 1976, Tripartite Consultation (Activities of the International Labor Organization) Convention, 1976, Tripartite Consultation (International Labor Organisation), Recommendation 152, as well as Recommendation 113 (Industry and National Level) Consultation, 1960. All three of these tools encourage dialogue between government, employer, and employee representatives (Engin, 2018:IX)

The COVID-19 pandemic is taking human lives, putting health systems under great pressure, and causing major global economic and social disruptions. Social dialogue is a key tool for managing complex situations for at least three reasons. First, policy design, crisis response, and recovery strategies can be developed through knowledge sharing among the tripartite body (actors); second, social dialogue builds ownership and commitment to these policies, facilitating their rapid and more effective implementation; and third, social dialogue helps build the confidence needed to overcome differences and increase social cohesion and resilience as we seek to rebuild the fabric of countries' economies and societies over the long term.

ILO assessments of countries' responses to the COVID-19 crisis indicate that social dialogue is used to good effect in the early stages of crisis response in many countries. Timing of engagement with social partners: Governments of many countries have included social partners from the beginning in the design of measures to address the crisis and its consequences (Germany, Morocco, the Republic of Korea, and Switzerland). In some cases, governments (e.g., the Republic of Korea) have called for support for workers' and employers' organizations. This has facilitated the rapid implementation of emergency measures adopted, so the involvement of the social partners at all stages of the policy response has been argued to increase the effectiveness of these policies (Policy Brief, 2020:1).

All forms and levels of social dialogue will be crucial in the current and future periods, despite the situation in each country and the different needs of each sector. There is no "ideal dialogue for all." Some policy recommendations for an ideal social dialogue environment can be listed as follows (Policy Brief, 2020:5):

- To maximize the effectiveness of social dialogue, starting the process as early as possible is essential. The social partners need to be involved in all phases of the social dialogue, from the initial needs assessment to the formulation, implementation, monitoring, and evaluation of measures.
- The highest level of participation of state officials in tripartite social dialogue with social partners increases the credibility of the process.
- Given that social partners have in-depth knowledge of the needs and realities of employers and workers, their active participation in decision-making can lead to the adoption of well-targeted and effective preventive measures to help workers and employers limit the spread of COVID-19.
- The social partners' organizations should also play an important role in providing support and advice to employers and workers on how best to confront and mitigate the effects of the crisis.
- The crisis presents an opportunity to overcome past barriers to social dialogue, as partners are willing to put aside their differences and focus on the fundamentals, taking into account the seriousness of the situation.
- Where social dialogue institutions have become dormant, they can be reactivated to deal with the problems associated with the COVID-19 crisis and its effects.

- Modern technology can facilitate virtual negotiations between the government and social partners to avoid the health risks associated with face-to-face meetings.
- Care should be taken to avoid any action that could undermine the trust and harmony built between governments and social partners in the early stages of the crisis.
- Measures adopted through social dialogue at the national level need to be followed up with complementary bilateral dialogue and collective bargaining at the sector and enterprise levels to better respond to the needs of specific industries or employers.

These suggestions, which are discussed for the post-COVID-19 period, can respond to the solution of problems that will arise in an ideal social dialogue environment. In addition, according to Crozet, social dialogue can facilitate the balanced adoption of new technologies, strengthen national governance systems in global supply chains, and help manage demographic change (2020:5–11). The importance of social dialogue can be emphasized as a mechanism that responds effectively to the solution of problems experienced in recent years. There are four basic prerequisites for the establishment of successful and sustainable social dialogue mechanisms:

1. Strong, independent, representative employee and employer organisations
2. Respect for fundamental rights to freedom of association and collective bargaining
3. Political will and commitment by all parties to participate in social dialogue in good faith
4. Appropriate institutional support. (Engin, 2018:43)

In addition to these (Giorginch and Molina, 2020:9), it draws attention to the balance of power between workers and employers, political will and government support, mutual trust among social partners, and the problem-solving capacities of social dialogue mechanisms at the national level.

However, a general trend has gradually replaced deliberative and consensual policymaking styles with the imposition on decision-making. In countries that come under the control of financial aid programs and, in turn, face social and political difficulties, tripartite social dialogue has completely disappeared or at least been interrupted, making it difficult for social partners to negotiate and dialogue with governments. However, tripartite social dialogue has improved since 2012 (Giorginch and Molina, 2020:7–8).

## SOCIAL DIALOGUE IN TURKIYE

Turkiye's social dialogue history dates back to the pre-Republican period. The first social dialogue attempt, called the Economic Council, was made in 1908 during the Second Constitutional Monarchy. The Council was chaired by the Minister of Commerce and Agriculture, the members of the Ayan and Mebusan councils, the teachers of the Darülfünun, the presidents and members of chambers of commerce, and people who had proven their knowledge in the field of economics. Since the Economic Council was established under the influence of the Committee of Union and Progress, it chose to consolidate the National Economy as a structure and to follow the statist economy instead of economic liberalism. The life of the Economic Council, which accepted the state's establishment of the sugar industry in its second meeting, was limited to the power of the Committee of Union and Progress (Görmüş, 2007:119). The Economic Council is not equivalent to today's Economic and Social Councils. While the Commerce and Industry sector is represented, the employees' representatives are not on the board. However, despite these shortcomings, it is considered important for the state to take the opinions of segments other than itself (Koray and Çelik, 2007:343).

After the War of Independence, the Izmir Economy Congress was held to maintain political and economic independence. A total of 1,135 delegates, consisting of representatives of tradespeople, artisans, workers, industrialists, bankers, and farmers, attended this Congress, which can be called the first social dialogue and sought social reconciliation before the proclamation of the Turkish Republic. İzmir Economic Congress has historical importance; it gave direction to the economic policies implemented in the first years of the Republic's history. It showed a remarkable example of dialogue and social reconciliation that brought together various segments of society in the pre-Republican period and was an exhibition of the wide participation of different segments of society (Görmüş, 2007:120). In addition, the Congress was a forum where social segments and the state were represented; a tripartite exchange of views and the economic policies to be followed in terms of social policy and social dialogue were effective until the 1930s (Koray and Çelik, 2007:344).

Although it is not a social dialogue ground, one of the mechanisms that should be mentioned is the Ali İktisat Council (Koray and Çelik, 2007:346). The Ali İktisat Council is the first Economic Council-type structure established in the post-Republican period. In the liberal conditions of the period, it could not be expected that the social parties would take part in this council due to the lack of capital accumulation necessary for the formation of the private sector in the economic field, the lack of democracy and freedom of association in the political field, and absence of the working class in the social field. Therefore, the council members were determined by the conditions of the period.

Turkiye became a member of the ILO in 1932. This development necessitated the regulation of worker-employer relations. Turkiye is a one-party country whose democracy has not yet developed. After the Second World War, Turkiye wanted to join the United Nations in 1946. For this reason, in the same year, it abolished the Law on Associations, which prohibited organizing based on class and transitioned to democratic and multiparty life. The Ministry of Labor was established in the same years, and the first Trade Union Law No. 5018 was established. With these developments, the first confederation TÜRK-İŞ was established in 1952. After that, the military coups of 1960 and 1980 had both positive and negative effects on the organization. Even though constitutions that do not impose any restrictions on the right to organize came along, pressures restricting social dialogue emerged (Görmüş, 2007:121; Koray and Çelik, 2007:348–358).

Since the early days of the Republic of Turkiye, bilateral or tripartite social dialogue has been adopted, and social partners have taken part in the management of many institutions.

The Labor Council and the Minimum Wage Determination Commission are examples of these. In addition to these institutions that survive today, there are many institutions established as tripartite and tripartite-plus social dialogue mechanisms, especially the Economic and Social Council, the Tripartite Advisory Board, and the Labor Council. At the national level, the Tripartite Advisory Board and the Labor Council, in which employee and employer organizations consult with the Ministry of Family, Labor and Social Services, perform a relatively effective function. At the same time, the Economic and Social Council has yet to be more successful than expected. A similar situation exists in terms of bilateral social dialogue. Since the beginning of the unionization process in Turkiye, strong communication and dialogue have yet to be established in general between the social partners. However, it cannot be said that there has been no effort to improve the dialogue between the social partners. It is observed that employee and employer unions carry out projects together, or confederations carry out activities with the Ministry of Family, Labor and Social Services in affiliated unions and member workplaces to improve the perception and methods of social dialogue. Although these efforts sometimes fail to yield results, it is important that social partners feel the need for dialogue.

Developing the implementation of framework agreements to strengthen the relationship of trust is the minimum condition for sustainable social dialogue. Improving democratic representation mechanisms is a prerequisite for social dialogue: acceptance of employees' information and consultation rights and establishment of social dialogue institutions in the workplace (Engin, 2018:45–46).

As we use it here, the concept of social dialogue depends on two conditions. The first condition is the presence of at least three parties, and the second is that these parties are willing to cooperate. The first condition presupposes that the state, employers, and workers are independent of each other and perform certain functions. Social dialogue cannot be mentioned in a country where a political party controls workers' and employers' organizations. The second condition is that the parties are willing to examine their problems together and seek compromises and solutions acceptable to them, despite their interests. Nor should the state monopolize the decision process or be content with a mere monitoring role, that is, it should play an active role alongside employers and workers in solving economic and social problems. The first condition of social dialogue is that the parties must be independent of each other and willing to cooperate but also have the power to enable them to fulfill their functions effectively. Social dialogue also requires a degree of centralization of decision processes in the economic and social fields. Particularly in industrial relations, there is a need for a centralized interaction between the parties and a strong bilateral collective bargaining that will serve as a unifying function between the upper and lower levels. For this, first of all, collective bargaining should be institutionally centralized to support agreements at the national level. Second, workers' and employers' top organizations should be able to coordinate sector- and enterprise-based bargaining informally but effectively (Dereli, 1997:115–118).

For social dialogue to be successful, there must also be certain stability and predictability in the economic and social environment. Tripartite cooperation is facilitated when Social Democratic parties or parties close to trade unions are in power or coalition. However, it cannot be said that any party or government has a monopoly on this issue. Especially if the economic situation is bad, the benefits of a social democratic party in power may disappear. Social dialogue gains effectiveness in proportion to the increase in the rate of organization and density of unionization in society. Again, strong participation, institutions, and traditions in the society are other factors that facilitate tripartite cooperation. These include an effective institutional framework and procedures and support services to be provided by public authorities, such as a technical secretariat (Ekin, 1997:124–126).

Çalış and Yıldırım (2003:112–114) argue that social dialogue in Turkiye can be realized by establishing and adopting the culture of democracy. There is a representation problem in the government-union-employer triangle, which takes place as a social partner. Political parties in Turkiye are seen as organizations managed by a narrow cadre, mostly in which the institutions and rules of intraparty democracy are not formed. The same can be said for most trade unions. The union management is not formed directly by its members but by predetermined delegates, similar to the delegation system of political parties. It is generally open to the influence of employers and political parties, far from pluralistic participation. This situation reveals a structure far from its member base. It includes managers who use the unions as a social ladder and confine themselves to wage unionism as a field of action. Unions reproduce an organizational structure in which managers prioritize individual and short-term interests over their members' interests. For these reasons, social dialogue in Turkiye should first come to the fore as a civil initiative and embrace all interest groups.

In light of all these suggestions, the ILO-supported "Improving Social Dialogue in Working Life" project was carried out between 2016 and 2019. The project's objectives are to support social dialogue at all levels in Turkiye, strengthen the capacities of social partners and relevant public institutions on social dialogue, and increase awareness of social dialogue at all levels with a holistic perspective. The target audience of the project: unions and confederations of workers, employers, and civil servants; organized workers and employers; unorganized workers and employers; educational institutions; teachers, academics, and students; Ministry of Labor and Social Security personnel (including İŞKUR and SGK); Ministry of Interior personnel (labor unions, local administrations, and security forces); Ministry of Justice personnel (judges and prosecutors, labor courts); local governments; Provincial Employment and Vocational Training Boards; and large-scale and medium-scale enterprises. The expected outputs from the project are: strengthening the capacity of the Ministry of Labor and Social Security, relevant institutions, and social partners; raising social and institutional awareness on freedom of association, collective bargaining, and social dialogue at all levels; and developing social dialogue mechanisms at all levels, to develop social dialogue in working life (ILO, 2022). In addition to creating various awareness programs within this project's scope, the due diligence of social dialogue in Turkiye has also been empirically tested. The findings are important because of the limited empirical studies on social dialogue in Turkiye.

According to Orhan and Çakmak (2017:61–64), the first attempt is the empirical study within the scope of the project. They made observations about the development of social dialogue in Turkiye. Accordingly, the first finding is that the employees do not fully perceive the functions of the unions. The second is a clear lack of knowledge of all actors, including trade union representatives, regarding social dialogue's definition, scope, parties, mechanisms, and functions. Third, actors want to learn about successful social dialogue examples. Fourth, according to gender, education, and seniority, the need for education is changing. Fifth, there is a consensus on the positive contributions of social dialogue in working life. Sixth, 63 percent of employers believe in the benefits of social dialogue. Finally, the seventh determination: employees sometimes emphasize individuality.

In light of these discussions, how social dialogue should be in Turkiye and its main deficiencies were evaluated. However, despite these discussions, there are many social dialogue mechanisms at the micro (local or institutional) and macro (national) levels in Turkiye.

According to Koray and Çelik (2007:395), there are about thirty mechanisms related to social dialogue with a legal basis in Turkiye. These are: Minimum Labor Determination Commission, Profession Advisory Commission, Social Insurance Supreme Health Board, Minimum Wage Determination Commission, Professional Standards Commission, Consumer Council, Work Council, Vocational Education Board, Turkish Employment Agency General Assembly, State Planning Organisation Special Commissions, National Productivity Center General Assembly, Turkish Employment Agency Board of Directors, Economic and Social Council, National Productivity Center Board of Directors, Turkish Employment Agency Provincial Employment Boards, Seafarer's Subsistence Determination Board, High Council for the Disabled, Turkiye-EU Joint Consultative Committee, Provincial Vocational Education Boards, Official Mediator Selection Board, National Occupational Health and Safety Council, Human Rights Advisory Board, Social Security Institution General Assembly, Tripartite Advisory Board, The Board Authorized to Use of Penalties Deducted from Workers' Wages, Social Security Institution Board of Directors, Tax Council, Labor Market Information Advisory Board, Social Security High Advisory Board, and High Board of Arbitration.

## EVALUATION OF THE 2010–2020 ACTIVITIES OF MACRO-LEVEL SOCIAL DIALOGUE MECHANISMS IN TURKIYE

These social dialogue mechanisms, which have a legal basis, have been established for different purposes and tasks. Within the scope of this study, the views of the Minimum Wage Determination Commission, the Tripartite Advisory Board, the Labor Council, the Economic and Social Council, and the EU progress reports for Turkiye on social dialogue, which carry out activities at the macro level, were evaluated.

### Minimum Wage Determination Commission

The Minimum Wage Determination Commission, one of the mechanisms that operate effectively in the meeting in Turkey, gained legal ground with the Minimum Wage Regulation based on Article 39 of the Labor Law No. 4857 dated May 22, 2003 (T.R. Official Gazette, 2004a: Art. 3).

In Article 8 of the same regulation, the establishment and meeting principles of the Commission were determined. According to this:

Commission; Under the chairmanship of one of the members to be determined by the Ministry;

a) Ministry General Director of Labor or his/her deputy,
b) Ministry General Director of Occupational Health and Safety or his/her deputy,
c) Head of the Economic Statistics Department of the State Institute of Statistics or his/her deputy (Department of Labor, Services, Price Statistics and Indexes)
d) Representative of the Undersecretariat of Treasury,
e) Head of the relevant department from the Undersecretariat of the State Planning Organization or an official to be authorized,
f) Five representatives to be elected by the highest worker organization, which has the highest number of workers, for different sectors,
g) Five representatives to be elected by the employer organization, which has the largest number of employers, for different sectors,

The Commission convenes upon the call of the ministry and works according to the agenda prepared by the ministry. The Commission meets with the participation of at least ten members and decides with the majority of their votes. The member who does not agree with the decision indicates the reason for not participating if he/she wishes. In the case of equality of votes, the party with the president is deemed to have obtained the majority. The decisions taken by the Commission at each meeting are written in the decision book and signed by the chairman and members. The Commission's decision on determining the minimum wage is final. This decision must be based on a justification to be prepared according to the information and documents collected (T.C. Official Gazette, 2004a: Art. 8). In addition, the Presidential Decree on the Presidency Organization in 2018 introduced some changes regarding the members of the Minimum Wage Determination Commission.

The Ministry of Labour and Social Security, the Ministry's general manager, the deputy director general of occupational health and safety, the representative of the Turkish Statistical Institute, the representative of the Ministry of Treasury and Finance, and the representative of the Ministry of commerce will determine the composition of the Minimum Wage Determination Commission, which will be chaired by one of its members. It is composed of five representatives to be elected for different sectors from the highest worker organization and five representatives to be elected for different sectors from the employer organization that has the highest number of employers. The Minimum Wage Determination Commission convenes with the participation of at least ten members. The board decides with the majority of members' votes. In the case of equality of votes, the party with the president is deemed to have achieved the majority (T.C. Official Gazette, 2018a: Art. 522/f). With this change, some new actors were added to the ministries or institutions whose names were changed, although the content of the Commission was mostly preserved. Thus, both in the Minimum Wage Regulation and the Presidential Decree on the Presidential Organization, the Commission tried to ensure equality of representation on the legal ground by forming five states, five employers, and five worker representatives.

The Commission's duties, authorities, and responsibilities are determined in Article 9 of the Minimum Wage Regulation. According to this article, in determining the wage, the Commission may cooperate with all relevant public institutions, organizations, and universities. It may receive suggestions and opinions from workers' and employers' organizations. In addition, the Commission may refer to the knowledge of experts when necessary. Discussions in the Commission and the work of the Commission are confidential. The chairman, members, rapporteurs, and persons, organizations falling within the scope of this article are obliged to conceal all kinds of information and documents they have learned due to their duties. The president's decisions are publicly announced (T.R. Official Gazette, 2004a: Art. 9). The secretariat and rapporteur services of the Commission are regulated in Article 10. According to this article, the secretariat and rapporteur services of the Commission are carried out by the ministry's General Directorate of Labor (T.R. Official Gazette, 2004a: Art. 10).

The Minimum Wage Determination Commission meets in December every year and determines the minimum wage to be applied in Turkey. The Commission decisions are included in the communiqués published in the Official Gazette. These communiqués also include the social parties' reasons for voting against the process of meeting the Commission and determining the minimum wage. The meeting decisions between 2010 and 2020 are analyzed in the table below:

Table 12.1 shows that between 2010 and 2020, workers' representatives mostly voted against the minimum wage determination commission decisions, and their justifications were added to the communiqués. In 2011, 2018, 2019, and 2020, the parties did not vote against the minimum wage determination. Especially after the Presidential Decree on the Presidency Organization in 2018, it is noteworthy that the representatives of workers and employers did not vote against it and did not provide reasons. Employer representatives only voted against the 2015 commission resolutions. The reason for this was justified as a 30 percent increase in the minimum wage despite the 8 percent inflation in 2015. Only in 2013 the representatives of

**Table 12.1 Minimum Wage Determination Commission Decisions**

| *Meeting Year* | *Number of Meetings* | *Actors Presenting Grounds to Vote Against* | *Grounds for the Opposition* |
|---|---|---|---|
| 2010 | 4 | Workers' Representatives (TÜRK-İŞ) | The amount and method of determination of the minimum wage |
| 2011 | 4 | No Grounds for Opposition | - |
| 2012 | 4 | Workers' Representatives (TÜRK-İŞ) | The amount and method of determination of the minimum wage |
| 2013 | 5 | Workers' and Employer Representatives | Not changing the sixteen-year-old criterion in determining the minimum wage according to age (Employer Representatives), amount and determination method of the minimum wage (Worker Representatives) |
| 2014 | 4 | Workers' Representatives (TÜRK-İŞ) | The amount and method of determination of the minimum wage |
| 2015 | 4 | Employer Representatives | Increasing the minimum wage by 30 percent while inflation is 8 percent |
| 2016 | 4 | Workers' Representatives (TÜRK-İŞ) | The amount and method of determination of the minimum wage |
| 2017 | 4 | Workers' Representatives (TÜRK-İŞ) | The amount and method of determination of the minimum wage |
| 2018 | 4 | No Grounds for Opposition | - |
| 2019 | 4 | No Grounds for Opposition | - |
| 2020 | 4 | No Grounds for Opposition | - |

*Source:* Compiled by the author from the Decisions of the Minimum Wage Determination Commission between 2010 and 2020.

the workers and employers jointly presented the reason for voting against it. Employer representatives proposed to increase the age of sixteen to twenty-one years in applying different minimum wages according to age and voted against it as the Commission did not accept it.

On the other hand, workers' representatives mostly presented a reason for dissenting votes regarding the amount and method of determining the minimum wage. Workers' representatives—in the years when they voted against, they voted against because the minimum wage was determined even below the calculations of TUIK, which calculates the minimum wage with scientific principles. Although the minimum wages calculated by the TUIK with the worker representatives' calculations were determined to be approximately the same amount in the years of opposition votes, the determination of the minimum wage below these minimum wage levels in the Commission is seen as the main reason for the worker representatives to vote against. In addition, they demanded that a minimum wage be determined at a level of "decent work," following some of the basic principles they had determined in the years they voted against. These principles include the following: living conditions, decent wages, considering the scientifically calculated TUIK data in determining the minimum wage, calculating the minimum wage annually without discrimination by sector, age, and gender, and considering the minimum wage above economic criteria as a social wage.

## Labor Council

The Labor Council is one of the oldest social dialogue mechanisms in Turkey. According to Law No. 4841 on the Establishment and Duties of the Ministry of Labor adopted in 1946, under the presidency of the Minister of Labor or the Undersecretary, a collective Labor Council is established by a fully authorized representative from the ministries and the representatives of workers and employers indicated in Article 12 of Law No. 4792. The Labor Council convenes at a time determined by the ministry. It gives its opinions by making examinations and discussions on the issues to be given by the ministry related to working life. Travel allowance is paid to the workers and employers of the Labor Council coming from outside of Ankara, following the principles to be set by the ministry (T.C. Official Gazette, 1946: Art. 17).

The Labor Council convened three times between 2010 and 2020: the 10th Labor Council in 2013, the 11th Labor Council in 2015, and the 12th Labor Council in 2019. Panel discussions on three of the top issues facing Turkey's working community—severity pay, subcontracting, and temporary work relationships through private employment offices—were held following the Labour Council Meeting on September 26–27, 2013, which drew in about 1,400 attendees. The meeting was held in three separate panels; approximately 600 people from universities, public institutions and organizations, trade unions and confederations, professional organizations, associations, and other relevant institutions attended. In the panels, academicians and representatives of social partners expressed their views, and the participants' current problems and solution proposals were discussed (ÇSGB, 2013:281).

On December 23, 2015, the 11th Labor Council Meeting was held as a panel on "employment policies" after an opening attended by approximately 600 people. At the meeting, approximately 300 people from universities, public institutions and organizations, trade unions and confederations, professional organizations, associations, and other relevant institutions attended. In the panels, the social partners expressed their views and solution proposals (ÇSGB, 2015:3).

The opening speeches and the panel organized according to the 11th Labor Council program took place between 12:00 and 18:00 (ÇSGB, 2015:6). There is no final declaration regarding the 11th Labor Council. A report was published in which only the speeches of the speakers and panelists were deciphered. These situations show that the 11th Labor Council is ineffective in social dialogue.

The 12th Labor Council convened in Ankara on May 23, 2019, with the agenda of "Working for a Brighter Future" to discuss the possible effects of changing trends in the world on working life and to understand the strategy that is developing on digital transformation in Turkiye (AÇSBH, 2019:1). The 12th Labor Council program was held between 14:30 and 20:00 (AÇSBH, 2019:5). As in the previous one, a final declaration was not published in the 12th Labor Council. Likewise, a report including the views of the speakers and panelists was published.

The tenth Labor Council, the first meeting held between 2010 and 2020, was partially productive for the parties. Discussing the views of the parties on the issues of "Severance Pay," "Subcontracting," and "Temporary Work Relationship Through Private Employment Offices" can be seen as a productive output. However, the fact that the 11th and 12th Labor Councils lasted for half a day reduced the effectiveness of these councils. In addition, the failure to publish a final report at the end of the 11th and 12th Labor Councils caused the parties to only convey their opinions to each other and be unable to prepare any action plans. In this respect, it has become a social dialogue mechanism where only opinions are shared.

## Tripartite Advisory Board

The Tripartite Advisory Board entered Turkiye's agenda by adopting the ILO's Tripartite Consultation (International Labor Standards) Convention No. 144. With Law 3851 adopted in 1992, this contract gained its legal basis and entered into force in 1993.

The tripartite advisory board is regulated in Article 114 of Labor Law No. 4857 following the spirit of the Tripartite Consultation Agreement No. 144.

To monitor the legislation studies and practices related to working life in the development of labor peace and industrial relations, and to ensure effective consultation between the government and employers, public officials, and trade union confederations, an advisory board based on tripartite representation is established. The working procedures and principles of the board are regulated by a regulation to be issued (T.C. Official Gazette, 2003: Art. 114). The regulation that regulates working procedures and principles of the board is regulated in the "Regulation on Working Procedures and Principles of the Tripartite Advisory Board on Working Life," which came into force in 2004.

According to Article 4 of the Regulation, the Tripartite Advisory Board:

Under the chairmanship of the Minister of Labor and Social Security or Undersecretary,

a) According to the agenda topics from the unit chiefs of the Ministry, affiliated and related institutions,
b) (Amendment: Official Gazette, 15/05/2004-25463) One from each of the trade union confederations and three representatives from the employers' confederation that has the most members,
c) (Amended: Official Gazette, 15/05/2004-25463) One representative from each public servants union confederation, occurs.

> Representatives from employers, public officials and trade union confederations must be senior managers. (Annex: Official Gazette, 15/05/2004-25463) The Board may convene with the participation of the representatives of the trade union and employer union confederations and public servants union confederations, or it may convene separately according to the agenda topics. (T.R. Official Gazette, 2004b: Art. 4)

The duties of the board are as follows:

a) Contributing to the formation of policies regarding working life,
b) To carry out studies that will strengthen reconciliation and cooperation between the parties,
c) To monitor the legislative studies and practices related to working life, to form opinions on new legislation and law amendments,
d) To ensure effective consultation, information and communication between the parties in participation in conferences and activities of the International Labor Organization,
e) To carry out studies in accordance with the provisions of "Convention No. 144 on Tripartite Consultation in the Development of the Application of International Labor Norms,"
f) To ensure the realization of effective consultation, information and communication between the parties for the harmonization of national legislation with the acquis on working life of the European Union,

g) Establishing commissions, determining their members, discussing reports, if needed,
h) Suggesting the organization of national and international seminars and meetings to the parties, sending representatives to meetings deemed appropriate,
i) Suggesting the parties research developing labor peace and industrial relations (T.C. Official Gazette, 2004b: Art. 5).

The board meets three times yearly, in January, May, and September. In addition, if the chairman or three board members make a written request, an extraordinary meeting can also be held (T.C. Official Gazette, 2004b: art. 7).

The chairman determines the meeting agenda by taking the opinions of the representative organizations. The meeting agenda, place, day and time, commission reports, and other documents, if any, are notified to the representative organizations fifteen days in advance (T.C. Official Gazette, 2004b: art. 8).

The duties and authorities of the board are similar to those of the Economic and Social Council (ESC). However, the board's area of interest is not as wide as the ESC and is limited to working life only. In addition, the Tripartite Advisory Board's creation of a platform that enables social partners to come together will certainly positively contribute to developing Turkey's reconciliation and cooperation culture. However, the fact that there is no obligation to consult the Tripartite Advisory Board in making policies and decisions regarding working life has also placed the work of the board under the government's discretion (Görmüş, 2007:133).

## Economic and Social Council

The ESC is a social dialogue mechanism that started to be discussed in Turkey before 1980 and whose legal basis was established in the following period. According to Çelik (2014:26), the structure of ESCs, which have undergone many changes in the historical process, can be examined in three periods. The first period is the period when the ESC was established and transformed with the Prime Ministry circular in 1995, the second period is the period of the ESC established with the Law numbered 4641 in 2001, and the third period is the period when the ESC attained its constitutional status after the September 12, 2010, referendum.

ESCs in Turkey were first introduced after the September 12, 1980, revolution, during the preparatory work of the 1982 constitution with the suggestions of the Turkish Confederation of Employers' Unions (TİSK), the Turkish Industrialists and Businessmen's Association (TÜSİAD), and academic circles. The ESC, whose constitutional status was discussed, was excluded from the draft constitution due to concerns such as "the collective bargaining system would be exposed to interventions, the unions would become dysfunctional, and all sacrifices would be demanded from the workers" (Görmüş, 2007:124–125).

According to Çelik (2014:27), the first period of ESC in Turkey can also be called the period of "An ESC for each government." In this period, it is seen that each government, sometimes the same government, changed the structure of the ESC several times.

Also Koray and Çelik (2007:409) highlight the structural changes in the ESC structure for each government between 1995 and 2001. In their point of view, the 52nd Government of the Turkish Republic in 1995 changed the structure of the ESC. The structure of ESC consisted of Government representatives thirteen members, employees representatives totally two members; (TURK-IS 2) Employers' representatives totally five members; TİSK (Turkish Confederation of Employer Associations) one member, TOBB (The Union of Chambers and Commodity Exchanges of Turkiye) two members, TZOB (Union of Chambers of Agriculture of Turkiye) one member, TESK (Confederation of Turkish Tradesmen and Craftsmen) one member; YOK (Council of Higher Education) two members. The 52nd Government of the Turkish Republic organized the structure of the ESC, totaling twenty-two members. The 53rd Government of Turkish Republic in 1996 changed the structure of the ESC. The structure of the ESC consisted of: Government representatives thirteen members, Employees representatives totally six members (TURK-IS two, DISK one, HAK-IS one, Public Employees 1), Employers' representatives totally eight members, TİSK (Turkish Confederation of Employer Associations) two members, TOBB (The Union of Chambers and Commodity Exchanges of Turkiye) two members, TZOB (Union of Chambers of Agriculture of Turkiye) one member, TESK (Confederation of Turkish Tradesmen and Craftsmen) one member, TUSIAD (Turkish Industry & Business Association) one member, TIM (Turkish Exporters Assembly) one member, YOK (Council of Higher Education) two members, Consumer Association one member. The 53rd Government of the Turkish Republic organized the structure of the ESC, totaling thirty members. The 54th Government of Turkish Republic in 1997 changed the structure of the ESC. The structure of the ESC consisted of: Government representatives ten members, Employee's representatives totally five members (TURK-IS 1(2), DISK one, HAK-IS one, Public Employees 1), Employers' representatives totally six members,TİSK (Turkish Confederation of Employer Associations) one member, TOBB (The Union of Chambers and Commodity Exchanges of Turkiye) one member, TZOB (Union of Chambers of Agriculture of Turkiye) one member, TESK (Confederation of Turkish Tradesmen and Craftsmen) one member, TIM (Turkish Exporters Assembly) one member, Banks Association one member, YOK (Council of Higher Education) one member, Consumer Association one member, Federation of the Disabled People one member. The 54th Government of the Turkish Republic organized the structure of the ESC, totaling twenty-four members. The 55th Government of the Turkish Republic in 1997 changed the structure of the ESC again. The structure of the ESC consisted of: Government representatives eleven members, Employee's representatives totally four members (TURK-IS two, DISK one, HAK-IS 1), Employers' representatives totally six members, TİSK (Turkish Confederation of Employer Associations) one member, TOBB (The Union of Chambers and Commodity Exchanges of Turkiye) two members, TZOB (Union of Chambers of Agriculture of Turkiye) one member, TESK (Confederation of Turkish Tradesmen and Craftsmen) one member. The 55th Government of the Turkish Republic organized the structure of the ESC, totaling twenty-one members. The 56th Government of the Turkish Republic in 1999 changed the structure of the ESC. The structure of the ESC consisted of: Government representatives nine members, Employees representatives totally four members (TURK-IS two, DISK one, HAK-IS 1), Employers representatives totally six members,TİSK (Turkish Confederation of Employer Associations) one member, TOBB (The Union of Chambers and Commodity Exchanges of Turkiye) two members, TZOB (Union of Chambers of Agriculture of Turkiye) one member, TESK (Confederation of Turkish Tradesmen and Craftsmen) one member. The 56th Government of the Turkish Republic organized the structure of the ESC, totaling nineteen members. The 57th Government of the Turkish Republic in 1999 changed the structure of the ESC again. The structure of the ESC consisted of: Government representatives eleven members, Employees representatives totally four members (TURK-IS two, DISK one, HAK-IS 1), Employers representatives totally six members, TİSK (Turkish Confederation of Employer Associations) one member, TOBB (The Union of Chambers and Commodity Exchanges of Turkiye) two members, TZOB (Union of Chambers of Agriculture of Turkiye) one member, TESK (Confederation of Turkish Tradesmen and Craftsmen) two members. The 57th Government of Turkish Republic organized the structure of the ESC, totaling twenty-one members. The 58th Government of Turkish Republic in 2001 changed the structure of the ESC. The structure of the ESC consisted of: Government representatives fifteen members, Employees representatives totally twelve members (TURK-IS three, DISK three, HAK-IS three, Public Employees three), Employers' representatives totally twelve members, TİSK (Turkish Confederation of Employer Associations) three members, TOBB (The Union of Chambers and Commodity Exchanges of Turkiye) three members, TZOB (Union of Chambers of Agriculture of Turkiye) three members, TESK (Confederation of Turkish Tradesmen and Craftsmen) three members. The 58th Government of Turkish republic organized the structure of the ESC totaling thirty-nine members.

The government's changes in the ESC structure can be seen. In almost every period, the weight of the government in the ESC stands out. It is understood that the structure of the ESC has narrowed even more, especially after 1997.

The legislative period, the second period of the ESC in Turkiye, started in 2001 with Law No. 4641 on the Establishment, Working Principles and Methods of the Economic and Social Council. The purpose of this law is to regulate the establishment, working principles, and methods of the Economic and Social Council, which was formed to determine a common opinion in consultation by creating a continuous and permanent environment that will ensure social reconciliation and cooperation in the formation of economic and social policies (T.R. Official Gazette, 2001: Art. 1). With Law numbered 4641, it was expected that the ESC structure, which the prime minister's circular could easily regulate before 2001, would be preserved. According to Çelik (2014:31), apart from stabilizing the structure of the ESC, this law did not make a fundamental transformation, and the ESC could not get rid of the image of a "showcase institution." According to Görmüş (2007:132), having the secretariat services of the ESC outsourced to a public institution (DPT performs according to Articles 9 and 10 of Law No. 4641) and the absence of a budget belonging to the council is incompatible with the autonomy of the ESC. Its mission needs to allocate a building to carry out ESC services, to have its secretariat, and, above all, to have an autonomous budget for the ESC. In addition, in Law numbered 4641, many issues like the functioning of the ESC, how the decisions regarding the agenda are taken, how the voting will be done, the appointment to the ESC membership, withdrawal from the membership, and so on have not been regulated. This situation creates the impression that the ESC was established as a "formality" to fulfill the relevant provisions of ILO and EU. In addition, according to Çalış and Yıldırım (2003:114), the ESC, which was historically formed as a result of state tradition that has made it a habit to govern its people with institutions from the top, will have the feature of being an institution where "dialogue of the deaf" is reproduced as long as its structure and functions do not change.

According to Law No. 4641, the Economic and Social Council; Under the chairmanship of the Prime Minister, Deputy Prime Ministers, State Minister responsible for the State Planning Organization, State Minister responsible for the Treasury, State Minister responsible for the Undersecretariat of Foreign Trade, State Minister responsible for the State Personnel Presidency, Minister of Finance, Minister of Agriculture and Rural Affairs, Minister of Labor and Social Security, Minister of Industry and Trade, Minister of Energy and Natural Resources, Undersecretary of the State Planning

Organization, Undersecretary of Customs, Head of State Personnel, Union of Chambers and Commodity Exchanges of Turkey, Confederation of Turkish Workers' Unions (TURKIS), Confederation of Turkish Employers' Unions, Confederation of Turkish Tradesmen and Craftsmen, Union of Chambers of Agriculture of Turkey, HAK-IS' Trade Union Confederation consists of three representatives each representing the Confederation of Progressive Trade Unions of Turkey (DISK) and other government representatives to be determined by the Prime Minister, representatives of nongovernmental organizations, and public officials (T.R. Official Gazette, 2001: Art. 2). This article states that the ESC's structure was changed to include a total of twelve employers' organizations, twelve workers' organizations, and fifteen government representatives. The government side retains its weight, even though the actor ratios are more egalitarian than they were during the cyclical period, according to the law.

The third term of the ESC in Turkey has passed into constitutional status with Law No. 5982, which was accepted with a referendum on September 12, 2010. The title of Article 166 of the Constitution is "Planning"; it was renamed the Economic and Social Council. In addition, the ESC is established to provide an advisory opinion to the government in formulating economic and social policies. The Law shall regulate the establishment and functioning of the Economic and Social Council. According to Çelik (2014:39–41), this provision narrowed the existing authority of the ESC. According to issue number 4641, the ESC can present the reports it has created to the Grand National Assembly of Turkey (GNAT), the president and the public, and the government. In addition, the ESC does not have a permanent secretariat, office, publication, or official website.

In 2014, the draft law of the Economic and Social Council came to the agenda. According to Article 2 of this draft law, under the chairmanship of the prime minister, it was envisaged to increase the number of members to fifty-seven, twenty from public institutions and organizations, eight from employees, twelve from the private sector, twelve from other social segments, and two from local governments and universities (Başbakanlık, 2014).

With the draft law, ESC members increased from thirty-nine to fifty-seven. Nevertheless, the composition of the ESC was being made even more anti-democratic. The representation of the employees, represented by twelve members, would be reduced to eight members with the draft. On the other hand, the representation of employer organizations, which twelve members still represent, was preserved. Instead of the triple representation system envisaged by the Law numbered 4641, the new draft law envisaged a 3+ system.

The bill envisages twelve members from other sections of society, two from local governments, and two from universities. The draft envisages twenty members from public institutions and organizations. Along with the prime minister, the government will be represented by twenty-one members in the fifty-seven-member ESC. As such, the representation of the government is more than each of the social segments. With the draft law, the proportional weight of the government in the ESC was not changed, but the representation of workers was reduced. In addition, the authority of the Economic and Social Council was also limited by the draft law. According to Article 3 of Law No. 4641, the duties and authorities of the ESC were discussed above. With the draft law, the duties of the Economic and Social Council were significantly limited, and it was turned into an organization that only offered advisory opinions to the government in parallel with the regulation in the Constitution. The duty of "ensuring participation of economic and social units in society in the formulation of economic and social policies of Government," which existed in Law numbered 4641, was removed from the law. The authority of the board to report to various public authorities and the public other than the government, to organize national and international seminars and meetings, and to conduct publications and research was also abolished.

Finally, the number of meetings of the board, which was supposed to meet four times a year according to Law numbered 4641, was reduced to twice a year. This draft law, which was not enacted, envisaged turning the council into an intensely political and administrative tutelage mechanism (Çelik, 2020:29).

In 2018, amendments were made to Law No. 4641 with the Decree Law (KHK) No. 703. The second article of the law states:

> *Article 2—(Amended: 2/7/2018-KHK/703/109 art.) "The President of the Economic and Social Council is the President of the Republic. If the President cannot attend the meetings, the Vice President or Minister to be appointed accompanies the meetings. The members of the Council are determined by the Presidency."* (T.R. Official Gazette, 2018b: md109)

Likewise, the fourth article of the Law is:

> *"The Presidency determines the working procedures and principles of the Council."* (T.R. Official Gazette, 2018b: art. 109)

It has been changed in form. In addition, with Decree-Law No. 703, some articles of the law (subparagraph (f) of the first paragraph of Article 3, Articles 5–11, brief first article) were repealed.

According to Çelik (2020:31), although the ESC, regulated by circulars in 1995, gained a legal and later a constitutional character, it returned to the circular period with the regulations made with the Decree-Law.

While these developments are taking place on the legal basis of the ESC in Turkey, the ESC has not been convened until today after it attained its constitutional status. After the last meeting held in 2009, the ESC could not take action. Today, although the social segments call for the convening of the ESC, the ESC cannot operate.

## SOCIAL DIALOGUE IN THE EUROPEAN COMMISSION PROGRESS/COUNTRY REPORTS

Since 1998, the European Commission has been publishing annual reports evaluating the progress made by candidate countries in compliance with the Copenhagen criteria. These reports were named "Progress Report" until 2016 and then "Country Report." Chapter 19 of these reports annually examines developments in candidate countries in the "Social Policy and Employment" field. In the same chapter, developments in the candidate countries regarding social dialogue are evaluated.

### Positive Developments Regarding Social Dialogue in Turkey According to EU Progress/Country Reports

In 2010, Amendments to the Constitution granted civil servants and other public employees the right to bargain and bargain collectively and subject disciplinary punishments to civil servants to judicial review. Removal of the ban on membership in more than one union at the same time and in the same sector and the abolition of the restriction of concluding a single collective agreement for the same period in the same workplace. With the constitutional amendments, the Economic and Social Council became a constitutional body that the government would consult while formulating policy on economic and social issues (EC, 2010:69).

In 2011, lifting the bans on contracted personnel working in state-owned enterprises to form unions or participate in union activities (EC, 2011:78).

In 2012, adopting the new law on public servants' unions allowed collective bargaining for the first time in the public sector (EC, 2012:82).

In 2013, entry into force of new trade unions and collective bargaining laws for the private sector. Facilitating the internal functioning of trade unions, simplifying membership procedures and requirements, limiting the prohibition of strikes, and reducing criminal penalties (EC, 2013:41).

In 2014, using the e-Government portal for union membership registration and withdrawal (EC, 2014:40).

In 2015, workers in small-sized companies are now legally protected against eviction for their union activities. Reducing the sector threshold from

3 percent to 1 percent to authorize independent unions to conclude collective bargaining agreements. The union membership rate in the private sector increased from 9.5 percent to 11.2 percent in 2015 (EC, 2015:57).

In 2016, the rate of unionized workers in the private sector rose slightly to 11.5 percent in 2016 but is still low (EC, 2016:59).

In 2017, the report has yet to be published.

In 2018 and 2019, there has been a setback in social dialogue.

In 2020, there is no progress that can be reported on social dialogue in Turkey.

## Negative Developments Regarding Social Dialogue in Turkey According to EU Progress/Country Reports

In 2010, the government attempted to address some of the key issues regarding trade union rights in the private sector, such as freedom of association and the right to collective bargaining in the workplace, in a new draft law that has failed to gain support from the social partners. The low number of workers is covered by collective bargaining agreements. Further strengthening the work of the main social dialogue mechanisms (Tripartite Advisory Board, Economic and Social Council) and the capacity of social partners (EC, 2010:69).

In 2011, inability to implement the constitutional amendments on workers' rights because the necessary changes were not made in the relevant union legislation. Failure of social partners to agree on key issues such as the right to organize at the workplace level and the collective bargaining threshold. Failure of the Economic and Social Council to meet during the reporting period. The capacity of the social partners needs to be developed. Not expanding the narrow scope of collective bargaining (EC, 2011:78).

In 2012, the high threshold for collective bargaining continues to significantly limit the possibility of collective bargaining, which hinders the full exercise of the right to collective bargaining. The failure of the authorities to share data on the number of employees in all sectors caused no new collective bargaining negotiations to be concluded for several months. The level of unionization and the coverage of collective agreements could be higher due to restrictive legal provisions and difficulties in enforcing trade union rights. The Economic and Social Council has not met since 2009 (EC, 2012:82).

In 2013, few workers benefited from collective bargaining and engaged in collective action, including strikes, due to the high and cumulative thresholds required for collective bargaining. Union member workers working in small workplaces are not adequately protected from the danger of dismissal due to their union activities. Many categories of public servants face restrictions on their right to organize, and the ban on strikes continues for public officials.

Ineffective functioning of tripartite and bilateral social dialogue mechanisms and the Economic and Social Council (EC, 2013:41).

In 2014, coverage of collective bargaining agreements was still low. The restrictive double threshold for collective bargaining agreements, uncertainties in protecting union members from dismissal, and gaps in organizing, collective bargaining, and the right to strike are still the most prominent issues in this area. With the amendment made in the Trade Unions and Collective Bargaining Agreement Law, the permanent setting of 1 percent (the ratio of union members to the workforce in the sector in which the workplace is included) for unions to make collective bargaining agreements continues to pose a significant obstacle to unions from making collective bargaining agreements (EC, 2014:40).

In 2015, the proportion of workers covered by collective bargaining agreements is still significantly low. This is due to the persistence of the "double threshold" limiting the unions' power to bargain collectively. Many informal workers do not have access to unions. Unlawful dismissals of union members and protracted lawsuits discourage workers from joining unions. The Economic and Social Council has not met since 2009 (EC, 2015:57).

In 2016, tripartite and bipartite social dialogue is still limited

The Economic and Social Council has been inactive since 2009. Legal deficiencies (such as a double threshold for collective bargaining and the lack of the right to strike for public servants) contradict European standards and ILO conventions. Informal workers, retirees and the unemployed, and a large segment of civil servants still lack the right to organize. Prohibition of large protests and demonstrations by trade unions, disproportionately restricting trade union rights. Numerous serious accusations of dismissal, harassment, retaliation, arrest, and police mistreatment of union officials by trade union confederations for their legitimate trade union activities. Closure of trade unions that have relations with FETO (EC, 2016:59).

In 2017, the report has yet to be published this year.

In 2018, five strikes were postponed and de facto banned. Cases of dismissal, ill-treatment, arrest, and police attacks on members engaged in legitimate trade union activities continued to be reported by unions. The Economic and Social Council has been inactive since 2009, and the tripartite advisory board met only once in 2017 (EC, 2018:84).

In 2019, the Economic and Social Council members, who have not met since 2009, will now be appointed by the president. The tripartite advisory committee, which remains the main tripartite social dialogue forum, met once in 2018. Managers and members of some unions continue to be subjected to arbitrary dismissals, ill-treatment, and detentions for their various peaceful union activities. Large-scale layoffs of public officials continued for their affiliation with terrorist groups linked to the 2016 coup attempt. The constitutional court ruled that the government's decision to postpone a strike in the metal sector in 2015 on the grounds of national security violated the right to strike (EC, 2019:96).

In 2020, Turkey held its 11th Labor Council Meeting in May 2019, bringing national social partners together. Focused on the ILO's future of work agenda, results still needed to be adopted. The Economic and Social Council has yet to meet since 2009. Other formal social dialogue mechanisms are either ineffective or lack genuine democratic participation from all parties, so they cannot support consensus building. It is reported that anti-union discrimination actions by employers are very strong. Managers and members of some unions continue to be subjected to arbitrary dismissals, ill-treatment, and detentions for their various peaceful union activities. These factors undermine the right to freedom of association (EC, 2020:95–96).

According to EU progress/country reports, it is seen that there has been very limited progress in the field of social dialogue between 2010 and 2020. It is seen in the reports that progress has yet to be made, especially after 2016. In addition, negative developments are widely covered. In particular, the inability of the ESC to convene within the relevant years has been frequently criticized. It should be noted that the ESC attained its constitutional status in 2010. Apart from the ESC, it is seen that other social dialogue mechanisms need to function more effectively, although they have legal grounds.

## CONCLUSION

The Republic of Turkey, in its centennial year, is a rich country in terms of social dialogue mechanisms. In Turkey, which wants to crown its political independence with its economic independence, various social dialogue mechanisms have been established both before and after the republic. Turkey, which had a single-party period from the first years of the republic until 1946, moved toward becoming a more democratic country by adopting a multiparty system in 1946 when it became a member of the United Nations. The prohibition of class-based organizations before 1946 made it difficult to represent the working life actors in an organized manner. However, efforts for dialogue with various mechanisms continued. After 1946, with the recognition of the organization as a right and the establishment of relevant state institutions, social dialogue efforts and mechanisms expanded in real terms. The military coups of 1960 and 1980 and the constitutions they brought positively and negatively impacted social dialogue efforts.

Developments related to social dialogue mechanisms, which tried to be functionalized with different mechanisms in the past, gained momentum in the 1990s. Social dialogue mechanisms such as the ESC, recommended by the ILO and widely used all over the world, were discussed and started to be implemented in these periods. The adventure started with the prime minister's circulars at the beginning and underwent constant changes with the legislation and constitutional process in 2010.

There are many legally regulated mechanisms according to the aims and objectives of the working life actors. However, many researchers mention that these mechanisms are not functional. Various discussions about this situation continue today.

The decisive role of the state in employment relations in Turkey has brought arbitrariness in implementing mechanisms related to social dialogue. The dominance of political power in employment relations is one of the main reasons for this situation. In addition, the limited number of empirical studies on social dialogue in Turkey prevents the working life actors' goals and objectives from being fully determined and thus preventing the mechanisms from functioning effectively. Social dialogue mechanisms in Turkey are regulated legally, but they need to function functionally in response to the demands of institutions such as the ILO or the EU. For this reason, social dialogue mechanisms in Turkey are called names such as "formality," "showcase," or "dialogue of the deaf."

To make social dialogue mechanisms functional in Turkey, it is important to increase the empirical studies on the perspectives, wishes, and demands of the working life actors, to train the actors on this issue, and to increase their awareness. However, balancing power in employment relations should also be discussed simultaneously. As long as the actors of working life do not enter into this mentality change, even if social dialogue mechanisms are organized with new laws and names, they will remain dysfunctional.

## NOTE

1. Dr. Sakarya University, Faculty of Political Sciences, Department of Labor Economics and Industrial Relations, cihand@sakarya.edu.tr.

## REFERENCES

AÇSHB, 2019, 12. Çalışma Meclisi Daha Parlak Bir Gelecek İçin Çalışmak, Çalışma Genel Müdürlüğü, Ankara.

Asgari Ücret Tespit Komisyonu Kararı, 2010, No:2010/1, Sayı: 27802, https://www.resmigazete.gov.tr/eskiler/2010/12/20101231-30.htm

Asgari Ücret Tespit Komisyonu Kararı, 2011, NO:2011/1, https://www.mevzuat.gov.tr/File/GeneratePdf?mevzuatNo=15683&mevzuatTur=Teblig&mevzuatTertip=5

Asgari Ücret Tespit Komisyonu Kararı, 2012, No: 2012/1, Sayı: 28512, https://www.resmigazete.gov.tr/eskiler/2012/12/20121229-19.htm

Asgari Ücret Tespit Komisyonu Kararı, 2013, No: 2013/1, www.resmigazete.gov.tr/eskiler/2020/12/20201230-2.pdf

Asgari Ücret Tespit Komisyonu Kararı, 2014, No: 2014/1, Sayı: 29222, https://www.resmigazete.gov.tr/eskiler/2014/12/20141231-7.htm

Asgari Ücret Tespit Komisyonu Kararı, 2015, No: 2015/1, https://www.resmigazete.gov.tr/eskiler/2015/12/20151231-11.pdf

Asgari Ücret Tespit Komisyonu Kararı, 2016, No: 2016/1, https://www.resmigazete.gov.tr/eskiler/2016/12/20161230-22.pdf

Asgari Ücret Tespit Komisyonu Kararı, 2017, No: 2017/1, https://www.resmigazete.gov.tr/eskiler/2017/12/20171230-10.pdf

Asgari Ücret Tespit Komisyonu Kararı, 2018, No: 2018/1, https://www.resmigazete.gov.tr/eskiler/2018/12/20181227-10.pdf

Asgari Ücret Tespit Komisyonu Kararı, 2019, No: 2019/1, Sayı: 30991, https://www.resmigazete.gov.tr/eskiler/2019/12/20191227-21.pdf

Asgari Ücret Tespit Komisyonu Kararı, 2020, No: 2020/1, Sayı: 31350, https://www.resmigazete.gov.tr/eskiler/2020/12/20201230-2.pdf

Başbakanlık, 2014, Ekonomik ve Sosyal Konsey'in Kuruluşu ve Görevleri Hakkındaki Kanun

Compston, Hugh, 2002, "Policy Concertation in Western Europe: A Configurational Approach." In Stefan Berger and Hugh Compston, eds. *Policy Concertation and Social Partnership in Western Europe: Lessons for the 21st Century*. Oxford: Berghahn Books.

Crozet, Marcel, 2020, *Social Dialogue and the Future of Work, Global Deal Together for Decent Work and Inclusive Growth Thematic Brief*. Madagascar: ILO.

Çalış, Ş., & Yıldırım, E., 2003, Sosyal Diyalog ve Ekonomik ve Sosyal Konsey. *Sendikal Notlar*, 20, 100–115.

Çelik, Aziz, 2014, Türkiye'de Sosyal Diyalog ve Ekonomik ve Sosyal Konsey: Bir Başarısızlık Öyküsü. 15. Çalışma Ekonomisi ve Endüstri İlişkileri Kongresi. Ankara: TÜRK-İŞ, 16–48.

Çelik, Aziz, 2020, Metruk Bir Anayasal Kurum Olarak Ekonomik ve Sosyal Konsey'in Tarihçesi. *Yönetim ve Çalışma Dergisi*, 4(1), 14–35.

ÇSGB, 2013, Çalışma ve Sosyal Güvenlik Bakanlığı 10. Çalışma Meclisi, Ankara.

ÇSGB, 2015, 11. Çalışma Meclisi, Çalışma Genel Müdürlüğü, Ankara.

Dereli, Toker, 1997, "Sosyal Diyalog: Ekonomik ve Sosyal Konsey Hakkında." *Ekonomik Yaklasim, Ekonomik Yaklasim Association*, 8(27), 113–130.

EC, 2010, Türkiye 2010 Yılı İlerleme Raporu, 09/11/2010, Brussels, https://www.ab.gov.tr/files/AB_Iliskileri/AdaylikSureci/IlerlemeRaporlari/turkiye_ilerleme_rap_2010.pdf

EC, 2011, Türkiye 2011 Yılı İlerleme Raporu, 12/10/2011, Brussels, https://www.ab.gov.tr/files/AB_Iliskileri/AdaylikSureci/IlerlemeRaporlari/2011_ilerleme_raporu_tr.pdf

EC, 2012, Türkiye 2012 Yılı İlerleme Raporu, 10/10/2012, Brussels, https://www.ab.gov.tr/files/2012_ilerleme_raporu_tr.pdf

EC, 2013, Türkiye 2013 Yılı İlerleme Raporu, 16/10/2013, Brussels, https://www.ab.gov.tr/files/2013%20ilerleme%20raporu/2013_ilerleme_raporu_tr.pdf

EC, 2014, Türkiye 2014 Yılı İlerleme Raporu, 08/10/2014, Brussels, https://www.ab.gov.tr/files/ilerlemeRaporlariTR/2014_ilerleme_raporu_tr.pdf

EC, 2015, Türkiye 2015 Yılı İlerleme Raporu, 10/11/2015, Brussels, https://www.ab.gov.tr/files/5%20Ekim/2015_ilerleme_raporu_tr.pdf

EC, 2016, 2016 Türkiye Raporu, 09/11/2016, Brussels, https://www.ab.gov.tr/files/pub/2016_ilerleme_raporu_tr.pdf

EC, 2018, 2018 Türkiye Raporu, 17/04/2018, Brussels, https://www.ab.gov.tr/siteimages/pub/komisyon_ulke_raporlari/2018_turkiye_raporu_tr.pdf

EC, 2019, 2019 Türkiye Raporu, 29/05/2019, Brussels, https://www.ab.gov.tr/siteimages/birimler/kpb/2019_trkiye_raporu-_tr.pdf

EC, 2020, 2020 Türkiye Raporu, 06/10/2020, Brussels, https://www.ab.gov.tr/siteimages/trkiye_raporustrateji_belgesi_2020/turkey_report_30.10.2020.pdf

Ekin, Nusret, (Ekim 1997); Diyalog Çağı, Mercek Dergisi, Sayı 8

Engin, Murat E., 2018, *AB Ülkelerinde İkili, Üçlü, Genişletilmiş Sosyal Diyalog Mekanizmaları ve İyi Uygulama Örnekleri.* Ankara: Çalışma Hayatında Sosyal Diyaloğun Geliştirilmesi Projesi.

Görmüş, A., 2007, "Türkiye'de Sosyal Diyaloğun Gelişimi." *Çalışma ve Toplum*, 3(14), 115–142.

Guardiancich, I., & Molina, O., 2020, *The Effectiveness of National Social Dialogue Institutions: From Theory to Evidence*, ILO Working Paper 16. Geneva: ILO.

ILO, 1999, Programme and Budget proposals for 2000-01: Approval of the detailed budget and further development of strategic budgeting, INTERNATIONAL LABOUR OFFICE, Programme, Financial and Administrative Committee, 276th Session, Geneva.

ILO, 2022, Çalışma Hayatında Sosyal Diyaloğun Geliştirilmesi Projesi, https://www.ilo.org/ankara/projects/WCMS_537299/lang--tr/index.htm

Ishikawa, J., 2003, *Key Features of National Social Dialogue: A Social Dialogue Resource Book Geneva.* International Labour Office, Geneva.

Koray, M., & Çelik, A., 2007, Avrupa Birliği ve Türkiye'de Sosyal Diyalog, Belediye-İş Yayınları, ISBN: 978-975-6024-2-7

Orhan, S., & Çakmak, B.Y., 2017, Sosyal Diyalog Durum Tespit ve Eğitim İhtiyaç Analizi Raporu, Türkiye Kooperatif, Ticaret, Eğitim ve Büro İşçileri Sendikası (Koop-iş) Sosyal Diyaloğun Geliştirilmesi: Çalışma Barışı ve Sürdürülebilir Üretimin Şifresi Projesi.

Policy Brief, 2020, The need for social dialogue in addressing the COVID-19 crisis, ILO Brief, May 2020.

Tasarısı, Sayı: 31853594-101-830-2953, https://www2.tbmm.gov.tr/d24/1/1-0946 .pdf

T.C. Resmi Gazete, 1946, Çalışma Bakanlığının kuruluş ve görevleri hakkında kanun, No:4841, Sayı 6219, https://www.resmigazete.gov.tr/arsiv/6219.pdf

T.C. Resmi Gazete, 2001, Ekonomik Ve Sosyal Konseyin Kuruluşu, Çalışma Esas Ve Yöntemleri Hakkında Kanun, No:4641, Sayı:24380, https://www.mevzuat.gov.tr/ MevzuatMetin/1.5.4641.pdf

T.C. Resmi Gazete, 2003, İş Kanunu, No: 4857, Sayı:25134, https://www.mevzuat .gov.tr/mevzuatmetin/1.5.4857.pdf

T.C. Resmi Gazete, 2004a, Asgari Ücret Yönetmeliği, Sayı 25540, https://www .mevzuat.gov.tr/File/GeneratePdf?mevzuatNo=5454&mevzuatTur=KurumVe KurulusYonetmeligi&mevzuatTertip=5

T.C. Resmi Gazete, 2004b, Çalışma Hayatına İlişkin Üçlü Danışma Kurulunun Çalışma Usul ve Esasları Hakkında Yönetmelik, https://www.mevzuat.gov.tr/ File/GeneratePdf?mevzuatNo=6250&mevzuatTur=KurumVeKurulusYonetmeligi &mevzuatTertip=5

T.C. Resmi Gazete, 2018a, Cumhurbaşkanlığı Teşkilatı Hakkında Cumhurbaşkanlığı Kararnamesi, Sayı 30474, https://www.mevzuat.gov.tr/MevzuatMetin/19.5.1.pdf

T.C. Resmi Gazete, 2018b, Anayasada Yapılan Değişikliklere Uyum Sağlanması Amacıyla Bazı Kanun ve Kanun Hükmünde Kararnamelerde Değişiklik Yapılması Hakkında Kanun Hükmünde Kararname, Sayı: KHK703, https://www.resmigazete .gov.tr/eskiler/2018/07/20180709M3-1.pdf

# *Chapter 13*

# A Glance at Turkey's OHS Outlook Within Law No. 6331

Zeynep Aca[1]

Occupational Health and Safety (OHS) Law No. 6331 was enacted in Turkey on June 30, 2012, upon the death of 3,888 workers between 2010 and 2012. Consequently, the OHS provisions were clustered under a single law incorporating all public and private sectors. The OHS provisions would apply to all employees, including employers, employer representatives, interns, and apprentices. Nevertheless, OHS-related problems have interestingly increased over the years despite this law. Ultimately, OHS and OHS-related defects in Turkey must be addressed in detail to uncover the reasons for the problems. This study attempts to discuss OHS in Turkey and the underlying causes of the issues in four sections. The first section introduces the history of OHS in Turkey. The improvements brought by OHS Law No. 6331 are elaborated on in the second section. The third section depicts the OHS outlook of Turkey in the last decade through seven focus areas: (1) years, (2) workplace sizes, (3) sectors, (4) occupational death rates, (5) working hours, (6) labor losses, and (7) causes of occupational accidents. The research is then wrapped up with an overview of current OHS-related problems.

## INTRODUCTION

Despite more than 100 years of legislation background regarding OHS, Turkey was able to cluster OHS-specific provisions under a single roof thanks to the Occupational Health and Safety Law No. 6331 on June 30, 2012. The law was enacted after 3,888 workers lost their lives between 2010 and 2012 and obliged all workplaces in public and private industries to related provisions on OHS. The law was taken into force primarily to eliminate vulnerabilities in OHS, mediate to establish a healthy working environment for all employees, raise awareness of OHS, resolve regulatory clutter, and introduce an efficient control mechanism to ensure a healthy working environment. Before its enactment, a report by the State Supervisory Board in 2011 listed the overall underlying causes of occupational accidents and diseases: lack of education, inadequate vocational education, poor infrastructure to prevent occupational accidents, employing workers with low education in hazardous jobs, employers' failure to fulfill the conditions stipulated in the legislation for on-the-job and in-service training, and perceiving relevant training as cost-raising and time-consuming activities (DDK, 2011: 575). Yet, the law adopts an understanding of preventing occupational accidents and diseases before they occur and eliminating them at the source. It was targeted to eliminate chronic OHS-related problems thanks to the law, and, therefore, the law has pioneered a new era in working life upon incorporating all workplaces into the scope of relevant OHS provisions. Nevertheless, the law has not given birth to the expected, and the problems in OHS have increased over the years, which mandates a detailed discussion of the general OHS outlook of Turkey. In this context, the present chapter addresses the reasons underlying the problems in OHS through the contemporary OHS outlook of Turkey and OHS-related statistics in the framework of Law No. 6331 within four sections. The first section reviews the OHS background of Turkey. The second section elaborates on what was brought new to OHS in Turkeyby Law No. 6331. The third section presents a glance at Turkey's OHS outlook by years, gender, workplace size, selected industries, and working hours. The research is then wrapped up with an overview of current OHS-related problems.

## OHS BACKGROUND OF TURKEY

The regulation of OHS as a legal norm in Turkey dates back to the "Mecelle," the first Turkish Civil Code enacted in 1860 in the second half of the nineteenth century (Dilik, 1985: 93). Since coal mines were at the heart of labor relations, the Ottoman Empire issued certain regulations for regional mines (Kılkış, 2018: 48). The Dilaver Pasha Regulation of 1867, circulated to ensure efficiency in coal mines and implemented for the mining workers primarily in the Zonguldak Coal Basin, is considered the very first official document related to OHS (Dilik, 1985: 93; Talas, 1992: 40; Kılkış, 2018: 49). Besides, the Maadin Regulation of 1869, embracing more advanced norms for mines in different regions of the country, included provisions to protect worker health and safety, pay compensation to workers having an occupational accident, and oblige employers to employ an occupational physician (Makal, Erdoğdu, & Çelik, 2018: 47; Dilik, 1985: 93; Talas, 1992: 40).

Immediately before the Republican period (1923), the republican Ankara government took several steps to accelerate industrialization and initiated more OHS-related regulations. The first regulation in this period was the Law on Mining Workers, dated 1921 and numbered 151. The law, limited to those employed in Eregli coal mines, is shown as the first labor law (Dilik; 1971: 17, 1985: 94; Deniz, 2007: 138). Similar to the regulations in the Ottoman Empire, this law also obliged employers to pay compensation to employees in the event of an occupational accident (Art. 6). However, due to the increase in occupational diseases caused by working conditions in the mines, the Regulation on the Provision of the Sanitary Needs of the Workers in the Eregli Coal Basin was issued in 1935 to meet the health-related needs of the workers. The first part of the regulation addressed OHS and included provisions for the treatment of workers in cases of diseases and accidents (İleri, 2013: 1455).

After the proclamation of the Republic, it was stipulated in the 1924 Constitution that the provisions on the right to work would be regulated by law. Accordingly, many laws enacted to regulate working life included OHS-related provisions (Dilik, 1971: 21; Kılkış, 2018: 50). For example, the Code of Obligations of 1926 regulated the employers' legal responsibilities regarding occupational accidents and diseases. The Public Health Law of 1930 required employers to hire a physician and construct a hospital based on the number of workers and workplace size (Gerek, 2008: 7; Arıcı, 1999: 44–45). Another significant legislation in these years was Labor Law No. 3008, dated 1936, introduced with many bylaws for the applicability of the provisions on OHS (Baybora, 2012: 8; Arıcı, 1999: 45–46). In addition, the law provided fundamental principles regarding social security and ensured workers have social security in case of a disability due to an occupational accident or disease. However, the idea of the social insurance system, which was thought to be accomplished gradually, had to be postponed due to the Second World War (Gökbayrak, 2010: 144). In 1945, the ministration of enforcing OHS across the country was assigned to the Ministry of Labor (Kılkış, 2018: 51; Baybora, 2012: 8). The same year also witnessed Law No. 4972 on Workers' Insurance Institution and Law No. 4772 on Occupational Accidents and Diseases and Maternity Insurance.[2]

OHS was first addressed constitutionally in 1961. Yet, it was not possible to trace detailed OHS regulations in the new labor law dated 1967 and numbered 931, causing great controversy. As expected, this law did not last long, and Labor Law No. 1475 was enacted in 1971 as a requirement of the constitution adopting the social state principle. The law introduced comprehensive regulations and held employers responsible for ensuring a healthy working environment. In addition, most of the OHS-related regulations and bylaws were issued in the same year (Kılkış, 2018: 52). In the process of harmonization with the European Union (EU), Law No. 1475 was repealed with Labor Law No. 4857 dated 2003. Moreover, the section titled "Occupational Health and Safety" in the 5th part of the Law extended the provisions on OHS, allowing for comprehensive bylaws and regulations (Baybora, 2018: 9). However, new regulations were still highly needed in OHS due to several reasons, such as considering only the EU directives while designing the domestic regulations, legislative incompatibilities with the conditions in Turkey, legislative insufficiency for current developments, and the increase in the number of occupational accidents (Süzek, 2000: 306–307; Süzek, 2011: 792). In this respect, the existing provisions for OHS were regulated by the Occupational Health and Safety Law No. 6331 in 2012.

## OCCUPATIONAL HEALTH AND SAFETY LAW NO. 6331 IN TURKEYAND ITS IMPLICATIONS IN OHS

In 2012, all OHS-related provisions were gathered under a single law, Law No. 6331. The law extended the scope of OHS with some exceptions in Article 2/2. Therefore, following the EU's Framework Directive on Occupational Health No. 1989/391, all jobs and workplaces in public and private sectors, including employers, employer representatives, interns, apprentices, and branches of activity, were included in the coverage of the law (Art. 2/1).

The law, enacted after 3,888 workers lost their lives between 2010 and 2012, primarily aimed to hinder the unstoppable rise in occupational accidents and diseases in Turkey. The law adopted a preventive approach in OHS, referring to preventing occupational accidents and diseases before they occur (Demir, 2014: 676). Yet, it is not the only reason for enacting the law. Despite having more than a century of legislation background regarding OHS, Türkiye had no exclusive law gathering the provisions on OHS under a single roof (Kılkış, 2018: 81; Centel, 2013: 79, 83). Furthermore, the regulations and bylaws on OHS in the Labor Law No. 4857 remained far from satisfying the needs in practice (Demircioğlu & Kaplan, 2013: 5) since not more than the translation of the relevant EU directives (Aydın, 2012: 10; Kılkış, 2018: 82). In addition, the nullity of all or critical articles of the regulations by the Council of State from time to time caused substantial uncertainties and gaps in OHS legislation (Aydın, 2012: 10). The regulations before Law No. 6331 were also highly criticized in terms of scope and compliance with the EU acquis, which were mostly resolved thanks to the enactment of Law No. 6331 (Demircioğlu & Kaplan, 2013: 5). Overall, some significant implications of Law No. 6331 in OHS may be summarized as follows:

- The obligation of ensuring OHS is primarily encumbered to employers (Art. 4) and the law is largely shaped upon this obligation (Kılkış, 2013: 22; Ger, 2012: 11; Demir, 2014: 676).
- As a result of the understanding of preventing OHS-related problems before they arise, the law envisages a risk assessment condition (Art. 4/1a, b, and c). Therefore, the law abandons the prescriptive approach of the past and adopts a proactive approach with preventive, improving, and remedial measures (Aydın, 2012: 11).
- Besides the implementation of OHS in all workplaces in the public and private sectors, the law also brings an obligation to employ occupational health specialists, healthcare personnel, and occupational physicians regardless of the nature of the job and the number of employees (Art. 6/1a).
- The law envisages state support for OHS measures in small-sized workplaces. Accordingly, excluding public institutions and organizations, "moderately hazardous" and "very hazardous" workplaces with fewer than ten employees may benefit from state consolidations (Art. 7/1).
- The law stipulates seeking employees' opinions in taking OHS measures (Art. 18) and assigning an "employee representative" to OHS-related issues (Art. 20/1).
- The law stipulates the establishment of an OHS committee in workplaces employing fifty or more workers and engaging in work lasting more than six months (Art. 22/1). Thus, unlike the previous legislation, the law removes the restriction on establishing the committee only in workplaces operating in industrial zones.
- The duties and authorities of labor inspectors are expanded (Art. 25/2).
- Employers shall confront increased administrative fines for OHS violations (Art. 26).

On the other hand, the government envisaged a gradual effective date for the law. In this respect, regarding Articles 6, 7, and 8 regulating the employment of occupational safety specialists, occupational physicians, and other health personnel, the effective date of the law was:

1) initially determined two years after the enactment date of the law for public institutions and "slightly hazardous" workplaces with fewer than 50 employees. However, the date was changed to "July 7, 2017," then "July 7, 2020," and then "December 31, 2023,"
2) envisaged one year after the enactment date of the law for "moderately hazardous" and "very hazardous" workplaces with fewer than 50 employees,
3) envisaged six months after the enactment date of the law for "other" workplaces.

# OHS OUTLOOK

This chapter presents Turkey's OHS outlook by years, gender, workplace size, selected industries, and working hours. While creating the subheadings, common data are considered to be the basis, leading to a symmetrical/simultaneous evaluation of Turkey's OHS outlook. Nevertheless, it should be noted that the present study offers an evaluation of the data only up to 2021 at most since the 2022 data were not shared with the public at the time of the study.

## Turkey's OHS Outlook by Years

Law No. 6331, enacted to adopt a preventive approach to OHS, primarily aimed to prevent occupational accidents, occupational diseases, and fatal injuries. However, despite fluctuations in some years from 2010 to 2020, there is a rising trend in occupational accidents, occupational diseases, and fatal occupational accidents (www.sgk.gov.tr).

For instance, the number of occupational accidents increased by 19.87 percent in 2018 compared to the previous year. Despite a 0.02 percent decrease in the number of occupational accidents in 2019 compared to the previous year, it increased by 220.69 percent in 2019 compared to 2013. The decrease in 2019 continued in 2020 for almost all kinds of work suspensions due to the COVID-19 pandemic. However, it can be asserted that occupational accidents tended to increase again with the gradual normalization in 2021 and the elevated production volume. Accordingly, there was no expected alleviation in occupational accidents in the years following the enactment of Law No. 6331. A similar case applies to occupational diseases and fatal injuries. There was a 210.82 percent increase in occupational diseases in 2019 compared to 2013. Despite a slight decline due to the pandemic (158.97 percent), occupational diseases with a specific diagnosis seem to have increased over the years, and a similar trend continued in 2021. One major reason for this picture may be that occupational accidents and diseases and fatal injuries have been notified to the Social Security Institution (SSI) electronically since 2013. Therefore, the data of the insured with an occupational accident, occupational disease, or fatal injury advised to SSI have been announced publicly since 2013 (İSG Genel Müdürlüğü, 2020: 18).

The OHS data in Turkey are largely compiled from the official notifications of employers. The SSI statistics also include the ones identified in the inspections by labor inspectors and those not reported but determined through lawsuits. Such records are exceptional and far from being decisive (Dertli, 2018). On the other hand, Law No. 6331 brought an obligation to record and report the OHS data of all employees (Kılkış, 2018: 69). In this context, although SSI has made an exception and taken the initiative to publish statistics on self-employed ones since 2017, the data of the institution cover "compulsory insurance holders" among the active insured. In addition, there are still difficulties in keeping complete and accurate records regarding OHS in Turkey[3] (Gerek, 2012: 13). Similarly, the OHS data on civil servants, immigrants, and unregistered labor are not included in the statistics, and fatal injuries of these groups are not shared in the statistics. Therefore, it is clear that the actual data on the numbers of occupational accidents diseases and fatal injuries are much higher (MMOB, 2020: 45,47). Fatal occupational injuries and occupational accidents leading to mass deaths are the most known to the public and the most scrutinized by experts (Dertli, 2018). However, minor accidents, disabilities, and injuries in the workplace are not reported to relevant authorities to avoid legal consequences (Ceylan, 2011: 21; Dertli, 2018). The data are much more problematic in terms of occupational diseases: such problems in Turkey stem from the deficiencies in the diagnosis, reporting, and definitive diagnosis of occupational diseases (Kılkış, 2018: 70). According to international standards, the incidence of occupational diseases is expected to be between 4 and 12 per 1,000 employees (ÇASGEM, 2013: 12; MMOB, 2018: 115; Dertli, 2018; MMOB, 2020: 100). Accordingly, for example, occupational disease cases should have been at least 60,813 among 15,203,423 people working as workers under a service contract and compulsory insurance in 2020 (www.sgk.gov.tr). Besides, occupational diseases in Türkiye are more likely to be closer to the upper limit than the lower limit when considering the typical characteristics of working life in Türkiye: the relative size of the informal economy, the prevalence of insecure employment, low unionization rates, the prevalence of low-wage employment and unprotected and unhealthy working environments, and length of shifts (Dertli, 2018).

## Turkey's OHS Outlook by Gender

The rate of men with fatal injuries predominates the figure. From 2010 to 2020, the rates of occupational accidents, occupational diseases, and fatal injuries by gender indicate that in all three cases, the average for men is above 80y percent (wwwsgk.gov.tr). In Turkey, women are prohibited by law from working in heavy and hazardous jobs. Thus, women cannot be employed in such industries as mining and construction, which are among the industries with elevated risks regarding occupational accidents and diseases. Similarly, the figure shows that the female employment rate remained behind the male employment rate. Therefore, it is not surprising that there is more OHS data on men who are more visible in working life. However, the other side of the coin tells another story. Women's gender-related positions and working conditions and areas in Turkey, on the one hand, lead to differences between women and men by types and numbers of occupational accidents diseases and fatal injuries. On the other hand, occupational accidents diseases and fatal injuries experienced by women are veiled (İSİG, 2020a), which is largely mediated by the prevalence of women's employment in the informal industry. For example, the data from the Occupational Health and Safety Assembly (OHS Assembly), which is a voluntary organization that regularly compiles OHS data in Turkey, reveal that thousands of women working in agriculture experience occupational accidents, catch an occupational disease, or lose their lives from fatal injuries (İSİG, 2020a). However, these facts are not reflected in the SSI statistics. A similar situation prevails in the accommodation and entertainment industry, where women are informally employed for long working hours (İSİG, 2018). The protection of women's health and safety is often shaped based on women's fertility in laws and policies in Turkey: "taking precautions against employing women in hazardous jobs." Aside from keeping women away from the dangers of working life, this situation poses threats to women's health and safety by creating illusions about the safety of the industry where they are employed. Exclusion of industries where women are prevalently employed unregistered (e.g., agriculture, accommodation and entertainment, textile, and paid domestic work) from OHS policies (İSİG, 2020a) causes severe deviations in the OHS data on women.

## Turkey's OHS Outlook by Workplace Size

Technological, financial, and competitive power problems are prioritized when generating policies in Turkey for labor-intensive small and medium enterprises (SMEs), which are known for more production and product diversity with less investment, creating employment with low investment costs, and responding quickly to changes in demand (Ar & İskender, 2005; Aydın, 2015: 48–49).

Micro businesses with one to nine employees and small businesses with fewer than fifty employees are common (98 percent) in Turkey, considering the SSI statistics by workplace size. This rate reaches 99.7 percent, together with workplaces employing 50–250 people (www.sgk.gov.tr).

Regarding the distribution of insured employees, the workplaces employing fewer than 250 workers dominate the data (80 percent). However, it should be noted that 20 percent of businesses employ more than 250 employees. Figure 4 presents the distribution of the insured by workplace size (www.sgk.gov.tr).

Considering occupational accidents,diseases and fatal injuries by workplace size may contribute to a more extensive assessment of Türkiye's OHS outlook.

There is a correlation between the number of occupational accidents and employees. Occupational accidents occurring in micro businesses employing one to nine people may not be fully reflected in the statistics due to the lack of inspection and notification. From 2010 to 2021, the figures reveal a dramatic increase in occupational accidents in large businesses with 250 or more employees. Moreover, a significant leap was recorded in occupational accidents, particularly between 2012 and 2013 when the law was enacted. In the relevant period, occupational accidents increased in all workplaces, regardless of size.

OHS expenditures are not at a desirable level in micro, small, and medium-sized workplaces (Gerek, 2012: 15). The relevant research shows that the measures to be taken are loosened as the scale of a workplace gets smaller (Gökbayrak, 2006). In addition to the limited financing opportunities in these businesses, based on a competitive and cost-oriented management approach, considering the expenditures an unnecessary cost item and giving up on OHS-related expenditures in periods of an economic recession may lead to deterioration in the relevant indicators (F. Yılmaz, 2009: 456; Alper, Kılkış, & Engin, 2015: 71). Other factors contributing to OHS-related problems are the absence of OHS culture among employers and employees, outdated technological equipment, and the failure to provide employees with protective equipment due to economic concerns. Besides, unregistered employment is common in Turkey. Although the rate of unregistered employment decreased gradually between 2010 and 2021 (from 43.3 percent to 28.7 percent), it is still alarming (TÜİK, 2020; TÜİK, 2022).

Two significant points should be noted on occupational accidents occurring in micro (one to nine employees) and small (ten to forty-nine) businesses. First, Law No. 6331 brought an agreement on providing OHS-related subsidies for workplaces with fewer than ten employees in hazardous classes. Moreover, allocating such grants does not lose its incentive even if considering the actual work instead of all the work performed in the workplace (Gerek, 2012: 17), counting on all hazardous and very hazardous workplaces owned by employers within the borders of Türkiye and their only registered employees in determining the number of employees (to encourage employers to hire their employees as registered), and 1.4 percent of the daily amount of the lower limit of the earning subject to premium in hazardous workplaces and 1.6 percent of this amount in very hazardous workplaces while calculating the amount of grant to be allocated (Alper, Kılkış, & Engin, 2015: 80). Second, as stated before, when Law No. 6331 entered into force, the obligation to employ an occupational health specialist and an occupational physician in less hazardous workplaces with fewer than fifty employees was postponed until 2024. Although government officials showed the reason for the postponement as a pandemic, it is known that the main reason was that employers could not complete their preparations for OHS and acquire the necessary certificates to fulfill their OHS-related obligations. Upon acquiring the relevant certificates, employers and their representatives will be able to perform all the duties of both an occupational safety specialist and an occupational physician, except for the procedures for employment and periodic health examinations (https://www.ttb.org.tr/). In fact, it may be proof that the health and safety of employees in less hazardous workplaces are left entirely at the mercy of employers.

Even though occupational accidents are prevalent in workplaces with 250 or more employees, the rate of fatal occupational accidents in these workplaces has decreased rapidly. A professional management approach rules financially potent large-scale workplaces. Hence, it is expected that the legislation regarding the implementation of OHS-related measures is better known and fulfilled in such workplaces. Yet, it is evident that such an advantage cannot prevent occupational accidents but leads to a decrease in fatal injuries. For instance, considering the distribution of fatal injuries, 17 percent of those losing their lives due to occupational accidents in 2020 were self-employed, and 83 percent were wage earners (İSİG, 2019, 2020b). It should be noted that the rate of fatal injuries is still high despite the recent decreasing trend.

According to the SSI statistics, the number of fatal occupational accidents in workplaces with ten to forty-nine employees is higher than in those employing more staff (www.sgk.gov.tr), which may be attributed to insufficient technological infrastructure, the absence of OHS committees, the lack of obligation to employ occupational safety specialists and physicians, the relatively weak financial structure of the businesses, and the lack of widespread unionization. In addition, employers do not employ professional managers and undertake all the work in most of these workplaces. Therefore, employers seem reluctant to spare enough time to take necessary OHS precautions and review and fulfill the requirements of the legislation (Yanık, 2021), which gives birth to increased numbers of fatal injuries (Gökbayrak, 2006).

Contrary to occupational accidents, the low number of fatal occupational injuries in workplaces with 250 or more employees compared to SMEs—excluding the 2013 data—implies that although occupational accidents have increased, fatal occupational injuries are relatively low in these workplaces.

The SSI data do not cover the fatalities from occupational diseases between 2013 and 2020 (the data of only those dying from an occupational disease in 2021 (thirty-five people) were shared); therefore, Figure 6 presents only the data on fatal occupational injuries. However, SSI publishes statistics on the death benefit of the beneficiaries of those who died from occupational diseases (i.e., Beneficiaries of Death Benefit for Deaths from Occupational Diseases) (MMOB, 2018: 55, 2020: 100). Across the world, the rates of fatality due to occupational diseases (56 percent) are higher than that of occupational fatal injuries (44 percent) (MMO, 2017: 102–103). Accordingly, 2 million lose their lives due to occupational diseases worldwide every year. Yet, the fact that such statistics are not recognized in Türkiye reveals the problematic nature of the data. Besides, different organizations released different statistics for the same period. According to OHS Assembly data, at least 1,736 employees (1,091 according to the SSI data) had fatal injuries in 2019; it was at least 2,427 employees (1,091 according to the SSI data) in 2020. The inconsistencies in the data also make it difficult to make reliable evaluations.

Occupational diseases in each workplace seem to vary over the years, as indicated by the SSI statistics. The SSI data between 2013 and 2021 demonstrate that, when excluding those diagnosed with occupational diseases following the expiration of their insurance period, the number of employees with an occupational disease in workplaces with 250 or more employees is higher than that of those employed in SMEs in recent years (www.sgk.gov.tr). On the other hand, while thousands of occupational accidents are recorded every year in Turkey, the low number of detected occupational diseases may be proof that occupational diseases exist but are ignored (Gökbayrak, 2006). Even though it was targeted in the National Occupational Health and Safety Document II (2009–2013) to "increase the expected but undetected number of cases by 500 percent," one cannot recognize a substantial increase in the data on occupational diseases. Employees often do not even realize that they have caught an occupational disease. Occupational diseases may occur over a long period and be confused with other diseases. In addition, the inadequacy of diagnosis systems and the legislation, the subsidiarity of admissions of occupational diseases to state hospitals, and the inadequate processes of state hospitals in keeping accurate and sufficient statistics—briefly the current approach and situation—show that occupational diseases are systematically concealed (Fişek, 1998; Ilıman, 2015: 24; MMOB, 2018: 71, 2020: 55–56).

## Turkey's OHS Outlook by Selected Industries

The OHS outlook by industries is limited to the five selected industries where the most occupational accidents and diseases and fatal occupational injuries have been recorded over the years.

From 2010 to 2021, 72.1 percent of occupational accidents occurred in the industries engaging in mining and quarrying; manufacturing; water supply, sewage, waste management, and remediation services; construction; accommodation; and food services. The highest number of occupational accidents in Turkeybelongs to the mining and quarrying industry by years, followed by the manufacturing industry. The construction industry, which is among those with the highest number of occupational accidents across the world, ranks fourth in Turkey. Even though employment in the mining and quarrying industry has constituted 0.99 percent of the total employment in the last twelve years (0.94 percent in 2021), the highest number of occupational accidents have occurred in this sector over the years, which may be because of ignoring the wrong practices and technical deficiencies in the sector.

The manufacturing sector, which ranks second regarding occupational accidents, has the highest employment rate among all sectors. The industry has undertaken an average of 27 percent of employment in the last twelve years. The high level of occupational accidents is reasonable considering the number of employees. An average of 5 percent of occupational accidents are reported in this sector, and most accidents in the industry occur in food production.

In the construction sector, the rate of occupational accidents has been recorded as 12.78 percent in the last twelve years, which makes it rank fourth in the rate of accidents per hundred thousand people. According to the ILO data, an average of 60,000 fatal occupational injuries occur every year in this labor-risk industry (MMOB, 2018: 1, 2020: 2). The relatively low rate of occupational accidents in this sector in Turkeymay refer to the problematic nature of reporting occupational accidents. It should also be noted this sector is among those where unregistered employment is most prevalent. Thus, the number of occupational accidents in this sector is more likely to be higher than presented in the figure.

It is undoubtedly undesirable to confront fatalities due to occupational accidents, albeit many factors may lead to such accidents. To exemplify, one reason for the disaster costing the lives of 301 miners in Soma in 2014 was that the interior design of the mine was not suitable for OHS standards (Gerek, 2015: 16; Karaahmetoğlu, 2019: 111–112). Other reasons can be listed as lack of or outdated ventilation and protective equipment and not supplying or performing maintenance on necessary equipment regularly (Gerek, 2015: 21; MMOB, 2014: 13–18). Moreover, the following factors play major roles in fatal injuries: nondetectable risks in the mines, unsatisfying inspection in the mines or number of inspectors, the lack of emergency plans (Gerek, 2015: 2, 15; Düzgün, 2016), perceiving OHS expenditures as unnecessary costs, deploying unqualified workforce to reduce costs, parcelling out the mining areas based on royalty applications, the inadequacy of gas measurement systems, and the inadequacy of warning and surveillance systems (Gerek, 2015: 15–22; Karaahmetoğlu, 2019: 113–115).

The highest number of fatal occupational accidents in Turkey occur in the following industries: agriculture, forestry, and fishing; mining and quarrying; electricity, gas, steam, and air conditioning supply; construction; and transportation and storage services.

From 2010 to 2021, about 60 percent of fatal occupational accidents occurred in agriculture, forestry, and fishing; mining and quarrying; electricity, gas, steam, and air conditioning supply; construction; and transportation and storage services. The high rate of fatal injuries was the driving motivation for the enactment of Law No. 6331. While enacting the law, it was especially emphasized that "occupational accidents" and resulting "fatalities" would be eliminated (MMOB, 2020: 188). However, the law has not brought what was initially expected. Instead, the number of fatal occupational accidents has increased over the years. In 2015, some amendments were made to the law called the "perfect law" after the mining disaster in Soma in 2014. The general picture of occupational accidents and diseases and fatal occupational accidents shows that the amendments have been far from bringing radical solutions. The unsatisfying inspection in workplaces is a significant factor in the negative course of OHS indicators. In 2019, the Ministry of Labor and Social Security (MoLSS) carried out 3,008 inspection works in workplaces, albeit only one-sixth of 1,000 workplaces were subjected to OHS-related inspection. Factors such as the prevalence of privatization and subcontracting, flexible employment policies, informality, de-unionization, and lack of control produce a complicated system for OHS (MMOB, 2021). In addition, the nonavailability of fatalities due to occupational diseases by sectors in the SSI data may suggest that occupational homicides are more prevalent than illustrated in the figure.

On the other hand, the mining and quarrying sector is not a popular industry regarding employment opportunities. Yet, it ranks first in the number of fatal occupational accidents per hundred thousand. Regardless of the number of employees, the construction sector takes the lead when fatal injuries are grouped by sector. In the last twelve years in Turkey, an average of 31 percent of fatal occupational accidents have been reported in the construction sector; about two out of five workers have a fatal injury daily in construction (MMOB, 2018: 191, 2020: 172). In the SSI statistical yearbooks, falls from height rank first in fatal occupational accidents in this sector (www.sgk.gov.tr).

As stated before, occupational diseases are neglected when compared to occupational accidents. Since they cover a more extended period, their follow-ups and severity may yield nonsignificant consequences.

In the last twelve years, 66 percent of occupational diseases have occurred in the following sectors: mining and quarrying; manufacturing; water supply, sewage, waste management, and remediation services; construction; and transportation and storage services. Considering the number of employees, occupational diseases are experienced the most (48 percent) in the manufacturing sector. The mining and quarrying sector accounts for 17.3 percent of occupational diseases, while it ranks first when considering the number of occupational diseases per hundred thousand. In the industry, respiratory diseases are prominent in the SSI statistics every year. When it comes to the manufacturing industry with twenty-four subsectors, the manufacture of other nonmetallic products is the subsector with the highest number of occupational diseases, according to the SSI statistics. About one-third (35 percent) of 510 occupational diseases in 2018, 28 percent of 671 occupational diseases in 2019, and 16 percent of 375 occupational diseases in 2020 occurred in this sector. Yet, the case above changed in 2021, and 18 percent of the 617 occupational diseases in the manufacturing sector occurred in the manufacturing of motor vehicles and trailers (www.sgk.gov.tr).

## Turkey's OHS Outlook by Length of Employment and Working Hours

In occupational accidents, there are organic associations between the length of employment and the features of the working environment, the conditions offered to employees, and their experience. In Turkey, from 2010 to 2020, excluding the data in 2010–2012, the most prevalent occupational accidents happened to those employed for at most one year. Similarly, more than 50 percent of those with an occupational accident every year consist of employees employed for one to thirty days and one month to one year. Therefore, it may be deduced that occupational accidents occur mostly in the first year of employment (www.sgk.gov.tr).

Law No. 6331 imposes specific OHS-related responsibilities to both employers and employees. Yet, the primary OHS-related responsibilities lie with employers. Thus, employers are obliged to ensure the health and safety of their employees (Art. 4/1). One of the obligations of employers is to inform and train their employees on relevant OHS measures (Art. 16, 17). According to the ILO Safety Culture Report published in 2002, all occupational diseases and 98 percent of occupational accidents are preventable. However, it is still necessary to inform employees about the conditions and risks of the working environment and emergencies. In addition, it is essential to provide the required training regarding the work and the machinery and equipment to be used while performing the work (G. Yılmaz, 2009: 28).

Moreover, a similar case appears regarding fatal occupational accidents by length of employment.

The data from 2013 to 2020 indicate that more than half of fatal occupational accidents happened to those employed for one to thirty days and one month to one year. On the other hand, when compared to other years, those with a length of employment of one to ten years lost their lives more in 2014. It may have been because a significant part of those losing their lives in the mine disaster in Soma in 2014 were employed for more than a year (www.sgk.gov.tr).

Turkey witnesses significant problems detecting and diagnosing occupational diseases arising from working conditions. Occupational diseases defined so far lack diversity. Moreover, occupational diseases are overlooked, and limited types of occupational diseases are not thoroughly investigated due to the unconsciousness of employees about such conditions, confusion with other diseases, and the subsidiarity of admissions of occupational diseases to state hospitals (Fişek, 1998). Hence, preventable occupational diseases cannot be detected accurately. Besides, current data on occupational diseases are far from reflecting the actual story. Overall, it can be claimed that our country has a long way to go regarding the diagnosis, detection, and registry of occupational diseases and raising awareness of occupational diseases among employees. On the other hand, employees began to be diagnosed with an occupational disease even after the expiry of their insurance as of 2013, which can be considered an improvement.

The time intervals with the most prevalent occupational accidents are during the daytime when employees often engage in intensive work. Each year, most accidents occur between 10:00 and 11:59 (particularly between 11:00 and 11:59). It may be inferred that employees have increased fatigue but decreased concentration before the lunch break. Another time interval in which the probability of occupational accidents increases due to elevated fatigue and reduced concentration is 14:00–15:59. The figure also reveals a relatively high rate of occupational accidents at the beginning of working hours. As expected, the least accidents occur between 12:00 and 13:59, which coincides with the lunch break. A similar case also applies to the time interval of 16:00–17:59. The daytime working hours often end at 17:00 or 17:30, referring to the decreased number of employees in this time interval in workplaces (www.sgk.gov.tr).

## OHS-RELATED PROBLEMS IN TURKEY

Despite more than a century of legislation background regarding OHS, the importance of OHS has gone hand in hand with industrialization in Turkey. Depending on unstoppable problems over the years, various regulations have been established for OHS, and the latest regulation in this domain was Law No. 6331, the first independent law concerning OHS. Since the fundamental indicators of OHS are occupational accidents and diseases and fatalities, it was assumed that occupational accidents and diseases and fatalities would be reduced by adopting a preventive approach in OHS, thanks to Law No. 6331. However, not only could this goal not be accomplished but also persisting OHS-related problems have continued during the period when the law is effective. Then, it is reasonable to list these problems within the framework of this study as follows.

Employers generally do not perform what they undertake for OHS and see OHS-oriented expenditures as unnecessary costs. It, unfortunately, applies to the state (e.g., poor inspections of workplaces for OHS). These two situations can be considered leading reasons for other OHS-related problems.

Over time, there has been no expected decrease in occupational accidents and diseases. Following the enactment of Law No. 6331, a massive accident occurred in the mining sector in 2014, resulting in the death of 301 workers. Interestingly, the most problematic factors regarding OHS have not made significant progress and maintained their OHS-related statistics over time. The current picture also applies to workplaces with fifty or fewer employees, which have persistently underperformed regarding OHS.

Another problem area of OHS in Turkeycan be shown as OHS data. There may be more than one reason why OHS data are far from demonstrating the actual picture of OHS in Turkey. Employers should keep a record of OHS data, reflecting the health status of employees and the general situation regarding OHS conditions, in line with the provisions of Law No. 6331, and it should be reported to the (SSI within three working days (ILO, 2016: 58). The SSI data mainly cover "compulsory insurance holders" among "active insurance holders" (those employed by one or more employers upon a service contract) in the scope of Article 4a of the Social Insurance and General Health Insurance Law No. 5510. On the other hand, the institution has been publishing OHS data of the insured within 4b since 2017 (neighborhood and village mukhtars and self-employed independent workers without a service contract). Nevertheless, not only are the data insufficient, but they also do not include OHS data of employees within 4c (public servants) (Aile, Çalışma ve Sosyal Hizmetler Bakanlığı, 2020: 9; MMOB, 2020: 54). Thus, the OHS data are not publicly known by sectors (i.e., by workplace size or the number of employees). In addition, unregistered employment in Turkey is relatively widespread, and the data on unregistered employees cannot be traced from the SSI statistics. In particular, the prevalence of unregistered employment of women results in shadowed OHS data for women. A similar case applies to the construction sector, and the OHS data cannot be fully traced due to widespread unregistered employment in this sector.

Poor diagnostic approaches to occupational diseases and confusion about occupational diseases with other conditions may appear as an OHS-related problem.

Employers are obliged to inform and train employees about OHS; however, the relevant statistics show that experienced employees are often less exposed to occupational accidents and that most occupational accidents and fatalities occur to those in their first month of employment in Turkey. On the other hand, the risk of developing an occupational disease increases with the length of employment.

Another OHS-related problem may be shown as the increased frequency of occupational accidents due to fatigue and reduced attention.

OHS-related problems can also be revealed with relevant statistics. As mentioned before, this research only considers the OHS data after the enactment of Law No. 6331. However, two-year data are also shared to uncover the situation before the law (only two-year pre-6331 data are shared to track the data more easily in the figures). Besides, considering that the SSI statistics cover only the data collected after 2007 (www.sgk.gov.tr), it can confidently be asserted that almost all of the available OHS data are demonstrated in the study.

## CONCLUSION

This chapter discussed Turkey's OHS outlook through the relevant statistics within the framework of Law No. 6331. In general, the scattered OHS-related legislation has been remedied to a large extent by Law No. 6331. However, the enactment of the law could not eliminate weaknesses in OHS. Although it has been ten years since the law came into force, there is still a lack of awareness of OHS. According to the relevant OHS statistics (despite incomplete data), one cannot still mention healthy working environments in workplaces and an exemplary implementation of control mechanisms for OHS. The understanding of preventing occupational accidents and diseases and fatal accidents before they occur is deemed a challenging goal to reach for now.

Above all, the state and employers need to take the necessary steps to enhance the positive understanding of OHS in Turkey. Yet, employers, who are primarily responsible for ensuring OHS, often adopt a cost-oriented approach toward OHS and regard expenditures in OHS as unnecessary due to highly competitive market conditions. It is particularly evident among SMEs. Unregistered employment, relatively widespread in Turkey, may lead employers to avoid their obligations arising from Law No. 6331. Nevertheless, the same picture regarding OHS in workplaces with 250 or more employees points out the insufficient awareness of OHS among employers and structural OHS-specific problems in Turkey. The statistics also reveal that occupational accidents have increased in high-risk industries such as mining and construction. Occupational accidents and fatal injuries are concentrated particularly among employees working for one month to one year.

The course of OHS in Turkey suggests that only legal regulations remain insufficient. Despite the major influence of mass fatalities on the enactment of Law No. 6331 and some amendments to the law following the Soma disaster in 2014, a satisfying OHS framework has not been established yet since the mining sector still ranks first regarding occupational accidents and diseases and fatal injuries. In addition, one can count major obstacles to the expected successes of OHS as statistics on the low rate of fatal occupational accidents in Turkey in the construction sector, which often ranks first in this category across the world, diagnostic issues in occupational diseases, nonavailability of fatalities due to occupational diseases in the SSI statistics, poor inspections of workplaces, and continuous postponement of the effective date of Law No. 6331 for public institutions and less hazardous workplaces with fewer than fifty employees.

To conclude, it is prudent to assert that Turkey's OHS outlook is not promising due to the lack of awareness and sufficient inspection, initiatives after accidents instead of taking preventive measures, the punitive nature of the system, and no encouraging rewards for those fulfilling their responsibilities.

## NOTES

1. Assoc. Prof. Dr., Bandırma Onyedi Eylül University, Faculty of Health Science, Department of Social Science, Bandırma, Turkey, zaca@bandirma.edu.tr.
2. In the following years, other insurance branches were also covered by relevant regulations. Hence, loose social insurance practices were regulated under the Social Insurance Law No. 506 of 1964. This trend was followed by Social Insurance and General Health Insurance Law No. 5510 in 2008.
3. Alternative organizations (e.g., the Occupational Health and Safety Assembly and the Umut Foundation) engage in collecting OHS data to fill the gap arising from the inadequacy of the official data.

## REFERENCES

Aca, Z. (2022), İnşaat İş Kolunda İnsana Yakışır İşe Yönelik Tehditler: Mikro Göstergelere İlişkin Bir Değerlendirme, Çalışma A. Özdemir (ed.), *Ekonomisi ve Endüstri İlişkileri Seçme Yazılar-VI içinde* (ss. 79–106), Sakarya: Değişim.

Alper, Y., Kılkış, İ. ve Engin, T. (2015), 6331 Sayılı Kanun Çerçevesinde Küçük İşyerlerine Yönelik Maddi Desteğin Önemi ve Etkinliği, *Business and Economics Research Journal*, 6(13), 69–86.

Ar, Aybeniz Akdeniz, İskender, H. (2005), Türkiye'de Kobi'ler Ve Kobi'lerde Planlama, Uygulama ve Denetim, https://www.mevzuatdergisi.com/2005/03a/06.htm, Erişim Tarihi: July 02, 2021.

Arıcı, K. (1999), *İş Sağlığı ve Güvenliği Dersleri*, Ankara: Tes-İş Eğitim Yayınları.

Atanur Karaahmetoğlu (2019), 6331 Sayılı İş Sağlığı ve Güvenliği Kanunu Bağlamında Soma Madenlerinin İş Sağlığı ve Güvenliği Açısından Değerlendirilmesi, *Journal of Social Policy Conferences*, 76, 89–128.

Aydın, T. Ş. (2015), *Küçük Ve Orta Ölçekli İşletmelerde İş Güvenliği Ve İşçi Sağlığı Uygulamalarının İş Kazalarının Önlenmesi Açısından İncelenmesi*, İstanbul

Gelişim Üniversitesi Sosyal Bilimler Enstitüsü, (Yayınlanmamış Yüksek Lisans Tezi).

Aydın, U. (2012), İş Sağlığı Güvenliği Kanunu Tasarısı Üzerine, *SİCİL İş Hukuku Dergisi*, 7(26), 10–19.

Baybora, D. (2012), İş Sağlığı ve Güvenliğine Genel Bakış, İş D. Baybora (ed.), *sağlığı ve güvenliği içinde* (ss. 2–21), Eskişehir: Anadolu Üniversitesi.

ÇASGEM (2013), *Meslek Hastalıkları*, Ankara: ÇASGEM.

Centel, T. (2013), İş Sağlığı ve Güvenliği Kanunu'nun Uygulama Alanı ve Kapsamı, *Marmara Üniversitesi Hukuk Fakültesi Hukuk Araştırmaları Dergisi*, 19(2), 79–84.

Ceylan, H. (2011), Türkiye'deki İş Kazalarının Genel Görünümü ve Gelişmiş Ülkelerle Kıyaslanması, *Uluslararası Mühendislik Araştırma ve Geliştirme Dergisi*, 3(2), 18–24.

DDK, Cumhurbaşkanlığı Devlet Denetleme Kurulu Madencilik Sektörü Araştırma Ve İnceleme Raporu [Presidency State Supervisory Board Mining Sector Research and Examination Report], V. 2011/3, Ankara, 2011.

Demir, F. (2014), İş Sağlığı ve Güvenliği Önlemlerinin Alınmasında İşverenin Sorumluluğu, *Marmara Üniversitesi Hukuk Fakültesi Hukuk Araştırmaları Dergisi*, 20(1), 675–704.

Demircioğlu, M. and ve Kaplan, H. A. (2013), 6331 Sayılı İş Sağlığı ve Güvenliği Yasası Çerçevesinde İşyerinde İş Sağlığı ve Güvenliği Örgütlenmesi, *SİCİL İş Hukuku Dergisi*, 8(30), 24–37.

Deniz, Ö. (2007), Cumhuriyet Dönemi Çalışma Hayatı, *Çağdaş Türkiye Tarihi Araştırmaları Dergisi*, 6(15), 131–150.

Dertli, N. (2018), SGK İş Kazası İstatistikleri, Alternatif Veri Kaynakları ve Veri Açığı, *Çalışma Ortamı Dergisi*, 155, 4–5.

Dilik, S. (1971), *Türkiye'de Sosyal Sigortalar İktisadi Açıdan Bir Tahlil Denemesi*, Ankara: Ankara Üniversitesi Siyasal Bilgiler Fakültesi Yayınları, No: 315.

Dilik, S. (1985), Atatürk Döneminde Sosyal Politika, *Ankara Üniversitesi SBF Dergisi*, 40(1), 93–102.

Düzgün, Ş. (2016), Kasti Körlük: Soma Faciası. https://bilimakademisi.org/wp-content/uploads/2016/02/soma-raporu-2016.pdf, Erişim Tarihi: July 13, 2021.

Fişek, G. (1998), Meslek Hastalıkları –Türkiye Sendikacılık Ansiklopedisi – Kültür Bakanlığı ve T. *Ekonomik ve Toplumsal Tarih Vakfı Ortak Yayını*, 2, 378–380, İstanbul.

Gerek, N. (2008), *İş Sağlığı ve Güvenliği*, Eskişehir: Anadolu Üniversitesi AOF Yayınları.

Gerek, N. (2012), İş Sağlığı ve Güvenliği Kanunun Düşündürdükleri, *Sicil İş Hukuku Dergisi*, 7(28), 10–19.

Gerek, N. (2015), Yeraltı Maden İşletmelerinde Çalışanlarla İlgili Yeni Düzenlemelerin Düşündürdükleri, *Kamu-İs*, 14(2), 1–27.

Gökbayrak, Ş. (2006), Küçük ve Orta Ölçekli İşletmelerde Risk Gruplarına Yönelik Sosyal Politikalar. https://sosyalpolitika.fisek.org.tr/kucuk-ve-orta-olcekli-isletmelerde-risk-gruplarina-yonelik-sosyal-politikalar/, Erişim Tarihi: July 02, 2021.

Gökbayrak, Ş. (2010), Türkiye'de Sosyal Güvenliğin Dönüşümü, *Çalışma ve Toplum*, 25(2), 141–162.

İleri T. (2013), Cumhuriyet'in İlk Yıllarında Maden İşçilerinin Çalışma Hayatına İlişkin Yapılan Düzenlemeler, *The Journal of Academic Social Science Studies*, 6(2), 1449–1467.

Ilıman, E. Z. (2015), Türkiye'de Meslek Hastalıkları, *Uluslararası Sağlık Yönetimi Ve Stratejileri Araştırma Dergisi*, 1(1), 21–36.

ILO (2016), *Occupational Safety and Health Profile Turkey*, Ministry of Labour and Social Security Publication Number: 62, Ankara: ILO.

İSİG (2018), İSİG Meclisi Kadın İşçiler Raporu, http://www.saglikcalisanisagligi.org /2666-isig-meclisi-kadin-isciler-raporu.html, Erişim Tarihi: July 02, 2021.

İSİG (2019), Yaşamak ve yaşatmak için direneceğiz! 2019 yılında en az 1736 işçi yaşamını yitirdi, http://isigmeclisi.org/20220-yasamak-ve-yasatmak-icin-direnec-egiz-2019-yilinda-en-az-1736-isci-yasa, Erişim Tarihi: July 02, 2021.

İSİG (2020a), Son yedi yılda en az 817 kadın işçi iş cinayetlerinde yaşamını yitirdi, http://isigmeclisi.org/20276-son-yedi-yilda-en-az-817-kadin-isci-is-cinayetlerinde -yasamini-yitirdi, Erişim Tarihi: July 02 2021.

İSİG (2020b), 2020 yılında en az 2427 işçi iş cinayetlerinde hayatını kaybetti... - 2020 Yılı İş Cinayetleri Raporu, http://isigmeclisi.org/20607-2020-yilinda-en-az-2427 -isci-is-cinayetlerinde-hayatini-kaybetti, Erişim Tarihi: July 02 2021.

Kılkış, İ. (2013), İş Sağlığı ve Güvenliği'nde Yeni Dönem:6331 Sayılı İş Sağlığı ve Güvenliği Kanunu (İSGK), İŞ, *GÜÇ Endüstri İlişkileri ve İnsan Kaynakları Dergisi*, 15(1), 17–41.

Kılkış, İ. (2018), *İş Sağlığı ve Güvenliği, 3. Baskı*, Bursa: Dora.

Makal A., Erdoğdu, S. ve Çelik, A. (2018), *Çalışma İlişkileri Tarihi* (Ahmet Makal, ed.), Eskişehir: Anadolu Üniversitesi Yayınları

MMOB (2018), İşçi Sağlığı Ve İş Güvenliği, Yayın No: MMO/689, Ankara.

MMOB (2020), İşçi Sağlığı Ve İş Güvenliği, Yayın No: MMO/718, Ankara.

MMMOB (2021), İş Cinayetleri Ve İşçi Katliamları Artarak Devam Ediyor, http:// www.tmmob.org.tr/icerik/cinayetleri-ve-isci-katliamlari-artarak-devam-ediyor, Erişim Tarihi: July 02, 2021.

MMOB Maden Mühendisleri Odası Araştırma Komisyonu (2014), Soma Faciası Ön Raporu, Ankara.SGK, "SGK İstatistik Yıllıkları" [Social Security Institution Statistical Yearbooks], http://www.sgk.gov.tr/wps/portal/sgk/tr/kurumsal/istatistik /sgk_istatistik_yilliklari, Erişim Tarihi: February 28, 2021.

Şardan, H. S. (2005), *İş Sağlığı ve Güvenliğinde Yeni Oluşumlar: Risk Değerlendirmesi ve OHSAS 18001*, Ankara: Çimento Endüstrisi İşverenleri Sendikası Yayınları.

Süzek, S. (2000, Nisan), İşçi Sağlığı ve İş Güvenliği Konusunda Somut Çözüm Önerileri, *Prof. Dr. Turhan ESENER'e Armağan, Kamu–İş İş Hukuku ve İktisat Dergisi, Ankara*, 5(3), ss. 305–324.

Süzek, S. (2011), *İş Hukuku* (7. Basım), İstanbul: Beta Yayınları

Talas, C. (1992), *Türkiye'nin Açıklamalı Sosyal Politika Tarihi*, Ankara: Bilgi Yayınevi.

TTB İşçi Sağlığı Ve İşyeri Hekimliği Kolu, İş Sağlığı ve Güvenliği Yasası'ndaki ertelemenin nedeni pandemi değildir!, https://www.ttb.org.tr/kollar/_isak/yazdir

.php?Tablo=tbl_haber&Guid=11970d92-ce66-11ea-ae98-95a88cc32d95, Erişim Tarihi: 02.07.2021.

TÜİK (2020), Labor Statistics, August 2020, Publishing Date: November 10, 2020, Issue: 33792, https://data.tuik.gov.tr/Bulten/Index?p=Isgucu-Istatistikleri-Agustos-2020-33792, Erişim Tarihi: July 02 2021.

TÜİK (2022), Labor Statistics, 2022, Publishing Date: February 15, 2022, Issue: 45643.

Yılmaz, F. (2009), Ülkemizde KOBİ'lerde İş Sağlığı ve Güvenliği: Avrupa Birliği Ülkeleriyle Karşılaştırılmalı Bir İnceleme, *Sosyal Siyaset Konferansları Dergisi, S,* 57, 449–479.

Yılmaz, G. (2009), İş Kazalarının Nedenleri ve Maliyeti, *Mühendis ve Makine Dergisi*, 50(592), 27–32.

## *Appendix A*

# Developments in Social Dialogue in Turkey According to EU Progress/Country *Reports*

**Table A.1 The Year of the EU Progress/Country Reports**

| *Report Year* | *Positive Developments* | *Negative Developments* |
|---|---|---|
| 2010 | Amendments to the Constitution granting civil servants and other public employees the right to bargain and bargain collectively and subject disciplinary punishments to civil servants to judicial review.<br>Removal of the ban on membership in more than one union at the same time and in the same sector and the abolition of the restriction of concluding a single collective agreement for the same period in the same workplace.<br>With the constitutional amendments, the Economic and Social Council became a constitutional body that the government would consult while formulating policy on economic and social issues (EC, 2010: 69). | The government attempts to address some of the key issues regarding trade union rights in the private sector, such as freedom of association and the right to collective bargaining in the workplace, in a new draft law that has failed to gain support from the social partners.<br>The low number of workers is covered by collective bargaining agreements.<br>Further strengthening the work of the main social dialogue mechanisms (Tripartite Advisory Board, Economic and Social Council) and the capacity of social partners (EC, 2010: 69). |
| 2011 | Lifting the bans on contracted personnel working in state-owned enterprises to form unions or participate in union activities (EC, 2011: 78). | Inability to implement the constitutional amendments on workers' rights because the necessary changes were not made in the relevant union legislation. |

(*Continued*)

**Table A.1 (Continued)**

| *Report Year* | *Positive Developments* | *Negative Developments* |
|---|---|---|
| | | Failure of social partners to agree on key issues such as the right to organize at the workplace level and the collective bargaining threshold.<br>Failure of the Economic and Social Council to meet during the reporting period.<br>The capacity of the social partners needs to be developed.<br>Not expanding the narrow scope of collective bargaining (EC, 2011: 78). |
| 2012 | Adopting the new law on public servants' unions allows collective bargaining for the first time in the public sector (EC, 2012: 82). | The high threshold for collective bargaining continues to significantly limit the possibility of collective bargaining, which hinders the full exercise of the right to collective bargaining.<br>The failure of the authorities to share data on the number of employees in all sectors caused no new collective bargaining negotiations to be concluded for several months.<br>The level of unionization and the coverage of collective agreements could be higher due to restrictive legal provisions and difficulties in enforcing trade union rights.<br>The Economic and Social Council has not met since 2009 (EC, 2012: 82). |
| 2013 | Entry into force of new Trade Unions and Collective Bargaining Laws for the private sector.<br>Facilitating the internal functioning of trade unions, simplifying membership procedures and requirements, limiting the prohibition of strikes, and reducing criminal penalties (EC, 2013: 41). | Few workers benefit from collective bargaining and engage in collective action, including strikes, due to the high and cumulative thresholds required for collective bargaining.<br>Union member workers working in small workplaces are not adequately protected from the danger of dismissal due to their union activities.<br>Many categories of public servants face restrictions on their right to organize, and the ban on strikes continues for public officials.<br>Ineffective functioning of tripartite and bilateral social dialogue mechanisms and the Economic and Social Council (EC, 2013: 41). |

**Table A.1 (Continued)**

| *Report Year* | *Positive Developments* | *Negative Developments* |
|---|---|---|
| 2014 | Using the e-Government portal for union membership registration and withdrawal (EC, 2014: 40). | Coverage of collective bargaining agreements is still low.<br>The restrictive double threshold for collective bargaining agreements, uncertainties in protecting union members from dismissal, and gaps in organizing, collective bargaining, and the right to strike are still the most prominent issues in this area.<br>With the amendment made in the Trade Unions and Collective Bargaining Agreement Law, the permanent setting of 1 percent (the ratio of union members to the workforce in the sector in which the workplace is included) for unions to make collective bargaining agreements continues to pose a significant obstacle to unions from making collective bargaining agreements (EC, 2014: 40). |
| 2015 | Workers in small-sized companies are now legally protected against eviction for their union activities.<br>Reducing the sector threshold from 3 percent to 1 percent to authorize independent unions to conclude collective bargaining agreements.<br>The union membership rate in the private sector increased from 9.5 percent to 11.2 percent in 2015 (EC, 2015: 57). | The proportion of workers covered by collective bargaining agreements is still significantly low.<br>This is due to the persistence of the "double threshold" limiting the unions' power to bargain collectively.<br>Many informal workers do not have access to unions.<br>Unlawful dismissals of union members and protracted lawsuits discourage workers from joining unions.<br>The Economic and Social Council has not met since 2009 (EC, 2015: 57). |
| 2016 | The rate of unionized workers in the private sector rose slightly to 11.5 percent in 2016 but is still low (EC, 2016: 59). | Tripartite and bipartite social dialogue is still limited. The<br>Economic and Social Council is inactive since 2009.<br>Legal deficiencies (such as a double threshold for collective bargaining and the lack of the right to strike for public servants) contradict European standards and ILO conventions. |

(*Continued*)

**Table A.1 (Continued)**

| *Report Year* | *Positive Developments* | *Negative Developments* |
|---|---|---|
| | | Informal workers, retirees and the unemployed, and a large segment of civil servants still lack the right to organize.<br>Prohibition of large protests and demonstrations by trade unions, disproportionately restricting trade union rights.<br>Numerous serious accusations of dismissal, harassment, retaliation, arrest, and police mistreatment of union officials by trade union confederations for their legitimate trade union activities.<br>Closure of trade unions that have relations with FETO (EC, 2016: 59). |
| 2017 | The report has yet to be published this year. | The report has yet to be published this year. |
| 2018 | There has been a setback in social dialogue. | In 2017, five strikes were postponed and de facto banned. Cases of dismissal, ill-treatment, arrest, and police attacks on members engaged in legitimate trade union activities continued to be reported by unions.<br>The Economic and Social Council has been inactive since 2009, and the tripartite advisory board met only once in 2017 (EC, 2018: 84). |
| 2019 | There has been a setback in social dialogue. | The Economic and Social Council members, who have not met since 2009, will now be appointed by the president.<br>The tripartite advisory committee, which remains the main tripartite social dialogue forum, met once in 2018.<br>Managers and members of some unions continue to be subjected to arbitrary dismissals, ill-treatment, and detentions for their various peaceful union activities.<br>Large-scale layoffs of public officials continued for their affiliation with terrorist groups linked to the 2016 coup attempt. |

**Table A.1 (Continued)**

| *Report Year* | *Positive Developments* | *Negative Developments* |
|---|---|---|
| | | The constitutional court ruled that the government's decision to postpone a strike in the metal sector in 2015 on the grounds of national security violated the right to strike (EC, 2019: 96). |
| 2020 | No progress can be reported on social dialogue. | Turkey held its 11th Labor Council Meeting in May 2019, bringing national social partners together. Focused on the ILO's future of work agenda, results still needed to be adopted. The Economic and Social Council has yet to meet since 2009. Other formal social dialogue mechanisms are either ineffective or lack genuine democratic participation from all parties, so they cannot support consensus building.<br>It is reported that anti-union discrimination actions by employers are very strong. Managers and members of some unions continue to be subjected to arbitrary dismissals, ill-treatment, and detentions for their various peaceful union activities. These factors undermine the right to freedom of association (EC, 2020: 95–96). |

*Source*: Compiled by the author from EU Progress/Country Reports between 2010 and 2020.

# Index

# About the Editors

**Meltem İNCE YENILMEZ** is a professor at the Department of Economics and deputy dean of the faculty of law at Izmir Democracy University who specializes in the economics of gender, labor economics, and social work. Prof. İnce Yenilmez was a visiting researcher at the University of California, Berkeley, between 2014 and 2015; was at Georg-Universität-Gottingen at summer school in 2015–2016; was a visiting researcher at Lund University; was a research associate at the University of Massachusetts, Amherst, in 2020–2022; and was visiting faculty at IIM Rohtak, India, in 2022. Prof. İnce Yenilmez has been a visiting professor at the University of Tohoku, Japan, since 2021. Prof. İnce Yenilmez is an economist focused on labor economics, discrimination, sustainability, social policy, behavioural economics, and care work. Prof. İnce-Yenilmez has eight books published by Routledge, Palgrave, Rowman & Littlefield, and Peter Lang, while the next book projects on cyberfeminism, migration economy, and economy, ecology, and environment will be published by 2024. For more information, please go to Prof. İnce Yenilmez's personal website: www.melteminceyenilmez.com.

**M. Çağlar ÖZDEMIR** graduated from the Gazi University Department of Labour Economics and Industrial Relations (LEIR). He started his academic career in 1999 as a research assistant at the Gazi University Department of LEIR. He completed his master's and doctorate degrees at Gazi University Social Sciences Institute. The master's thesis concerns the social security of workers who do not work full-time. In his doctoral dissertation, he studied the comparative analysis of Turkey's ICT sector labor market with India and Ireland. For his postdoctoral studies, he was at Oxford University UK from 2010 to 2011 and at Korkyt Ata Kyzylorda University in Kazakhstan from 2017 to 2018. Özdemir has worked at Sakarya University's Department of Labour Economics and Industrial Relations since 2011. He received the title of Associate Professor in 2013 and Professor in 2020. Courses: Labor Economics, Income Distribution and Poverty, Wage Policy, Social Project Management, Socioeconomic Analysis (Master), International Labor Market Analysis (Master), Research Methods (Master/Dr), Welfare Analysis and Measurement (Dr), and Green Economics and Sustainable Social Policy (Dr).

# About the Contributors

*Zeynep ACA* (orcid.org/ 0000-0002-3399-5310) is a graduate of Ankara University, School of Political Sciences, Department of Labor Economics and Industrial Relations. She started her academic life in 2009 as a research assistant at Uludağ University, Department of Labor Economics and Industrial Relations. She was granted a master's degree in Labor and Social Security Law and a PhD in Labor Economics and Industrial Relations at Uludağ University, Graduate School of Social Sciences. She continued her postdoctoral studies at Strathclyde University in Scotland between March, 2015 and February, 2016 (with a TUBITAK scholarship). She is an associate professor at Bandırma Onyedi Eylül University, Department of Social Work, since 2019.

*Beril BAYKAL* (orcid.org/ 0000-0002-0769-459X) graduated with a PhD degree from the Gazi University of the Institute of Social Sciences, Labor Economics and Industrial Relations Program, in 2015. She has been working as an assistant professor in the Department of Labor Economics and Industrial Relations at Kocaeli University since 2016. Her academic research topics have focused on work organizational psychology and social policy.

*Ufuk BİNGÖL* (orcid.org/ 0000-0003-1834-842X) is an associate professor at Bandırma Onyedi Eylül University since 2018 after a professional career at Turkish Navy as an IT Specialist. He graduated from Anadolu University, Department of Public Administration. He has completed his postgraduate studies in Human Resources and Industrial Relations and his doctorate in Labor Economics and Social Policy at Sakarya University Institute of Social Sciences. His main interests are qualitative and quantitative data analysis on policy debates in economics and social sciences. Lectures: Labor Economics,

Labor Market Policies in Turkey, Globalization and Welfare State, Current Issues in Turkish Economics (MSc), International Integrations and Globalization (MSc).

*Cihan DURMUŞKAYA* (orcid.org/ 0000-0001-7878-8641) is a graduate of Ankara University, School of Political Sciences, Department of Labor Economics and Industrial Relations. He started his academic life in 2012 as a research assistant at Sakarya University, Department of Labor Economics and Industrial Relations. He was granted a master's degree in labor economics and social policy and a PhD in labor economics and industrial relations at Sakarya University, Graduate School of Social Sciences. Dr. Durmuşkaya has been working at Sakarya University, Department of Labor Economics and Industrial Relations since 2012. He lectures Industrial Relations (U), Research Methods (U), Sociology of Work (U), Conflict Management and Dispute Resolution (P), Career Planning (P), and Industrial Relations in SMEs (P).

*Ekrem ERDOĞAN* (orcid.org/ 0000-0002-3480-4758) is a graduate of Sakarya University, Faculty of Economics and Administrative Sciences, Department of Labor Economics and Industrial Relations. He started his academic life in 2001 as a research assistant at Sakarya University, Department of Labor Economics, and Industrial Relations. He was granted a master's degree in labor economics and social policy and a PhD in labor economics and industrial relations at Sakarya University, Graduate School of Social Sciences. He received the title of Dr. in 2010, Assist. Prof. in 2010, Associate Professor in 2017, and Professor in 2022. Professor Dr. Erdogan has been working at Sakarya University, Department of Labor Economics and Industrial Relations since 2001. He lectures on Industrial Relations, Sociology of Work, History of Labor Relations, Comparative Industrial Relations, and New Types of Employment.

*Suheyla ERIKLI SELEK* (orcid.org/ 0000-0002-5817-6469) completed her MBA and PhD at Gazi University, in the field of Labor Economics and Industrial Relations, between 2012 and 2019. The subject of the master's thesis is youth poverty, and the subject of the doctoral thesis is long-term youth unemployment. She started her academic career at Recep Tayyip Erdogan University as a research assistant in 2010. Erikli worked as a research assistant at Gazi University between 2012 and 2019. Her research areas are social policy, labor markets, gender at work, poverty, youth unemployment, youth poverty, and the education-employment relationship. Erikli has worked at Ankara Yildirim Beyazit University since 2019 and got the title of Associate Professor in 2022.

*Volkan IŞIK* (orcid.org/ 0000-0003-3690-969X) has completed his MBA and PhD degrees in Labor Economics and Industrial Relations at Gazi University Institute of Social Sciences. He started his academic career at Gazi University as a research assistant in 2008. In 2011, he was selected as a scholarship student for the "Migration and Labour in a Global Economy" training program organized by Linköping University REMESO Institute of Migration, Ethnicity, and Society in Sweden. His research areas are social policy, labor markets, social entrepreneurship, youth unemployment, development, and the education-employment relationship. Isik, who has worked in the Department of Vocational School of Social Sciences at Hacettepe University since 2018, got the title of Associate Professor in 2020.

*Eylül KABAKÇI GÜNAY* (orcid.org/ 0000-0001-5547-4316) holds bachelor's, master's, and PhD degrees in economics from Anadolu University. Dr. Kabakçı Günay's areas of research are economic growth, development economics, and international economics. Throughout her career, Dr. Kabakçı Günay took part in various international and national projects, participated in seminars, and gave lectures in diversified areas of economics. Dr. Kabakçı Günay serves as an Associate Professor at Izmir Democracy University.

*Hakan METE* (orcid.org/ 0000-0002-8887-1809) graduated from the Anadolu University Public Administration undergraduate program. He has completed his master's degree in Human Resource Management and Industrial Relations and his doctorate in Labor Economics and Industrial Relations at Sakarya University Institute of Social Sciences. Mete has been working in the Turkish Naval Forces since 2002 as a senior IT specialist. He works in the fields of informatics, education, labor compliance, and employment policies. Lectures: Information Technology Computer Systems, Network Technologies, and Software (IHO/FIG/ICA Cat-B Hydrographic Survey Course in Turkish Naval Forces Office of Navigation, Hydrography and Oceanography).

*Menekşe ŞAHIN* (orcid.org/ 0000-0002-9312-770X) was born in Kayseri, Turkey, in 1975. She graduated from Gazi University, Faculty of Economic and Administrative Sciences, in 1997. She completed her postgraduate degree in 2002 at Gazi University Social Sciences Institute on Labor Economics and Industrial Relations. She obtained her PhD title in Labor Economics with the study of "A field research for the decent work in the context of social policy and in terms of evaluation decent work performance in Turkey: Example of Çorum." She has currently been working as an associate professor at Hittites University. Her major field of study is Social Policy and Employment.

*Hülya YILMAZ* (orcid.org/ 0000-0003-2672-2362) graduated from the Gazi University Labour Economics and Industrial Relations (LEIR) undergraduate program. She started her working life in 2003 as an expert at the Ministry of Treasury and Finance. She has completed her master's degree in Labor and Social Security Law and her doctorate in Labor Economics and Industrial Relations at Gazi University Institute of Social Sciences. She has studies on youth employment, social exclusion, and social exclusion of disadvantaged groups in working life. There are articles published in national peer-reviewed journals called "Comparative Evaluation of Social Inclusion Policies Implemented in Turkey with EU Member States," "Dimensions of Youth Unemployment in Turkey and Recommendations to This Problem," and a book chapter called "Social Policy and Social Innovation."

www.ingramcontent.com/pod-product-compliance
Ingram Content Group UK Ltd.
Pitfield, Milton Keynes, MK11 3LW, UK
UKHW041833031026
15587UKWH00002B/738

9 781666 956177